Praise for *Google BigQuery: The Definitive Guide*

This book is essential to the rapidly growing list of businesses that are migrating their
existing enterprise data warehouses from legacy technology stacks to Google Cloud.
Lak and Jordan provide a comprehensive coverage of BigQuery so that you can use it not
only as your Enterprise Data Warehouse, for business analytics— but also use SQL to
query real-time data streams; access BigQuery from managed Hadoop and Spark clusters;
and use machine learning to automatically categorize and run forecasting and
predictions on your data.

—*Thomas Kurian, CEO, Google Cloud*

Every once in a great while a piece of software or service comes along that changes
everything. BigQuery has changed the way enterprises can think about their data, all of it.
Designed from the beginning to handle the world's largest datasets, BigQuery has gone on
to be one of the best platforms for analyzing and learning from data. Announced in June
2016, "Standard SQL" is one of the most clean, complete, powerful, implementations of
SQL ever designed. Powerful features include deeply nested data, user defined functions
in JavaScript and SQL, geospatial data, integrated machine learning, and URL addressable
data sharing, just to name a few. There is no better place to learn about BigQuery than
from this book by Jordan and Lak, two of the people who know BigQuery best.

—*Lloyd Tabb, Cofounder and CTO, Looker*

Even though I've been using BigQuery for over seven years, I was pleased to discover that
this book taught me things I never knew about it! It provides invaluable insights into best
practices and techniques, and explains concepts in an easy to understand fashion. The
code examples are a great way to follow the content in a practical, hands-on manner, and
they kept the book fun and engaging. This book will undoubtedly become the go-to
reference for BigQuery users.

—*Graham Polley, Managing Consultant, Servian*

BigQuery can handle a lot of data very fast and at a low cost. The platform is there to help you get all your data in one place for faster insights. This book is a deep dive into key parts of BigQuery. In this quest along with two prominent legendary Googlers—Lak Lakshmanan and Jordan Tigani—you'll learn the essentials of BigQuery as well as advanced topics like machine learning. I'm a huge BigQuery advocate. Having used the tool firsthand, I can say that it will easily make your big data life a lot easier. This was an amazing read and now the BigQuery journey starts for you! Jump in!

—*Mikhail Berlyant, SVP Technology, Viant Inc.*

Google BigQuery: The Definitive Guide

Data Warehousing, Analytics, and Machine Learning at Scale

Valliappa Lakshmanan and Jordan Tigani

Beijing · Boston · Farnham · Sebastopol · Tokyo

Google BigQuery: The Definitive Guide
by Valliappa Lakshmanan and Jordan Tigani

Published by O'Reilly Media, Inc., 1005 Gravenstein Highway North, Sebastopol, CA 95472.

O'Reilly books may be purchased for educational, business, or sales promotional use. Online editions are also available for most titles (*http://oreilly.com*). For more information, contact our corporate/institutional sales department: 800-998-9938 or *corporate@oreilly.com*.

Editor: Nicole Taché
Production Editor: Kristen Brown
Copyeditor: Octal Publishing, LLC
Proofreader: Arthur Johnson

Indexer: Ellen Troutman-Zaig
Interior Designer: David Futato
Cover Designer: Karen Montgomery
Illustrator: Rebecca Demarest

October 2019:   First Edition

Revision History for the First Edition
2019-10-23:   First Release
2020-06-12:   Second Release

See *http://oreilly.com/catalog/errata.csp?isbn=9781492044468* for release details.

978-1-492-04446-8

[LSI]

Table of Contents

Preface

Enterprises are becoming increasingly data driven, and a key component of any enterprise's data strategy is a data warehouse—a central repository of integrated data from all across the company. Traditionally, the data warehouse was used by data analysts to create analytical reports. But now it is also increasingly used to populate real-time dashboards, to make ad hoc queries, and to provide decision-making guidance through predictive analytics. Because of these business requirements for advanced analytics and a trend toward cost control, agility, and self-service data access, many organizations are moving to cloud-based data warehouses such as Google BigQuery.

In this book, we provide a thorough tour of BigQuery, a serverless, highly scalable, low-cost enterprise data warehouse that is available on Google Cloud. Because there is no infrastructure to manage, enterprises can focus on analyzing data to find meaningful insights using familiar SQL.

Our goal with BigQuery has been to build a data platform that provides leading-edge capabilities, takes advantage of the many great technologies that are now available in cloud environments, and supports tried-and-true data technologies that are still relevant today. For example, on the leading edge, Google's BigQuery is a serverless compute architecture that decouples compute and storage. This enables diverse layers of the architecture to perform and scale independently, and it gives data developers flexibility in design and deployment. Somewhat uniquely, BigQuery supports native machine learning and geospatial analysis. With Cloud Pub/Sub, Cloud Dataflow, Cloud Bigtable, Cloud AI Platform, and many third-party integrations, BigQuery interoperates with both traditional and modern systems, at a wide range of desired throughput and latency. And on the tried-and-true front, BigQuery supports ANSI-standard SQL, columnar optimization, and federated queries, which are key to the self-service ad hoc data exploration that many users demand.

Who Is This Book For?

This book is for data analysts, data engineers, and data scientists who want to use Big-Query to derive insights from large datasets. Data analysts can interact with BigQuery through SQL and via dashboarding tools like Looker, Data Studio, and Tableau. Data engineers can integrate BigQuery with data pipelines written in Python or Java and using frameworks such as Apache Spark and Apache Beam. Data scientists can build machine learning models in BigQuery, run TensorFlow models on data in BigQuery, and delegate distributed, large-scale operations to BigQuery from within a Jupyter notebook.

Conventions Used in This Book

The following typographical conventions are used in this book:

Italic
: Indicates new terms, URLs, email addresses, filenames, and file extensions.

`Constant width`
: Used for program listings, as well as within paragraphs to refer to program elements such as variable or function names, databases, data types, environment variables, statements, and keywords.

`Constant width bold`
: Shows commands or other text that should be typed literally by the user.

`Constant width italic`
: Shows text that should be replaced with user-supplied values or values determined by context.

> This element signifies a tip or suggestion.

> This element signifies a general note.

This element indicates a warning or caution.

Using Code Examples

Supplemental material (code examples, exercises, etc.) is available for download at *https://github.com/GoogleCloudPlatform/bigquery-oreilly-book*.

If you have a technical question or a problem using the code examples, please send email to *bookquestions@oreilly.com*.

This book is here to help you get your job done. In general, if example code is offered with this book, you may use it in your programs and documentation. You do not need to contact us for permission unless you're reproducing a significant portion of the code. For example, writing a program that uses several chunks of code from this book does not require permission. Selling or distributing examples from O'Reilly books does require permission. Answering a question by citing this book and quoting example code does not require permission. Incorporating a significant amount of example code from this book into your product's documentation does require permission.

We appreciate, but generally do not require, attribution. An attribution usually includes the title, author, publisher, and ISBN. For example: "*Google BigQuery: The Definitive Guide* by Valliappa Lakshmanan and Jordan Tigani (O'Reilly). Copyright 2020 Valliappa Lakshmanan and Jordan Tigani, 978-1-492-04446-8."

If you feel your use of code examples falls outside fair use or the permission given above, feel free to contact us at *permissions@oreilly.com*.

O'Reilly Online Learning

 For more than 40 years, *O'Reilly Media* has provided technology and business training, knowledge, and insight to help companies succeed.

Our unique network of experts and innovators share their knowledge and expertise through books, articles, and our online learning platform. O'Reilly's online learning platform gives you on-demand access to live training courses, in-depth learning paths, interactive coding environments, and a vast collection of text and video from O'Reilly and 200+ other publishers. For more information, please visit *http://oreilly.com*.

How to Contact Us

Please address comments and questions concerning this book to the publisher:

O'Reilly Media, Inc.
1005 Gravenstein Highway North
Sebastopol, CA 95472
800-998-9938 (in the United States or Canada)
707-829-0515 (international or local)
707-829-0104 (fax)

We have a web page for this book, where we list errata, examples, and any additional information. You can access this page at *https://oreil.ly/google_bigquery_tdg*.

To comment or ask technical questions about this book, send email to *bookquestions@oreilly.com*.

For news and more information about our books and courses, see our website at *http://www.oreilly.com*.

Find us on Facebook: *http://facebook.com/oreilly*

Follow us on Twitter: *http://twitter.com/oreillymedia*

Follow the authors on Twitter: *https://twitter.com/lak_gcp* and *https://twitter.com/jrdntgn*

Watch us on YouTube: *http://www.youtube.com/oreillymedia*

Acknowledgments

We (Lak and Jordan) were extremely fortunate in our reviewers—Elliott Brossard, Evan Jones, Graham Polley, Rebecca Ward, and Tegan Tigani reviewed every chapter of this book and made numerous suggestions for improvement. Elliott kept our SQL queries lean and clean. We benefited from Evan's experience using BigQuery in Google Finance. Graham brought a valuable customer perspective to many of our discussions involving cost and regionalization. Rebecca kept us factual, and Tegan made sure our language was simple and straightforward. Besides these five, many Googlers (Chad Jennings, Haris Khan, Misha Brukman, Daniel Gundrum, Mosha Pashumansky, Amir Hormati, and Mingge Deng) reviewed parts of the manuscript in their areas of expertise. Any errors that remain are ours, of course.

Thanks also to our respective families, teammates, and managers (Rochana Golani and Sudhir Hasbe) for their support. Nicole Taché and Kristen Brown, our editors at O'Reilly, were a pleasure to work with. The text is immeasurably better because of the eagle-eyed work of Bob Russell, our copyeditor. This book was Saptarshi Mukherjee's idea, and it was he who pushed the two of us to collaborate on a new BigQuery book. Finally, we would like to thank BigQuery users (and competitors!) for pushing us to make BigQuery better, and the BigQuery engineering team for making magic happen.

We are donating 100% of the royalties from this book to United Way of King County (*https://www.uwkc.org*), where we both live. We strongly encourage you to get involved with a local charity to give, volunteer, and take action to help solve your community's toughest challenges.

Updates to First Edition

There are new features and improvements being made to BigQuery at a breakneck pace. We will post links to articles that explain new features and updates to BigQuery at *https://github.com/GoogleCloudPlatform/bigquery-oreilly-book*. Periodically, we will summarize those articles in updates to this book.

This book was published in November 2019, and the first update was applied in June 2020. Included in this update were new or expanded sections on scripting, reservations, materialized views, column-level security, dynamic SQL, machine learning, table-level access controls, and federated queries.

## CHAPTER 1

What Is Google BigQuery?

Data Processing Architectures

Google BigQuery is a serverless, highly scalable data warehouse that comes with a built-in query engine. The query engine is capable of running SQL queries on terabytes of data in a matter of seconds, and petabytes in only minutes. You get this performance without having to manage any infrastructure and without having to create or rebuild indexes.

BigQuery has legions of fans. Paul Lamere, a Spotify engineer, was thrilled that he could finally talk about how his team uses BigQuery to quickly analyze large datasets: "Google's BigQuery is *da bomb*," he tweeted in February 2016 (*https://twitter.com/ plamere/status/702168809445134336*). "I can start with 2.2Billion 'things' and compute/summarize down to 20K in < 1 min." The scale and speed are just two notable features of BigQuery. What is more transformative is not having to manage infrastructure because the simplicity inherent in serverless, ad hoc querying can open up new ways of working.

Companies are increasingly embracing data-driven decision making and fostering an open culture where the data is not siloed within departments. BigQuery, by providing the technological means to enact a cultural shift toward agility and openness, plays a big part in increasing the pace of innovation. For example, Twitter recently reported in its blog (*https://blog.twitter.com/engineering/en_us/topics/infrastructure/2019/ democratizing-data-analysis-with-google-bigquery.html*) that it was able to democratize data analysis with BigQuery by providing some of its most frequently used tables to Twitter employees from a variety of teams (Engineering, Finance, and Marketing were mentioned).

For Alpega Group, a global logistics software company, the increased innovation and agility offered by BigQuery were key. The company went from a situation in which

real-time analytics was impossible to being able to provide fast, customer-facing analytics in near real time. Because Alpega Group does not need to maintain clusters and
infrastructure, its small tech team is now free to work on software development and
data capabilities. "That was a real eye opener for us," says the company's lead archi-
tect, Aart Verbeke (*https://cloud.google.com/customers/alpega*). "In a conventional
environment we would need to install, set up, deploy and host every individual building block. Here we simply connect to a surface and use it as required."

Imagine that you run a chain of equipment rental stores. You charge customers based
on the length of the rental, so your records include the following details that will
allow you to properly invoice the customer:

1. Where the item was rented
2. When it was rented
3. Where the item was returned
4. When it was returned

Perhaps you record the transaction in a database every time a customer returns an
item.[1]

From this dataset, you would like to find out how many "one-way" rentals occurred
every month in the past 10 years. Perhaps you are thinking of imposing a surcharge
for returning the item at a different store and you would like to find out what fraction
of rentals would be affected. Let's posit that wanting to know the answer to such questions is a frequent occurrence—it is important for you to be able to answer such ad
hoc questions because you tend to make data-driven decisions.

What kind of system architecture could you use? Let's run through some of the
options.

Relational Database Management System

When recording the transactions, you are probably recording them in a relational,
online transaction processing (OLTP) database such as MySQL or PostgreSQL. One
of the key benefits of such databases is that they support querying using Structured
Query Language (SQL)—your staff doesn't need to use high-level languages like Java
or Python to answer questions that arise. Instead, it is possible to write a query, such
as the following, that can be submitted to the database server:

---

[1] In reality, you'll need to start the record keeping at the time customers borrow the equipment, so that you will
know whether customers have absconded with the equipment. However, it's rather early in this book to worry
about that!

```
SELECT
  EXTRACT(YEAR FROM starttime) AS year,
  EXTRACT(MONTH FROM starttime) AS month,
  COUNT(starttime) AS number_one_way
FROM
  mydb.return_transactions
WHERE
  start_station_name != end_station_name
GROUP BY year, month
ORDER BY year ASC, month ASC
```

Ignore the details of the syntax for now; we cover SQL queries later in this book. Instead, let's focus on what this tells us about the benefits and drawbacks of an OLTP database.

First, notice that SQL goes beyond just being able to get the raw data in database columns—the preceding query parses the timestamp and extracts the year and month from it. It also does aggregation (counting the number of rows), some filtering (finding rentals where the starting and ending locations are different), grouping (by year and month), and sorting. An important benefit of SQL is the ability to specify what we want and let the database software figure out an optimal way to execute the query.

Unfortunately, queries like this one are quite inefficient for an OLTP database to carry out. OLTP databases are tuned toward data consistency; the point is that you can read from the database even while data is simultaneously being written to it. This is achieved through careful locking to maintain data integrity. For the filtering on station_name to be efficient, you would need to create an *index* on the station name column. If the station name is indexed, then and only then does the database do special things to the storage to optimize searchability—this is a tradeoff, slowing writing down a bit to improve the speed of reading. If the station name is not indexed, filtering on it will be quite slow. Even if the station name is an index, this particular query will be quite slow because of all the aggregating, grouping, and ordering. OLTP databases are not built for this sort of ad hoc[2] query that requires traversal through the entire dataset.

MapReduce Framework

Because OLTP databases are a poor fit for ad hoc queries and queries that require traversal of the entire dataset, special-purpose analyses that require such traversal might be coded in high-level languages like Java or Python. In 2003, Jeff Dean and Sanjay Ghemawat observed that they and their colleagues at Google were implementing hundreds of these special-purpose computations to process large amounts of raw

---

2 In this book, we use "ad hoc" query to refer to a query that is written without any attempt to prepare the database ahead of time by using features such as indexes.

data. Reacting to this complexity, they designed an abstraction that allowed these computations to be expressed in terms of two steps: a *map* function that processed a key/value pair to generate a set of intermediate key/value pairs, and a *reduce* function that merged all intermediate values associated with the same intermediate key.[3] This paradigm, known as *MapReduce*, became hugely influential and led to the development of Apache Hadoop.

Although the Hadoop ecosystem began with a library that was primarily built in Java, custom analysis on Hadoop clusters is now typically carried out using Apache Spark (*http://spark.apache.org/*). Spark programs can be written in Python or Scala, but among the capabilities of Spark is the ability to execute ad hoc SQL queries on distributed datasets.

So, to find out the number of one-way rentals, you could set up the following data pipeline:

1. Periodically export transactions to comma-separated values (CSV) text files in the Hadoop Distributed File System (HDFS).

2. For ad hoc analysis, write a Spark program that does the following:

   a. Loads up the data from the text files into a "DataFrame"

   b. Executes an SQL query, similar to the query in the previous section, except that the table name is replaced by the name of the DataFrame

   c. Exports the result set back to a text file

3. Run the Spark program on a Hadoop cluster.

Although seemingly straightforward, this architecture imposes a couple of hidden costs. Saving the data in HDFS requires that the cluster be large enough. One underappreciated fact about the MapReduce architecture is that it usually requires that the compute nodes access data that is local to them. The HDFS must, therefore, be sharded across the compute nodes of the cluster. With both data sizes and analysis needs increasing dramatically but independently, it is often the case that clusters are underprovisioned or overprovisioned.[4] Thus, the need to execute Spark programs on a Hadoop cluster means that your organization will need to become expert in

---

3 Jeffrey Dean and Sanjay Ghemawat, "MapReduce: Simplified Data Processing on Large Clusters," OSDI '04: Sixth Symposium on Operating Systems Design and Implementation, San Francisco, CA (2004), pp. 137–150. Available at *https://research.google.com/archive/mapreduce-osdi04.pdf*.

4 On Google Cloud Platform, Cloud Dataproc (the managed Hadoop offering) addresses this conundrum in a different way. Because of the high bisectional bandwidth available within Google datacenters, Cloud Dataproc clusters are able to be job specific—the data is stored on Google Cloud Storage and read over the wire on demand. This is possible only if bandwidths are high enough to approximate disk speeds. Don't try this at home.

managing, monitoring, and provisioning Hadoop clusters. This might not be your core business.

BigQuery: A Serverless, Distributed SQL Engine

What if you could run SQL queries as in a Relational Database Management System (RDBMS) system, obtain efficient and distributed traversal through the entire dataset as in MapReduce, and not need to manage infrastructure? That's the third option, and it is what makes BigQuery so magical. BigQuery is serverless, and you can run queries without the need to manage infrastructure. It enables you to carry out analyses that process aggregations over the entire dataset in seconds to minutes.

Don't take our word for it, though. Try it out now. Navigate to *https://console.cloud.google.com/bigquery* (logging into Google Cloud Platform and selecting your project if necessary), copy and paste the following query in the window,[5] and then click the "Run query" button:

```
SELECT
  EXTRACT(YEAR FROM starttime) AS year,
  EXTRACT(MONTH FROM starttime) AS month,
  COUNT(starttime) AS number_one_way
FROM
  `bigquery-public-data.new_york_citibike.citibike_trips`
WHERE
  start_station_name != end_station_name
GROUP BY year, month
ORDER BY year ASC, month ASC
```

When we ran it, the BigQuery user interface (UI) reported that the query involved processing 2.51 GB and gave us the result in about 2.7 seconds, as illustrated in Figure 1-1.

---

5 For your copy and pasting convenience, you can find all of the code and query snippets in this book (including the query in the example (*https://github.com/GoogleCloudPlatform/bigquery-oreilly-book/blob/master/01_intro/queries.txt*)) in the GitHub repository for this book (*https://github.com/GoogleCloudPlatform/bigquery-oreilly-book*).

Figure 1-1. Running a query to compute the number of one-way rentals in the BigQuery web UI

The equipment being rented out is bicycles, and so the preceding query totals up one-way bicycle rentals in New York month by month over the extent of the dataset. The dataset itself is a public dataset (meaning that anyone can query the data held in it) released by New York City as part of its Open City initiative. From this query, we learn that in July 2013, there were 815,324 one-way Citibike rentals in New York City.

Note a few things about this. One is that you were able to run a query against a dataset that was already present in BigQuery. All that the owner of the project hosting the data had to do was to give you[6] "view" access to this dataset. You didn't need to start up a cluster or log in to one. Instead, you just submitted a query to the service and received your results. The query itself was written in SQL:2011, making the syntax familiar to data analysts everywhere. Although we demonstrated on gigabytes of data, the service scales well even when it does aggregations on terabytes to petabytes of data. This scalability is possible because the service distributes the query processing among thousands of workers almost instantaneously.

Working with BigQuery

BigQuery is a data warehouse, implying a degree of centralization and ubiquity. The query we demonstrated in the previous section was applied to a single dataset. However, the benefits of BigQuery become even more apparent when we do joins of datasets from completely different sources or when we query against data that is stored outside BigQuery.

Deriving Insights Across Datasets

The bicycle rental data comes from New York City. How about joining it against weather data from the US National Oceanic and Atmospheric Administration (NOAA) to learn whether there are fewer bicycle rentals on rainy days?[7]

```
-- Are there fewer bicycle rentals on rainy days?
WITH bicycle_rentals AS (
  SELECT
    COUNT(starttime) as num_trips,
    EXTRACT(DATE from starttime) as trip_date
  FROM `bigquery-public-data.new_york_citibike.citibike_trips`
  GROUP BY trip_date
),

rainy_days AS
(
SELECT
  date,
  (MAX(prcp) > 5) AS rainy
FROM (
  SELECT
    wx.date AS date,
    IF (wx.element = 'PRCP', wx.value/10, NULL) AS prcp
  FROM
```

---

6 Not you specifically. This is a public dataset, and the owner of the dataset gave this permission to all authenticated users. You can be less permissive with your data, sharing the dataset only with those within your
  domain or within your team.

7 This code can be downloaded from the book's GitHub repository.

```
    `bigquery-public-data.ghcn_d.ghcnd_2016` AS wx
  WHERE
    wx.id = 'USW00094728'
)
GROUP BY
 date
)

SELECT
  ROUND(AVG(bk.num_trips)) AS num_trips,
  wx.rainy
FROM bicycle_rentals AS bk
JOIN rainy_days AS wx
ON wx.date = bk.trip_date
GROUP BY wx.rainy
```

Ignore the specific syntax of the query. Just notice that, in the bolded lines, we are joining the bicycle rental dataset with a weather dataset that comes from a completely different source. Running the query satisfyingly yields that, yes, New Yorkers are wimps—they ride the bicycle nearly 20% fewer times when it rains:[8]

```
Row num_trips  rainy
  1  39107.0   false
  2  32052.0   true
```

What does being able to share and query across datasets mean in an enterprise context? Different parts of your company can store their datasets in BigQuery and quite easily share the data with other parts of the company and even with partner organizations. The serverless nature of BigQuery provides the technological means to break down departmental silos and streamline collaboration.

ETL, EL, and ELT

The traditional way to work with data warehouses is to start with an Extract, Transform, and Load (ETL) process, wherein raw data is extracted from its source location, transformed, and then loaded into the data warehouse. Indeed, BigQuery has a native, highly efficient columnar storage format[9] that makes ETL an attractive methodology. The data pipeline, typically written in either Apache Beam or Apache Spark, extracts the necessary bits from the raw data (either streaming data or batch files), transforms what it has extracted to do any necessary cleanup or aggregation, and then loads it into BigQuery, as demonstrated in Figure 1-2.

---

8 Keep in mind that both authors live in Seattle, where it rains 150 days each year.

9 You can find more details on the columnar storage format in "How BigQuery Came About" on page 12.

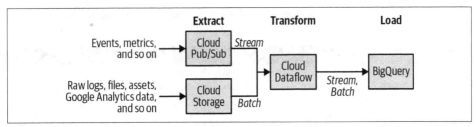

Figure 1-2. The reference architecture for ETL into BigQuery uses Apache Beam pipelines executed on Cloud Dataflow and can handle both streaming and batch data using the same code

Even though building an ETL pipeline in Apache Beam or Apache Spark tends to be quite common, it is possible to implement an ETL pipeline purely within BigQuery. Because BigQuery separates compute and storage, it is possible to run BigQuery SQL queries against CSV (or JSON or Avro) files that are stored as-is on Google Cloud Storage; this capability is called *federated querying*. You can take advantage of federated queries to extract the data using SQL queries against data stored in Google Cloud Storage, transform the data within those SQL queries, and then materialize the results into a BigQuery native table.

If transformation is not necessary, BigQuery can directly ingest standard formats like CSV, JSON, or Avro into its native storage—an EL (Extract and Load) workflow, if you will. The reason to end up with the data loaded into the data warehouse is that having the data in native storage provides the most efficient querying performance.

We strongly recommend that you design for an EL workflow if possible, and drop to an ETL workflow only if transformations are needed. If possible, do those transformations in SQL, and keep the entire ETL pipeline within BigQuery. If the transforms will be difficult to implement purely in SQL, or if the pipeline needs to stream data into BigQuery as it arrives, build an Apache Beam pipeline and have it executed in a serverless fashion using Cloud Dataflow. Another advantage of implementing ETL pipelines in Beam/Dataflow is that, because this is programmatic code, such pipelines integrate better with Continuous Integration (CI) and unit testing systems.

Besides the ETL and EL workflows, BigQuery makes it possible to do an Extract, Load, and Transform (ELT) workflow. The idea is to extract and load the raw data as-is and rely on BigQuery views to transform the data on the fly. An ELT workflow is particularly useful if the schema of the raw data is in flux. For example, you might still be carrying out exploratory work to determine whether a particular timestamp needs to be corrected for the local time zone. The ELT workflow is useful in prototyping and allows an organization to start deriving insights from the data without having to make potentially irreversible decisions too early.

The alphabet soup can be confusing, so we've prepared a quick summary in Table 1-1.

Table 1-1. Summary of workflows, sample architectures, and the scenarios in which they would be used

Workflow	Architecture	When you'd use it
EL	Extract data from files on Google Cloud Storage. Load it into BigQuery's native storage. You can trigger this from Cloud Composer, Cloud Functions, or scheduled queries.	Batch load of historical data. Scheduled periodic loads of log files (e.g., once a day).
ETL	Extract data from Pub/Sub, Google Cloud Storage, Cloud Spanner, Cloud SQL, etc. Transform the data using Cloud Dataflow. Have Dataflow pipeline write to BigQuery	When the raw data needs to be quality controlled, transformed, or enriched before being loaded into BigQuery. When the data loading needs to happen continuously, i.e., if the use case requires streaming. When you want to integrate with continuous integration/ continuous delivery (CI/CD) systems and perform unit testing on all components.
ELT	Extract data from files in Google Cloud Storage. Store data in close-to-raw format in BigQuery. Transform the data on the fly using BigQuery views.	Experimental datasets where you are not yet sure what kinds of transformations are needed to make the data usable. Any production dataset where the transformation can be expressed in SQL.

The workflows in Table 1-1 are in the order that we usually recommend.

Powerful Analytics

The benefits of a warehouse derive from the kinds of analyses that you can do with the data held within it. The primary way you interact with BigQuery is via SQL, and because BigQuery is an SQL engine, you can use a wide variety of Business Intelligence (BI) tools such as Tableau, Looker, and Google Data Studio to create impactful analyses, visualizations, and reports on data held in BigQuery. By clicking the "Explore in Data Studio" button in the BigQuery web UI, for example, we can quickly create a visualization of how our one-way bike rentals vary by month, as depicted in Figure 1-3.

BigQuery provides full-featured support for SQL:2011, including support for arrays and complex joins. The support for arrays in particular makes it possible to store hierarchical data (such as JSON records) in BigQuery without the need to flatten the nested and repeated fields. Besides the support for SQL:2011, BigQuery has a few extensions that make it useful beyond the core set of data warehouse use cases. One of these extensions is support for a wide range of spatial functions that enable location-aware queries, including the ability to join two tables based on distance or overlap criteria.[10] BigQuery is, therefore, a powerful engine to carry out descriptive analytics.

---

10 For example, to compute conversion metrics based on the distance that a customer would need to travel to purchase a product.

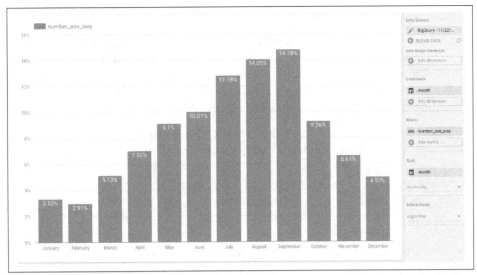

Figure 1-3. Visualization in Data Studio of how one-way rentals vary by month; nearly 15% of all one-way bicycle rentals in New York happen in September

Another BigQuery extension to standard SQL supports creating machine learning models and carrying out batch predictions. We cover the machine learning capability of BigQuery in detail in Chapter 9, but the gist is that you can train a BigQuery model and make predictions without ever having to export data out of BigQuery. The security and data locality advantages of being able to do this are enormous. BigQuery is, therefore, a data warehouse that supports not just descriptive analytics but also predictive analytics.

A warehouse also implies being able to store different types of data. Indeed, BigQuery can store data of many types: numeric and textual columns, for sure, but also geospatial data and hierarchical data. Even though you can store flattened data in BigQuery, you don't need to—schemas can be rich and quite sophisticated. The combination of location-aware queries, hierarchical data, and machine learning make BigQuery a powerful solution that goes beyond conventional data warehousing and business intelligence.

BigQuery supports the ingest both of batch data and of streaming data. You can stream data directly into BigQuery via a REST API. Often, users who want to transform the data—for example, by adding time-windowed computations—use Apache Beam pipelines executed by the Cloud Dataflow service. Even as the data is streaming into BigQuery, you can query it. Having common querying infrastructure for both historical (batch) data and current (streaming) data is extremely powerful and simplifies many workflows.

Simplicity of Management

Part of the design consideration behind BigQuery is to encourage users to focus on insights rather than on infrastructure. When you ingest data into BigQuery, there is no need to think about different types of storage, or their relative speed and cost tradeoffs; the storage is fully managed. As of this writing, the cost of storage automatically drops to lower levels if a table is not updated for 90 days.[11]

We have already talked about how indexing is not necessary; your SQL queries can filter on any column in the dataset, and BigQuery will take care of the necessary query planning and optimization. For the most part, we recommend that you write queries to be clear and readable and rely on BigQuery to choose a good optimization strategy. In this book, we talk about performance tuning, but performance tuning in BigQuery consists mainly of clear thinking and the appropriate choice of SQL functions. You will not need to do database administration tasks like replication, defragmentation, or disaster recovery; the BigQuery service takes care of all that for you.

Queries are automatically scaled to thousands of machines and executed in parallel. You don't need to do anything special to enable this massive parallelization. The machines themselves are transparently provisioned to handle the different stages of your job; you don't need to set up those machines in any way.

Not having to set up infrastructure leads to less hassle in terms of security. Data in BigQuery is automatically encrypted, both at rest and in transit. BigQuery takes care of the security considerations behind supporting multitenant queries and providing isolation between jobs. Your datasets can be shared using Google Cloud Identity and Access Management (IAM), and it is possible to organize the datasets (and the tables and views within them) to meet different security needs, whether you need openness or auditability or confidentiality.

In other systems, provisioning infrastructure for reliability, elasticity, security, and performance often takes a lot of time to get right. Given that these database administration tasks are minimized with BigQuery, organizations using BigQuery find that it frees their analysts' time to focus on deriving insights from their data.

How BigQuery Came About

In late 2010, the site director of the Google Seattle office pulled several engineers (one of whom is an author of this book) off their projects and gave them a mission: to build a data marketplace. We tried to craft the best way to come up with a viable marketplace. The chief issue was data sizes, because we didn't want to provide just a

---

11 We believe all mentions of price to be correct as of the writing of this book, but please do refer to the relevant policy and pricing sheets (*https://cloud.google.com/bigquery/pricing*), as these are subject to change.

download link. A data marketplace is infeasible if people need to download terabytes of data in order to work with it. How would you build a data marketplace that didn't require users to start by downloading the datasets to their own machines?

Enter a principle popularized by Jim Gray, the database pioneer (*https://en.wikipe dia.org/wiki/Jim_Gray_(computer_scientist)*). When you have "big data," Gray said, "you want to move the computation to the data, rather than move the data to the computation." Gray elaborates:

> The other key issue is that as the datasets get larger, it is no longer possible to just FTP or grep them. A petabyte of data is very hard to FTP! So at some point, you need indices and you need parallel data access, and this is where databases can help you. For data analysis, one possibility is to move the data to you, but the other possibility is to move your query to the data. You can either move your questions or the data. Often it turns out to be more efficient to move the questions than to move the data.[12]

In the case of the data marketplace that we were building, users would not need to download the datasets to their own machines if we made it possible for them to bring their computations to the data. We would not need to provide a download link, because users could work on their data without the need to move it around.[13]

We, the Googlers who were tasked with building a data marketplace, made the decision to defer that project and focus on building a compute engine and storage system in the cloud. After ensuring that users could do something with the data, we would go back and add data marketplace features.

In what language should users write their computation when bringing computation to the data on the cloud? We chose SQL because of three key characteristics. First, SQL is a versatile language that allows a large range of people, not just developers, to ask questions and solve problems with their data. This ease of use was extremely important to us. Second, SQL is "relationally complete," meaning that any computation over the data can be done using SQL. SQL is not just easy and approachable. It is also very powerful. Finally, and quite important for a choice of a cloud computation language, SQL is not "Turing complete" in a key way: it always terminates.[14] Because it always terminates, it is ok to host SQL computation without worrying that someone will write an infinite loop and monopolize all the compute power in a datacenter.

---

12 Jim Gray on eScience: A Transformed Scientific Method", from *The Fourth Paradigm: Data-Intensive Scientific Discovery*, ed. Tony Hey, Stewart Tansley, and Kristin Tolle (Microsoft, 2009), xiv. Available at *https://oreil.ly/M6zMN*.

13 Today, BigQuery does provide the ability to export tables and results to Google Cloud Storage, so we did end up building the download link after all! But BigQuery is not just a download link—most uses of BigQuery involve operating on the data in place.

14 SQL does have a RECURSIVE keyword, but like many SQL engines, BigQuery does not support this. Instead, BigQuery offers better ways to deal with hierarchical data by supporting arrays and nesting.

Next, we had to choose an SQL engine. Google had a number of internal SQL engines that could operate over data, including some that were very popular. The most advanced engine was called Dremel; it was used heavily at Google and could process terabytes' worth of logs in seconds. Dremel was quickly winning people over from building custom MapReduce pipelines to ask questions of their data.

Dremel had been created in 2006 by engineer Andrey Gubarev, who was tired of waiting for MapReduces to finish. Column stores were becoming popular in the academic literature, and he quickly came up with a column storage format (Figure 1-4) that could handle the Protocol Buffers (Protobufs) that are ubiquitous throughout Google.

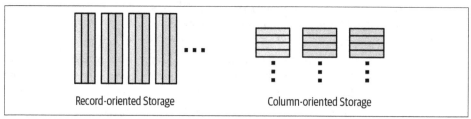

Record-oriented Storage   Column-oriented Storage

Figure 1-4. Column stores can reduce the amount of data being read by queries that process all rows but not all columns

Although column stores are great in general for analytics, they are particularly useful for logs analysis at Google because many teams operate over a type of Protobuf that has hundreds of thousands of columns. If Andrey had used a typical record-oriented store, users would have needed to read the files row by row, thus reading in a huge amount of data in the form of fields that they were going to discard anyway. By storing the data column by column, Andrey made it so that if a user needed just a few of the thousands of fields in the log Protobufs, they would need to read only a small fraction of the overall data size. This was one of the reasons why Dremel was able to process terabytes' worth of logs in seconds.

The other reason why Dremel was able to process data so fast was that its query engine used distributed computing. Dremel scaled to thousands of workers by structuring the computation as a tree, with the filters happening at the leaves and aggregation happening toward the root.

By 2010, Google was scanning petabytes of data per day using Dremel, and many people in the company used it in some form or another. It was the perfect tool for our nascent data marketplace team to pick up and use.

As the team productized Dremel, added a storage system, made it self-tuning, and exposed it to external users, the team realized that a cloud version of Dremel was perhaps even more interesting than their original mission. The team renamed itself "BigQuery," following the naming convention for "Bigtable," Google's NoSQL database.

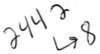

At Google, Dremel is used to query files that sit on Colossus, Google's file store for storing data. BigQuery added a storage system that provided a table abstraction, not just a file abstraction. This storage system was key in making BigQuery simple to use and always fast, because it allowed key features like ACID (Atomicity, Consistency, Isolation, Durability) transactions and automatic optimization, and it meant that users didn't need to manage files.

Initially, BigQuery retained its Dremel roots and was focused on scanning logs. However, as more customers wanted to do data warehousing and more complex queries, BigQuery added improved support for joins and advanced SQL features like analytic functions. In 2016, Google launched support for standard SQL in BigQuery, which allowed users to run queries using standards-compliant SQL rather than the awkward initial "DremelSQL" dialect.

BigQuery did not start out as a data warehouse, but it has evolved into one over the years. There are good things and bad things about this evolution. On the positive side, BigQuery was designed to solve problems people have with their data, even if they don't fit nicely into data warehousing models. In this way, BigQuery is more than just a data warehouse. On the downside, however, a few data warehousing features that people expect, like a Data Definition Language (DDL; e.g., CREATE statements) and a Data Manipulation Language (DML; e.g., INSERT statements), were missing until recently. That said, BigQuery has been focusing on a dual path: first, adding differentiated features that Google is in a unique position to provide; and second, becoming a great data warehouse in the cloud.

What Makes BigQuery Possible?

From an architectural perspective, BigQuery is fundamentally different from on-premises data warehouses like Teradata or Vertica as well as from cloud data warehouses like Redshift and Microsoft Azure Data Warehouse. BigQuery is the first data warehouse to be a scale-out solution, so the only limit on speed and scale is the amount of hardware in the datacenter.

This section describes some of the components that go into making BigQuery successful and unique.

Separation of Compute and Storage

In many data warehouses, compute and storage reside together on the same physical hardware. This colocation means that in order to add more storage, you might need to add more compute power as well. Or to add more compute power, you'd also need to get additional storage capacity.

If everyone's data needs were similar, this wouldn't be a problem; there would be a consistent golden ratio of compute to storage that everyone would live by. But in practice, one or the other of the factors tends to be a limitation. Some data warehouses are limited by compute capacity, so they slow down at peak times. Other data warehouses are limited by storage capacity, so maintainers need to figure out what data to throw out.

When you separate compute from storage as BigQuery does, it means that you never need to throw out data, unless you no longer want it. This might not sound like a big deal, but having access to full-fidelity data is immensely powerful. You might decide you want to calculate something in a different way, so you can go back to the raw data to requery it. You would not be able to do this if you had discarded the source data due to space constraints. You might decide that you want to dig into why some aggregate value exhibits strange behavior. You couldn't do this if you had deleted the data that contributed to the aggregation.

Scaling compute is equally powerful. BigQuery resources are denominated in terms of "slots," which are, roughly speaking, about half of a CPU core (we cover slots in detail in Chapter 6). BigQuery uses slots as an abstraction to indicate how many physical compute resources are available. Queries running too slow? Just add more slots. More people want to create reports? Add more slots. Want to cut back on your expenses? Decrease your slots.

Because BigQuery is a multitenant system that manages large pools of hardware resources, it is able to dole out the slots on a per-query or per-user basis. It is possible to reserve hardware for your project or organization, or you can run your queries in the shared on-demand pool. By sharing resources in this way, BigQuery can devote very large amounts of computing power to your queries. If you need more computing power than is available in the on-demand pool, you can purchase more via the Big-Query Reservation API.

Several BigQuery customers have reservations in the tens of thousands of slots, which means that if they run only one query at a time, those queries can consume tens of thousands of CPU cores at once. With some reasonable assumptions about numbers of CPU cycles per processed row, it is pretty easy to see that these instances can process billions or even trillions of rows per second.

In BigQuery, there are some customers that have petabytes of data but use a relatively small amount of it on a daily basis. Other customers store only a few gigabytes of data but perform complex queries using thousands of CPUs. There isn't a one-size-fits-all approach that works for all use cases. Fortunately, the separation of compute and storage allows BigQuery to accommodate a wide range of customer needs.

Storage and Networking Infrastructure

BigQuery differs from other cloud data warehouses in that queries are served primarily from spinning disks in a distributed filesystem. Most competitor systems need to cache data within compute nodes to get good performance. BigQuery, on the other hand, relies on two systems unique to Google, the Colossus File System (*https://cloud.google.com/files/storage_architecture_and_challenges.pdf*) and Jupiter networking (*https://cloudplatform.googleblog.com/2015/06/A-Look-Inside-Googles-Data-Center-Networks.html*), to ensure that data can be queried quickly no matter where it physically resides in the compute cluster.

Google's Jupiter networking fabric relies on a network configuration where smaller (and hence cheaper) switches are arranged to provide the capability for which a much larger logical switch would otherwise be needed. This topology of switches, along with a centralized software stack and custom hardware and software, allows one petabit of bisection bandwidth within a datacenter. That is equivalent to 100,000 servers communicating at 10 Gb/sec, and it means that BigQuery can work without the need to colocate the compute and storage. If the machines hosting the disks are at the other end of the datacenter from the machines running the computation, it will effectively run just as fast as if the two machines were in the same rack.

The fast networking fabric comes in handy in two ways: to read in data from a disk, and to shuffle between query stages. As discussed earlier, the separation of compute and storage in BigQuery enables any machine within the datacenter to ingest data from any storage disk. This requires, however, that the necessary input data to the queries be read over the network at very high speeds. The details of shuffle are described in Chapter 6, but it suffices for now to understand that running complex distributed queries usually requires moving large amounts of data between machines at intermediate stages. Without a fast network connecting the machines doing the work, shuffle would become a bottleneck that slows down the queries significantly.

The networking infrastructure provides more than just speed: it also allows for dynamic provisioning of bandwidth. Google datacenters are connected through a backbone network called B4 (*https://www.usenix.org/conference/atc15/technical-session/presentation/mandal*) that is software-defined to allocate bandwidth in an elastic manner to different users, and to provide reliable quality of service for high-priority operations. This is crucial for implementing high-performing, concurrent queries.

Fast networking isn't enough, however, if the disk subsystem is slow or lacks enough scale. To support interactive queries, the data needs to be read from the disks fast enough so that they can saturate the network bandwidth available. Google's distributed filesystem is called Colossus and can coordinate hundreds of thousands of disks by constantly rebalancing old, cold data and distributing newly written data evenly across disks.[15] This means that the effective throughput is tens of terabytes per

---

15 To read more about Colossus, see *http://www.pdsw.org/pdsw-discs17/slides/PDSW-DISCS-Google-Keynote.pdf* and *https://www.wired.com/2012/07/google-colossus/*.

second. By combining this effective throughput with efficient data formats and storage, BigQuery provides the ability to query petabyte-sized tables in minutes.

Managed Storage

BigQuery's storage system is built on the idea that when you're dealing with structured storage, the appropriate abstraction is the table, not the file. Some other cloud-based and open source data processing systems expose the concept of the file to users, which puts users on the hook for managing file sizes and ensuring that the schema remains consistent. Even though creating files of an appropriate size for a static data store is possible, it is notoriously difficult to maintain optimal file sizes for data that is changing over time. Similarly, it is difficult to maintain a consistent schema when you have a large number of files with self-describing schemas (e.g., Avro or Parquet)—typically, every software update to systems producing those files results in changes to the schema. BigQuery ensures that all the data held within a table has a consistent schema and enforces a proper migration path for historical data. By abstracting the underlying data formats and file sizes from the user, BigQuery can provide a seamless experience so that queries are always fast.

There is another advantage to BigQuery managing its own storage: BigQuery can continue to become faster in a way that is transparent to the end user. For example, improvements in storage formats can be applied automatically to user data. Similarly, improvements in storage infrastructure become immediately available. Because Big-Query manages all of the storage, users don't need to worry about backup or replication. Everything from upgrades and replication to backup and restoration are handled transparently and automatically by the storage management system.

One key advantage of working with structured storage at the abstraction level of a table (rather than of a file) and of providing storage management to these tables transparently to the end user is that tables allow BigQuery to support database-like features, such as DML. You can run a query that updates or deletes rows in a table and leave it to BigQuery to determine the best way to modify the storage to reflect this information. BigQuery operations are ACID; that is, all queries will commit completely or not at all. Rest assured that your queries will never see the intermediate state of another query, and queries started after another query completes will never see old data. You do have the ability to fine-tune the storage by specifying directives that control how the data is stored, but these operate at the abstraction level of tables, not files. For example, it is possible to control how tables are partitioned and clustered (we cover these features in detail in Chapter 7) and thereby improve the performance and/or reduce the cost of queries against those tables.

Managed storage is strongly typed, which means that data is validated at entry to the system. Because BigQuery manages the storage and allows users to interact with this storage only via its APIs, it can count on the underlying data not being modified outside of BigQuery. Thus, BigQuery can guarantee to not throw a validation error at read time about any of the data present in its managed storage. This guarantee also implies an authoritative schema, which is useful when figuring out how to query your tables. Besides improving query performance, the presence of an authoritative schema helps when trying to make sense of what data you have because a BigQuery schema contains not just type information but also annotations and table descriptions about how the fields can be used.

One downside of managed storage is that it is more difficult to directly access and process the data using other frameworks. For example, had the data been available at the abstraction level of files, you might have been able to directly run a Hadoop job over a BigQuery dataset. BigQuery addresses this issue by providing a structured parallel API to read the data. This API lets you read at full speed from Spark or Hadoop jobs, but it also provides extra features, like projection, filtering, and dynamic rebalancing.

Integration with Google Cloud Platform

Google Cloud follows the design principle called "separation of responsibility," wherein a small number of high-quality, highly focused products integrate tightly with each other. It is, therefore, important to consider the entire Google Cloud Platform (GCP) when comparing BigQuery with other database products.

A number of different GCP products extend the usefulness of BigQuery or make it easier to understand how BigQuery is being used. We talk about many of these related products in detail in this book, but it is worth being aware of the general separation of responsibilities:

- Stackdriver monitoring and audit logs provide ways to understand BigQuery usage in your organization. In March 2020, Stackdriver was rebranded as Cloud Logging and Cloud Monitoring.

- Cloud Dataproc provides the ability to read, process, and write to BigQuery tables using Apache Spark programs. Because of this, BigQuery can function as the storage layer for a Hadoop-based data lake. On Google Cloud, the line between data warehouse and data lake is blurred.

- Federated queries allow BigQuery to query data held in Google Cloud Storage, Cloud SQL (a relational database), Bigtable (a NoSQL database), Spanner (a distributed database), or Google Drive (which offers spreadsheets). Because of federated queries, BigQuery can function as the processing engine for a data lake whose storage layer is on Cloud Storage.

- Google Cloud Data Loss Prevention API (*https://cloud.google.com/dlp*) helps you to manage sensitive data and provides the capability to redact or mask Personally Identifiable Information (PII) from your tables.

- Other machine learning APIs extend what it is possible on data held in BigQuery; for example, the Cloud Natural Language API can identify people, places, sentiment, and more in free-form text (such as those of customer reviews) held in some table column.

- AutoML Tables and AutoML Text can create high-performing custom machine learning models from data held in BigQuery tables.

- Cloud Data Catalog provides the ability to discover data held across your organization.

- You can use Cloud Pub/Sub to ingest streaming data and Cloud Dataflow to transform and load it into BigQuery. You can use Cloud Dataflow to carry out streaming queries as well. You can, of course, interactively query the streaming data within BigQuery itself.[16]

- Data Studio provides charts and dashboards driven from data in BigQuery. Looker provides an enterprise Business Intelligence (BI) data platform with a semantic layer. Third-party tools such as Tableau also support BigQuery as a backend.

- Cloud AI Platform provides the ability to train sophisticated machine learning programs from data held in BigQuery. It also provides the way to tune the hyperparameters of BigQuery ML models and deploy them for online prediction.

- Cloud Scheduler and Cloud Functions allow for scheduling or triggering of BigQuery queries as part of larger workflows.

- Cloud Data Fusion provides drag-and-drop data integration tools and connectors. Cloud Dataflow provides the ability to create stateful ETL pipelines.

- Cloud Composer allows for orchestration of BigQuery jobs along with tasks that need to be performed in Cloud Dataflow or other processing frameworks, whether on Google Cloud or on-premises in a hybrid cloud setup.

Taken together, BigQuery and the GCP ecosystem have features that span several other database products from other cloud vendors; you can use them as an analytics warehouse but also as an ELT system, a data lake (queries over files), or a source of BI. The rest of this book paints a broad picture of how you can use BigQuery in all of its aspects.

---

16 The separation of responsibility here is that Cloud Dataflow is better for ongoing, routine processing while BigQuery is better for interactive, ad hoc processing. Both Cloud Dataflow and BigQuery handle batch data as well as streaming data, and it is possible to run SQL queries within Cloud Dataflow.

Security and Compliance

The integration with GCP goes beyond just interoperability with other products. Cross-cutting features provided by the platform provide consistent security and compliance.

The fastest hardware and most advanced software are of little use if you can't trust them with your data. BigQuery's security model is tightly integrated with the rest of GCP, so it is possible to take a holistic view of your data security. BigQuery uses Google's IAM access-control system to assign specific permissions to individual users or groups of users. BigQuery also ties in tightly with Google's Virtual Private Cloud (VPC) policy controls, which can protect against users who try to access data from outside your organization, or who try to export it to third parties. Both IAM and VPC controls are designed to work across Google Cloud products, so you don't need to worry that certain products create a security hole.

BigQuery is available in every region where Google Cloud has a presence, enabling you to process the data in the location of your choosing. As of this writing, Google Cloud has more than two dozen datacenters around the world, and new ones are being opened at a fast rate. If you have business reasons for keeping data in Australia or Germany, it is possible to do so. Just create your dataset with the Australian or German region code, and all of your queries against the data will be done within that region.

Some organizations have even stronger data location requirements that go beyond where data is stored and processed. Specifically, they want to ensure that their data cannot be copied or otherwise leave their physical region. GCP has physical region controls that apply across products; you can create a "VPC service controls" policy that disallows data movement outside of a selected region. If you have these controls enabled, users will not be able to copy data across regions or export to Google Cloud Storage buckets in another region.

Summary

BigQuery is a highly scalable data warehouse that provides fast SQL analytics over large datasets in a serverless way. Although users appreciate the scale and speed of BigQuery, company executives often appreciate the transformational benefits that come from being able to do ad hoc querying in a serverless way, opening up data-driven decision making to all parts of the company.

To ingest data into BigQuery, you can use an EL pipeline (commonly used for periodic loads of log files), an ETL pipeline (commonly used when data needs to be enriched or quality controlled), or an ELT pipeline (commonly used for exploratory work).

BigQuery is designed for data analytics (OLAP) workloads and provides full-featured support for SQL:2011. BigQuery can achieve its scale and speed because it is built on innovative engineering ideas such as the use of columnar storage, support for nested and repeated fields, and separation of compute and storage, about which Google went on to publish papers. BigQuery is part of the GCP ecosystem of big data analytics tools and integrates tightly with both the infrastructure pieces (such as security, monitoring, and logging) and the data processing and machine learning pieces (such as streaming, Cloud DLP, and AutoML) of the platform.

## CHAPTER 2

Query Essentials

BigQuery is first and foremost a data warehouse, by which we mean that it provides persistent storage for structured and semi-structured data (like JSON objects). The four basic CRUD operations are supported on this persistent storage:

Create

To insert new records. This is implemented through load operations, by the SQL INSERT statement, and through a streaming insert API. You can also use SQL to create database objects like tables, views, and machine learning models as part of BigQuery's support of the Data Definition Language (DDL). We go into examples of each later.

Read

To retrieve records. This is implemented by the SQL SELECT statement as well as the bulk read API.

Update

To modify existing records. This is implemented by the SQL UPDATE and MERGE statements, which are part of BigQuery's support of the Data Manipulation Language (DML). Note that, as we discussed in Chapter 1, BigQuery is an analytics tool and is not meant to be used for frequent updates.

Delete

To remove existing records. This is implemented by SQL DELETE, which is also a DML operation.

BigQuery is a tool for data analysis, and the majority of queries you can expect to write will be the aforementioned Read operations. Reading and analyzing your data is accomplished by the SELECT statement, which is the focus of this chapter. We cover creating, updating, and deleting data in later chapters.

Simple Queries

BigQuery supports a dialect of SQL that is compliant with SQL:2011 (*https://www.iso.org/standard/53681.html*). When the specification is ambiguous or otherwise lacking, BigQuery follows the conventions set by existing SQL engines. There are other areas in which there is no specification at all, such as with machine learning; in these cases, BigQuery defines its own syntax and semantics.

What's Legacy SQL?

For a long time, BigQuery supported only a limited subset of SQL with some Google enhancements. This was because BigQuery was based on an internal SQL query engine at Google (called Dremel) that was originally built to process log data held in Protocol Buffers (Protobufs).[1] Because it was not built as a general-purpose SQL engine, Dremel could use a dialect of SQL (now referred to as *legacy SQL*) that was well suited to Protobufs, which are used to hold hierarchical structures. For example, the legacy SQL dialect distinguished between records (the complete hierarchical structure pertaining to a log message) and rows (slices through the structure).[2] Therefore, COUNT(*) in Dremel counts the number of non-NULL values in the most repeated field. Even though such features made certain types of queries much easier to write, Dremel took some getting used to because it was not standard SQL.

In this book, we focus exclusively on standard SQL. The BigQuery user interface (UI) in the Google Cloud Platform (GCP) Cloud Console defaults to standard SQL, and new features are not being backported to legacy SQL. However, some older tools and user interfaces default to legacy SQL for backward compatibility reasons. If that is the case for any tool that you are using, preface the query with #standardsql on the first line, as shown in the following example:

```
#standardsql
SELECT DISTINCT gender
FROM `bigquery-public-data`.new_york_citibike.citibike_trips
```

If the BigQuery service receives a query string whose first line consists of #standardsql, the query engine will treat what follows as standard SQL even if the client itself does not know about standard SQL.

---

1 This is a data format that is very popular within Google because it provides efficient storage in a programming-language-neutral way. It is now open source; see *https://developers.google.com/protocol-buffers/*.

2 For more details on Dremel, see *https://ai.google/research/pubs/pub36632*.

Retrieving Rows by Using SELECT

The `SELECT` statement allows you to retrieve the values of specified columns from a table. For example, consider the New York bicycle rentals dataset (*https://bigquery.cloud.google.com/table/bigquery-public-data:new_york.citibike_trips*)—it contains several columns relating to bicycle rentals, including the trip duration and the gender of the person renting the bicycle. We can pull out the values of these columns by using the `SELECT` statement (lines beginning with double dashes or # are comments):

```
-- simple select
SELECT
  gender, tripduration
FROM
  `bigquery-public-data`.new_york_citibike.citibike_trips
LIMIT 5
```

The result looks something like this:

Row	gender	tripduration
1	male	371
2	male	1330
3	male	830
4	male	555
5	male	328

The result set has two columns (`gender` and `tripduration`) in the order specified in the `SELECT`. There are five rows in the result set because we limited it to five in the final line of the query. BigQuery distributes the task of fetching rows to multiple workers, each of which can read a different shard (or part) of the dataset, so if you run the previous query, you might get a different set of five rows.

Note that using a `LIMIT` constrains only the amount of data displayed to you and not the amount of data the query engine needs to process. You are typically charged based on the amount of data processed by your queries, and this usually implies that the more columns your query reads, the higher your cost will be. The number of rows processed will usually be the total size of the table that you are reading, although there are ways to optimize this (which we cover in Chapter 7). We examine performance and pricing considerations in later chapters.

The values are being retrieved from the following:

```
bigquery-public-data.new_york_citibike.citibike_trips
```

Here, `bigquery-public-data` is the project ID, `new_york_citibike` is the dataset, and `citibike_trips` is the table. The project ID indicates ownership of the persistent storage associated with the dataset and its tables. The owner of `bigquery-public-data` is paying the storage costs associated with the `new_york` dataset. The cost of the query is paid by the project within which the query is issued. If you run the preceding query, you pay the query costs. Datasets provide for Identity and Access Management (IAM). The person who created the `new_york_citibike` dataset[3] in BigQuery made it public, which is why we were able to list the tables (*https://bigquery.cloud.google.com/ dataset/bigquery-public-data:new_york*) in the dataset and query one of those tables. The `citibike_trips` table contains all of the bicycle trips. The project, dataset, and table are separated by dots. The backtick is needed as an escape character in this case because the hyphen (-) in the project name (`bigquery-public-data`) would otherwise be interpreted as subtraction. Most developers simply enclose the entire string within backticks, as shown here:

```
-- simple select
SELECT
  gender, tripduration
FROM
  `bigquery-public-data.new_york_citibike.citibike_trips`
LIMIT 5
```

Although this is simpler, you lose the ability to use the table name (`citibike_trips`) as an alias. So it is worth developing the habit of putting the backticks only around the project name and avoiding the use of hyphens when you create your own datasets and tables.

For a long time, our recommendation was that tables in BigQuery be stored in denormalized form (i.e., a single table often containing all of the data you'd need without the need for joining multiple tables). However, with improvements in the service, this is no longer necessary. It is possible now to achieve good performance even with a star schema.

Table 2-1 reviews the three key components of the name `bigquery-public-data`.new_york_citibike.citibike_trips.

Table 2-1. Summary of BigQuery objects and descriptions

BigQuery object	Name	Description
Project	`bigquery-public-data`	Owner of the persistent storage associated with the dataset and its tables. The project also governs the use of all other GCP products as well.
Dataset	`new_york_citibike`	Datasets are top-level containers that are used to organize and control access to tables and views. A user can own multiple datasets.

---

3 The "person" in this case is one of the members of the Google Cloud Platform public datasets team. See Google Cloud Public Datasets (*https://cloud.google.com/public-datasets/*) for what else is available.

BigQuery object	Name	Description
Table/View	`citibike_trips`	A table or view must belong to a dataset, so you need to create at least one dataset before loading data into BigQuery.[a]

[a] See *https://cloud.google.com/bigquery/docs/datasets-intro*.

Distinguishing between each of these three will be critical later when we discuss geographic location, data access, and sharing of data.

Aliasing Column Names with AS

By default, the names of the columns in the result set match those of the table from which the data is retrieved. It is possible to alias the column names by using AS:

```
-- Aliasing column names
SELECT
  gender, tripduration AS rental_duration
FROM
  `bigquery-public-data`.new_york_citibike.citibike_trips
LIMIT 5
```

This now yields the following (your results might be a different set of five):

Row	gender	rental_duration
1	male	432
2	female	1186
3	male	799
4	female	238
5	male	668

Aliasing is useful when you are transforming data. For example, without the alias, a statement such as

```
SELECT
  gender, tripduration/60
FROM
  `bigquery-public-data`.new_york_citibike.citibike_trips
LIMIT 5
```

would result in an automatically assigned column name for the second column in the result set:

Row	gender	f0_
1	male	6.183333333333334
2	male	22.166666666666668
3	male	13.833333333333334
4	male	9.25

Row	gender	f0_
5	male	5.466666666666667

You can assign the second column a more descriptive name by adding an alias to your query:

```
SELECT
  gender, tripduration/60 AS duration_minutes
FROM
  `bigquery-public-data`.new_york_citibike.citibike_trips
LIMIT 5
```

This yields a result similar to the following:

Row	gender	duration_minutes
1	male	6.183333333333334
2	male	22.166666666666668
3	male	13.833333333333334
4	male	9.25
5	male	5.466666666666667

Filtering with WHERE

To find rentals of less than 10 minutes, we could filter the results returned by SELECT by using a WHERE clause:

```
SELECT
  gender, tripduration
FROM
  `bigquery-public-data`.new_york_citibike.citibike_trips
WHERE tripduration < 600
LIMIT 5
```

As expected, the result set now consists only of rows for which the trip duration is less than 600 seconds:

Row	gender	tripduration
1	male	178
2	male	518
3	male	376
4	male	326
5	male	516

The WHERE clause can include Boolean expressions. For example, to find trips rented by females and lasting between 5 and 10 minutes, you could use this:

```
SELECT
  gender, tripduration
FROM
  `bigquery-public-data`.new_york_citibike.citibike_trips
WHERE tripduration >= 300 AND tripduration < 600 AND gender = 'female'
LIMIT 5
```

The OR keyword also works, as does NOT. For example, to find nonfemale riders (i.e., male riders and those whose gender is unknown), the WHERE clause could be as follows:

```
WHERE tripduration < 600 AND NOT gender = 'female'
```

It is also possible to use parentheses to control the order of evaluation. To find female riders who take short trips as well as all male riders, you could use this:

```
WHERE (tripduration < 600 AND gender = 'female') OR gender = 'male'
```

The WHERE clause operates on the columns in the FROM clause; thus, it is not possible to reference aliases from the SELECT list in the WHERE clause. In other words, to retain only trips shorter than 10 minutes, it is not possible to use the following:

```
SELECT
  gender, tripduration/60 AS minutes
FROM
  `bigquery-public-data`.new_york_citibike.citibike_trips
WHERE minutes < 10 -- CAN NOT REFERENCE ALIAS IN WHERE
LIMIT 5
```

Instead, you need to repeat the transformation in the WHERE clause (we explore better alternatives later):

```
SELECT
  gender, tripduration / 60 AS minutes
FROM
  `bigquery-public-data`.new_york_citibike.citibike_trips
WHERE (tripduration / 60) < 10
LIMIT 5
```

SELECT *, EXCEPT, REPLACE

For cost and performance reasons (which we cover in detail in Chapter 7), it is better to select only the columns that you want. If, however, you do want to select all of the columns in the table, you can use SELECT *:

```
SELECT
  *
FROM
  `bigquery-public-data`.new_york_citibike.citibike_stations
WHERE name LIKE '%Riverside%'
```

The WHERE clause uses the LIKE operator to look for stations that have Riverside anywhere in their name.

To select all except for a few columns, use SELECT EXCEPT:

```
SELECT
  * EXCEPT(short_name, last_reported)
FROM
  `bigquery-public-data`.new_york_citibike.citibike_stations
WHERE name LIKE '%Riverside%'
```

This query returns the same result as the previous one except that two of the columns (short_name and last_reported) are omitted.

To select all of the columns but replace a column with another, you can use SELECT REPLACE. For example, you can add 5 to the number of bikes reported to be available using the following:

```
SELECT
  * REPLACE(num_bikes_available + 5 AS num_bikes_available)
FROM
  `bigquery-public-data`.new_york_citibike.citibike_stations
```

Subqueries with WITH

You can reduce the repetitiveness and retain the use of the alias by using a subquery:

```
SELECT * FROM (
  SELECT
    gender, tripduration / 60 AS minutes
  FROM
    `bigquery-public-data`.new_york_citibike.citibike_trips
)
WHERE minutes < 10
LIMIT 5
```

The outer SELECT operates on the inner subquery that is enclosed within parentheses. Because the alias happens in the inner query, the outer query can use the alias in its WHERE clause.

Queries with parentheses can become quite difficult to read. A better approach is to use a WITH clause to provide names to what would otherwise have been subqueries:

```
WITH all_trips AS (
  SELECT
    gender, tripduration / 60 AS minutes
  FROM
    `bigquery-public-data`.new_york_citibike.citibike_trips
)

SELECT * from all_trips
```

```
    WHERE minutes < 10
    LIMIT 5
```

In BigQuery, the WITH clause behaves like a named subquery and does not create temporary tables. We will refer to all_trips as a "from_item"—it's not a table, but you can select from it.

Sorting with ORDER BY

To control the order of rows in the result set, use ORDER BY:

```
SELECT
    gender, tripduration/60 AS minutes
FROM
    `bigquery-public-data`.new_york_citibike.citibike_trips
WHERE gender = 'female'
ORDER BY minutes DESC
LIMIT 5
```

By default, rows in results are not ordered. If an order column is specified, the default is ascending order. By asking for the rows to be listed in descending order and limiting to 5, we get the five longest trips by women in the dataset:

Row	gender	minutes
1	female	250348.9
2	female	226437.93333333332
3	female	207988.71666666667
4	female	159712.05
5	female	154239.0

Note that we are ordering by minutes, which is an alias—because the ORDER BY is carried out after the SELECT, it is possible to use aliases in ORDER BY.

Aggregates

In the example in the previous section, when we converted seconds to minutes by dividing by 60, we operated on every row in the table and transformed it. It is also possible to apply a function to aggregate all of the rows so that the result set contains only one row.

Computing Aggregates by Using GROUP BY

To find the average duration of trips by male riders, you could do the following:

```
SELECT
    AVG(tripduration / 60) AS avg_trip_duration
FROM
```

```
    `bigquery-public-data`.new_york_citibike.citibike_trips
WHERE
    gender = 'male'
```

This yields the following:

Row	avg_trip_duration
1	13.415553172043886

This indicates that the average bicycle trip taken by male riders in New York is about 13.4 minutes. Because the dataset is continuously updated, though, your result might be different.

How about female riders? Although you could run the previous query twice, once for male riders and the next for females, it seems wasteful to traverse through the dataset a second time, changing the WHERE clause. Instead, you can use a GROUP BY:

```
SELECT
    gender, AVG(tripduration / 60) AS avg_trip_duration
FROM
    `bigquery-public-data`.new_york_citibike.citibike_trips
WHERE
    tripduration is not NULL
GROUP BY
    gender
ORDER BY
    avg_trip_duration
```

This yields the following result:

Row	gender	avg_trip_duration
1	male	13.415553172043886
2	female	15.977472148805207
3	unknown	31.4395230232542

The aggregates have now been computed on each group separately. The SELECT expression can include the thing being grouped by (gender) and aggregates (AVG). Note that there are actually three genders in the dataset: male, female, and unknown.

Counting Records by Using COUNT

To see how many rides went into the previous averages, you can simply add a COUNT():

```
SELECT
    gender,
    COUNT(*) AS rides,
    AVG(tripduration / 60) AS avg_trip_duration
```

```
FROM
  `bigquery-public-data`.new_york_citibike.citibike_trips
WHERE
  tripduration IS NOT NULL
GROUP BY
  gender
ORDER BY
  avg_trip_duration
```

This gives us the result shown here:

Row	gender	rides	avg_trip_duration
1	male	35611787	13.415553172043888
2	female	11376412	15.97747214880521
3	unknown	6120522	31.439523023254207

Filtering Grouped Items by Using HAVING

It is possible to post-filter the grouped operations via the HAVING clause. To learn which genders take trips that, on average, last longer than 14 minutes, you can use this:

```
SELECT
  gender, AVG(tripduration / 60) AS avg_trip_duration
FROM
  `bigquery-public-data`.new_york_citibike.citibike_trips
WHERE tripduration IS NOT NULL
GROUP BY
  gender
HAVING avg_trip_duration > 14
ORDER BY
  avg_trip_duration
```

This yields the following:

Row	gender	avg_trip_duration
1	female	15.977472148805209
2	unknown	31.439523023254203

Note that, even though it is possible to filter the gender or trip duration with a WHERE clause, it is not possible to use it to filter by average duration, because the average duration is computed only after the items have been grouped (try it!).

Finding Unique Values by Using DISTINCT

What values of gender are present in the dataset? Although you could use GROUP BY, a simpler way to get a list of distinct values of a column is to use SELECT DISTINCT:

```
SELECT DISTINCT
  gender
FROM
  `bigquery-public-data`.new_york_citibike.citibike_trips
```

This yields a result set with just four rows:

Row	gender
1	male
2	female
3	unknown
4	

Four rows? What is the fourth row? Let's explore:

```
SELECT
  bikeid,
  tripduration,
  gender
FROM
  `bigquery-public-data`.new_york_citibike.citibike_trips
WHERE gender = ""
LIMIT 100
```

This yields the result shown here:

Row	bikeid	tripduration	gender
1	*null*	*null*	
2	*null*	*null*	
3	*null*	*null*	
...			

In this particular case, a blank gender value seems to indicate missing or poor-quality data. We discuss missing data (NULL values) and how you can account for and transform them in Chapter 3, but briefly: if you want to filter for NULLs in a WHERE clause, use the IS NULL or IS NOT NULL operators because other comparison operators (=, !=, <, >) applied to a NULL return NULL and therefore will never match the WHERE condition.

Going back to our original query for DISTINCT genders, it's important to note that the DISTINCT modifies the entire SELECT, not just the gender column. To see what we mean, add a second column to the query's SELECT list:

```
SELECT DISTINCT
  gender,
  usertype
FROM
```

```
    `bigquery-public-data`.new_york_citibike.citibike_trips
  WHERE gender != ''
```

This results in six rows; that is, you get a row for every combination of unique gender and user type (subscriber or customer) that exists in the dataset:

Row	gender	usertype
1	male	Subscriber
2	unknown	Customer
3	female	Subscriber
4	female	Customer
5	male	Customer
6	unknown	Subscriber

A Brief Primer on Arrays and Structs

In this section, we provide a brief primer on arrays so that we can illustrate many of the data types and functions in the next chapter on small, illustrative datasets. The combination of ARRAY (the square brackets in the query that follows) and UNNEST gives us a quick way to experiment with queries, functions, and data types.

For example, if you want to know how the SPLIT function of a string behaves, simply try it out:

```
SELECT
  city, SPLIT(city, ' ') AS parts
FROM (
  SELECT * from UNNEST([
      'Seattle WA', 'New York', 'Singapore'
  ]) AS city
)
```

Here's the result of this quick query:

Row	city	parts
1	Seattle WA	Seattle
		WA
2	New York	New
		York
3	Singapore	Singapore

This ability to hardcode an array of values in the SQL query itself allows you to play with arrays and data types without the need to find an appropriate dataset or wait for long queries to finish. Even better, this processes 0 bytes and therefore does not incur BigQuery charges.[4]

Another way to quickly experiment with a set of values employs `UNION ALL` to combine single row `SELECT` statements:

```
WITH example AS (
  SELECT 'Sat' AS day, 1451 AS numrides, 1018 AS oneways
  UNION ALL SELECT 'Sun', 2376, 936
  UNION ALL SELECT 'Mon', 1476, 736
)

SELECT * from example
WHERE numrides < 2000
```

This yields the two rows in the small inline dataset that have fewer than 2,000 rides:

Row	day	numrides	oneways
1	Sat	1451	1018
2	Mon	1476	736

In the next chapter, we use such inline datasets with hardcoded numbers to illustrate various aspects of the way different data types and functions behave.

The purpose of this section is to quickly introduce arrays and structs so that we can use them in illustrative examples. We review these concepts in greater detail in Chapter 8, so feel free to quickly skim the remainder of this section for now.

Creating Arrays by Using ARRAY_AGG

Consider finding the number of trips by gender and year:

```
SELECT
  gender
  , EXTRACT(YEAR from starttime) AS year --
  , COUNT(*) AS numtrips
FROM
  `bigquery-public-data`.new_york_citibike.citibike_trips
WHERE gender != 'unknown' and starttime IS NOT NULL
GROUP BY gender, year
HAVING year > 2016
```

This returns the following:

---

4 We believe all mentions of price to be correct as of the writing of this book, but please do refer to the relevant policy and pricing sheets (*https://cloud.google.com/bigquery/pricing*) because these are subject to change.

Row	gender	year	numtrips
1	male	2017	9306602
2	male	2018	3955871
3	female	2018	1260893
4	female	2017	3236735

What's with the leading commas in the SELECT clause? At the time this book was first published (October 2019), BigQuery Standard SQL did not support a trailing comma, and so moving the comma to the next line allowed the data analyst to easily reorder or comment lines and still have a working query:

```
SELECT
  gender
  , EXTRACT(YEAR from starttime) AS year
  -- comment out this line , COUNT(1) AS numtrips
FROM etc.
```

BigQuery now supports trailing commas, and so this is no longer needed, but it will take us a while to break this habit.[5]

What would be required, though, if we want to get a time-series of the number of trips associated with each gender over the years—in other words, the following result?

Row	gender	numtrips
1	male	9306602
		3955871
2	female	3236735
		1260893

To get this, you would need to create an array of the numbers of trips. You can represent that array in SQL using the ARRAY type and create such an array by using ARRAY_AGG:

```
SELECT
  gender
  , ARRAY_AGG(numtrips order by year) AS numtrips
FROM (
  SELECT
    gender
    , EXTRACT(YEAR from starttime) AS year
```

---

5 For an entertaining data-driven examination of the correlation between project success and the use of leading commas, see *https://oreil.ly/mFZKh*.

```
    , COUNT(1) AS numtrips
  FROM
    `bigquery-public-data`.new_york_citibike.citibike_trips
  WHERE gender != 'unknown' and starttime IS NOT NULL
  GROUP BY gender, year
  HAVING year > 2016
)
GROUP BY gender
```

Normally, when you group by gender, you compute a single scalar value for the group, such as the AVG(numtrips) to find the average number of trips across all years. ARRAY_AGG allows you to collect the individual values and put them into an ordered list, or ARRAY.

The ARRAY type is not limited to the results of queries. Because BigQuery can ingest hierarchical formats such as JSON, it is possible that the input data contains JSON arrays—for example:

```
[
  {
    "gender": "male",
    "numtrips": [
      "9306602",
      "3955871"
    ]
  },
  {
    "gender": "female",
    "numtrips": [
      "3236735",
      "1260893"
    ]
  }
]
```

Creating a table by ingesting such a JSON file will result in a table whose numtrips column is an ARRAY type. An array is an ordered list of non-NULL elements; for instance, ARRAY<INT64> is an array of integers.

Technically, NULL elements in arrays are permissible as long as you don't try to save them to a table. Thus, for example, the following *will not* work, because you are trying to save the array [1, NULL, 2] to the temporary table that holds the results:

```
WITH example AS (
    SELECT true AS is_vowel, 'a' as letter, 1 as position
    UNION ALL SELECT false, 'b', 2
    UNION ALL SELECT false, 'c', 3
)
SELECT ARRAY_AGG(IF(position = 2, NULL, position)) as
positions from example
```

However, the following will work because the intermediate array with a NULL element is not being saved:

```
WITH example AS (
    SELECT true AS is_vowel, 'a' as letter, 1 as position
    UNION ALL SELECT false, 'b', 2
    UNION ALL SELECT false, 'c', 3
)
SELECT ARRAY_LENGTH(ARRAY_AGG(IF(position = 2, NULL,
position))) from example
```

Array of STRUCT

A STRUCT is a group of fields in order. The fields can be named (if omitted, BigQuery will assign them names), which we recommend for readability:

```
SELECT
  [
    STRUCT('male' as gender, [9306602, 3955871] as numtrips)
    , STRUCT('female' as gender, [3236735, 1260893] as numtrips)
  ] AS bikerides
```

This results in the following:

Row	bikerides.gender	bikerides.numtrips
1	male	9306602
		3955871
	female	3236735
		1260893

TUPLE

We could have left out the STRUCT keyword and the names of the fields, in which case we would have ended up with a tuple or anonymous struct. BigQuery assigns arbitrary names for unnamed columns and struct fields in the result of a query; thus

```
SELECT
  [
    ('male', [9306602, 3955871])
    , ('female', [3236735, 1260893])
  ]
```

yields this result:

Row	f0_._field_1	f0_._field_2
1	male	9306602
		3955871
	female	3236735
		1260893

Obviously, leaving out aliases for the field names makes subsequent queries unreadable and unmaintainable. Do not do this except for throwaway experimentation.

Working with Arrays

Given an array, we can find the length of the array and retrieve individual items:

```
SELECT
  ARRAY_LENGTH(bikerides) as num_items
  , bikerides[ OFFSET(0) ].gender as first_gender
FROM
(SELECT
  [
    STRUCT('male' as gender, [9306602, 3955871] as numtrips)
    , STRUCT('female' as gender, [3236735, 1260893] as numtrips)
  ] AS bikerides)
```

This yields the following:

Row	num_items	first_gender
1	2	male

Offsets are numbered starting at zero, which is why OFFSET(0) gives us the first item in the array.[6]

---

6 You can also use ORDINAL(1) to work with 1-based indexing. We look at arrays in more detail in Chapter 8.

UNNEST an Array

In the query

```
SELECT
    [
        STRUCT('male' as gender, [9306602, 3955871] as numtrips)
        , STRUCT('female' as gender, [3236735, 1260893] as numtrips)
    ]
```

the SELECT returns exactly one row containing an array, and so both genders are part of the same row (look at the Row column):

Row	f0_.gender	f0_.numtrips
1	male	9306602
		3955871
	female	3236735
		1260893

UNNEST is a function that returns the elements of an array as rows, so you can UNNEST the result array to get a row corresponding to each item in the array:

```
SELECT * from UNNEST(
    [
        STRUCT('male' as gender, [9306602, 3955871] as numtrips)
        , STRUCT('female' as gender, [3236735, 1260893] as numtrips)
    ])
```

This yields the following:

Row	gender	numtrips
1	male	9306602
		3955871
2	female	3236735
		1260893

Notice that UNNEST is actually a from_item—you can SELECT from it. You can select just parts of the array as well. For example, we can get only the numtrips column by using this:

```
SELECT numtrips from UNNEST(
    [
        STRUCT('male' as gender, [9306602, 3955871] as numtrips)
        , STRUCT('female' as gender, [3236735, 1260893] as numtrips)
    ])
```

This gives us the following results:

Row	numtrips
1	9306602
	3955871
2	3236735
	1260893

Joining Tables

Data warehouse schemas often rely on a primary "fact" table that contains events, and satellite "dimension" tables that contain extended, slowly changing information. For example, a retail schema might have a "Sales" table as the fact table and then "Products" and "Customers" tables as dimensions. When using this type of schema, the majority of queries will require a JOIN operation, such as to return the names of all the products purchased by a particular customer.

BigQuery supports all of the common join types from relational algebra: inner joins, outer joins, cross joins, anti-joins, semi-joins, and anti-semi-joins. Although it can sometimes be faster to avoid a JOIN, BigQuery can efficiently join tables of almost any size. Chapter 7 discusses more about how to optimize JOIN performance, but for now, we describe only the basic JOIN operation.

The JOIN Explained

In Chapter 1, we looked at an example of a JOIN across tables in two different datasets produced by two different organizations. Let's revisit that for a refresher:

```
WITH bicycle_rentals AS (
  SELECT
    COUNT(starttime) as num_trips,
    EXTRACT(DATE from starttime) as trip_date
    FROM `bigquery-public-data`.new_york_citibike.citibike_trips
  GROUP BY trip_date
),

rainy_days AS
(
SELECT
  date,
  (MAX(prcp) > 5) AS rainy
FROM (
  SELECT
    wx.date AS date,
    IF (wx.element = 'PRCP', wx.value/10, NULL) AS prcp
  FROM
    `bigquery-public-data`.ghcn_d.ghcnd_2016 AS wx
  WHERE
    wx.id = 'USW00094728'
```

```
  )
GROUP BY
  date
)

SELECT
  ROUND(AVG(bk.num_trips)) AS num_trips,
  wx.rainy
FROM bicycle_rentals AS bk
JOIN rainy_days AS wx
ON wx.date = bk.trip_date
GROUP BY wx.rainy
```

In Chapter 1, we asked you to ignore the syntax, but let's parse it now.

The first WITH pulls out the number of trips by day from the citibike_trips table into a from_item called bicycle_rentals. This is not a table, but it is something from which we can select. Hence, we will refer to it as a "from_item." The second from_item is called rainy_days and is created from the Global Historical Climate Network (GHCN) observation in each day. This from_item marks each day as being rainy or not depending on whether at least five mm of precipitation was observed at weather station 'USW00094728', which happens to be in New York.

So now we have two from_items. Let's visualize them separately:

```
WITH bicycle_rentals AS (
  SELECT
    COUNT(starttime) as num_trips,
    EXTRACT(DATE from starttime) as trip_date
  FROM `bigquery-public-data`.new_york_citibike.citibike_trips
  GROUP BY trip_date
)
SELECT * from bicycle_rentals LIMIT 5
```

The bicycle_rentals from_item looks like this:

Row	num_trips	trip_date
1	31287	2013-09-16
2	22477	2015-12-30
3	37812	2017-09-02
4	54230	2017-11-15
5	25719	2013-11-07

Similarly, the rainy_days from_item looks like this:

Row	date	rainy
1	2016-10-11	false
2	2016-12-13	false

Row	date	rainy
3	2016-09-28	false
4	2016-01-25	false
5	2016-05-24	false

We can now join these from_items using the join condition that the `trip_date` in one is the same as the date in the second:

```
SELECT
  bk.trip_date,
  bk.num_trips,
  wx.rainy
FROM bicycle_rentals AS bk
JOIN rainy_days AS wx
ON wx.date = bk.trip_date
LIMIT 5
```

This creates a table in which columns from the two tables are joined by date:

Row	trip_date	num_trips	rainy
1	2016-07-13	55486	false
2	2016-04-25	42308	false
3	2016-09-27	61346	true
4	2016-07-15	48572	false
5	2016-05-20	52543	false

Given this, finding the average number of trips on rainy and nonrainy dates is straightforward.

What we have illustrated is called an *inner join*, and it is the type of JOIN used if no join type is specified.

Here's how the JOIN works:

- Create two from_items. These can be anything: any two of a table, a subquery, an array, or a WITH statement from which you can select.
- Identify a join condition. The join condition does not need to be an equality condition; any Boolean condition that uses the two from_items will do.
- Select the columns that you want. If identically named columns exist in both from_items, use aliases (bk, wx in the previous example query) to clearly specify from which from_item the column needs to come.
- If not using an inner join, specify a join type.

The only requirement for carrying out such a join is that all the datasets used to create the from_items are in the same BigQuery region (all BigQuery public datasets are in the US region).

INNER JOIN

There are several types of joins. The INNER JOIN (or simply JOIN), to which the previous example defaulted, creates a common set of rows to select from:

```
WITH from_item_a AS (
  SELECT 'Dalles' as city, 'OR' as state
  UNION ALL SELECT 'Tokyo', 'Tokyo'
  UNION ALL SELECT 'Mumbai', 'Maharashtra'
),

from_item_b AS (
  SELECT 'OR' as state, 'USA' as country
  UNION ALL SELECT 'Tokyo', 'Japan'
  UNION ALL SELECT 'Maharashtra', 'India'
)

SELECT from_item_a.*, country
FROM from_item_a
JOIN from_item_b
ON from_item_a.state = from_item_b.state
```

The first from_item has a list of cities, and the second from_item identifies the country each of the states belongs to. Joining the two yields a dataset with three columns:

Row	city	state	country
1	Dalles	OR	USA
2	Tokyo	Tokyo	Japan
3	Mumbai	Maharashtra	India

Again, the join condition does not need to be an equality check. Any Boolean condition will do, although it's best to use an equality condition if possible because BigQuery will return an error if the JOIN cannot be executed efficiently.

For example, we might have a business rule that shipping from one country to another involves a surcharge. To get a list of countries for which there will be a surcharge from a given location, we could have specified this:

```
SELECT from_item_a.*, country AS surcharge
FROM from_item_a
JOIN from_item_b
ON from_item_a.state != from_item_b.state
```

We would obtain the following:

Row	city	state	surcharge
1	Dalles	OR	Japan
2	Dalles	OR	India
3	Tokyo	Tokyo	USA
4	Tokyo	Tokyo	India
5	Mumbai	Maharashtra	USA
6	Mumbai	Maharashtra	Japan

Notice that we get a row for each time that the join condition is met. Because there are two rows for which the state doesn't match, we get two rows for each row in the original from_item_a. If the join condition is not met for some row, that row's data items will not make it to the output.

CROSS JOIN

The CROSS JOIN, or cartesian product, is a join with no join condition. All rows from both from_items are joined. This is the join that we would get if the join condition of an INNER JOIN always evaluated to true.

For example, suppose that you organized a tournament and have a table of the winners of each event in the tournament, and another table containing the gifts for each event. You can give each winner the gift corresponding only to their event by doing an INNER JOIN (this is the default JOIN):

```
WITH winners AS (
  SELECT 'John' as person, '100m' as event
  UNION ALL SELECT 'Hiroshi', '200m'
  UNION ALL SELECT 'Sita', '400m'
),
gifts AS (
  SELECT 'Google Home' as gift, '100m' as event
  UNION ALL SELECT 'Google Hub', '200m'
  UNION ALL SELECT 'Pixel3', '400m'
)
SELECT winners.*, gifts.gift
FROM winners
INNER JOIN gifts
USING (event)
```

This would provide the following result:

Row	person	event	gift
1	John	100m	Google Home
2	Hiroshi	200m	Google Hub
3	Sita	400m	Pixel3

On the other hand, if you want to give each gift to each winner (i.e., each winner gets all three gifts), you could do a CROSS JOIN:

```
WITH winners AS (
  SELECT 'John' as person, '100m' as event
  UNION ALL SELECT 'Hiroshi', '200m'
  UNION ALL SELECT 'Sita', '400m'
),
gifts AS (
  SELECT 'Google Home' as gift
  UNION ALL SELECT 'Google Hub'
  UNION ALL SELECT 'Pixel3'
)
SELECT person, gift
FROM winners
CROSS JOIN gifts
```

This yields a row for each potential combination:

Row	person	gift
1	John	Google Home
2	John	Google Hub
3	John	Pixel3
4	Hiroshi	Google Home
5	Hiroshi	Google Hub
6	Hiroshi	Pixel3
7	Sita	Google Home
8	Sita	Google Hub
9	Sita	Pixel3

Even though we wrote

```
SELECT from_item_a.*, from_item_b.*
FROM from_item_a
CROSS JOIN from_item_b
```

we could also have written this:

```
SELECT from_item_a.*, from_item_b.*
FROM from_item_a, from_item_b
```

Therefore, a CROSS JOIN is also termed a *comma cross join*.

OUTER JOIN

Suppose that we have winners in events for which there is no gift, and gifts for events that didn't take place in our tournament:

```
WITH winners AS (
  SELECT 'John' as person, '100m' as event
```

```
      UNION ALL SELECT 'Hiroshi', '200m'
      UNION ALL SELECT 'Sita', '400m'
      UNION ALL SELECT 'Kwame', '50m'
    ),
    gifts AS (
      SELECT 'Google Home' as gift, '100m' as event
      UNION ALL SELECT 'Google Hub', '200m'
      UNION ALL SELECT 'Pixel3', '400m'
      UNION ALL SELECT 'Google Mini', '5000m'
    )
```

In an INNER JOIN (on the event column), the winner of the 50-meter dash doesn't receive a gift, and the gift for the 5,000-meter event goes unclaimed. In a CROSS JOIN, as we noted, every winner receives every gift. OUTER JOINs control what happens if the join condition is not met. Table 2-2 summarizes the various types of joins and the resulting output.

Table 2-2. Summary of types of joins and their outputs

Syntax	What happens	Output		
SELECT person, gift FROM winners INNER JOIN gifts ON winners.event = gifts.event	Only rows that meet the join condition are retained	Row	person	gift
		1	John	Google Home
		2	Hiroshi	Google Hub
		3	Sita	Pixel3
SELECT person, gift FROM winners FULL OUTER JOIN gifts ON winners.event = gifts.event	All rows are retained even if the join condition is not met	Row	person	gift
		1	John	Google Home
		2	Hiroshi	Google Hub
		3	Sita	Pixel3
		4	Kwame	*null*
		5	*null*	Google Mini
SELECT person, gift FROM winners LEFT OUTER JOIN gifts ON winners.event = gifts.event	All the winners are retained, but some gifts are discarded	Row	person	gift
		1	John	Google Home
		2	Hiroshi	Google Hub
		3	Sita	Pixel3
		4	Kwame	*null*
SELECT person, gift FROM winners RIGHT OUTER JOIN gifts ON winners.event = gifts.event	All the gifts are retained, but some winners aren't	Row	person	gift
		1	John	Google Home
		2	Hiroshi	Google Hub
		3	Sita	Pixel3
		4	*null*	Google Mini

Saving and Sharing

The BigQuery web UI offers the ability to save and share queries. This is handy for collaboration because you can send colleagues a link to the query text that enables them to execute the query immediately. Be aware, though, that if someone has your query, they might not be able to execute it if they don't have access to your data. We discuss how to share and limit access to your datasets in Chapter 10.

Query History and Caching

We should note that BigQuery retains, for audit and caching purposes, a history of the queries that you submitted to the service (regardless of whether the queries succeeded), as illustrated in Figure 2-1.

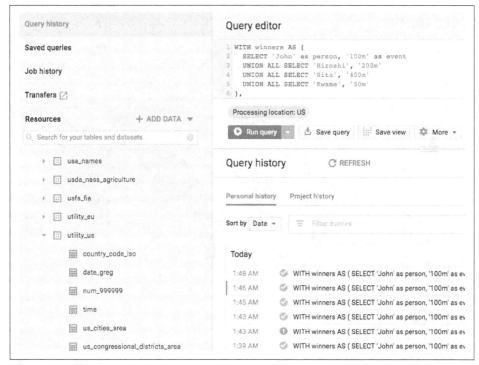

Figure 2-1. The history of queries submitted to the BigQuery service is available via the "Query history" tab in the web UI

This history includes all queries submitted by you to the service, not just those submitted via the web UI. Clicking any of the queries provides the text of the query and the ability to open the query in the editor so that you can modify and rerun it. In addition, the historical information includes the amount of data processed by the query and the execution time. As of this writing, the history is limited to 1,000 queries and six months.

The actual results of the query are stored in a temporary table that expires after about 24 hours. If you are within that expiry window, you will also be able to browse the results of the query from the web UI. Your personal history is available only to you.

Administrators of the project to which your query was billed will also see your query text in the project's history.

This temporary table is also used as a cache if the exact same query text is submitted to the service and the query does not involve dynamic elements such as `CURRENT_TIMESTAMP()` or `RAND()`. Cached query results incur no charges, but note that the algorithm to determine whether a query is a duplicate simply does a string match—even an extra whitespace can result in the query being reexecuted.

Saved Queries

You can save any query by loading it into the query editor, clicking the "Save query" button, and then giving the query a name, as shown in Figure 2-2. BigQuery then provides a URL to the query text.

Figure 2-2. Save a query by clicking the "Save query" button in the web UI

You can also choose to make the saved query shareable, in which case anyone who has the URL will be directed to a page with the query text prepopulated.

When you share a query, all that you share is the text of the query; you do not share access to any data. Dataset permissions to execute the query must be provided independently using the IAM controls (we discuss these in Chapter 10). Also, unlike most BigQuery features, the ability to save and share queries is available only from the web UI. As of this writing, there is no REST API or client library available for this.

The list of saved queries is available from the UI. You can turn off link sharing at any time to make the query text private again, as illustrated in Figure 2-3.

Figure 2-3. You can turn off link sharing at any time to make the query text private again

Views Versus Shared Queries

One of the advantages of sharing a query link (as opposed to simply copying the text of the query into an email) is that you can continue to edit the query so that your collaborators always get the latest version of the query. This is useful when the envisioned use case is that they might want to examine the query text, modify it, and then run the query.

The query text does not need to be syntactically correct; you can save and share incomplete query text or template queries that need to be completed by the end user. These capabilities are helpful when you're collaborating with colleagues.

If you expect the person to whom you are sending the query to subset or query the results of your query, it is better to save your query as a view and send your colleague a link to the view. Another advantage of views over shared queries is that views are placed into datasets and offer fine-grained IAM controls. Views can also be materialized.

We look at authorized views and at dynamically filtering them based on the user in Chapter 10.

Summary

In this chapter, you saw how BigQuery supports SQL:2011: selecting records (SELECT), aliasing column names (AS), filtering (WHERE), using subqueries (parentheses and WITH), sorting (ORDER), aggregating (GROUP, AVG, COUNT, MIN, MAX, etc.), filtering grouped items (HAVING), filtering unique values (DISTINCT), and joining (INNER/CROSS/OUTER JOIN). There is also support for arrays (ARRAY_AGG, UNNEST) and structs (STRUCT). You also looked at how to review the history of queries (the text of the query, not the results) submitted to the service. This history is available, you learned, to the user who submitted the query, and to project administrators. And you learned that it is possible to share query text through a link.

## CHAPTER 3

Data Types, Functions, and Operators

In the bike rental queries in the previous chapters, when we divided the trip duration by 60, we were able to do so because trip duration was a numeric type. Trying to divide the gender by 60 would not have worked because gender is a string. The functions and operations you have at your disposal might be restricted based on the type of data to which you are applying them.

BigQuery supports several data types to store numeric, string, time, geographic, structured, and semi-structured data:

INT64
> This is the only integer type. It can represent numbers ranging from approximately 10^{-19} to 10^{19}. For real-valued numbers, use FLOAT64, and for Booleans, use BOOL.

NUMERIC
> NUMERIC offers 38 digits of precision and 9 decimal digits of scale and is suitable for exact calculations, such as in finance.

STRING
> This is a first-class type and represents variable-length sequences of Unicode characters. BYTES are variable-length sequences of characters (not Unicode).

TIMESTAMP
> This represents an absolute point in time.

DATETIME
> This represents a calendar date and time. DATE and TIME are also available separately.

GEOGRAPHY

GEOGRAPHY represents points, lines, and polygons on the surface of the Earth.

STRUCT *and* ARRAY

See the description for each of these in Chapter 2.

Numeric Types and Functions

As just stated, there is only one integer type (INT64) and only one floating-point type (FLOAT64). Both of these types support the typical *arithmetic* operations (+, −, /, *— for add, subtract, divide, and multiply, respectively). Thus, we can find the fraction of bike rentals that are one-way by simply dividing one column by the other:

```
WITH example AS (
  SELECT 'Sat' AS day, 1451 AS numrides, 1018 AS oneways
  UNION ALL SELECT 'Sun', 2376, 936
)
SELECT *, (oneways/numrides) AS frac_oneway from example
```

This yields the following:

Row	day	numrides	oneways	frac_oneway
1	Sat	1451	1018	0.7015851137146796
2	Sun	2376	936	0.3939393939393939

Besides the arithmetic operators, *bitwise* operations (<< and >> for shifting, & and | for bitwise AND and OR, etc.) are also supported on integer types.

To operate on data types, we can use *functions*. Functions perform operations on the values that are input to them. As with other programming languages, functions in SQL encapsulate reusable logic and abstract away the complexity of their implementation. Table 3-1 presents the various types of functions.

Table 3-1. Types of functions

Type of function	Description	Example
Scalar	A function that operates on one or more input parameters and returns a single value. A scalar function can be used wherever its return data type is allowed.	ROUND(3.14) returns 3, which is a FLOAT64, and so the ROUND function can be used wherever a FLOAT64 is allowed. SUBSTR("hello", 1, 2) returns "he" and is an example of a scalar function that takes three input parameters.
Aggregate	A function that performs a calculation on a collection of values and returns a single value. Aggregate functions are often used with a GROUP BY to perform a computation over a group of rows.	MAX(tripduration) computes the maximum value within the tripduration column. Other aggregate functions include SUM(), COUNT(), AVG(), etc.

Type of function	Description	Example
Analytic	Analytic functions operate on a collection of values but return an output for each value in the collection. A window frame is used to specify the set of rows to which the analytic function applies.	`row_number()`, `rank()`, etc. are analytic functions. We look at these in Chapter 8.
Table-valued	A function that returns a result set and can therefore be used in FROM clauses.	You can call UNNEST on an array and then select from it.
User-defined	A function that is not built in, but whose implementation is specified by the user. User-defined functions can be written in SQL (or JavaScript) and can themselves return any of the aforementioned types.	`CREATE TEMP FUNCTION lastElement(arr ANY TYPE) AS (` `  arr[ORDINAL(ARRAY_LENGTH(arr))] );`

Mathematical Functions

Had we wanted to round off the end-result of the query that computed the fraction of bike rentals that were one-way, we would have used one of the many built-in mathematical functions (*https://cloud.google.com/bigquery/docs/reference/standard-sql/mathematical_functions*) that work on integer and floating-point types:

```
WITH example AS (
  SELECT 'Sat' AS day, 1451 AS numrides, 1018 AS oneways
  UNION ALL SELECT 'Sun', 2376, 936
)
SELECT *, ROUND(oneways/numrides, 2) AS frac_oneway from example
```

This returns the following:

Row	day	numrides	oneways	frac_oneway
1	Sat	1451	1018	0.7
2	Sun	2376	936	0.39

Standard-Compliant Floating-Point Division

The division operator fails if the denominator is zero or if the result overflows. Rather than protect the division by checking for zero values beforehand, it is better to use a special function for division whenever the denominator could be zero, as is the case in the previous example. A better form of that query would be this:

```
WITH example AS (
  SELECT 'Sat' AS day, 1451 AS numrides, 1018 AS oneways
  UNION ALL SELECT 'Sun', 2376, 936
  UNION ALL SELECT 'Wed', 0, 0
)
SELECT
```

```
    *, ROUND(IEEE_Divide(oneways, numrides), 2)
  AS frac_oneway from example
```

The IEEE_Divide function follows the standard set by the Institute of Electrical and Electronics Engineers (IEEE) and returns a special floating-point number called Not-a-Number (NaN) when a division by zero is attempted.

Also try the previous query using the standard division operator and using SAFE_DIVIDE (discussed shortly).[1] Recall that, for your copy-pasting convenience, all the queries in this book are available in the book's GitHub repository (*https://www.github.com/GoogleCloudPlatform/bigquery-oreilly-book/*).

SAFE Functions

You can make any scalar function return NULL instead of raising an error by prefixing it with SAFE. For example, the following query will raise an error because the logarithm of a negative number is undefined:

```
SELECT LOG(10, -3), LOG(10, 3)
```

However, by prefixing the LOG with SAFE, like so:

```
SELECT SAFE.LOG(10, -3), SAFE.LOG(10, 3)
```

you will get NULL for the result of LOG(10, -3):

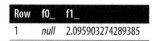

The SAFE prefix works for mathematical functions, string functions (for example, the SUBSTR function would normally raise an error if the starting index is negative, but it returns NULL if invoked as SAFE.SUBSTR), and time functions. It is, however, restricted to scalar functions and will not work for aggregate functions, analytic functions, or user-defined functions.

Comparisons

Comparisons are carried out using operators. The operators <, <=, >, >=, and != (or <>) are used to obtain the results of comparison. NULL, followed by NaN, is assumed to be smaller than valid numbers (including -inf) for the purposes of ordering. However, comparisons with NaN always return false and comparisons with NULL always return NULL. This can lead to seemingly paradoxical results:

---

1 The standard division operator raises a division-by-zero error. SAFE_DIVIDE returns NULL for the entry when division by zero is attempted.

```
WITH example AS (
  SELECT 'Sat' AS day, 1451 AS numrides, 1018 AS oneways
  UNION ALL SELECT 'Sun', 2376, 936
  UNION ALL SELECT 'Mon', NULL, NULL
  UNION ALL SELECT 'Tue', IEEE_Divide(-3,0), 0 -- this is -inf,0
)
SELECT * from example
ORDER BY numrides
```

This query returns the following:

Row	day	numrides	oneways
1	Mon	*null*	*null*
2	Tue	-Infinity	0
3	Sat	1451.0	1018
4	Sun	2376.0	936

However, filtering for fewer than 2000 rides with

```
SELECT * from example
WHERE numrides < 2000
```

yields only two results, not three:

Row	day	numrides	oneways
1	Sat	1451.0	1018
2	Tue	-Infinity	345

This is because the WHERE clause returns only those rows for which the result is true, and when NULL is compared to 2000, the result is NULL and not true.

Note that the operators & and | exist in BigQuery but are used only for bitwise operations. The ! symbol, as in !=, means NOT, but it does not work as a standalone—you cannot say !gender to compute the logical negative of gender, as you can in other languages. An alternate way to specify not-equals is to write <>, but be consistent on whether you use != or <>.

Precise Decimal Calculations with NUMERIC

INT64 and FLOAT64 are designed to be flexible and fast, but they are limited by the fact that they are stored in a base-2 (0s and 1s) form in a 64-bit area of computer memory when being used for calculations. This is a trade-off well worth making in most applications, but financial and accounting applications often require exact calculations for numbers represented in decimal (base-10).

The NUMERIC data type in BigQuery provides 38 digits to represent numbers, with 9 of those digits appearing after the decimal point. It uses 16 bytes for storage and can represent decimal fractions exactly, thus making it suitable for financial calculations.

For example, imagine that you needed to compute the sum of three payments. You'd want the results to be exact. When using FLOAT64 values, however, the tiny differences between how the number is represented in memory and how the number is represented in decimals can add up:

```
WITH example AS (
  SELECT 1.23 AS payment
  UNION ALL SELECT 7.89
  UNION ALL SELECT 12.43
)
SELECT
  SUM(payment) AS total_paid,
  AVG(payment) AS average_paid
FROM example
```

Look at what we get:

Row	total_paid	average_paid
1	21.549999999999997	7.183333333333334

In financial and accounting applications, these imprecisions can add up and make balancing the books tricky.

Watch what happens when we change the data type of payment to be NUMERIC:

```
WITH example AS (
  SELECT NUMERIC '1.23' AS payment
  UNION ALL SELECT NUMERIC '7.89'
  UNION ALL SELECT NUMERIC '12.43'
)
SELECT
  SUM(payment) AS total_paid,
  AVG(payment) AS average_paid
FROM example
```

The problem goes away. The sum of the payments is now precise (the average cannot be represented precisely even in NUMERIC because it is a repeating decimal):

Row	total_paid	average_paid
1	21.55	7.183333333

Note that NUMERIC types need to be directly ingested into BigQuery as strings (NUMERIC '1.23'); otherwise, the floating-point representation will obviate any of the precision gains to be had.

Working with BOOL

Boolean variables are those that can be either `True` or `False`. Because SQL is case insensitive, `TRUE`, `true`, and so on also work.

Logical Operations

Recall from the section on filtering within the `WHERE` clause that the `WHERE` clause can include Boolean expressions that include `AND`, `OR`, and `NOT`, as well as parentheses to control the order of execution. We used this query to illustrate these options:

```
SELECT
  gender, tripduration
FROM
  `bigquery-public-data`.new_york_citibike.citibike_trips
WHERE (tripduration < 600 AND gender = 'female') OR gender = 'male'
```

You could use comparison operators with Boolean variables, as in the following:

```
WITH example AS (
  SELECT NULL AS is_vowel, NULL as letter, -1 as position
  UNION ALL SELECT true, 'a', 1
  UNION ALL SELECT false, 'b', 2
  UNION ALL SELECT false, 'c', 3
)
SELECT * from example WHERE is_vowel != false
```

This gives us the following:

Row	is_vowel	letter	position
1	true	a	1

However, it is often simpler to use the `IS` operator when comparing against built-in constants, as shown in this example:

```
WITH example AS (
  SELECT NULL AS is_vowel, NULL as letter, -1 as position
  UNION ALL SELECT true, 'a', 1
  UNION ALL SELECT false, 'b', 2
  UNION ALL SELECT false, 'c', 3
)
SELECT * from example WHERE is_vowel IS NOT false
```

This yields the following:

Row	is_vowel	letter	position
1	null	null	-1
2	true	a	1

Note that the two queries yield different results. The comparators (=, !=, <, etc.) return NULL for comparisons against NULL, whereas the IS operator doesn't.

 NULLs typically represent missing values or values that were not collected. They have no value and are not zero, empty strings, or blanks. If your dataset has NULLs, you must tread carefully since comparisons with NULL always return NULL, and so the WHERE clause will filter out NULL values. Use the IS operator to check where a value is NULL.

It is simpler and more readable to use Boolean variables directly:

```
WITH example AS (
  SELECT NULL AS is_vowel, NULL as letter, -1 as
position
  UNION ALL SELECT true, 'a', 1
  UNION ALL SELECT false, 'b', 2
  UNION ALL SELECT false, 'c', 3
)

SELECT * from example WHERE is_vowel
```

The result here is like is_vowel IS TRUE:

Row	is_vowel	letter	position
1	true	a	1

Of course, such readability depends on naming the Boolean variables well!

Conditional Expressions

It is not just in the WHERE clause that Booleans are useful. It is possible to simplify many queries by using conditional expressions in the SELECT. For example, suppose that you need to compute the sales price of each item in a catalog based on the desired markup and tax rate corresponding to the item. If your catalog is missing values for some of the necessary information, you might want to impute a default markup or default tax rate. You can achieve this with the IF function:

```
WITH catalog AS (
  SELECT 30.0 AS costPrice, 0.15 AS markup, 0.1 AS taxRate
  UNION ALL SELECT NULL, 0.21, 0.15
  UNION ALL SELECT 30.0, NULL, 0.09
  UNION ALL SELECT 30.0, 0.30, NULL
  UNION ALL SELECT 30.0, NULL, NULL
)
SELECT
  *, ROUND(
    costPrice *
```

```
      IF(markup IS NULL, 1.05, 1+markup) *
      IF(taxRate IS NULL, 1.10, 1+taxRate)
    , 2) AS salesPrice
  FROM catalog
```

This yields a valid `salesPrice` for all items except those for which we don't know the cost:

Row	costPrice	markup	taxRate	salesPrice
1	30.0	0.15	0.1	37.95
2	*null*	0.21	0.15	*null*
3	30.0	*null*	0.09	34.34
4	30.0	0.3	*null*	42.9
5	30.0	*null*	*null*	34.65

The way the `IF` function works is that the first parameter is the condition to be evaluated. If the condition is true, the second parameter is used, or else the third parameter is used. Because this function occurs in the `SELECT`, it is carried out row by row.

Cleaner NULL-Handling with COALESCE

What if you want to do the imputation if a single value is missing, but not if more than one value is missing? In other words, if you have no tax rate, you are willing to impute a 10% tax rate, but not if you also don't know the markup on the item.

A convenient way to keep evaluating expressions until we get to a non-NULL value is to use COALESCE:

```
WITH catalog AS (
    SELECT 30.0 AS costPrice, 0.15 AS markup, 0.1 AS taxRate
    UNION ALL SELECT NULL, 0.21, 0.15
    UNION ALL SELECT 30.0, NULL, 0.09
    UNION ALL SELECT 30.0, 0.30, NULL
    UNION ALL SELECT 30.0, NULL, NULL
)
SELECT
  *, ROUND(COALESCE(
  costPrice * (1+markup) * (1+taxrate),
  costPrice * 1.05 * (1+taxrate),
  costPrice * (1+markup) * 1.10,
  NULL
  ),2) AS salesPrice
FROM catalog
```

This yields the following (only the last row is different from the previous computation):

Row	costPrice	markup	taxRate	salesPrice
1	30.0	0.15	0.1	37.95
2	null	0.21	0.15	null
3	30.0	null	0.09	34.34
4	30.0	0.3	null	42.9
5	30.0	null	null	null

The COALESCE short-circuits the calculation whenever possible—that is, later expressions are not evaluated after a non-NULL result is obtained. Therefore, the final NULL in the COALESCE is not required, but it makes the intent clearer.

BigQuery supports the IFNULL function as a simplification of COALESCE when you have only two inputs. IFNULL(a, b) is the same as COALESCE(a, b) and yields b if a is NULL. In other words, IFNULL(a, b) is the same as IF(a IS NULL, b, a).

The very first query in this section on conditional expressions could have been simplified as follows:

```
SELECT
  *, ROUND(
    costPrice *
    (1 + IFNULL(markup, 0.05)) *
    (1 + IFNULL(taxrate,0.10))
  , 2) AS salesPrice
FROM catalog
```

Casting and Coercion

Consider this example dataset in which the number of hours worked by an employee is stored as a string in order to accommodate reasons for a leave of absence (this is a bad schema design, but bear with us):

```
WITH example AS (
  SELECT 'John' as employee, 'Paternity Leave' AS hours_worked
  UNION ALL SELECT 'Janaki', '35'
  UNION ALL SELECT 'Jian', 'Vacation'
  UNION ALL SELECT 'Jose', '40'
)
```

Now suppose that you want to find the total number of hours worked. This won't work because the hours_worked is a string, not a numeric type:

```
WITH example AS (
  SELECT 'John' as employee, 'Paternity Leave' AS hours_worked
  UNION ALL SELECT 'Janaki', '35'
  UNION ALL SELECT 'Jian', 'Vacation'
  UNION ALL SELECT 'Jose', '40'
)
SELECT SUM(hours_worked) from example
```

We need to explicitly convert the hours_worked to an INT64 before doing any aggregation. Explicit conversion is called *casting*, and it requires the explicit use of the CAST() function. If casting fails, BigQuery raises an error. To have it return NULL instead, use SAFE_CAST. For example, the following raises an error:

```
SELECT CAST("true" AS bool), CAST("invalid" AS bool)
```

Now try using SAFE_CAST:

```
SELECT CAST("true" AS bool), SAFE_CAST("invalid" AS bool)
```

You should see the following:

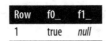

Row	f0_	f1_
1	true	*null*

Implicit conversion is called *coercion*, and this happens automatically when a data type is used in a situation for which another data type is required. For example, when we use an INT64 in a situation when a FLOAT64 is needed, the integer will be coerced into a floating-point number. The only coercions done by BigQuery are to convert INT64 to FLOAT64 and NUMERIC, and NUMERIC to FLOAT64. Every other conversion is explicit and requires a CAST.

With the problem of the total number of hours worked, not all of the hours_worked strings can be converted to integers, so you should use a SAFE_CAST:

```
WITH example AS (
  SELECT 'John' as employee, 'Paternity Leave' AS hours_worked
  UNION ALL SELECT 'Janaki', '35'
  UNION ALL SELECT 'Jian', 'Vacation'
  UNION ALL SELECT 'Jose', '40'
)
SELECT SUM(SAFE_CAST(hours_worked AS INT64)) from example
```

This yields the following:

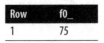

Row	f0_
1	75

Had it simply been a schema problem and all the rows contained numbers but were stored as strings, you could have used a simple CAST:

```
WITH example AS (
  SELECT 'John' as employee, '0' AS hours_worked
  UNION ALL SELECT 'Janaki', '35'
  UNION ALL SELECT 'Jian', '0'
  UNION ALL SELECT 'Jose', '40'
)
SELECT SUM(CAST(hours_worked AS INT64)) from example
```

Using COUNTIF to Avoid Casting Booleans

Consider this example dataset:

```
WITH example AS (
  SELECT true AS is_vowel, 'a' as letter, 1 as position
  UNION ALL SELECT false, 'b', 2
  UNION ALL SELECT false, 'c', 3
)
SELECT * from example
```

Here's the result of the query:

Row	is_vowel	letter	position
1	true	a	1
2	false	b	2
3	false	c	3

Now suppose that you want to find the total number of vowels. You might be tempted to do something simple, such as the following:

```
SELECT SUM(is_vowel) as num_vowels from example
```

This won't work, however (try it!), because SUM, AVG, and others are not defined on Booleans. You could cast the Booleans to an INT64 before doing the aggregation, like so:

```
WITH example AS (
  SELECT true AS is_vowel, 'a' as letter, 1 as position
  UNION ALL SELECT false, 'b', 2
  UNION ALL SELECT false, 'c', 3
)
SELECT SUM(CAST (is_vowel AS INT64)) as num_vowels from example
```

This would yield the following:

Row	num_vowels
1	1

However, you should try to avoid casting as much as possible. In this case, a cleaner approach is to use the IF statement on the Booleans:

```
WITH example AS (
  SELECT true AS is_vowel, 'a' as letter, 1 as position
  UNION ALL SELECT false, 'b', 2
  UNION ALL SELECT false, 'c', 3
)
SELECT SUM(IF(is_vowel, 1, 0)) as num_vowels from example
```

An even cleaner approach is to use `COUNTIF`:

```
WITH example AS (
  SELECT true AS is_vowel, 'a' as letter, 1 as position
  UNION ALL SELECT false, 'b', 2
  UNION ALL SELECT false, 'c', 3
)
SELECT COUNTIF(is_vowel) as num_vowels from example
```

String Functions

String manipulation is a common requirement for data wrangling, so BigQuery provides a library of built-in string functions (*https://cloud.google.com/bigquery/docs/ reference/standard-sql/string_functions*)—for example:

```
WITH example AS (
  SELECT * from unnest([
      'Seattle', 'New York', 'Singapore'
  ]) AS city
)
SELECT
  city
  , LENGTH(city) AS len
  , LOWER(city) AS lower
  , STRPOS(city, 'or') AS orpos
FROM example
```

This example computes the length of the string, makes the string lowercase, and finds the location of a substring in the "city" column, which gives us the following result:

Row	city	len	lower	orpos
1	Seattle	7	seattle	0
2	New York	8	new york	6
3	Singapore	9	singapore	7

The substring "or" occurs in "New York" and in "Singapore," but not in "Seattle."

Two particularly useful functions for string manipulation are `SUBSTR` and `CONCAT`. `SUBSTR` extracts a substring, and `CONCAT` concatenates the input values. The following query finds the position of the @ symbol in an email address, extracts the username, and concatenates the city in which the individual lives:

```
WITH example AS (
  SELECT 'armin@abc.com' AS email, 'Annapolis, MD' as city
  UNION ALL SELECT 'boyan@bca.com', 'Boulder, CO'
  UNION ALL SELECT 'carrie@cab.com', 'Chicago, IL'
)

SELECT
```

```
  CONCAT(
    SUBSTR(email, 1, STRPOS(email, '@') - 1), -- username
    ' from ', city) AS callers
FROM example
```

Here's what the result looks like:

Row	callers
1	armin from Annapolis, MD
2	boyan from Boulder, CO
3	carrie from Chicago, IL

Internationalization

Strings in BigQuery are Unicode, so avoid assumptions that rely on English. For example, the "upper" case is a no-op in Japanese, and the default UTF-8 encoding that is carried out by the cast as bytes is insufficient for languages such as Tamil, as demonstrated here:

```
WITH example AS (
  SELECT * from unnest([
    'Seattle', 'New York', 'சிங்கப்பூர்', '東京'
  ]) AS city
)
SELECT
  city
  , UPPER(city) AS allcaps
  , CAST(city AS BYTES) as bytes
FROM example
```

As you can see, this simply doesn't work as presumably intended:

Row	city	allcaps	bytes
1	Seattle	SEATTLE	U2VhdHRsZQ==
2	New York	NEW YORK	TmV3IFlvcms=
3	சிங்கப்பூர்	சிங்கப்பூர்	4K6a4K6/4K6Z4K+N4K6V4K6q4K+N4K6q4K+C4K6w4K+N
4	東京	東京	5p2x5Lqs

BigQuery supports three different ways to represent strings—as an array of Unicode characters, as an array of bytes, and as an array of Unicode code points (INT64):

```
WITH example AS (
  SELECT * from unnest([
    'Seattle', 'New York', 'சிங்கப்பூர்', '東京'
  ]) AS city
)
SELECT
```

```
    city
  , CHAR_LENGTH(city) as char_len
  , TO_CODE_POINTS(city)[ORDINAL(1)] as first_codept
  , ARRAY_LENGTH(TO_CODE_POINTS(city)) as num_codepts
  , CAST (city AS BYTES) as bytes
  , BYTE_LENGTH(city) as byte_len
FROM example
```

Note the difference between the results for CHAR_LENGTH and BYTE_LENGTH on the same strings, and how the number of code points is the same as the number of characters:

Row	city	char_len	first_codept	num_codepts	bytes	byte_len
1	Seattle	7	83	7	U2VhdHRsZQ==	7
2	New York	8	78	8	TmV3IFlvcms=	8
3	சிங்கப்பூர்	11	2970	11	4K6a4K6/4K6Z4K+N4K6V4K6q4K+N4K6q4K+C4K6w4K+N	33
4	東京	2	26481	2	5p2x5Lqs	6

Because of these differences, you need to recognize which columns might contain text in different languages, and be aware of language differences when using string manipulation functions.

Printing and Parsing

You can simply cast a string as an INT64 or a FLOAT64 in order to parse it, but customizing the string representation will require the use of FORMAT:

```
SELECT
  CAST(42 AS STRING)
  , CAST('42' AS INT64)
  , FORMAT('%03d', 42)
  , FORMAT('%5.3f', 32.457842)
  , FORMAT('%5.3f', 32.4)
  , FORMAT('**%s**', 'H')
  , FORMAT('%s-%03d', 'Agent', 7)
```

Here is the result of that query:

Row	f0_	f1_	f2_	f3_	f4_	f5_	f6_
1	42	42	042	32.458	32.400	**H**	Agent-007

FORMAT works similarly to C's printf (*http://www.cplusplus.com/reference/cstdio/printf/*), and it accepts the same format specifiers. A few of the more useful specifiers are demonstrated in the preceding example. Although FORMAT also accepts dates and timestamps, it is better to use `FORMAT_DATE` and `FORMAT_TIMESTAMP` so that the display formats can be locale-aware.

String Manipulation Functions

Manipulating strings is such a common need in Extract, Transform, and Load (ETL) pipelines that these BigQuery convenience functions are worth having on speed dial:

```
SELECT
  ENDS_WITH('Hello', 'o') -- true
  , ENDS_WITH('Hello', 'h') -- false
  , STARTS_WITH('Hello', 'h') -- false
  , STRPOS('Hello', 'e') -- 2
  , STRPOS('Hello', 'f') -- 0 for not-found
  , SUBSTR('Hello', 2, 4) -- 1-based
  , CONCAT('Hello', 'World')
```

The result of this query is as follows:

Row	f0_	f1_	f2_	f3_	f4_	f5_	f6_
1	true	false	false	2	0	ello	HelloWorld

Note how `SUBSTR()` behaves. The first parameter is the starting position (it is 1-based), and the second parameter is the desired number of characters in the substring.

Transformation Functions

Another set of functions that is worth becoming familiar with are those that allow you to manipulate the string:

```
SELECT
  LPAD('Hello', 10, '*') -- left pad with *
  , RPAD('Hello', 10, '*') -- right pad
  , LPAD('Hello', 10) -- left pad with spaces
  , LTRIM('   Hello   ') -- trim whitespace on left
  , RTRIM('   Hello   ') -- trim whitespace on right
  , TRIM ('   Hello   ') -- trim whitespace both ends
  , TRIM ('***Hello***', '*') -- trim * both ends
  , REVERSE('Hello') -- reverse the string
```

Let's look at the result of this query:

Row	f0_	f1_	f2_	f3_	f4_	f5_	f6_	f7_
1	*****Hello	Hello*****	Hello	Hello	Hello	Hello	Hello	olleH

Regular Expressions

Regular expressions provide much more powerful semantics than the convenience functions. For instance, STRPOS and others can find only specific characters, whereas you can use REGEXP_CONTAINS for more powerful searches.

For example, you could do the following to determine whether a column contains a US zip code (the short form of which is a five-digit number and the long form of which has an additional four digits separated by either a hyphen or a space):

```
SELECT
  column
  , REGEXP_CONTAINS(column, r'\d{5}(?:[-\s]\d{4})?') has_zipcode
  , REGEXP_CONTAINS(column, r'^\d{5}(?:[-\s]\d{4})?$') is_zipcode
  , REGEXP_EXTRACT(column, r'\d{5}(?:[-\s]\d{4})?') the_zipcode
  , REGEXP_EXTRACT_ALL(column, r'\d{5}(?:[-\s]\d{4})?') all_zipcodes
  , REGEXP_REPLACE(column, r'\d{5}(?:[-\s]\d{4})?', '*****') masked
FROM (
  SELECT * from unnest([
      '12345', '1234', '12345-9876',
      'abc 12345 def', 'abcde-fghi',
      '12345 ab 34567', '12345 9876'
  ]) AS column
)
```

Here's what this query yields:

Row	column	has_zipcode	is_zipcode	the_zipcode	all_zipcodes	masked
1	12345	true	true	12345	12345	*****
2	1234	false	false	*null*		1234
3	12345-9876	true	true	12345-9876	12345-9876	*****
4	abc 12345 def	true	false	12345	12345	abc ***** def
5	abcde-fghi	false	false	*null*		abcde-fghi
6	12345 ab 34567	true	false	12345	12345	***** ab *****
					34567	
7	12345 9876	true	true	12345 9876	12345 9876	*****

There are a few things to note:

- The regular expression \d{5} matches any string consisting of five decimal numbers.
- The second part of the expression, in parentheses, looks for an optional (note the ? at the end of the parentheses) group (?:) of four decimal numbers (\d{4}), which is separated from the first five numbers by either a hyphen or by a space (\s).

- The presence of \d, \s, and others in the string could cause problems, so we prefix the string with an r (for raw), which makes it a string literal.

- The second expression illustrates how to find an exact match: simply insist that the string in question must start (^) and end ($) with the specified string.

- To extract the part of the string matched by the regular expression, use REGEXP_EXTRACT. This returns NULL if the expression is not matched, and only the first match if there are multiple matches.

- REGEXP_EXTRACT_ALL returns all the matches. If there is no match, it returns an empty array.

- REGEXP_REPLACE replaces every match with the replacement string.

The regular expression support in BigQuery follows that of Google's open source RE2 library (*https://github.com/google/re2*). To see the syntax accepted by this library, visit *https://github.com/google/re2/wiki/Syntax*. Regular expressions can be cryptic, but they are a rich topic that is well worth mastering.[2]

Summary of String Functions

Because strings are so common in data analysis, it is worth learning the broad contours of the available functions. You can always refer to the BigQuery documentation (*https://cloud.google.com/bigquery/docs/reference/standard-sql/string_functions*) for the exact syntax. Table 3-2 separates them into their respective categories.

Table 3-2. Categories of string functions

Category	Functions	Notes
Representations	CHAR_LENGTH, BYTE_LENGTH, TO_CODE_POINTS, CODE_POINTS_TO_STRING, SAFE_CONVERT_BYTES_TO_STRING, TO_HEX, TO_BASE32, TO_BASE64, FROM_HEX, FROM_BASE32, FROM_BASE64, NORMALIZE	Normalize allows, for example, different Unicode space characters to be made equivalent.
Printing and parsing	FORMAT, REPEAT, SPLIT	The syntax of FORMAT is similar to C's printf: format("%03d", 12) yields 012. For locale-aware conversions, use FORMAT_DATE, etc.

---

2 Start with *Mastering Regular Expressions* (*http://shop.oreilly.com/product/9781565922570.do*) by Jeffrey Friedl (O'Reilly).

Category	Functions	Notes
Convenience	ENDS_WITH, LENGTH, STARTS_WITH, STRPOS, SUBSTR, CONCAT	The LENGTH function is equivalent to CHAR_LENGTH for Strings and to BYTE_LENGTH for Bytes.
Transformations	LPAD, LOWER, LTRIM, REPLACE, REVERSE, RPAD, RTRIM, TRIM, UPPER	The default trim characters are Unicode whitespace, but it is possible to specify a different set of trim characters.
Regular expressions	REGEXP_CONTAINS, REGEXP_EXTRACT, REGEXP_EXTRACT_ALL, REGEXP_REPLACE	See *https://github.com/google/re2/wiki/Syntax* for the syntax accepted by BigQuery.

Working with TIMESTAMP

A timestamp represents an absolute point in time regardless of location. Thus a timestamp of 2017-09-27 12:30:00.45 (Sep 27, 2017, at 12:30 UTC) represents the same time as 2017-09-27 13:30:00.45+1:00 (1:30 p.m. at a time zone that is an hour behind):

```
SELECT t1, t2, TIMESTAMP_DIFF(t1, t2, MICROSECOND)
FROM (SELECT
  TIMESTAMP "2017-09-27 12:30:00.45" AS t1,
  TIMESTAMP "2017-09-27 13:30:00.45+1" AS t2
)
```

This returns the following:

Row	t1	t2	f0_
1	2017-09-27 12:30:00.450 UTC	2017-09-27 12:30:00.450 UTC	0

Parsing and Formatting Timestamps

BigQuery is somewhat forgiving when it comes to parsing the timestamp. The date and time parts of this string representation can be separated either by a T or by a space in accordance with ISO 8601 (*https://www.iso.org/iso-8601-date-and-time-format.html*). Similarly, the month, day, hour, and so on might or might not have leading zeros. However, best practice is to use the canonical representation shown in the previous paragraph. As that string representation would indicate, this timestamp can represent only four-digit years; years before the common era cannot be represented using TIMESTAMP.

You can use PARSE_TIMESTAMP to parse a string that is not in the canonical format:

```
SELECT
  fmt, input, zone
  , PARSE_TIMESTAMP(fmt, input, zone) AS ts
FROM (
  SELECT '%Y%m%d-%H%M%S' AS fmt, '20181118-220800' AS input, '+0' as zone
```

```
    UNION ALL SELECT '%c', 'Sat Nov 24 21:26:00 2018', 'America/Los_Angeles'
    UNION ALL SELECT '%x %X', '11/18/18 22:08:00', 'UTC'
)
```

Here is what this would yield:

Row	fmt	input	zone	ts
1	%Y%m%d%-H%M%S	20181118-220800	+0	2018-11-18 22:08:00 UTC
2	%c	Sat Nov 24 21:26:00 2018	America/Los_Angeles	2018-11-25 05:26:00 UTC
3	%x %X	11/18/18 22:08:00	UTC	2018-11-18 22:08:00 UTC

The first example uses format specifiers for the year, month, day, and so on to create a timestamp from the provided string. The second and third examples use preexisting specifiers for commonly encountered date-time formats.[3]

Conversely, you can use FORMAT_TIMESTAMP to print out a timestamp in any desired format:

```
SELECT
  ts, fmt
  , FORMAT_TIMESTAMP(fmt, ts, '+6') AS ts_output
FROM (
  SELECT CURRENT_TIMESTAMP() AS ts, '%Y%m%d-%H%M%S' AS fmt
  UNION ALL SELECT CURRENT_TIMESTAMP() AS ts, '%c' AS fmt
  UNION ALL SELECT CURRENT_TIMESTAMP() AS ts, '%x %X' AS fmt
)
```

This results in the following:

Row	ts	fmt	ts_output
1	2018-11-25 05:42:13.939840 UTC	%Y%m%d-%H%M%S	20181125-114213
2	2018-11-25 05:42:13.939840 UTC	%c	Sun Nov 25 11:42:13 2018
3	2018-11-25 05:42:13.939840 UTC	%x %X	11/25/18 11:42:13

The preceding example uses the function CURRENT_TIMESTAMP() to retrieve the system time at the time the query is executed. In both PARSE_TIMESTAMP and FOR MAT_TIMESTAMP, the time zone is optional; if omitted, the time zone is assumed to be UTC.

---

3 For the full list of specifiers, consult the documentation (*https://cloud.google.com/bigquery/docs/reference/ standard-sql/timestamp_functions#supported_format_elements_for_timestamp*).

Extracting Calendar Parts

Given a timestamp, it is possible to extract information about the Gregorian calendar corresponding to the timestamp. For example, we can extract information about Armistice Day[4] using this:

```
SELECT
  ts
  , FORMAT_TIMESTAMP('%c', ts) AS repr
  , EXTRACT(DAYOFWEEK FROM ts) AS dayofweek
  , EXTRACT(YEAR FROM ts) AS year
  , EXTRACT(WEEK FROM ts) AS weekno
FROM (
  SELECT PARSE_TIMESTAMP('%Y%m%d-%H%M%S', '19181111-054500') AS ts
)
```

Here is the result:

Row	ts	repr	dayofweek	year	weekno
1	1918-11-11 05:45:00 UTC	Mon Nov 11 05:45:00 1918	2	1918	45

The week is assumed to begin on Sunday, and days prior to the first Sunday of the year are assigned to week 0. This is not internationally safe. Hence, if you're in a country (such as Israel) where the week begins on Saturday, it is possible to specify a different day for the start of the week:

```
EXTRACT(WEEK('SATURDAY') FROM ts)
```

The number of seconds from the Unix epoch (January 1, 1970) is not available through EXTRACT. Instead, special functions exist to convert to and from the Unix epoch:

```
SELECT
  UNIX_MILLIS(TIMESTAMP "2018-11-25 22:30:00 UTC")
  , UNIX_MILLIS(TIMESTAMP "1918-11-11 22:30:00 UTC") --invalid
  , TIMESTAMP_MILLIS(1543185000000)
```

This yields the following:

Row	f0_	f1_	f2_
1	1543185000000	-1613784600000	2018-11-25 22:30:00 UTC

Note that the second one overflows and yields a negative number, but no error is raised.

---

4 According to *https://en.wikipedia.org/wiki/Armistice_Day*, the agreement was signed at 5:45 a.m. on November 11, 1918. In Winter 1918, unlike now, France was in the UTC time zone; see *https://www.timeand date.com/time/zone/france/paris*.

Arithmetic with Timestamps

It is possible to add or subtract time durations from timestamps. It is also possible to find the time difference between two timestamps. In all of these functions, you need to specify the units in which the durations are expressed:

```
SELECT
    EXTRACT(TIME FROM TIMESTAMP_ADD(t1, INTERVAL 1 HOUR)) AS plus_1h
    , EXTRACT(TIME FROM TIMESTAMP_SUB(t1, INTERVAL 10 MINUTE)) AS minus_10min
    , TIMESTAMP_DIFF(CURRENT_TIMESTAMP(),
                TIMESTAMP_SUB(CURRENT_TIMESTAMP(), INTERVAL 1 MINUTE),
                SECOND) AS plus_1min
    , TIMESTAMP_DIFF(CURRENT_TIMESTAMP(),
                TIMESTAMP_ADD(CURRENT_TIMESTAMP(), INTERVAL 1 MINUTE),
                SECOND) AS minus_1min
FROM (SELECT
    TIMESTAMP "2017-09-27 12:30:00.45" AS t1
    )
```

This returns the timestamps an hour from now, 10 minutes ago, and the time difference in seconds corresponding to one minute from now and one minute earlier:

Row	plus_1h	minus_10min	plus_1min	minus_1min
1	13:30:00.450000	12:20:00.450000	60	-60

Date, Time, and DateTime

BigQuery has three other functions for representing time: DATE, TIME, and DATETIME. DATE is useful for when you are tracking only the day in which something happens, and any more precision is unnecessary. TIME is useful to represent the time of day that things happen, and to perform mathematical operations with those times. With TIME, you can answer questions like, "What time will it be eight hours from the starting time?" DATETIME is a TIMESTAMP rendered in a specific time zone, so it is useful when you have an unambiguous time zone in which an event occurred and you don't need to do time zone conversions.

Counterparts to most of the TIMESTAMP functions are available for DATETIME. Thus, you can call DATETIME_ADD, DATETIME_SUB, and DATETIME_DIFF, as well as PARSE_DATETIME and FORMAT_DATETIME. You can also EXTRACT calendar parts from a DATETIME. The two types are quite interoperable—it is possible to extract a DATETIME from a TIMESTAMP and cast a DATETIME to a TIMESTAMP:

```
SELECT
    EXTRACT(DATETIME FROM CURRENT_TIMESTAMP()) as dt
    , CAST(CURRENT_DATETIME() AS TIMESTAMP) as ts
```

The following shows the result:

Row	dt	ts
1	2018-11-25T07:03:15.055141	2018-11-25 07:03:15.055141 UTC

Note that the canonical representation of a DATETIME has the letter T separating the date part and the time part, whereas the representation of a TIMESTAMP uses a space. The TIMESTAMP also explicitly includes the time zone, whereas the time zone is implicit in the DATETIME. But for the most part, you can use DATETIME and TIMESTAMP interchangeably in BigQuery.

DATE is just the date part of a DATETIME (or a TIMESTAMP, interpreted in some time zone), and TIME is the time part. Because many real-world scenarios might happen on a certain date (i.e., at multiple times throughout that day), many database tables contain just a DATE. So there is some benefit to being able to directly parse and format dates. On the other hand, there is very little need for the TIME type other than as the "missing" part of a DATETIME.

For the most part, therefore, our advice is to just use TIMESTAMP and DATE. There is, however, one practical wrinkle to using TIMESTAMP. Timestamps in BigQuery are stored using eight bytes with microsecond resolution. This means that you can store years 0 through 9999, and any microsecond in between. In some other databases (e.g., MySQL), TIMESTAMP is stored using four bytes and DATETIME using eight bytes. In those systems, the range of a TIMESTAMP is within the limits of the Unix epoch time (years 1970 to 2038), which means that you cannot even store the birthdays of 60-year-old people or the expiry dates of 30-year mortgages. So, whereas a TIMESTAMP might work in BigQuery, you might not be able to use the same schema in MySQL, and this might make moving queries and data between BigQuery and MySQL challenging.

Working with GIS Functions

We look at geography functions in much more detail in Chapter 8, which looks at advanced features. In this section, we provide only a brief introduction.

The GEOGRAPHY type can be used to represent points, lines, and polygons on the surface of the Earth (i.e., there is no height associated with them). Because the Earth is a lumpy mass, points on its surface can be represented only on spherical and ellipsoidal approximations of the surface. In BigQuery, the geographic positions of the points and the vertices of the lines and polygons are represented in the WGS84 ellipsoid (*https://en.wikipedia.org/wiki/World_Geodetic_System*). Practically speaking, this is the same ellipsoid as used by the Global Positioning System (GPS), so you will be able to take the longitude and latitude positions reported by most sensors and use them directly in BigQuery.

The simplest geography is a point specified by its longitude and latitude. So, for example,

```
ST_GeogPoint(-122.33, 47.61)
```

represents a point at 47.61N and 122.33W—Seattle, Washington.

The BigQuery public datasets include a table that contains polygons corresponding to each of the US states and territories. We can therefore write a query to find out which state the geographic point is in:

```
SELECT
  state_name
FROM `bigquery-public-data`.utility_us.us_states_area
WHERE
  ST_Contains(
    state_geom,
    ST_GeogPoint(-122.33, 47.61))
```

As anticipated, this returns the following:

Row	state_name
1	Washington

The query uses the `ST_Contains` function to determine whether the state's geometry (stored as the `state_geom` column in the BigQuery dataset) contains the point we are interested in. The spatial functions that BigQuery supports follow the SQL/MM 3 specification (*https://oreil.ly/9AgOe*) and are similar to what the PostGIS library (*https://oreil.ly/x8kNM*) provides for Postgres.

Summary

To summarize what we've covered in this chapter, Table 3-3 presents the data types that BigQuery supports.

Table 3-3. Data types supported by BigQuery

Data type	Sample functions and operators supported	Notes
INT64	Arithmetic operations (+, −, /, *, for add, subtract, divide, and multiply, respectively).	Approximately 10^{-19} to 10^{19}.
NUMERIC	Arithmetic operations.	38 digits of precision and 9 decimal digits of scale; this is suitable for financial calculations.
FLOAT64	Arithmetic operations. Also: IEEE_DIVIDE.	IEEE-754 behavior if one of the values is NaN or ± inf.

Data type	Sample functions and operators supported	Notes
BOOL	Conditional statements. MIN, MAX. However, SUM, AVG, etc. are not supported (you'd need to cast the Booleans to INT64 first).	Is either True and False. SQL is case insensitive, so TRUE, true, and so on also work.
STRING	Use special String functions (*https://cloud.google.com/bigquery/docs/reference/standard-sql/string_functions*) such as CONCAT, LENGTH, etc. to operate on strings.	Strings are Unicode characters and are variable length.
BYTES		Variable length characters. Many String operations are also defined on BYTES.
TIMESTAMP	CURRENT_TIMESTAMP() represents "now." You can extract month, year, dayofweek, etc. from a timestamp. Arithmetic on timestamps is supported via special functions (*https://cloud.google.com/bigquery/docs/reference/standard-sql/timestamp_functions*), not through arithmetic operators.	Absolute point in time, to microsecond precision, represented in a subset of ISO 8601. This is the recommended way to store times in BigQuery.
DATE	CURRENT_DATE() represents the current date in the UTC time zone, whereas CURRENT_DATE("America/Los_Angeles") represents the current date in the Los Angeles time zone. Like TIMESTAMP, arithmetic on dates is supported via special functions (*https://cloud.google.com/bigquery/docs/reference/standard-sql/date_functions*).	2018-3-14 (or 2018-03-14) is March 14, 2018, independent of time zone (*https://cloud.google.com/bigquery/docs/reference/standard-sql/data-types#timestamp-type*). Because this represents different 24-hour blocks in different time zones, use TIMESTAMP to represent an absolute point in time. You can then construct a DATE from a TIMESTAMP relative to a particular time zone.
DATETIME	As with DATE.	2018-03-14 3:14:57 or 2018-03-14T03:14:57.000000 is, like DATE, independent of time zone. Most applications will want to use TIMESTAMP.
TIME	As with DATETIME, except that the DATE part is absent.	Independent of a specific date or time zone. This ranges from 00:00:00 to 23:59:59.999999.
GEOGRAPHY	Topological functions on geographies are supported via special functions (*https://cloud.google.com/bigquery/docs/reference/standard-sql/geography_functions*).	Points, lines, and polygons on the surface of the Earth (i.e., there is no height). The representations are in the WGS84 ellipsoid; this is the same ellipsoid as used by the Global Positioning System (GPS). The simplest geography is a point specified by its longitude and latitude.

Data type	Sample functions and operators supported	Notes
STRUCT	You can deference the fields by name.	A collection of fields in order. The field name is optional; that is, you could have either: `STRUCT<INT64, STRING>` or `STRUCT<id INT64, name STRING>`.
ARRAY	You can deference the items by offset, aggregate the items in the array, or unnest them to get the items one by one.	Ordered list of non-null elements; e.g., `ARRAY<INT64>`. Arrays of arrays are not allowed, but you can get around this by creating an array of STRUCT in which the struct itself contains an array; i.e., `ARRAY<STRUCT<ARRAY<INT64>>>` (We cover arrays in Chapter 2).

You can use all data types, except for arrays and structs, in ORDER BY and GROUP BY.

## CHAPTER 4

Loading Data into BigQuery

In the previous chapter, we wrote the following query:

```
SELECT
  state_name
FROM `bigquery-public-data`.utility_us.us_states_area
WHERE
  ST_Contains(
    state_geom,
    ST_GeogPoint(-122.33, 47.61))
```

We also learned that the city at the location (-122.33, 47.61) is in the state of Washington. Where did the data for the `state_name` and `state_geom` come from?

Note the `FROM` clause in the query. The owners of the `bigquery-public-data` project had already loaded the state boundary information into a table called `us_states_area` in a dataset called `utility_us`. Because the team shared the `utility_us` dataset with all authenticated users of BigQuery (more restrictive permissions are available), we were able to query the `us_states_area` table that is in that dataset.

But how did they get the data into BigQuery in the first place? In this chapter, we look at various ways to load data into BigQuery, starting with the basics.

The Basics

Data values such as the boundaries of US states change rarely,[1] and the changes are small enough that most applications can afford to ignore them. In data warehousing lingo, we call this a *slowly changing dimension*. As of this writing, the last change of

---

[1] Six to eight changes every decade—see *https://oreil.ly/Merow*.

US state boundaries occurred on January 1, 2017, and affected 19 home owners and one gas station.[2]

State boundary data is, therefore, the type of data that is often loaded just once. Analysts query the single table and ignore the fact that the data could change over time. For example, a retail firm might care only about which state a home is in currently to ensure that the correct tax rate is applied to purchases from that home. So when a change does happen, such as through a treaty between states or due to a change in the path of a river channel, the owners of the dataset might decide to replace the table with more up-to-date data. The fact that queries could potentially return slightly different results after an update compared to what was returned before the update is ignored.

Ignoring the impact of time on the correctness of the data might not always be possible. If the state boundary data is to be used by a land title firm that needs to track ownership of land parcels, or if an audit firm needs to validate the state tax paid on shipments made in different years, it is important that there be a way to query the state boundaries as they existed in years past. So even though the first part of this chapter covers how to do a one-time load, carefully consider whether you would be better off planning on periodically updating the data and allowing users of the data to know about the version of the data that they are querying.

Loading from a Local Source

The US government issues a "scorecard" for colleges to help consumers compare the cost and perceived value of higher education. Let's load this data into BigQuery as an illustration. The raw data is available on *catalog.data.gov*. For convenience, we also have it available as *04_load/college_scorecard.csv.gz* in the GitHub repository for this book (*https://github.com/GoogleCloudPlatform/bigquery-oreilly-book/*). The comma-separated values (CSV) file was downloaded from data.gov and compressed using the open source software utility gzip.

---

2 See *https://abc7ny.com/news/border-of-north-and-south-carolina-shifted-on-january-1st/1678605/* and *https://www.nytimes.com/2014/08/24/opinion/sunday/how-the-carolinas-fixed-their-blurred-lines.html*.

Why did we compress the file? The raw, uncompressed file is about 136 MB, whereas the gzipped file is only 18 MB. Because we are about to send the file over the wire to BigQuery, it makes sense to optimize the bandwidth being transferred. The BigQuery load command can handle gzipped files, but it cannot load parts of a gzipped file in parallel. Loading would be much faster if we were to hand BigQuery a splittable file, either an uncompressed CSV file that is already on Cloud Storage (so that the network transfer overhead is minimized) or data in a format such as Avro for which each block is internally compressed but the file as a whole can be split across workers.

A splittable file can be loaded by different workers starting at different parts of the file, but this requires that the workers be able to "seek" to a predictable point in the middle of the file without having to read it from the beginning. Compressing the entire file using gzip doesn't allow this, but a block-by-block compression such as Avro does. Therefore, using a compressed, splittable format such as Avro is an unmitigated good. However, if you have CSV or JSON files that are splittable only when uncompressed, you should measure whether the faster network transfer is counterbalanced by the increased load time.

From Cloud Shell, you can page through the gzipped file using `zless`:

```
zless college_scorecard.csv.gz
```

Here are detailed steps:

1. Open Cloud Shell in your browser by visiting *https://console.cloud.google.com/cloudshell*.

2. In the terminal window, type: `git clone https://github.com/GoogleCloudPlatform/bigquery-oreilly-book`.

3. Navigate to the folder containing the college scorecard file: `cd bigquery-oreilly-book/04_load`.

4. Type the command **`zless college_scorecard.csv.gz`**, and then use the space bar to page through the data. Type the letter **q** to quit.

The file contains a header line with the names of the columns. Each of the lines following the header contains one row of data.

To load the data into BigQuery, first create a dataset called `ch04` to hold the data:

```
bq --location=US mk ch04
```

The bq command-line tool provides a convenient point of entry to interact with the BigQuery service on Google Cloud Platform (GCP), although everything you do with bq you also can do using the REST API. And you can accomplish most things using the GCP Cloud Console. We are asking it here to make (mk) a dataset named ch04.

Datasets in BigQuery function like top-level folders that are used to organize and control access to tables, views, and machine learning models. The dataset is created in the current project,[3] and it is to this project that storage costs for tables in this dataset will be billed (queries are charged to the project of the querier).

We also specify that the dataset should be created in the US location (this is the default, so we could have omitted that). Location choices include multiregional locations (such as US, EU) and specific regions (e.g., us-east4, europe-west2 and australia-southeast1).[4] Be careful when choosing a region for loading data: as of this writing, queries cannot join tables held in different regions. In this book, we will use the US multiregion location so that our queries can join against tables in the public datasets that are located in the United States.

Then, from the directory containing your clone of the GitHub repository, load the data in the file as a table in BigQuery:

```
bq --location=US \
    load \
    --source_format=CSV --autodetect \
    ch04.college_scorecard \
    ./college_scorecard.csv.gz
```

In this case, we are asking bq to load the dataset, informing the tool that the source format is CSV and that we would like the tool to autodetect the schema (i.e., the data types of individual columns). We then specify that the table to be created is called college_scorecard in the dataset ch04 and that the data is to be loaded from college_scorecard.csv.gz in the current directory.

When we did this, though, we ran into an issue:

```
Could not parse 'NULL' as int for field HBCU (position 26) starting at location
11945910
```

---

3 This is set through a drop-down box in the GCP Cloud Console, or when you last did a gcloud init. Typically, a project corresponds to a workload or to a small team.

4 For an updated list, see *https://cloud.google.com/bigquery/docs/locations*.

This caused the load job to fail with the following error:[5]

```
CSV table encountered too many errors, giving up. Rows: 591; errors: 1.
```

The problem is that, based on most of the data in the CSV file, BigQuery's schema autodetection expects that the 26th column (whose name is HBCU) should be an integer, but the 591st row of the file has the text NULL in that field—this usually signifies that the college in question did not answer the survey question corresponding to this field.[6]

There are several ways in which we can fix this problem. For example, we could edit the data file itself if we knew what the value ought to be. Another fix could be to specify explicitly the schema for each column and change the column type of the HBCU column to be a string so that NULL is an acceptable value. Alternatively, we could ask BigQuery to ignore a few bad records by specifying, for example, --max_bad_records=20. Finally, we could instruct the BigQuery load program that this particular file uses the string NULL to mark nulls (the standard way in CSV is to use empty fields to represent nulls).

Let's apply the last method, because it seems to be the most appropriate:[7]

```
bq --location=US \
    load --null_marker=NULL \
    --source_format=CSV --autodetect \
    ch04.college_scorecard \
    ./college_scorecard.csv.gz
```

You can find the full list of bq load options by typing bq load --help. By default, bq load will append to a table. Here, you want to replace the existing table, so you should add --replace:

```
bq --location=US \
    load --null_marker=NULL --replace \
    --source_format=CSV --autodetect \
    ch04.college_scorecard \
    ./college_scorecard.csv.gz
```

You can also specify --replace=false to append rows to an existing table.

---

5 The autodetect algorithm continues to handle more and more corner cases, and so this might not happen for you. In general, though, schema autodetection will never be perfect. Regardless of the details of what aspect of the schema is not correctly captured, our larger point is this: use the autodetected schema as a starting point and build on top of it, as we do in this section.

6 It is possible for an integer column to be nullable, but the file is encoding NULL values in a nonstandard way. BigQuery is interpreting the text NULL as a string, which is why the load fails.

7 The NULL string in the file represents a lack of data for that field, and this is what a NULL value in our BigQuery table should mean as well.

Loading or Streaming?

Loading data into BigQuery does not incur any charges, although you will be charged for storage after the data is loaded.[8] If you are on flat-rate pricing, loading data into BigQuery uses computational resources that are separate from the slots that are paid for by the flat rate. Therefore, if you do not need near-real-time data in your data warehouse, a frugal way to get data into BigQuery is to set up a scheduled Cloud Storage transfer (which we cover later in this chapter). If transformations are needed, you can use Cloud Composer or Cloud Functions to load data into BigQuery every day.

All that the bq command does is to invoke a REST API exposed by the BigQuery service. So you can load the data in many other ways as well. Those methods invoke the same REST API. Client libraries in a number of languages, including Java, Python, and Node.js, are available—these provide convenient, programmatic ways to upload the data. We discuss the use of client libraries in Chapter 5.

If you do need data in near real time, you should stream data into BigQuery (*https://cloud.google.com/bigquery/streaming-data-into-bigquery*). Even though streaming incurs charges, you should prefer to use streaming over frequent loads if you need near-real-time data. It is not a good idea to load data using a large number of small load jobs frequently (for example, to issue a load every minute). Tables that are loaded so frequently can end up with significant fragmentation and high metadata overhead, causing queries over them to be slow until BigQuery performs an optimization pass at some point in the future. Streaming, unlike frequent small loads, batches rows on the backend for a period of time before writing them to storage, thus limiting the fragmentation and keeping querying performant. Streamed data is available for querying immediately, whereas loads can take a while to complete. Moreover, if you rely on frequent small batch loads, any sort of throttling or backups in the systems that produce these files can result in unexpected delays in data being available.

It is worth noting that you can do one-time loads from the BigQuery web user interface (UI). Click your project, and you will be presented with a button to create a dataset (ch04, in our case); click the dataset, and you will be presented with a button to create a table. You can then follow the prompts to upload the file as a BigQuery table. As of this writing, however, use of the web UI to load data from a local file is limited to data whose size is less than 10 MB and 16,000 rows. Hence, it would not work for the college scorecard dataset unless we had staged it in Google Cloud Storage first.

---

8 As we've noted in earlier chapters, we believe all mentions of price to be correct as of the writing of this book, but please do refer to the relevant policy and pricing sheets (*https://cloud.google.com/bigquery/pricing*), as these are subject to change.

Even if you did not (or cannot) use the web UI to load the data, it is a good idea to look at the created table using the web UI to ensure that details about the table as well as the autodetected schema are correct. It is also possible to edit some details about the table even after it has been created. For example, it is possible to specify that the table should automatically expire after a certain number of days, add columns, or relax a required field to become nullable.

 You can also set an expiration date using the `ALTER TABLE SET OPTIONS` statement—for example:

```
ALTER TABLE ch04.college_scorecard
  SET OPTIONS (
    expiration_timestamp=
      TIMESTAMP_ADD(CURRENT_TIMESTAMP(), INTERVAL 7 DAY),
    description="College Scorecard table that expires
      seven days from now"
  )
```

For more details, see *https://cloud.google.com/bigquery/docs/refer ence/standard-sql/data-definition-language#alter_table_set_options_statement*.

Regardless of how the table is loaded, anyone who is allowed to access the dataset in which the table is located can query it. The default is to make a newly created dataset visible only to people with project-level view permissions. You can, however, share the dataset[9] with specific individuals (identified by their Google account), a domain (e.g., xyz.com), or a Google group. We discuss using Identity and Access Management (IAM) to share datasets in Chapter 10. For now, though, anyone with view access to the project holding the dataset can query it:

```
SELECT
  INSTNM
  , ADM_RATE_ALL
  , FIRST_GEN
  , MD_FAMINC
  , MD_EARN_WNE_P10
  , SAT_AVG
FROM
  ch04.college_scorecard
WHERE
  SAFE_CAST(SAT_AVG AS FLOAT64) > 1300
  AND SAFE_CAST(ADM_RATE_ALL AS FLOAT64) < 0.2
  AND SAFE_CAST(FIRST_GEN AS FLOAT64) > 0.1
```

---

9 As of this writing, this capability does not exist in the "new" UI; you must access it through the bq command-line tool.

```
ORDER BY
    CAST(MD_FAMINC AS FLOAT64) ASC
```

This query pulls out institution name (INSTNM), admission rate, and other information for colleges whose average SAT score is more than 1300 and whose admission rate is less than 20%, which is a plausible definition of "elite" colleges. It also filters by colleges that admit first-generation college goers at a rate greater than 10% and ranks them in ascending order of median family income, thus finding elite colleges that admit culturally or economically disadvantaged students. The query also pulls the median earnings of students 10 years after entry:

Row	INSTNM	ADM_RATE_ALL	FIRST_GEN	MD_FAMINC	MD_EARN_WNE_P10	SAT_AVG
1	University of California–Berkeley	0.1692687830816	0.3458005249	31227	64700	1422
2	Columbia University in the City of New York	0.06825366802669	0.2504905167	31310.5	83300	1496
3	University of California–Los Angeles	0.17992627069775	0.3808913934	32613.5	60700	1334
4	Harvard University	0.05404574677902	0.25708061	33066	89700	1506
5	Princeton University	0.06521516568269	0.2773972603	37036	74700	1493

Look, however, at the query itself. Notice how several of the WHERE clauses need a cast:

```
SAFE_CAST(ADM_RATE_ALL AS FLOAT64)
```

Had we not included the cast, we would have received an error:

```
No matching signature for operator > for argument types: STRING, INT64.
```

Had we simply cast as a float, it would have failed on a row where the value was a string (PrivacySuppressed) that cannot be cast as a float:

```
Bad double value: PrivacySuppressed; while executing the filter ...
```

This is because the automatic schema detection did not identify the admission rate column as numeric. Instead, that column is being treated as a string because, in some of the rows, the value is suppressed for privacy reasons (e.g., if the number of applications is very small) and replaced by the text PrivacySuppressed. Indeed, even the median family income is a string (it happens to always be numeric for colleges that meet the criteria we outlined), and so we need to cast it before ordering.[10]

---

10 Strings are sorted lexically. If stored as a string, "100" would be less than "20" for the same reason that "abc" comes before "de" when the two strings are sorted. When sorted numerically, 20 is less than 100, as you would expect.

Specifying a Schema

Inevitably in real-world datasets, we will need to do some cleanup and transformations before loading the data into BigQuery. Although later in this chapter we look at building more sophisticated data processing pipelines to do this, a simple way is to use Unix tools to replace privacy-suppressed data with NULLs:

```
zless ./college_scorecard.csv.gz | \
    sed 's/PrivacySuppressed/NULL/g' | \
    gzip > /tmp/college_scorecard.csv.gz
```

Here, we are using a string editor (`sed`) to replace all occurrences of `PrivacySup` `pressed` by `NULL`, compressing the result and writing it to a temporary folder. Now, instead of loading the original file, we can load the cleaner file.

When presented with the cleaner file, BigQuery correctly identifies many more of the columns as integers or floats, but not `SAT_AVG` or `ADM_RATE_ALL`; those columns are still autodetected as strings. This is because the algorithm to autodetect the schema does not look at all the rows in the file; it looks at only a sample of them. Because a large number of rows have a null `SAT_AVG` (fewer than 20% of colleges report SAT scores), the algorithm was unable to infer the type of the field. The safe choice is to treat any column that the tool is not sure of as a string.

It is therefore best practice to not autodetect the schema of files that you receive in production—you will be at the mercy of whatever data happens to have been sampled. For production workloads, insist on the data type for a column by specifying it at the time of load.

You can use the autodetect feature to avoid starting to write a schema from scratch. You can display the schema of the table as it currently exists:

```
bq show --format prettyjson --schema ch04.college_scorecard
```

You can also save the schema to a file:

```
bq show --format prettyjson --schema ch04.college_scorecard > schema.json
```

Automating the Creation of Schema

We haven't covered table metadata yet (we do so in Chapter 8), but you can automate the creation of the schema by using SQL itself. Here is a query to obtain the schema of all the tables in the dataset ch04:

```
SELECT
  table_name
  , column_name
  , ordinal_position
  , is_nullable
  , data_type
FROM
  ch04.INFORMATION_SCHEMA.COLUMNS
```

You can then use the TO_JSON_STRING function to create the JSON of the schema in the necessary format, thus avoiding the need to drop to the command line:

```
SELECT
  TO_JSON_STRING(
    ARRAY_AGG(STRUCT(
      IF(is_nullable = 'YES', 'NULLABLE', 'REQUIRED') AS
mode,
      column_name AS name,
      data_type AS type)
    ORDER BY ordinal_position), TRUE) AS schema
FROM
  ch04.INFORMATION_SCHEMA.COLUMNS
WHERE
  table_name = 'college_scorecard'
```

This yields a JSON string of the form:

```
[
  {
     "mode": "NULLABLE",
     "name": "INSTNM",
     "type": "STRING"
  },
  {
     "mode": "NULLABLE",
     "name": "ADM_RATE_ALL",
     "type": "FLOAT64"
  },
  ...
```

Now, you can open the schema file in your favorite text editor (if you don't have a preference, use the pen icon in Cloud Shell to open up the default editor) and change the type of the columns you care about. Specifically, change the four columns in the WHERE clause (SAT_AVG, ADM_RATE_ALL, FIRST_GEN, and MD_FAMINC) to be FLOAT64:

```
{
  "mode": "NULLABLE",
  "name": "FIRST_GEN",
  "type": "FLOAT64"
},
```

In addition, also change (for now) the T4APPROVALDATE to be a string, because it is in a nonstandard date format:[11]

```
{
  "mode": "NULLABLE",
  "name": "T4APPROVALDATE",
  "type": "STRING"
},
```

With the schema updated, we can load the data with this schema rather than with the autodetect:

```
bq --location=US \
    load --null_marker=NULL --replace \
    --source_format=CSV \
    --schema=schema.json --skip_leading_rows=1 \
    ch04.college_scorecard \
    ./college_scorecard.csv.gz
```

Because we are supplying a schema, we need to instruct BigQuery to ignore the first row of the CSV file (which contains the header information).

After the table has been loaded, we can repeat the query of the previous section:

```
SELECT
  INSTNM
  , ADM_RATE_ALL
  , FIRST_GEN
  , MD_FAMINC
  , MD_EARN_WNE_P10
  , SAT_AVG
FROM
  ch04.college_scorecard
WHERE
  SAT_AVG > 1300
  AND ADM_RATE_ALL < 0.2
  AND FIRST_GEN > 0.1
ORDER BY
  MD_FAMINC ASC
```

---

11 The file contains D/M/YYYY, whereas the standard format for a date is YYYY-MM-DD (which matches ISO 8601). Although autodetect can look at multiple rows and infer whether 12/11/1965 is the 12th of November or the 11th of December, we don't want the schema-based BigQuery load making any such assumptions. The transformation pipeline that we build later in this chapter converts the dates into the standard format. For now, let's just treat it as a string.

Notice that, because SAT_AVG, ADM_RATE_ALL, and the others are no longer strings, our query is much cleaner because we no longer need to cast them to floating-point numbers. The reason they are no longer strings is that we made a decision on how to deal with the privacy-suppressed data (treat them as being unavailable) during the Extract, Transform, and Load (ETL) process.

Copying into a New Table

The table as loaded contains many columns that we do not need. It is possible to create a cleaner, more purposeful table from the original table by using the CREATE TABLE statement and populating the new table with only the columns of interest:

```
CREATE OR REPLACE TABLE ch04.college_scorecard_etl AS
SELECT
    INSTNM
    , ADM_RATE_ALL
    , FIRST_GEN
    , MD_FAMINC
    , SAT_AVG
    , MD_EARN_WNE_P10
FROM ch04.college_scorecard
```

By using a robust ETL pipeline and making decisions early, downstream queries are cleaner and more concise. The trade-off is that the ETL process involves extra work (determining the data types and specifying the schema) and might involve irrevocable decisions (e.g., there is no way to get back whether a field is unavailable because it was not collected, because it was suppressed due to privacy reasons, or because it was deleted). Later in this chapter, we discuss how an ELT pipeline in SQL can help us delay making irrevocable decisions.

Data Management (DDL and DML)

Why cover data management in a chapter on loading data? Because loading data is typically only part of the task of managing data. If data is loaded by mistake, you might need to delete it. Sometimes you need to delete data because of regulations and compliance.

 Even though we normally want you to try all the commands and queries in this book, don't try the ones in this section, because you will lose your data!

The easiest way to delete a table (or view) as a whole is from the BigQuery UI. You can also carry out the delete from the bq command-line tool:

```
bq rm ch04.college_scorecard
bq rm -r -f ch04
```

The first line removes a single table, whereas the second one removes recursively (-r) and without prompting (-f, for force) the dataset ch04 and all of the tables it contains.

You can also delete a table (or view) by using SQL:

```
DROP TABLE IF EXISTS ch04.college_scorecard_gcs
```

It is also possible to specify that a table needs to be expired at a certain time in the future. You can so this with the ALTER TABLE SET OPTIONS statement:

```
ALTER TABLE ch04.college_scorecard
  SET OPTIONS (
    expiration_timestamp=TIMESTAMP_ADD(CURRENT_TIMESTAMP(),
                                        INTERVAL 7 DAY),
    description="College Scorecard expires seven days from now"
  )
```

The DROP TABLE and ALTER TABLE statements, like the CREATE TABLE statement, are examples of Data Definition Language (DDL) statements.

It is possible to delete only specific rows from a table—for example:

```
DELETE FROM ch04.college_scorecard
WHERE SAT_AVG IS NULL
```

Similarly, it is also possible to INSERT rows into an existing table instead of replacing the entire table. For example, it is possible to insert more values into the college_scorecard table using the following:

```
INSERT ch04.college_scorecard
  (INSTNM
    , ADM_RATE_ALL
    , FIRST_GEN
    , MD_FAMINC
    , SAT_AVG
    , MD_EARN_WNE_P10
  )
  VALUES ('abc', 0.1, 0.3, 12345, 1234, 23456),
         ('def', 0.2, 0.2, 23451, 1232, 32456)
```

It is possible to use a subquery to extract values from one table and copy them into another:

```
INSERT ch04.college_scorecard
SELECT *
FROM ch04.college_scorecard_etl
WHERE SAT_AVG IS NULL
```

The DELETE, INSERT, and MERGE statements are examples of Data Manipulation Language (DML) statements.

As of this writing, BigQuery does not support an `SQL COPY` statement. To copy tables, use `bq cp` to copy one table to another:

```
bq cp ch04.college_scorecard
someds.college_scorecard_copy
```

You are not billed for running a query, but you will be billed for the storage of the new table. The `bq cp` command supports appending (specify `-a` or `--append_table`) and replacement (specify `-noappend_table`).

You can also use the idiomatic Standard SQL method of using either `CREATE TABLE AS SELECT` or `INSERT VALUES`, depending on whether the destination already exists. However, `bq cp` is faster (because it copies only the table metadata) and doesn't incur query costs.

Loading Data Efficiently

Although BigQuery can load data from CSV files, CSV files are inefficient and not very expressive (for example, there is no way to represent arrays and structs in CSV). If you have a choice, you should choose to export your data in a different format. What format should you choose?

An efficient and expressive format is Avro (*https://avro.apache.org/*). Avro uses self-describing binary files that are broken into blocks and can be compressed block by block. Because of this, it is possible to parallelize the loading of data from Avro files and the export of data into Avro files. Because the blocks are compressed, the file sizes will also be smaller than the data size might indicate. In terms of expressiveness, the Avro format is hierarchical and can represent nested and repeated fields, something that BigQuery supports but CSV files don't have an easy way to store. Because Avro files are self-describing, you never need to specify a schema.

There are two drawbacks to Avro files. One is that they are not human readable. If readability and expressiveness are important to you, use newline-delimited JSON files[12] to store your data. JSON supports the ability to store hierarchical data but requires that binary columns be base-64 encoded. However, JSON files are larger than even the equivalent CSV files because the name of each field is repeated on every line. The second drawback is that Avro files are stored row by row. This makes Avro files not as efficient for federated queries.

---

12 Newline-delimited JSON often goes by the name of jsonl, or "JSON lines format."

The Parquet file format was inspired by Google's original Dremel ColumnIO format, [13] and like Avro, Parquet is binary, block oriented, compact, and capable of representing hierarchical data. However, whereas Avro files are stored row by row, Parquet files are stored column by column. Columnar files are optimized for reading a subset of the columns; loading data requires reading all columns, and so columnar formats are somewhat less efficient at the loading of data. However, the columnar format makes Parquet a better choice than Avro for federated queries, a topic that we discuss shortly. Optimized Row Columnar (ORC) files are another open source columnar file format. ORC is similar to Parquet in performance and efficiency.

Therefore, if you have a choice of file formats, we recommend Avro if you plan to load the data into BigQuery and discard the files. We recommend Parquet if you will be retaining the files for federated queries. Use JSON for small files where human readability is important.

Impact of compression and staging via Google Cloud Storage

For formats such as CSV and JSON that do not have internal compression, you should consider whether you should compress the files using gzip. Compressed files are faster to transmit and take up less space, but they are slower to load into Big-Query. The slower your network, the more you should lean toward compressing the data.

If you are on a slow network or if you have many files or very large files, it is possible to set up a multithreaded upload of the data using `gsutil cp`. After the data is all on Google Cloud Storage, then you can invoke `bq load` from the Cloud Storage location:

```
gsutil -m cp *.csv gs://BUCKET/some/location
bqload … gs://BUCKET/some/location/*.csv
```

This experiment captures the various trade-offs involved with compression and with staging the college scorecard data on Cloud Storage before invoking `bq load`. Table 4-1 examines this further. Your results will vary, of course, depending on your network and the actual data you are loading.[14] Therefore, you should carry out a similar measurement for your loading job and choose the method that provides you with the best performance on the measures you care about.

---

13 See *https://blog.twitter.com/engineering/en_us/a/2013/dremel-made-simple-with-parquet.html*. In Chapter 6, we discuss Capacitor, BigQuery's backend storage format, which is the successor to ColumnIO.

14 Try it out by running the *load_*.sh* scripts in the *04_load* of the GitHub repository for this book.

Table 4-1. Trade-offs involved with compression and staging the college scorecard data on Google Cloud Storage before invoking `bq load`

Compressed file	Stage on GCS?	GCS size	Network time (if separate)	Time to load into BigQuery	Total time
Yes	No	None	N/A	105 seconds	105 seconds
No	No	None	N/A	255 seconds	255 seconds
Yes	Yes	16 MB	47 sec	42 seconds	89 seconds
No	Yes	76 MB	139 sec	28 sec	167 sec

Staging the file on Google Cloud Storage involves paying storage costs at least until the BigQuery load job finishes. However, storage costs are generally quite low and so, on this dataset and this network connection (see Table 4-1), the best option is to stage compressed data in Cloud Storage and load it from there. Even though it is faster to load uncompressed files into BigQuery, the network time to transfer the files dwarfs whatever benefits you'd get from a faster load.

As of this writing, the loading of compressed CSV and JSON files is limited to files less than 4 GB in size because BigQuery has to uncompress the files on the fly on workers whose memory is finite. If you have larger datasets, split them across multiple CSV or JSON files. Splitting files yourself can allow for some degree of parallelism when doing the loads, but depending on how you size the files, this can lead to suboptimal file sizes in the table until BigQuery decides to optimize the storage.

Price and quota

BigQuery does not charge for loading data. Ingestion happens on a set of workers that is distinct from the cluster providing the slots used for querying. Hence, your queries (even on the same table into which you are ingesting data) are not slowed down by the fact that data is being ingested.

Data loads are atomic. Queries on a table will either reflect the presence of all the data that is loaded in through the `bq load` operation or reflect none of it. You will not get query results on a partial slice of the data.

The drawback of loading data using a "free" cluster is that load times can become unpredictable and bottlenecked by preexisting jobs. As of this writing, load jobs are limited to 1,000 per table and 100,000 per project per day (*https://cloud.google.com/bigquery/quotas#load_jobs*). In the case of CSV and JSON files, cells and rows are limited to 100 MB, whereas in Avro, blocks are limited to 16 MB. Files cannot exceed 5 TB in size. If you have a larger dataset, split it across multiple files, each smaller than 5 TB. However, a single load job can submit a maximum of 15 TB of data split across a maximum of 10 million files. The load job must finish executing in less than six hours or it will be cancelled.

Federated Queries and External Data Sources

You can use BigQuery without first loading the data. It is possible to leave the data in-place, specify the structure of the data, and use BigQuery as just the query engine. In contrast to the queries thus far for which BigQuery queried its own native storage, we discuss the use of "federated queries" to query "external data sources" in this section and explain when you might want to use such queries.

Currently supported external data sources include Google Cloud Storage, Cloud Bigtable, Cloud SQL, and Google Drive. You will notice that all of these sources are external to BigQuery but are, nevertheless, within the Google Cloud perimeter. This is necessary because otherwise the network overhead and security considerations would make the queries either slow or infeasible.

How to Use Federated Queries

There are three steps to querying data in an external data source:

1. Create a table definition using bq mkdef.
2. Make a table using bq mk, passing in the external table definition.
3. Query the table as normal.

As with querying data in native storage, you can do this either in the web UI or by using a programmatic interface. To use the web UI, follow the just-listed steps to create a table, but make sure to specify that you want an external table, not a native one, as demonstrated in Figure 4-1.

Figure 4-1. You can create an external table from the web UI by following the "Create Table" workflow but specifying "External table" as the table type

Using the command-line interface, create a table definition using bq mkdef. As with bq load, you have the option of using --autodetect:

```
bq mkdef --source_format=CSV \
    --autodetect \
    gs://bigquery-oreilly-book/college_scorecard.csv
```

This prints a table definition file to standard output. The normal course of action is to redirect this to a file and use that table definition to make a table using bq mk:

```
bq mkdef --source_format=CSV \
    --autodetect \
    gs://bigquery-oreilly-book/college_scorecard.csv \
    > /tmp/mytable.json
bq mk --external_table_definition=/tmp/mytable.json \
    ch04.college_scorecard
```

With these two steps, you can query the table college_scorecard as in the previous section, except that the queries will happen on the CSV file stored in Google Cloud Storage—the data is not ingested into BigQuery's native storage.

Wildcards

Many big data frameworks such as Apache Spark, Apache Beam, and others shard their output across hundreds of files with names such as *course_grades.csv-00095-of-00313*. When loading such files, it would be convenient if we could avoid having to list each file individually.

Indeed, it is possible to use a wildcard in the path to bq mkdef (and bq load) so that you can match multiple files:

```
bq mkdef --source_format=CSV \
    --autodetect \
    gs://bigquery-oreilly-book/college_* \
    > /tmp/mytable.json
```

This creates a table that refers to all the files matched by the pattern.

Temporary table

It is also possible to condense the three steps (mkdef, mk, and query) by passing in the table definition parameters along with a query, thus ensuring that the table definition will be used only for the duration of the query:

```
LOC="--location US"
INPUT=gs://bigquery-oreilly-book/college_scorecard.csv

SCHEMA=$(gsutil cat $INPUT | head -1 | awk -F, '{ORS=","}{for (i=1; i <= NF; i++){
print $i":STRING"; }}' | sed 's/,$//g'| cut -b 4- )

bq $LOC query \
    --external_table_definition=cstable::${SCHEMA}@CSV=${INPUT} \
    'SELECT SUM(IF(SAT_AVG != "NULL", 1, 0))/COUNT(SAT_AVG) FROM cstable'
```

In the preceding query, the external table definition consists of the temporary table name (cstable), two colons, the schema string, the @ symbol, the format (CSV), an equals sign, and the Google Cloud Storage URL corresponding to the data file(s). If you already have a table definition file, you can specify it directly:

```
--external_table_definition=cstable::${DEF}
```

It is possible to specify a JSON schema file as well as to query JSON, Avro, and other supported formats directly from Cloud Storage, Cloud Bigtable, and other supported data sources.

While undeniably convenient, federated queries leave much to be desired in terms of performance. Because CSV files are stored row-wise and the rows themselves are stored in some arbitrary order, much of the efficiency that we commonly associate with BigQuery is lost. It is also not possible for BigQuery to estimate how much data it is going to need to scan before running the query.

Loading and querying Parquet and ORC

As previously mentioned, Parquet and ORC are columnar data formats. Therefore, federated querying of these formats will provide better query performance than if the data was stored in row-based formats such as CSV or JSON (queries will still be slower than BigQuery's native Capacitor storage, however).

Because Parquet and ORC are self-describing (i.e., the schema is implicit in the files themselves), it is possible to create table definitions without specifying a schema:

```
bq mkdef --source_format=PARQUET gs://bucket/dir/files* > table_def.json
bq mk --external_table_definition=table_def.json <dataset>.<table>
```

As with querying external tables created from CSV files, querying this table works like querying any other table in BigQuery.

Even though Parquet and ORC files provide better query performance than row-based file formats, they are still subject to the limitations of external tables.

Loading and querying Hive partitions

Apache Hive (*https://hive.apache.org/*) allows for reading, writing, and managing an Apache Hadoop–based data warehouse using a familiar SQL-like query language. Cloud Dataproc, on Google Cloud, enables Hive software to work on distributed data stored in Hive partitions on Google Cloud Storage. A common public cloud migration pattern is for on-premises Hive workloads to be moved to Cloud Dataproc and for newer workloads to be written using BigQuery's federated querying capability. This way, the current Hive workloads work as-is, whereas newer workloads can take advantage of the serverless, large-scale querying capability provided by BigQuery.

You can load Hive partitions on Google Cloud Storage by specifying a Hive partitioning mode to bq load:

```
bq load --source_format=ORC --autodetect \
    --hive_partitioning_mode=AUTO <dataset>.<table> <gcs_uri>
```

The Cloud Storage URI in the case of Hive tables needs to encode the table path prefix without including any partition keys in the wildcard. Thus, if the partition key for a Hive table is a field named `datestamp`, the Cloud Storage URI should be of the following form:

```
gs://some-bucket/some-dir/some-table/*
```

This is true even if the files themselves all begin with the following:

```
gs://some-bucket/some-dir/some-table/datestamp=
```

As of this writing, the `AUTO` partitioning mode can detect the following types: `STRING`, `INTEGER`, `DATE`, and `TIMESTAMP`. It is also possible to request that the partition keys be detected as strings (this can be helpful in exploratory work):

```
bq load --source_format=ORC --autodetect \
  --hive_partitioning_mode=STRINGS <dataset>.<table> <gcs_uri>
```

As with CSV files from Google Cloud Storage, federated querying of Hive partitions requires the creation of a table definition file, and the options closely mirror that of load:

```
bq mkdef --source_format=ORC --autodetect \
    --hive_partitioning_mode=AUTO <gcs_uri> > table_def.json
```

After the table definition file is created, querying is the same whether the underlying external dataset consists of CSV files or Hive partitions.

In addition to ORC, as shown earlier, data in other formats is also supported. For example, to create a table definition of data stored in newline-delimited JSON, you can use this:

```
bq mkdef --source_format=NEWLINE_DELIMITED_JSON --autodetect --
hive_partitioning_mode=STRINGS <gcs_uri> <schema> > table_def.json
```

Note that in the preceding command, the partition keys are being autodetected, but not the data types of the partition keys, because we explicitly specify that they ought to be treated as strings and not the data types of the other columns, since we pass in an explicit schema.

We started this section by saying that a common use case for querying Hive partitions is to support cloud migration efforts where significant Hive workloads already exist but allow future workloads to be implemented using BigQuery. Although Apache Hive allows full management (reading and writing) of the data, BigQuery's external tables are read-only. Moreover, even though BigQuery can handle the data being modified (e.g., from Hive) while a federated query is running, it does not currently support concepts such as reading data at a specific point in time. Because external tables in BigQuery have these limitations, it is better over time to move the data to BigQuery's native storage and rewrite the Hive workloads in BigQuery. When the data is in BigQuery's native storage, features such as DML, streaming, clustering, table copies, and more all become possible.

When to Use Federated Queries and External Data Sources

Querying external sources is slower than querying data that is natively in BigQuery, thus federated queries are typically not recommended in the long term for frequently accessed data. There are, however, situations for which federated queries can be advantageous:

- Carrying out exploratory work using federated queries to determine how best to transform the raw data before loading it into BigQuery. For example, evidence of actual analysis workloads could dictate the transformations present in production tables. You might also treat original, external data sources as staging, and use federated queries to transform the data and write it to production tables.

- Keeping data in Google Sheets if the spreadsheet will be edited interactively, and using federated queries exclusively if the results of those queries need to reflect the live data in that sheet.

- Keeping data in an external data source if ad hoc SQL querying of the data is relatively infrequent. For example, you might keep the data in Cloud Bigtable if the predominant use of that data is for low-latency, high-volume streaming ingest and if most queries on the data can be accomplished using key prefixes.

For large, relatively stable, well-understood datasets that will be updated periodically and queried often, BigQuery native storage is a better choice. In the rest of this section, we look at the implementation details of each of these situations, beginning with exploratory work using federated queries.

Exploratory work using federated queries

Autodetect is a convenience feature that works by sampling a few (on the order of hundreds) rows of the input files to determine the type of a column. It is not foolproof unless you are using self-describing file formats, such as Avro, Parquet, or ORC. To ensure that your ETL pipeline works properly, you should verify the value of every row to ensure that the data type for each column is correct. For example, it is possible that a column contains integers except for a handful of rows that have floats. If so, then it's quite likely that the autodetect will detect the column as being an integer because the chance of selecting one of the rows containing the floating-point value is rather low. You won't learn there is a problem until you issue a query that does a table scan of this column's values.

The best practice is to use self-describing file formats, in which case you don't need to worry about how BigQuery interprets the data. If you need to use CSV or JSON, we recommend that you explicitly specify a schema. Although it is possible to specify the schema in an accompanying JSON file, it is also possible to pass in the schema on the command line of bq mkdef by creating a string with this format:

```
FIELD1:DATATYPE1,FIELD2:DATATYPE2,...
```

If you are unsure of the quality of your data, you should specify everything as a STRING. Note that this is the default data type, so the formatting command becomes just this:

```
FIELD1,FIELD2,FIELD3,,...
```

Why treat everything as a string? Even if you believe that some of the fields are integers and others are floats, it is best to validate this assumption. Define everything as a string and learn what transformations you need to carry out as you query the data and discover errors.

We can extract the column names by using the first line of the CSV file to create a schema string of the desired format:[15]

```
INPUT=gs://bigquery-oreilly-book/college_scorecard.csv
SCHEMA=$(gsutil cat $INPUT | head -1 | cut -b 4- )
```

If we are going to specify the schema, we should ask that the first row be skipped and that the tool allow empty lines in the file. We can do this by piping the table definition through sed, a line editor:[16]

```
LOC="--location US"
OUTPUT=/tmp/college_scorecard_def.json
bq $LOC \
    mkdef \
    --source_format=CSV \
    --noautodetect \
    $INPUT \
    $SCHEMA \
 | sed 's/"skipLeadingRows": 0/"skipLeadingRows": 1/g' \
 | sed 's/"allowJaggedRows": false/"allowJaggedRows": true/g' \
 > $OUTPUT
```

We define that we are operating in the US location and that we want to save the output (the table definition) to the /tmp folder.

At this point, we have a table that we can query. Note two things: this table is defined on an external data source, so we are able to start querying the data without the need to wait for the data to be ingested; and all of the columns are strings—we have not made any irreversible changes to the raw data.

---

15 This particular file includes a "byte order marker" (\u0eff) as its first character, so we remove the first few bytes using cut: cut -b 4-.

16 The complete script is called *load_external_gcs.sh* and is located in the GitHub repository for this book.

Let's begin our data exploration by trying to do a cast:

```
SELECT
  MAX(CAST(SAT_AVG AS FLOAT64)) AS MAX_SAT_AVG
FROM
  `ch04.college_scorecard_gcs`
```

The query fails with the following error message:

```
Bad double value: NULL
```

This indicates that we need to handle the nonstandard way that missing data is encoded in the file. In most CSV files, missing data is encoded as an empty string, but in this one, it is encoded as the string NULL.

We could fix this problem by checking before we do the cast:

```
WITH etl_data AS (
  SELECT
   SAFE_CAST(SAT_AVG AS FLOAT64) AS SAT_AVG
  FROM
   `ch04.college_scorecard_gcs`
)
SELECT
  MAX(SAT_AVG) AS MAX_SAT_AVG
FROM
  etl_data
```

Notice that we have started a WITH clause containing all the ETL operations that need to be performed on the dataset. Indeed, as we go through exploring the dataset and culminate with the query of the previous section, we learn that we need a reusable function to clean up numeric data:

```
CREATE TEMP FUNCTION cleanup_numeric(x STRING) AS
(
  IF ( x != 'NULL' AND x != 'PrivacySuppressed',
       CAST(x as FLOAT64),
       NULL )
);

WITH etl_data AS (
  SELECT
    INSTNM
    , cleanup_numeric(ADM_RATE_ALL) AS ADM_RATE_ALL
    , cleanup_numeric(FIRST_GEN) AS FIRST_GEN
    , cleanup_numeric(MD_FAMINC) AS MD_FAMINC
    , cleanup_numeric(SAT_AVG) AS SAT_AVG
    , cleanup_numeric(MD_EARN_WNE_P10) AS MD_EARN_WNE_P10
  FROM
    `ch04.college_scorecard_gcs`
)

SELECT
```

```
    *
FROM
  etl_data
WHERE
  SAT_AVG > 1300
  AND ADM_RATE_ALL < 0.2
  AND FIRST_GEN > 0.1
ORDER BY
  MD_FAMINC ASC
LIMIT 10
```

At this point, we can export the cleaned-up data (note the SELECT *) into a new table (note the CREATE TABLE) for just the columns of interest by running the following query:

```
CREATE TEMP FUNCTION cleanup_numeric(x STRING) AS
(
  IF ( x != 'NULL' AND x != 'PrivacySuppressed',
       CAST(x as FLOAT64),
       NULL )
);

CREATE TABLE ch04.college_scorecard_etl
OPTIONS(description="Cleaned up college scorecard data") AS

WITH etl_data AS (
  SELECT
    INSTNM
    , cleanup_numeric(ADM_RATE_ALL) AS ADM_RATE_ALL
    , cleanup_numeric(FIRST_GEN) AS FIRST_GEN
    , cleanup_numeric(MD_FAMINC) AS MD_FAMINC
    , cleanup_numeric(SAT_AVG) AS SAT_AVG
    , cleanup_numeric(MD_EARN_WNE_P10) AS MD_EARN_WNE_P10
  FROM
    `ch04.college_scorecard_gcs`
)

SELECT * FROM etl_data
```

It is also possible to script this out by removing the CREATE TABLE statement from the preceding query, invoking bq query and passing in a --destination_table.

ELT in SQL for experimentation

In many organizations, there are many more data analysts than there are engineers. Thus, the needs of the data analysis teams usually greatly outpace what the data engineers can deliver. In such cases, it can be helpful if data analysts themselves can create an experimental dataset in BigQuery and get started with analysis tasks.

The organization can then use the evidence of actual analytics workloads to prioritize what data engineers focus on. For example, as a data engineer, you might not yet know what fields you need to extract out of a log file. So you might set up an external data source as an experiment and allow data analysts to query the raw data on Google Cloud Storage directly.

If the raw log files are in JSON format, with each of the rows having a different structure because the logs come from different applications, the analysts could define the entire log message as a single BigQuery string column and use `JSON_EXTRACT` and string manipulation functions to pull out the necessary data. At the end of a month, you could analyze the BigQuery query logs for which fields they actually did access, and how they did such access, and then build a pipeline to routinely load those fields into BigQuery.

For example, you can export BigQuery audit logs from Stackdriver in JSON format with the entire log message in a nested column named `protopayload_auditlog.meta dataJson`. Here is a query to count log messages with the root element `tableData Read` and use the count to rank datasets in terms of the number of times each dataset is accessed:

```
SELECT
  REGEXP_EXTRACT(protopayload_auditlog.resourceName,
'^projects/[^/]+/datasets/([^/]+)/tables') AS datasetRef,
  COUNTIF(JSON_EXTRACT(protopayload_auditlog.metadataJson, "$.tableDataRead")
         IS NOT NULL) AS dataReadEvents,
FROM `ch04.cloudaudit_googleapis_com_data_access_2019*`
WHERE
  JSON_EXTRACT(protopayload_auditlog.metadataJson, "$.tableDataRead")
         IS NOT NULL
GROUP BY datasetRef
ORDER BY dataReadEvents DESC
LIMIT 5
```

The method `JSON_EXTRACT` takes the column name (`protopayload_auditlog.metada taJson`) as the first parameter and a JSONPath[17] as the second parameter.

If the original data is in a relational database management system (RDBMS), it is possible to export the data periodically as a tab-separated values (TSV) file to Google Cloud Storage. For example, if you are using MySQL with a database named `somedb`, the relevant command would be as follows:

```
mysql somedb < select_data.sql | \
      gsutil cp - gs://BUCKET/data_$(date -u "+%F-%T").tsv
```

The `select_data.sql` would contain a query to pull just the most recent records (here, those from the previous 10 days):

---

17 For the grammar of a JSONPath, see *https://restfulapi.net/json-jsonpath/*.

```
select * from my_table
where transaction_date >= DATE_SUB(CURDATE(), INTERVAL 10 DAY)
```

Given these periodically exported files, it is straightforward for an analyst to get started querying the data using federated queries. After the value of the dataset is proven, the data can be loaded routinely and/or in real time through a data pipeline.

The reason that this is not always suitable for operationalization is that it doesn't handle the case of mutations to the database. If data that is more than 10 days old is updated, the tab-separated dumps will not be synchronized. Realistically, dumps to TSV files work only for small datasets (on the order of a few gigabytes) where the original database fields themselves do not need to be transformed or corrected before they are used for analytics queries.

If you do want to operationalize synchronization from an operational database to BigQuery, there are a number of third-party companies that partner with Google, each with a menu of connectors and transformation options.[18] These tools can do change data capture (CDC) to allow you to stream changes from a database to a Big-Query table.

External query in Cloud SQL

BigQuery supports external queries, not just federated queries. Whereas a federated query allows you to query an external data source using BigQuery, an external query allows you to run the query in the external database and seamlessly join the results against data in BigQuery. At the time of writing, MySQL and PostgresSQL databases in Cloud SQL (the managed relational database service in Google Cloud) are supported.

There is an initial one-time setup to create a connection resource in BigQuery and grant users permission to use this connection resource. Once this connection resource has been set up, it can be used from an EXTERNAL_QUERY as follows:

```
SELECT * FROM EXTERNAL_QUERY(connection_id, cloud_sql_query);
```

In this example, connection_id is the name of the database connection resource that you created in BigQuery using the web UI, a REST API, or the command-line tool.

The performance of the external query depends on the speed of the external database and, because it involves an intermediate temporary table, will usually be slower than queries that are purely in Cloud SQL or purely in BigQuery. Still, there is a tremendous benefit to being able to query data residing in an RDBMS in real time without

---

18 These partners include Alooma, Informatica, and Talend. For a full, and current, list of BigQuery partners, visit *https://cloud.google.com/bigquery/partners/*.

having to move data around, thus avoiding unnecessary ETL, scheduling, and orchestration.

For example, suppose we wish to create a report of gift cards belonging to customers who have not made any recent purchases. The date of the latest order for each customer is available in Cloud SQL and updated in real time. The balance associated with every gift card our store has ever issued, however, is available in BigQuery. We can join the result of an external query of the orders data in Cloud SQL with the gift card balance data in BigQuery to create an up-to-date report without having to move any data around:

```
SELECT
    c.customer_id
    , c.gift_card_balance
    , rq.latest_order_date
FROM ch04.gift_cards AS c
LEFT OUTER JOIN EXTERNAL_QUERY(
  'connection_id',
  '''SELECT customer_id, MAX(order_date) AS latest_order_date
  FROM orders
  GROUP BY customer_id''') AS rq ON rq.customer_id = c.customer_id
WHERE c.gift_card_balance > 100
ORDER BY rq.latest_order_date ASC;
```

Interactive Exploration and Querying of Data in Google Sheets

Google Sheets is part of G Suite, a set of productivity and collaboration tools from Google Cloud. It provides the means of creating, viewing, editing, and publishing spreadsheets. A spreadsheet contains tabular values in individual cells; some of these values are data and some are the result of computations carried out on the values of other cells. Google Sheets brings spreadsheets online—multiple people can collaboratively edit a spreadsheet, and you can access it from a variety of devices.

Loading Google Sheets data into BigQuery

Google Sheets is an external source, so loading and querying a Google Sheets spreadsheet is a federated query; it works similarly to querying a CSV file from Google Cloud Storage. We create a table definition in BigQuery to point to the data in Google Sheets, and then we can query that table as if it were a native BigQuery table.

Let's begin by creating a Google Sheets spreadsheet that we can query. Open a web browser, and then, in the URL navigation bar, type **https://sheets.new --**. Visiting this URL opens a blank spreadsheet.

Type in the following data (or download the corresponding CSV file (*https://oreil.ly/ckBA5*) from GitHub and do a File > Import of the data into Google Sheets):

Student	Home state	SAT score
Aarti	KS	1111
Billy	LA	1222
Cao	MT	1333
Dalia	NE	1444

Next, navigate to the BigQuery section of the GCP Cloud Console, create a dataset (if necessary), and create a table, specifying that the source of the table is on Drive and its URL, and that it is a Google Sheet. Ask for the schema to be autodetected, as demonstrated in Figure 4-2.

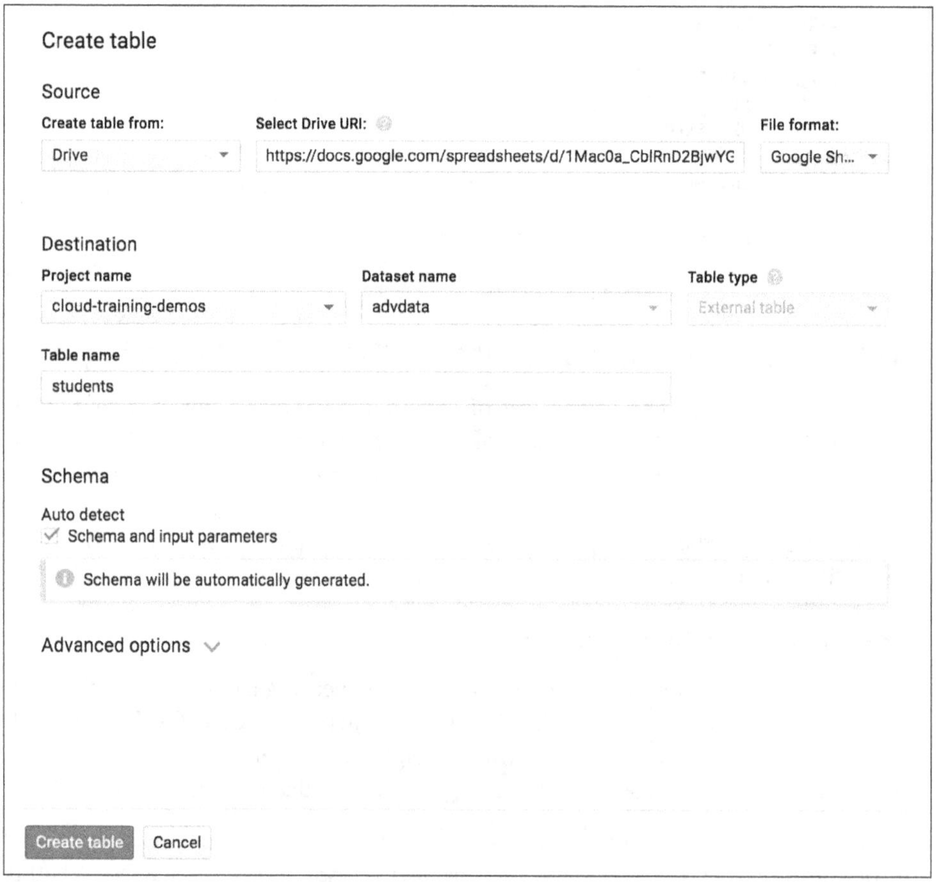

Figure 4-2. The "Create table" dialog box allows you to specify that the external data source is Google Sheets

After you do this, you can query the spreadsheet like any other BigQuery table:

```
SELECT * from advdata.students
```

Try changing the spreadsheet and verify that the returned results reflect the current state of the table (the results of federated queries on external datasets are not cached).

Even though querying a spreadsheet using SQL like this is possible, it is unlikely that you'd want to do this, because it's usually more convenient to use the interactive filtering and sorting options built into Google Sheets. For example, you can click the Explore button and type in the natural language query "average SAT score of students in KS," which returns the results shown in Figure 4-3.

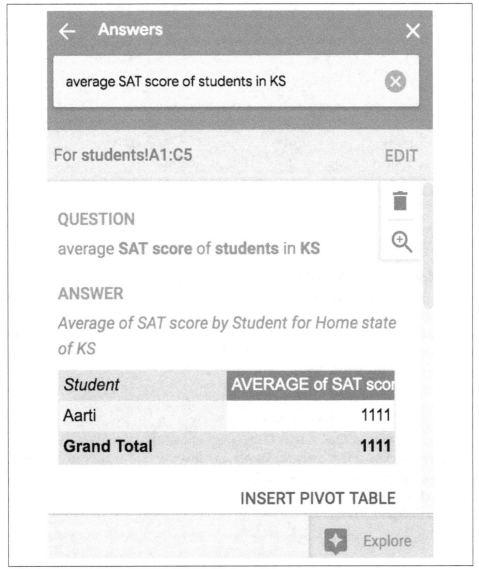

Figure 4-3. Natural language query in Google Sheets

There are several broad use cases for the tie between Google Sheets and BigQuery:

- Populating a spreadsheet with data from BigQuery
- Exploring BigQuery tables using Sheets
- Querying Sheets data using SQL

Let's look at these three cases.

Populating a Google Sheets spreadsheet with data from BigQuery

The BigQuery data connector in Google Sheets allows you to query BigQuery tables[19] and use the results to populate a spreadsheet. This can be extremely useful when sharing data with nontechnical users. In most businesses, nearly all office workers know how to read/interpret spreadsheets. They don't need to have anything to do with BigQuery or SQL to be able to use Google Sheets and work with the data in the sheet.

From Google Sheets, click Data > Data Connectors > BigQuery, select your project, and write a query to populate the spreadsheet from the BigQuery table of college scorecard data:

```
SELECT
  *
FROM
  ch04.college_scorecard_etl
```

Exploring BigQuery tables using Sheets

One of the reasons that you might want to populate a Google Sheets spreadsheet with data from a BigQuery table is that Sheets is a familiar interface for business users creating charts, formulas, and pivot tables. For example, from the college scorecard data in Sheets, it is quite straightforward to create a formula to rank colleges by the increase in median income experienced by their graduates:

1. In a new column, enter the following formula:

   ```
   =ArrayFormula(IF(ISBLANK(D2:D), 0, F2:F/D2:D))
   ```

   Note that the spreadsheet has now been populated with the ratio of the value in the F-column to the value in the D-column—that is, by the increase in income.

2. From the Data menu, create a filter on the newly created column and turn off blanks and zeros.

---

19 As of this writing, there are size restrictions on the BigQuery table.

---

3. Sort the spreadsheet Z to A based on this column.

Selecting the first few rows of the sheet, we can quickly create a chart to showcase the best colleges in terms of economic improvement of the student body, as illustrated in Figure 4-4.

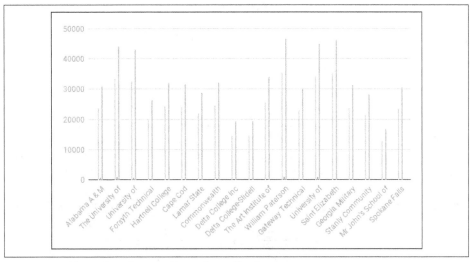

Figure 4-4. Chart that shows colleges that offer the greatest economic improvement to their graduates

In addition to interactively creating the charts you want, you can use the machine learning features of Google Sheets to further explore your data.

In Google Sheets, click the Explore button and notice the charts that are automatically created through machine learning.[20] For example, the automatically generated insight depicted in Figure 4-5 captures a striking inequality.

---

20 Due to continuing changes and improvements in the products, the graphs you see might be different.

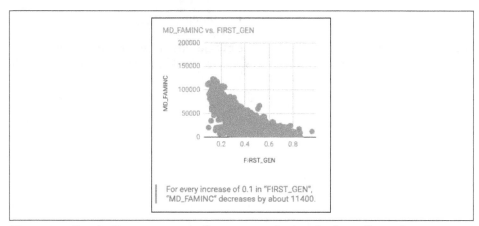

Figure 4-5. Google Sheets automatically generates the insight that colleges that serve first-generation college students also have poorer student bodies; for every 10% increase in first-generation college students, median family income decreases by $11,400

Figure 4-6 shows a subsequent automatically created chart that puts the SAT_AVG in context.

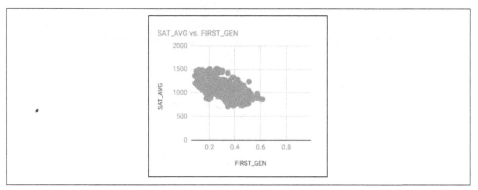

Figure 4-6. Colleges that serve first-generation college students tend to have lower SAT averages

We can even ask for specific charts using natural language. Typing "histogram of sat_avg where first_gen more than 0.5" in the "Ask a question" box returns the answer displayed in Figure 4-7.

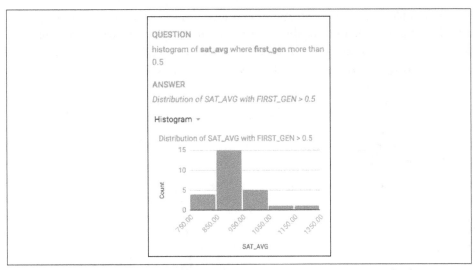

Figure 4-7. Getting the charts we want by simply asking for them in Google Sheets

Exploring BigQuery tables as a data sheet in Google Sheets

In the previous section, we loaded the entire BigQuery table into Google Sheets, but this was possible only because our college scorecard dataset was small enough. Loading the entire BigQuery table into Google Sheets is obviously not feasible for larger BigQuery tables.

Google Sheets does allow you to access, analyze, visualize, and share even large Big-Query datasets as a BigQuery Data Sheet. To try this out, start a new Google Sheets document and navigate via the menu by clicking Data > Data Connectors > BigQuery Data Sheet.

Choose your Cloud project (that should be billed), and navigate via the menu to the table you want to load into the Data Sheet by clicking bigquery-public-data > usa_names > usa_1910_current > Connect. This table contains nearly six million rows and is too large to load in its entirety. Instead, BigQuery acts as a cloud backend for the data shown in Sheets.

Unlike when loading the entire table into Sheets (as in the previous section), only the first 500 rows of a Data Sheet are loaded in the UI. These 500 rows are best thought of as a preview of the full dataset. Another difference is in editing: if the entire table is loaded, Google Sheets holds a copy of the data; thus, you can edit cells and save the changed spreadsheet. On the other hand, if BigQuery is acting as a cloud backend, cells are not editable—users can filter and pivot the BigQuery Data Sheet, but they cannot edit the data. When users do filtering and pivoting, these actions happen on the entire BigQuery table, not just the preview that is shown in Sheets.

As an example of the kind of analysis that is possible, let's create a Pivot table by clicking the Pivot table button. In the Pivot table editor, choose `state` as the Rows, and select `year` as the Columns. For Values, choose `number`, and ask Sheets to summarize by `COUNTUNIQUE` and show as `Default`, as shown in Figure 4-8.

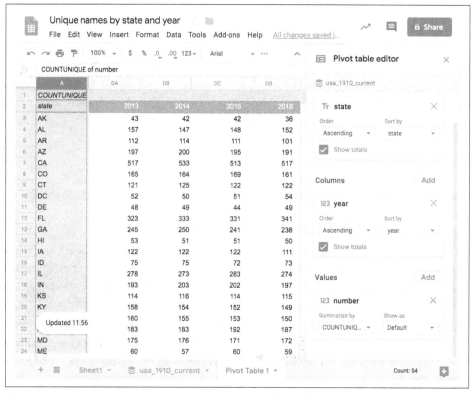

Figure 4-8. Creating a Pivot table from a BigQuery Data Sheet

As Figure 4-8 illustrates, we get a table of the number of unique baby names in each state, broken down by year.

Joining Sheets data with a large dataset in BigQuery

Both BigQuery and Google Sheets are capable of storing and providing access to tabular data. However, BigQuery is primarily an analytics data warehouse, whereas Google Sheets is primarily an interactive document. As we saw in the earlier sections, the familiarity of Sheets and the exploration and charting capabilities makes loading BigQuery data into Sheets very powerful.

However, there is a practical limitation on the size of BigQuery datasets that you can load into Sheets. For example, BigQuery holds information on Stack Overflow questions, answers, and users. Even with BigSheets, these petabyte-scale datasets are much too large to load directly into Google Sheets. However, it is still possible to write queries that join a small dataset in Sheets with such large datasets in BigQuery and proceed from there. Let's look at an example.

From the previous section, we have a spreadsheet with college scorecard data. Let's assume that we don't already have the data in BigQuery. We could create a table in BigQuery using the spreadsheet as a source, calling the resulting table `college_score card_gs`, as depicted in Figure 4-9.

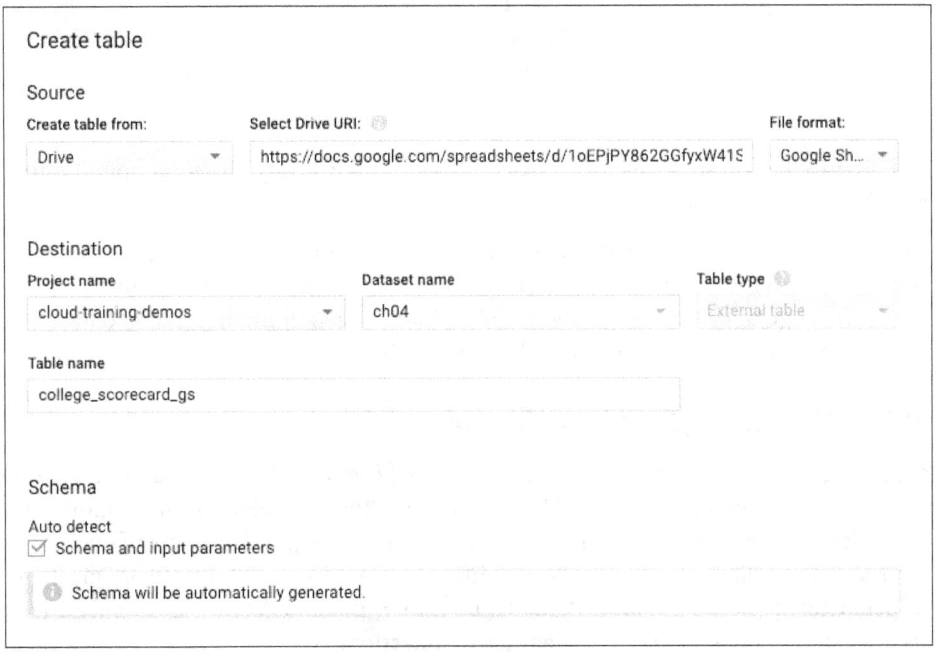

Figure 4-9. Creating a table in BigQuery using a Google Sheets spreadsheet as a source

Now we can issue a query in BigQuery that joins this relatively small table (7,700 rows) with a massive table consisting of Stack Overflow data (10 million rows) to find which colleges are most commonly listed in Stack Overflow users' profiles:

```
SELECT INSTNM, COUNT(display_name) AS numusers
FROM `bigquery-public-data`.stackoverflow.users, ch04.college_scorecard_gs
WHERE REGEXP_CONTAINS(about_me, INSTNM)
GROUP BY INSTNM
ORDER BY numusers DESC
LIMIT 5
```

This yields the following:[21]

---

21 This query will be slow because we are doing a regular expression match and doing so 77 billion times.

Row	INSTNM	numusers
1	Institute of Technology	2364
2	National University	332
3	Carnegie Mellon University	169
4	Stanford University	139
5	University of Maryland	131

The first two entries are suspect,[22] but it appears that Carnegie Mellon and Stanford are well represented on Stack Overflow.

The result of this query is again small enough to load directly into Google Sheets and perform interactive filtering and charting. Thus the SQL querying capability of Sheets data from BigQuery is particularly useful to join a small, human-editable dataset (in Google Sheets) with large enterprise datasets (in BigQuery).

SQL Queries on Data in Cloud Bigtable

Cloud Bigtable is a fully managed NoSQL database service that scales up to petabytes of data. Cloud Bigtable is meant to be used in situations for which some combination of low latency (on the order of milliseconds), high throughput (millions of operations per second), replication for high availability, and seamless scalability (from gigabytes to petabytes) is desired. Cloud Bigtable, therefore, finds heavy use in finance (trade reconciliation and analytics, payment fraud detection, etc.), Internet of Things (IoT) applications (for centralized storage and processing of real-time sensor data), and advertising (real-time bidding, placement, and behavioral analysis). Although Cloud Bigtable itself is available only on GCP, it supports the open source Apache HBase API, enabling easy migration of workloads in a hybrid cloud environment.

NoSQL Queries based on a row-key prefix

Cloud Bigtable provides high-performance queries that look up rows or sets of rows that match a specific row-key, a row-key prefix, or a range of prefixes. Even though Cloud Bigtable requires an instance, consisting of one or more logical clusters, to be provisioned and available in your project, it uses that cluster only for compute (and not for storage)—the data itself is stored on Colossus, and the nodes themselves need

---

22 Most likely, the rows include data from multiple colleges, such as National University of Singapore, National University of Ireland, Massachusetts Institute of Technology, Georgia Institute of Technology, and so on.

only to know about the location of row-ranges on Colossus. Because the data is not stored on the Cloud Bigtable nodes, it is possible to easily scale the Cloud Bigtable cluster up and down without expensive data migration.

In financial analysis, a common pattern is to store time-series data in Cloud Bigtable as it arrives in real- time and support low-latency queries on that data based on the row-key (e.g., all buy orders, if any, for GOOG stock in the past 10 minutes). This allows dashboards that require recent data to provide automatic alerts and actions based on recent activity. Cloud Bigtable also supports being able to quickly obtain a range of data (e.g., all the buy orders for GOOG stock in any given day), a necessity for financial analytics and reporting. Prediction algorithms themselves need to be trained on historical data (e.g., the time-series of ask prices for GOOG over the past five years), and this is possible because machine learning frameworks like TensorFlow can read and write directly from and to Cloud Bigtable. These three workloads (real-time alerting, reporting, and machine learning training) can occur on the same data, with the cluster potentially being scaled up and down with workload spikes due to the separation of compute and storage.

All three workloads in the previous paragraph involve obtaining ask prices for Google stock. Cloud Bigtable will provide efficient retrieval of records if the row-key with which the time-series data is stored is of the form GOOG#buy#20190119-090356.0322234—that is, the security name and the timestamp. Then the queries of ask prices, whether over the previous 10 minutes or over the past five years, all involve requesting records that fall within a range of prefixes.

What if, though, we desire to perform ad hoc analytics over all of the Cloud Bigtable data, and our query is not of a form that will result in retrieving only a subset of records—what if, in other words, our query does not filter based on the row-key prefix? Then the NoSQL paradigm of Cloud Bigtable falls down, and it is better to resort to the ad hoc SQL querying capabilities offered by BigQuery instead, with the understanding that BigQuery results will be subject to higher latency.

Ad hoc SQL queries on Cloud Bigtable data

Just as BigQuery can directly query files in certain formats (CSV, Avro, etc.) in Google Cloud Storage by treating it as an external data source, BigQuery can directly query data in Cloud Bigtable. Just as with data in Cloud Storage, data in Cloud Bigtable can be queried using either a permanent table or a temporary table. A permanent table can be shared by sharing the dataset that it is part of; a temporary table is valid only for the duration of a query and so cannot be shared.

A table in Cloud Bigtable is mapped to a table in BigQuery. In this section, we use a time-series of point-of-sale data to illustrate. To follow along, run the script *setup_data.sh* (*https://github.com/GoogleCloudPlatform/bigquery-oreilly-book/tree/master/04_load/bigtable*) in the GitHub repository for this book to create a Cloud

Bigtable instance populated with some example data. Because the setup script creates a Cloud Bigtable instance with a cluster, remember to delete the instance when you are done.

We begin by using the BigQuery UI to create an external table in BigQuery to point to the data in Cloud Bigtable, as shown in Figure 4-10. The location is a string of the form `https://googleapis.com/bigtable/projects/[PROJECT_ID]/instances/[INSTANCE_ID]/tables/[TABLE_NAME]`. The `PROJECT_ID`, `INSTANCE_ID`, and `TABLE_NAME` refer to the project, instance, and table in Cloud Bigtable.[23]

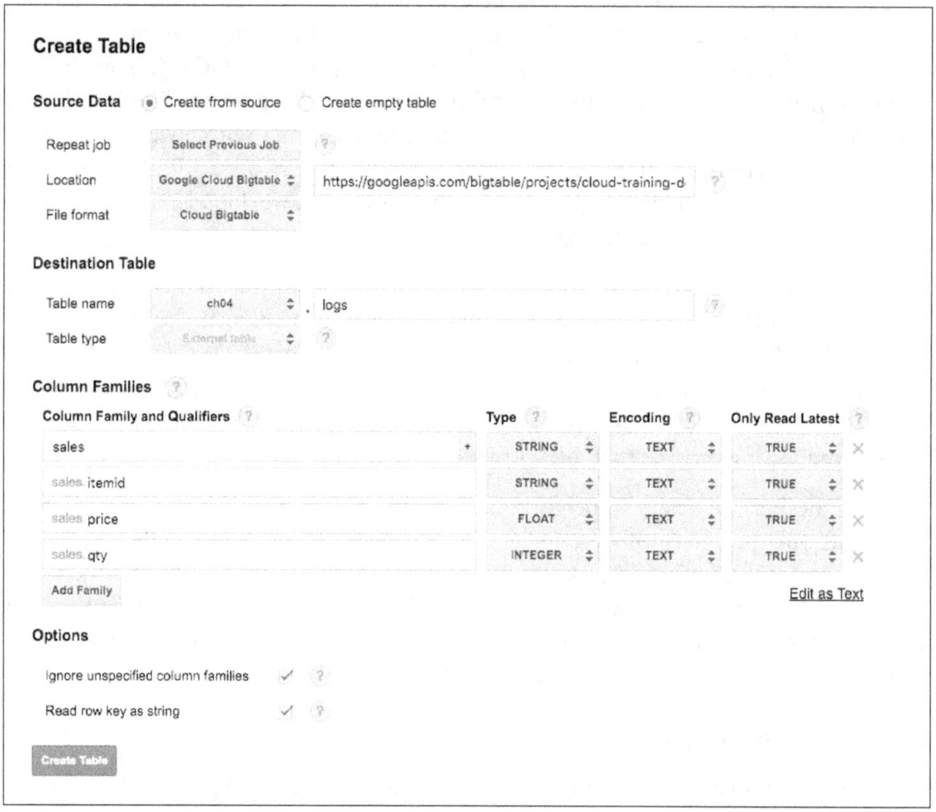

Figure 4-10. Creating an external table in BigQuery to point to data in Cloud Bigtable.[24]

---

23 If you followed along by running the *setup_data.sh* file in the GitHub repository, the `project_id` will be your unique project ID, the `instance_id` will be bqbook-instance, and the `table_name` will be logs-table.

24 As of this writing, this capability is available only in the "old" UI at *https://bigquery.cloud.google.com/* and not in the "new" UI that is part of the GCP Cloud Console (*https://console.cloud.google.com/bigquery*).

Data in Cloud Bigtable consists of records, each of which has a row-key and data tied to the row-key that is organized into column families, which are key/value pairs, where the key is the name of the column family and the value is a set of related columns.

Cloud Bigtable does not require every record to have every column family and every column allowed in a column family; in fact, the presence or absence of a specific column can itself be considered data. Therefore, BigQuery allows you to create a table that is tied to data in Cloud Bigtable without explicitly specifying any column names. If you do that, BigQuery exposes the values in a column family as an array of columns and each column as an array of values written at different timestamps.

In many cases, the column names are known beforehand, and if that is the case, it is better to supply the known columns in the table definition. In our case, we know the schema of each record in the logs-table of Cloud Bigtable:

- A row-key, which is the store ID followed by the timestamp of each transaction
- A column family named "sales" to capture sales transactions at the register
- Within the sales column family, we capture:
  — The item ID (a string)
  — The price at which the item was sold (a floating-point number)
  — The number of items bought in this transaction (an integer)

Notice from Figure 4-10 that we have specified all of this information in the Column Families section of the table definition.

Cloud Bigtable treats all data simply as byte strings, so the schema (string, float, integer) are meant more for BigQuery so that we can avoid the need to cast the values each time in our queries. Avoiding the cast is also the reason why we ask for the row-key to be treated as a string. When the BigQuery table is created, each of the columns in Cloud Bigtable is mapped to a column in BigQuery of the appropriate type:

sales.price	RECORD	NULLABLE	Describe this field...
sales.price.cell	RECORD	NULLABLE	Describe this field...
sales.price.cell.timestamp	TIMESTAMP	NULLABLE	Describe this field...
sales.price.cell.value	FLOAT	NULLABLE	Describe this field...

With the BigQuery table in place, it is now possible to issue a good, old-fashioned SQL query to aggregate the total number of itemid 12345 that have been sold:

```
SELECT SUM(sales.qty.cell.value) AS num_sold
FROM ch04.logs
WHERE sales.itemid.cell.value = '12345'
```

Improving performance

When we issue a federated query on data held in Google Cloud Storage, the work is carried out by BigQuery workers. On the other hand, when we issue a federated query on data held in Cloud Bigtable, the work is carried out on the Cloud Bigtable cluster. The performance of the second query is, therefore, limited by the capacity of the Cloud Bigtable cluster and the load on it at the time that the query is being submitted.

As with any analytics query, the overall query speed also depends on the number of rows that need to be read and the size of the data being read. BigQuery does try to limit the amount of data that needs to be read by reading only the column families referenced in the query, and Cloud Bigtable will split the data across nodes to take advantage of the distribution of row-key prefixes across the full dataset.

 If you have data that has a high update frequency or you need low-latency point lookups, Cloud Bigtable will provide the best performance for queries that can filter on a range of row-key prefixes. It can be tempting to think of BigQuery as providing an end run around Cloud Bigtable performance by supporting ad hoc point lookups of Cloud Bigtable data that aren't limited by row-keys. However, this pattern often gives disappointing performance, and you should benchmark it on your workload before deciding on a production architecture.

BigQuery stores data in a column-oriented order, which is optimized for table scans, whereas Cloud Bigtable stores data in a row-major order, which is optimized for small reads and writes. Queries of external data stored in Cloud Bigtable do not provide the benefits of BigQuery's internal column-based storage and will be performant only if they read a subset of rows, not if they do a full table scan. Hence, you should be careful to ensure that your BigQuery federated queries filter on the Bigtable row-key; otherwise, they will need to read the entire Cloud Bigtable table every time.

The knob you do have under your control is the number of nodes in your Cloud Bigtable cluster. If you are going to routinely issue SQL queries against your Cloud Bigtable data, monitor the Cloud Bigtable CPU usage and increase the number of Cloud Bigtable nodes if necessary.

As with federated queries over Google Cloud Storage, consider whether it is advantageous to set up an ELT pipeline when performing analytics over data in Cloud Bigtable; that is, consider extracting data from Cloud Bigtable using a federated query and loading it into a BigQuery table for further analysis and transformations. This approach, illustrated in Figure 4-11, allows you to carry out your analytics workload in an environment where you are not at the mercy of the operational load on Cloud

Bigtable. Analytics on an internal BigQuery table can be carried out on thousands of machines rather than a much smaller cluster. The analytics queries will, therefore, finish more quickly in BigQuery (assuming that these analytics cannot be achieved using row-key prefixes) than if you use federated queries on an external table. The drawback is, of course, that the extracted data is duplicated in both Cloud Bigtable and BigQuery. Still, storage tends to be inexpensive, and the advantages of scale and speed might be enough compensation.

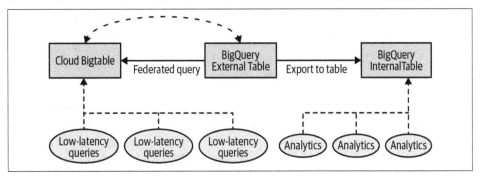

Figure 4-11. Use a federated query to export selected tables to a BigQuery internal table and have your analytics workloads query the internal table

It is possible to schedule such data ingest into internal BigQuery tables to happen periodically. We look at that in the next section.

 If you started a Cloud Bigtable instance to experiment with, delete it now so as not to run up charges.

Transfers and Exports

So far, we have looked at loading data on a one-off basis and avoiding the movement of data by using federated queries. In this section, we look at turn-key services to transfer data into BigQuery from a variety of sources on a periodic basis.

Data Transfer Service

The BigQuery Data Transfer Service allows you to schedule recurring data loads from a variety of data sources into BigQuery. As with most BigQuery capabilities, you can access the BigQuery Data Transfer Service using the web UI or the command-line tool, or through a REST API. For repeatability, we show you the command-line tool.

After you configure a data transfer, BigQuery will automatically load data on the schedule you specify. However, in case there is a problem with the original data, you can also initiate data backfills to recover from any outages or gaps. This is called *refreshing*, and you can initiate it from the web UI.

The Data Transfer Service supports loading data from a number of Software as a Service (SaaS) applications, such as Google Ads, Google Play, Amazon Redshift, and YouTube, as well as from Google Cloud Storage. We look at how to set up routine ingest of files that show up in Cloud Storage, noting along the way any differences with data transfer of a SaaS dataset, using YouTube channel reports as a running example.

Data locality

As we discussed earlier in the chapter, BigQuery datasets are created in a specific region (such as `asia-northeast1`, which is Tokyo) or in a multiregional location (e.g., EU).[25] When you set up a Data Transfer Service to a dataset, it processes and stages data in the same location as the target BigQuery dataset.

If your Cloud Storage bucket is in the same region as your BigQuery dataset, the data transfer does not incur charges. Transferring data between regions (e.g., from a Cloud Storage bucket in one region to a BigQuery dataset in a different region) will incur network charges, whether the transfer happens via loads, exports, or data transfers.

BigQuery Data Transfer Service needs to be enabled (you can do this from the BigQuery web UI), and you need to have been granted the `bigquery.admin` role in order to create transfers and write data to the destination dataset.

Setting up destination table

The data transfer service does not have the ability to create a new table, autodetect schema, and so on. Instead, you need to provide a template table that has the desired schema. If you are writing all the data to a column-partitioned table, specify the partitioning column as a `TIMESTAMP` or `DATE` column when you create the destination table schema. We cover partitions in detail in Chapter 7.

Here, we illustrate the process on the college scorecard dataset. We have it stored in the US multiregion, so you should create a dataset in the US multiregion if you want to try out the following steps.

In BigQuery, run the following query:

---

25 See *https://cloud.google.com/bigquery/docs/locations* for BigQuery dataset locations and *https://cloud.google.com/storage/docs/bucket-locations* for Cloud Storage locations.

```
CREATE OR REPLACE TABLE
ch04.college_scorecard_dts
AS
SELECT * FROM ch04.college_scorecard_gcs
LIMIT 0
```

This is an example of a DDL statement. It will save the result of the SELECT query (which will have no rows and not incur any charges) as a table named college_score card_dts in the ch04 dataset.

Creating Tables in SQL

DDL statements allow you to create and modify BigQuery tables and views using standard SQL query syntax. For example, the following query creates a new table named ch04.college_scorecard_valid_sat and populates it with rows from ch04.college_scorecard_gcs, where the SAT_AVG column is valid:

```
CREATE TABLE
    ch04.college_scorecard_valid_sat
    AS
    SELECT * FROM ch04.college_scorecard_gcs
    WHERE LENGTH(SAT_AVG) > 0
```

The CREATE TABLE DDL statement will return an error if the table already exists. Other options for the behavior when the table already exists include CREATE OR REPLACE (to replace the existing table) and CREATE IF NOT EXISTS (to leave the existing table as is).

Instead of providing a SELECT statement, it is also possible to create an empty table with some desired schema:

```
CREATE TABLE ch04.payment_transactions
(
  PAYEE STRING OPTIONS(description="Id of payee"),
  AMOUNT NUMERIC OPTIONS(description="Amount paid")
)
```

By running the DDL query from the BigQuery command-line UI or invoking it using the REST API, it is possible to script out or programmatically create a table.

Create a transfer job

On the command line, issue the following command to set up a transfer job:

```
bq mk --transfer_config --data_source=google_cloud_storage \
  --target_dataset=ch04 --display_name ch04_college_scorecard \
  --params='{"data_path_template":"gs://bigquery-oreilly-book/college_*.csv",
"destination_table_name_template":"college_scorecard_dts", "file_format":"CSV",
"max_bad_records":"10", "skip_leading_rows":"1", "allow_jagged_rows":"true"}'
```

This command specifies that the data source is to be Google Cloud Storage (if you're transferring from YouTube Channel, for example, the data source would be youtube_channel (*https://cloud.google.com/bigquery/docs/youtube-channel-transfer*)) and that the target dataset is ch04. The display name is used as a human-readable name on various user interfaces to refer to the transfer job.

In the case of YouTube, the destination tables are automatically partitioned on the time of import and named appropriately. However, in the case of Cloud Storage, you will need to explicitly specify this in the destination table name. For example, specifying mytable_{run_time|"%Y%m%d"} as the destination table name template indicates that the table name should start with mytable and have the job runtime appended using the datetime formatting parameters specified.[26] A convenient shortcut is ytable_{run_date}. This simply uses the date in the format YYYYMMDD. It is also possible to supply a time offset. For example, to name the table based on the timestamp 45 minutes after the runtime, we could specify the following:

```
{run_time+45m|"%Y%m%d"}_mytable_{run_time|"%H%M%s"}
```

This yields a table name of the form 20180915_mytable_004500.

The parameters themselves are specific to the data source. In the case of transferring files from Google Cloud Storage, we should specify the following:

- The input data path, with an optional wildcard.
- The destination table name template.
- The file format. The transfer service from Cloud Storage supports all of the data formats that the federated querying capability supports (CSV, JSON, Avro, Parquet, etc.). In the case that the file format is CSV, we can specify CSV-specific options, such as the number of header lines to skip.

The parameters for the YouTube Channel data transfer include the page_id (in YouTube) and table_suffix (in BigQuery).

When you run the bq mk command, as just shown, you will get a URL as part of an OAuth2 workflow; provide the necessary token by signing in via the browser, and the transfer job will be created.

You can also initiate a Data Transfer Service from the web UI. Initiate a transfer and choose the data source, as illustrated in Figure 4-12.

---

26 For a list of available formatting options, see the BigQuery docs for formatting datetime columns (*https://cloud.google.com/bigquery/docs/reference/standard-sql/functions-and-operators#supported-format-elements-for-datetime*).

Figure 4-12. You can initiate a data transfer from the web UI as well

Note that we have not specified a schedule; by default, the job will run every 24 hours, starting "now." It is possible to edit the schedule of the transfer job from the BigQuery web UI, as demonstrated in Figure 4-13.

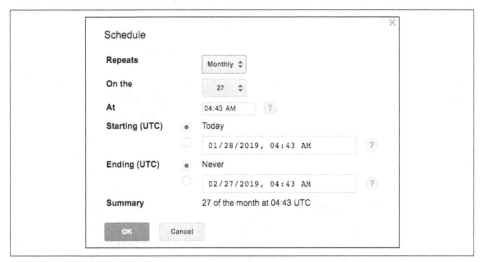

Figure 4-13. Editing the schedule of the transfer job from the web UI

The price of data transfers varies by the source. As of this writing, data transfers from YouTube Channel costs $5 per channel per month, whereas data transfers from Cloud Storage incur no charge. However, because the Data Transfer Service uses load jobs to load Cloud Storage data into BigQuery, this is subject to the BigQuery limits on load jobs (*https://cloud.google.com/bigquery/quotas#load_jobs*).

Scheduled queries

BigQuery supports the scheduling of queries to run on a recurring basis and saving the results in BigQuery tables. In particular, you can use a federated query to extract data from an external data source, transform it, and load it into BigQuery. Because such scheduled queries can include DDL and DML statements, it is possible to build sophisticated workflows purely in SQL.

You can open the dialog box to set up a scheduled query by clicking the Schedule Query button in the BigQuery UI, as shown in Figure 4-14.[27]

Figure 4-14. Schedule a query from the BigQuery user interface

Scheduled queries are built on top of the Data Transfer Service, so many of the features are similar. Thus you can specify the destination table using the same parameter settings (e.g., run_date and run_time) as for the Data Transfer Service (see the previous section).

Cross-region dataset copy

BigQuery supports the scheduling of cross-region dataset copies via the Data Transfer Service. In the Data Transfer Service web UI, choose Cross Region Copy as the Source. You will also need to specify as the source dataset the name of the dataset from which tables are to be copied into the destination dataset, as depicted in Figure 4-15.

Because the source and destination datasets are both BigQuery datasets, the initiator needs to have permission to initiate data transfers, list tables in the source dataset, view the source dataset, and edit the destination dataset.

A cross-region copy can also be initiated from bq mk by specifying cross_region_copy as the data source.

---

27 As of this writing, this is available only in the "classic UI."

Figure 4-15. Initiate a scheduled cross-region dataset copy from the Data Transfer Service UI by specifying that the source is a cross-region copy

Exporting Cloud Logging Logs

Log data from GCP virtual machines (VMs) and services[28] can be stored, monitored, and analyzed using Cloud Logging logs. Cloud Logging thus serves as a unified view of all the activity in your GCP account. It is helpful, therefore, to export Cloud Logging and Firebase logs to BigQuery. You can do this by using the command-line interface, a REST API, or the web UI, which is shown in Figure 4-16.

To export all the logs from the BigQuery service, click the Create Export button at the top of the Cloud Logging Logs Viewer (*https://console.cloud.google.com/logs/*) and then fill in the following information:

- Select BigQuery and All Logs to view the logs from BigQuery. Do you see your recent activity?
- Provide a sink name, perhaps `bq_logs`.
- Specify the sink service: BigQuery, because we want to export to BigQuery.
- Specify the sink destination: `ch04`, the dataset to which we want to export.

---

28 Also from VMs and services running in Amazon Web Services.

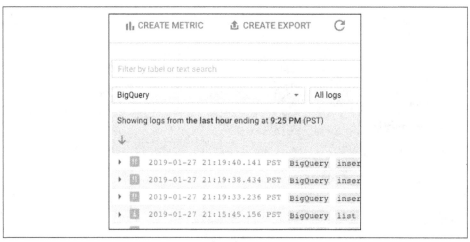

Figure 4-16. To view logs from the BigQuery ingest jobs in the previous section, for example, you would go to the Cloud Logging section of the GCP Cloud Console

Let's look at the logs generated by running a query. Go to the BigQuery UI and try running a query:

```
SELECT
  gender, AVG(tripduration / 60) AS avg_trip_duration
FROM
  `bigquery-public-data`.new_york_citibike.citibike_trips
GROUP BY
  gender
HAVING avg_trip_duration > 14
ORDER BY
  avg_trip_duration
```

In the BigQuery UI, if you now do (change the date appropriately)

```
SELECT protopayload_auditlog.status.message FROM
ch04.cloudaudit_googleapis_com_data_access_20190128
```

you will find a list of BigQuery log messages, including a message about reading the results of the preceding query. Depending on your date filter, you should also see the logs corresponding to earlier operations that you carried out.

Note a few things about the export capability:

- The schema and even the table name were set by Cloud Logging. We simply specified the destination dataset.

- The data was updated in near real time. This is an example of a streaming buffer —a BigQuery table updated in real time by Cloud Logging (although the typical latency of BigQuery queries implies that the data you see is a few seconds old).

To avoid running up charges for this streaming pipeline, go to the Cloud Logging section of the console and delete the sink.

Using Cloud Dataflow to Read/Write from BigQuery

As we've discussed, BigQuery supports federated querying from sources such as Google Sheets. Its Data Transfer Service supports sources such as Google Ads and YouTube. Products such as Stackdriver Logging and Firestore provide the ability to export their data to BigQuery.

What if you are using a product such as MySQL that does not provide an export capability and is not supported by the Data Transfer Service? One option is to use Cloud Dataflow. Cloud Dataflow is a fully managed service on GCP that simplifies the execution of data pipelines that are built using the open source Apache Beam API by handling operational details such as performance, scaling, availability, security, and compliance, so that users can focus on programming instead of managing server clusters. You can use Dataflow for transforming and enriching data both in streaming (real time) mode as well as in batch (historical) mode with the same reusable code across both streaming and batch pipelines.

Using a Dataflow template to load directly from MySQL

Although you could write your own Cloud Dataflow pipelines (we do that in "Writing a Dataflow job" on page 129), Dataflow template pipelines are available on GitHub (*https://github.com/GoogleCloudPlatform/DataflowTemplates*) for many common needs. Looking at the list of available templates, it appears that the Jdbc to BigQuery template might fit our requirements and allow us to transfer data from our MySQL database to BigQuery.

Open the GCP Cloud Console and navigate to the Cloud Dataflow section. Next, select "Create job from template," choose "Jdbc to BigQuery," and then fill out the resulting form with information about the source database table in MySQL and the destination table in BigQuery, as illustrated in Figure 4-17.

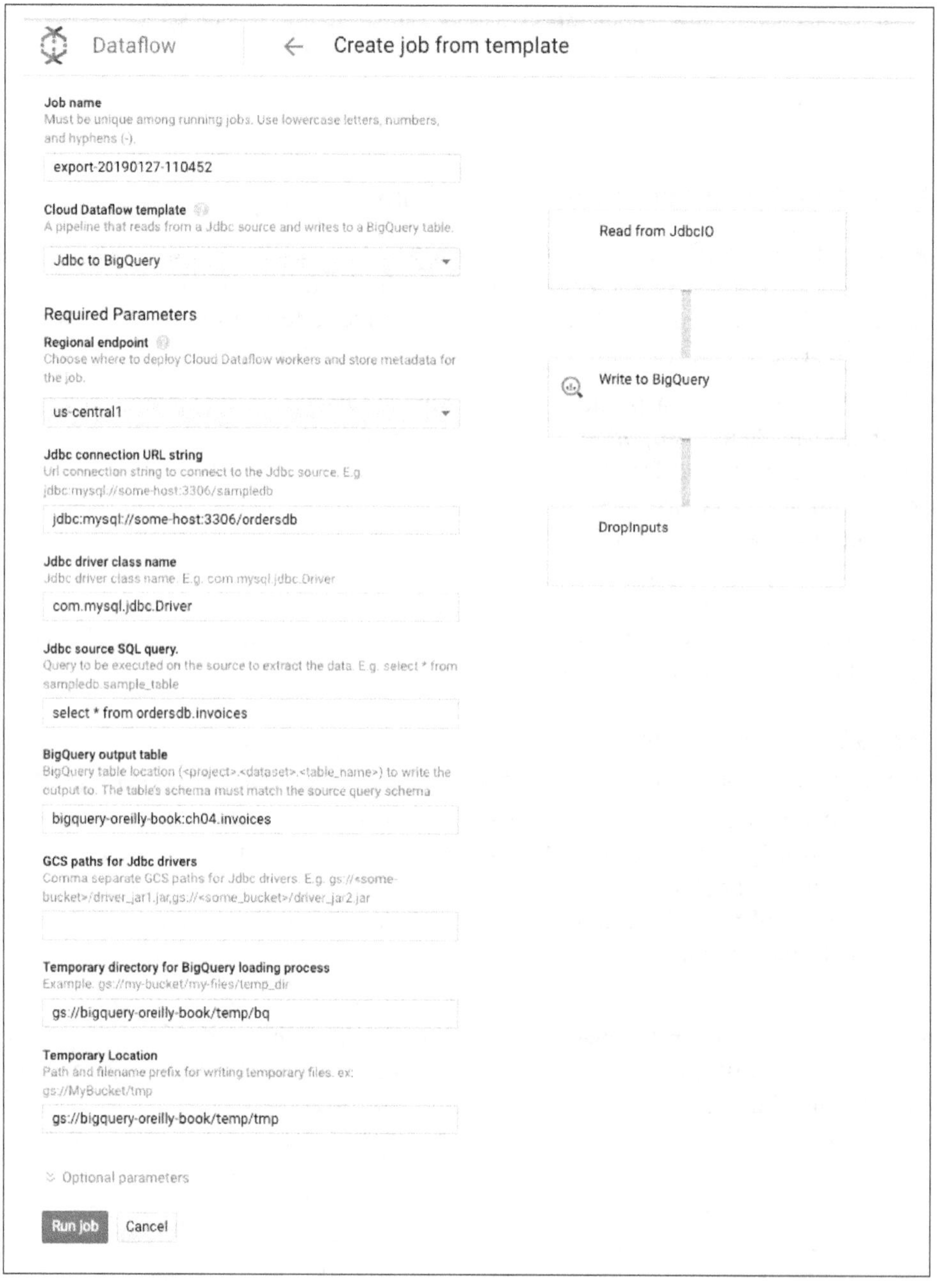

Figure 4-17. Creating a Dataflow job from a template to transfer data from MySQL to BigQuery

When you click the "Run job" button, a Dataflow job is launched. It will execute the JDBC query you specified and write the resulting rows to BigQuery.

Writing a Dataflow job

If you have a format for which there is no federated querying, no Data Transfer Service, no export capability, and no prebuilt Dataflow template, you can write your own Dataflow pipeline to load the data into BigQuery.

Even though both federated querying and a Data Transfer Service exist for CSV files on Google Cloud Storage, we will use CSV files to demonstrate what this looks like. The code is written to the Apache Beam API and can be written in Python, Java, or Go. Here, we use Python.

The crux of the code is to extract the input data, transform it by extracting and cleaning up the desired fields, and load it into BigQuery:

```
INPATTERNS = 'gs://bigquery-oreilly-book/college_*.csv'
RUNNER = 'DataflowRunner'
with beam.Pipeline(RUNNER, options = opts) as p:
  (p
    | 'read' >> beam.io.ReadFromText(INPATTERNS, skip_header_lines=1)
    | 'parse_csv' >> beam.FlatMap(parse_csv)
    | 'pull_fields' >> beam.FlatMap(pull_fields)
    | 'write_bq' >> beam.io.gcp.bigquery.WriteToBigQuery(bqtable, bqdataset,
schema=get_output_schema())
  )
```

In this code, we create a Beam pipeline, specifying that it will be executed by Cloud Dataflow. Other options for the RUNNER include DirectRunner (executed on the local machine) and SparkRunner (executed by Apache Spark on a Hadoop cluster, such as Cloud Dataproc on GCP).

The first step of the pipeline is to read all of the files that match the specified input patterns. These files can be on local disk or on Google Cloud Storage. The data from the text files is streamed line by line to the next step of the pipeline, where the parse_csv method is applied to each line:

```
def parse_csv(line):
  try:
    values = line.split(',')
    rowdict = {}
    for colname, value in zip(COLNAMES, values):
      rowdict[colname] = value
    yield rowdict
  except:
    logging.warn('Ignoring line ...')
```

The `parse_csv` method splits the line based on commas and converts the values into a dictionary, where the key is the name of the column and the value is the value of the cell.

This dictionary is next sent to the method `pull_fields`, which will extract the data of interest (the INSTNM column and a few numeric fields) and transform it:

```
def pull_fields(rowdict):
  result = {}
  # required string fields
  for col in 'INSTNM'.split(','):
    if col in rowdict:
      result[col] = rowdict[col]
    else:
      logging.info('Ignoring line missing {}', col)
      return

  # float fields
  for col in \
  'ADM_RATE_ALL,FIRST_GEN,MD_FAMINC,SAT_AVG,MD_EARN_WNE_P10'.split(','):
    try:
      result[col] = (float) (rowdict[col])
    except:
      result[col] = None
  yield result
```

These dictionaries with the extracted fields are streamed into BigQuery row by row. The BigQuery sink (`beam.io.gcp.bigquery.WriteToBigQuery`) requires the name of the table, the name of the dataset, and an output schema of the following form:

```
INSTNM:string,ADM_RATE_ALL:FLOAT64,FIRST_GEN:FLOAT64,...
```

The BigQuery table is created if needed, and rows are appended. Other options exist as well, for example, to truncate the table (i.e., to replace it).

Running the Python program[29] will launch a Dataflow job that will read the CSV file, parse it line by line, pull necessary fields, and write the transformed data to BigQuery.

Even though we demonstrated the Dataflow program on a batch pipeline (i.e., the input is not unbounded), essentially you can use the same pipeline to parse, transform, and write out records received in a streaming mode (e.g., from Cloud Pub/Sub), as will be the case in many logging and IoT applications. The Dataflow approach thus provides a way to transform data on the fly and load it into BigQuery.

Note that Dataflow uses streaming inserts to load the data into BigQuery, whether you are operating in batch mode or in streaming mode. Streaming inserts offer the advantage that the data shows up in a timely manner, into a streaming buffer, and can

---

29 See *04_load/dataflow.ipynb* in the book's GitHub repository.

be queried even as the data is being written. The disadvantage is that, unlike Big-Query load jobs, streaming inserts are not free. Recall that loading data into Big-Query might be free, but because of performance reasons, there are limits on how many load jobs you can do. Streaming inserts provide a way to avoid the limits and quotas placed on load jobs without sacrificing query performance.

Using the Streaming API directly

We presented Apache Beam on Cloud Dataflow as a way to extract, transform, and load data in BigQuery in streaming mode, but it is not the only data processing framework that is capable of writing to BigQuery. If your team is more familiar with Apache Spark, writing the ETL pipeline in Spark and executing it on a Hadoop cluster (such as Cloud Dataproc on GCP) is a viable alternative to Dataflow. This is because client libraries exist for a variety of different languages, and BigQuery supports a streaming API.

We cover the client library and streaming in greater detail in Chapter 5, but here is a snippet that illustrates how to load data using the Streaming API in Python after you have a client:

```
# create an array of tuples and insert as data becomes available
rows_to_insert = [
    (u'U. Puerto Rico', 0.18,0.46,23000,1134,32000),
    (u'Guam U.', 0.43,0.21,28000,1234,33000)
]
errors = client.insert_rows(table, rows_to_insert) # API request
```

As new data becomes available, the `insert_rows()` method on the BigQuery client is invoked. This method in turn invokes the REST API's `tabledata.insertAll` method. The data is held in a streaming buffer by BigQuery and is available immediately for querying, although it can take up to 90 minutes for the data to become available for exporting.

Moving On-Premises Data

In Chapter 1, we discussed that one of the key factors that makes BigQuery tick is the separation of compute and storage across a petabit-per-second bandwidth network. BigQuery works best on datasets that are within the datacenter and behind the Google Cloud firewall—if BigQuery had to read its data from across the public internet or a slower network connection, it would not be as performant. Therefore, for BigQuery to work well, it is essential that the data be in the cloud.

BigQuery is a highly scalable analytics platform and is the recommended place to store structured data except that meant for real-time, transactional use. So if Big-Query is the place to store all structured data that will be used for data analytics, how do you move your on-premises data into BigQuery?

Data Migration Methods

If you have a good network with fast interconnect speeds to Google Cloud, you could use bq load to load the data into BigQuery. As discussed in this chapter, it is preferable that the data being loaded is already present on Google Cloud Storage. You can use the command-line tool gsutil to copy the data from on-premises to Cloud Storage.

When copying many files, especially large files, to Google Cloud Storage, use the -m option to enable multithreading. Multithreading will allow the gsutil tool to copy files in parallel:

```
gsutil -m cp /some/dir/myfiles*.csv gs://bucket/some/dir
```

Because it is likely that data continues to be collected, moving data is often not a one-time process but an ongoing one. One approach to handling this is to launch a Cloud Function to automatically invoke bq load whenever a file shows up on Cloud Storage.[30] As the frequency of file arrival increases (and as those files grow smaller), you are better off using Cloud Pub/Sub[31] rather than Cloud Storage to store the incoming data as messages that will be processed by a Cloud Dataflow pipeline and streamed directly into BigQuery.

These three approaches—gsutil, Cloud Functions, and Cloud Dataflow—are shown in the first three rows of Table 4-2 and work when the network connection is quite good.

Table 4-2. The recommended migration method for different situations

What you want to migrate	Recommended migration method
Relatively small files	gsutil cp -m bq load
Loading occasional (e.g., once per day) files into BigQuery when they are available	gsutil cp Cloud Function invokes bq load
Loading streaming messages into BigQuery	Post data to Cloud Pub/Sub and then use Cloud Dataflow to stream into BigQuery Typically, you have to implement the pipeline in Python, Java, Go, etc. Alternately, use the Streaming API from the client library. This will be covered in more detail in Chapter 5.
Hive partitions	Migrate Hive workload to Cloud Dataproc Query Hive partitions as external table
Petabytes of data or poor network	Transfer appliance bq load

---

30 We cover how to do so programmatically in Chapter 5.

31 A message bus service—see *https://cloud.google.com/pubsub/*.

What you want to migrate	Recommended migration method
Region to region or from other clouds	Cloud Storage Transfer Service
Load from a MySQL dump	Open source Dataflow templates that can be configured and run
Transfer from Google Cloud Storage, Google Ads, Google Play, etc. to BigQuery	BigQuery Data Transfer Service Set this up in BigQuery. All of the Data Transfer Service functions work similarly.
Migrate from other data warehouses such as Amazon Redshift, Teradata, etc.	BigQuery Data Transfer Service migrates data and schema. Depending on the source data warehouse, it could use migration agents that reside in the source data warehouse and may support both one-time and incremental transfers.
Stackdriver Logging, Firestore, etc.	These tools provide capability to export to BigQuery. Set this up in the other tool (Stackdriver, Firestore, etc.).

Although data migration using `gsutil` to stage the data on Cloud Storage and then invoking `bq load` might be easy to do if you have only a few small datasets, it is more difficult if you have many datasets or if your datasets are large. As data size increases, the incidence of errors also increases. Therefore, migrating large datasets requires paying attention to details—for example, check-summing data at capture and ingest, working with firewalls so that they don't block transfers or drop packets, avoiding exfiltration of sensitive data, and ensuring that your data is encrypted and protected against loss during and after migration.

Another issue with the `gsutil` method is that it is quite likely that your business will not be able to dedicate bandwidth for data transfers because such dedicated bandwidth is often too expensive and will disrupt routine operations that convey data over the corporate network.

For cases in which it is not possible to copy data to Google Cloud because of data size or network limitations, consider using the Transfer Appliance. This is a rackable, high-capacity storage server that is shipped to you, and then you fill it up and ship it back to Google Cloud or one of its authorized partners. The Transfer Appliance is best used for lots of data (hundreds of terabytes to petabytes) for which your network situation won't meet transfer demands.

If your data is held not on-premises but in another public cloud (such as in an Amazon Web Services Simple Storage Service bucket), you can use the Cloud Storage Transfer Service to migrate the data. Common use cases include running an application on Amazon Web Services but analyzing its log data in BigQuery. The Cloud Storage Transfer Service is also a great way to transfer large amounts of data between regions at Google.

The BigQuery Data Transfer Service automates loading data into BigQuery from Google properties like YouTube, Google Ads, and more. Other tools such as Stackdriver Logging and Firestore provide the capability to export to BigQuery.

The BigQuery Data Transfer Service also supports automatic migration of data and schema from other data warehouse products like Amazon Redshift and Teradata. In the case of Teradata, an on-premises migration agent connects to the local data warehouse and copies the data to BigQuery. Both one-time and incremental transfers are supported. Partition-by-partition extraction is also supported. At the time of writing, only data and schema are migrated, not ETL pipelines and stored procedures, although there are partner tools that can carry out automatic SQL translation and data warehouse virtualization. See the documentation (*https://cloud.google.com/bigquery-transfer/docs/migrations*) for details of what is supported for each source data warehouse.

Although you can carry out data migration yourself, it is unlikely to be something that your IT department has much experience with given that migration is often just a one-time task. It might be advantageous to use a GCP authorized partner[32] to carry out the data migration.

Summary

The `bq` command-line tool provides a single point of entry to interact with the Big-Query service on GCP. After your data is on Google Cloud Storage, you can do a one-time load of the data using the `bq load` utility. It supports schema autodetection, but it can also use a specific schema that you supply. Depending on whether your load job is CPU-bound or I/O-bound, it might be advantageous to either compress the data or leave it uncompressed.

It is possible to leave the data in place, specify the structure of the data, and use Big-Query as just the query engine. These are called external datasets, and queries over external datasets are called federated queries. Use federated queries for exploratory work, or where the primary use of the data is in the external format (e.g., low-latency queries in Cloud Bigtable or interactive work in Sheets). EXTERNAL_QUERY provides the ability to do real-time joins against MySQL and Postgres databases without any data movement. For large, relatively stable, well-understood datasets that will be updated periodically and queried often, BigQuery native storage is a better choice. Federated queries are also useful in an Extract, Load, and Transform (ELT) workflow for which the data is not yet well understood.

---

32 See *https://cloud.google.com/bigquery/providers/*. As this book was being written, GCP announced its intent to acquire Alooma, a provider of cloud migration services—see *https://cloud.google.com/blog/topics/inside-google-cloud/google-announces-intent-to-acquire-alooma-to-simplify-cloud-migration*.

It is possible to set up a scheduled transfer of data from a variety of platforms into BigQuery. Other tools also support mechanisms to export their data into BigQuery. For routine loading of data, consider using Cloud Functions; for ongoing, streaming loads, use Cloud Dataflow. It is also possible to schedule queries (including federated queries) to run periodically and have these queries load data into tables.

Developing with BigQuery

So far, we have mostly used the BigQuery web user interface (UI) and the bq command-line tool to interact with BigQuery. In this chapter, we look at ways to programmatically interact with the service. This can be useful to script out or automate tasks that involve BigQuery. Programmatic access to BigQuery is also essential when developing applications, dashboards, scientific graphics, and machine learning models for which BigQuery is only one of the tools being used.

We begin by looking at BigQuery client libraries that allow you to programmatically query and manipulate BigQuery tables and resources. Although you can programmatically access BigQuery using these low-level APIs, you want to be aware of customizations and higher-level abstractions available for particular environments (Jupyter notebooks and shell scripts). These customizations, which we cover in the second half of this chapter, are easier to use, handle error conditions appropriately, and cut out a lot of boilerplate code.

Developing Programmatically

The recommended approach for accessing BigQuery programmatically is to use the Google Cloud Client Library in your preferred programming language. The REST API is helpful in understanding what happens under the hood when you send a request to the BigQuery service, but the BigQuery client library is more practical. So feel free to skim the section on the REST API.

Accessing BigQuery via the REST API

You can send a query to the BigQuery service by making a direct HTTP request to the server because BigQuery, like all Google Cloud services, exposes a traditional JSON/REST interface (*https://cloud.google.com/bigquery/docs/reference/rest/v2/*).

JSON/REST is an architectural style of designing distributed services for which each request is stateless (i.e., the server does not maintain session state or context; instead, each request contains all the necessary information) and both request and response objects are in a self-describing text format called JSON. Because HTTP is a stateless protocol, REST services are particularly well suited to serving over the web. JSON maps directly to in-memory objects in languages like JavaScript and Python.

REST APIs provide the illusion that the objects referred to by the API are static files in a collection, and they provide Create, Read, Update, Delete (CRUD) operations that map to HTTP verbs. For example, to create a table in BigQuery you use POST, to inspect the table you use GET, to update it you use PATCH, and to delete it you use DELETE. There are some methods, like Query, that don't map exactly to CRUD operations, so these are often referred to as Remote Procedure Call (RPC)–style methods.

All BigQuery URIs begin with the prefix `https://www.googleapis.com/bigquery/v2`. Notice that it uses HTTPS rather than HTTP, thus stipulating that requests should be encrypted on the wire. The `v2` part of the URI is the version number. Although some Google APIs revise their version number frequently, BigQuery has adamantly stuck with v2 for several years and is likely to do so for the foreseeable future.[1]

Dataset manipulation

The REST interface involves issuing HTTP requests to specific URLs. The combination of the HTTP request method (GET, POST, PUT, PATCH, or DELETE) and a URL specifies the operation to be performed. For example, to delete a dataset, the client would issue an HTTP DELETE request to the URL (inserting the ID of the dataset and the project in which it is held):

```
.../projects/<PROJECT>/datasets/<DATASET>
```

Here, the "..." refers to `https://www.googleapis.com/bigquery/v2`. All BigQuery REST URLs are relative to this path.

 When you type in a URL in a web browser's navigation toolbar, the browser issues an HTTP GET to that URL. To issue an HTTP DELETE, you need a client that gives you the option of specifying the HTTP method to invoke. One such client tool is `curl`; we look at how to use this shortly.

---

1 Other APIs, especially non-REST APIs such as gRPC ones, will have a different API prefix.

We know that we need to send a DELETE request to that URL because the BigQuery REST API documentation (*https://cloud.google.com/bigquery/docs/reference/rest/v2/*) specifies the HTTP request details, as illustrated in Figure 5-1.

Datasets

For Datasets Resource details, see the resource representation page.

Method	HTTP request	Description
URIs relative to https://www.googleapis.com/bigquery/v2, unless otherwise noted		
delete	DELETE /projects/*projectId*/datasets/*datasetId*	Deletes the dataset specified by the datasetId value. Before you can delete a dataset, you must delete all its tables, either manually or by specifying deleteContents. Immediately after deletion, you can create another dataset with the same name.
get	GET /projects/*projectId*/datasets/*datasetId*	Returns the dataset specified by datasetID.
insert	POST /projects/*projectId*/datasets	Creates a new empty dataset.
list	GET /projects/*projectId*/datasets	Lists all datasets in the specified project to which you have been granted the READER dataset role.

Figure 5-1. The BigQuery REST API specifies that issuing an HTTP DELETE request to the URL /projects/<PROJECT>/datasets/<DATASET> will result in the dataset being deleted if it is empty

Table manipulation

Deleting a table similarly involves issuing an HTTP DELETE to the URL:

```
.../projects/<PROJECT>/datasets/<DATASET>/tables/<TABLE>
```

Note that both of these requests employ the HTTP DELETE method, and it is the URL path that differentiates them. Of course, not everyone who visits the URL will be able to delete the dataset or table. The request will succeed only if the request includes an access token, and if the access token (covered shortly) represents appropriate authorization in the BigQuery or Cloud Platform scopes.[2]

---

2 Specifically, *https://www.googleapis.com/auth/bigquery* or *https://www.googleapis.com/auth/cloud-platform* have to be allowed.

As an example of a different HTTP method type, it is possible to list all the tables in a dataset by issuing an HTTP GET, as follows:

```
.../projects/<PROJECT>/datasets/<DATASET>/tables
```

Listing the tables in a dataset requires only a read-only scope—full access to Big-Query (such as to delete tables) is not necessary, although, of course, the greater authority (e.g., BigQuery scope) also provides the lesser permissions.

We can try this using a Unix shell:[3]

```bash
#!/bin/bash
PROJECT=$(gcloud config get-value project)
access_token=$(gcloud auth application-default print-access-token)
curl -H "Authorization: Bearer $access_token" \
    -H "Content-Type: application/json" \
    -X GET
"https://www.googleapis.com/bigquery/v2/projects/$PROJECT/datasets/ch04/tables"
```

The access token is a way to get application-default credentials. These are temporary credentials that are issued by virtue of being logged into the Google Cloud Software Development Kit (SDK). The access token is placed into the header of the HTTP request, and because we want to list the tables in the dataset ch04, we issue a GET request to the URL using the curl command:

```
.../projects/$PROJECT/datasets/ch04/tables
```

Using SQL Instead of a Client API

This chapter shows how to access BigQuery programmatically through a client API. However, consider whether you are better off using SQL queries to retrieve this information. For example, you can create and delete tables via CREATE TABLE and DROP TABLE statements, respectively. Using SQL might allow you to stay within the tool you regularly use to explore and analyze data, without having to integrate a programming or scripting tool into your workflow.

You can list the tables in the dataset used in Chapter 4 in SQL by querying an INFORMA TION_SCHEMA view:

```sql
SELECT
  table_name, creation_time
FROM
  ch04.INFORMATION_SCHEMA.TABLES
```

---

3 This is the file *05_devel/rest_list.sh* in the GitHub repository for this book (*https://github.com/GoogleCloudPlat form/bigquery-oreilly-book*). You can run it anywhere that you have the Cloud SDK and curl installed (such as in Cloud Shell). Because we have not created it in this chapter yet, I'm using the dataset (ch04) that we loaded in the previous chapter.

We examine the use of INFORMATION_SCHEMA and SQL alternatives to the client API in Chapter 8. However, for now, Table 5-1 presents the mapping between client API functions and SQL.

Table 5-1. Client API functions and SQL alternatives

Client API capability	SQL alternative
Creating tables (or views: just replace TABLE with VIEW)	CREATE TABLE CREATE TABLE IF NOT EXISTS CREATE OR REPLACE TABLE
Update table (or view)	ALTER TABLE SET OPTIONS ALTER TABLE IF EXISTS SET OPTIONS
Update table data	INSERT INTO DELETE FROM UPDATE MERGE
Delete table (or view)	DROP TABLE
Dataset metadata	Query: INFORMATION_SCHEMA.SCHEMATA INFORMATION_SCHEMA.SCHEMATA_OPTIONS
Table (or view) metadata	Query: INFORMATION_SCHEMA.TABLES INFORMATION_SCHEMA.TABLE_OPTIONS INFORMATION_SCHEMA.COLUMNS INFORMATION_SCHEMA.COLUMN_FIELD_PATHS
Jobs metadata	Query: INFORMATION_SCHEMA.JOBS_BY_USER INFORMATION_SCHEMA.JOBS_BY_PROJECT INFORMATION_SCHEMA.JOBS_BY_ORGANIZATION

In many situations, using SQL might be a better alternative from a tooling and familiarity perspective.

Querying

In some cases, issuing an HTTP GET request to a BigQuery URL is not enough. More information is required from the client. In such cases, the API requires that the client issue an HTTP POST and send along a JSON request in the body of the request.

For example, to run a BigQuery SQL query and obtain the results, issue an HTTP POST request to

```
.../projects/<PROJECT>/queries
```

and send in a JSON of the following form:

```
{
  "useLegacySql": false,
  "query": \"${QUERY_TEXT}\"
}
```

Here, `QUERY_TEXT` is a variable that holds the query to be performed:

```
read -d '' QUERY_TEXT << EOF
SELECT
  start_station_name
  , AVG(duration) as duration
  , COUNT(duration) as num_trips
FROM \`bigquery-public-data\`.london_bicycles.cycle_hire
GROUP BY start_station_name
ORDER BY num_trips DESC
LIMIT 5
EOF
```

We are using the heredoc syntax (*http://tldp.org/LDP/abs/html/here-docs.html*) in Bash to specify that the string `EOF` marks the point at which our query begins and ends.

The `curl` request now is a POST that includes the request as its data:[4]

```
curl -H "Authorization: Bearer $access_token" \
    -H "Content-Type: application/json" \
    -X POST \
    -d "$request" \
    "https://www.googleapis.com/bigquery/v2/projects/$PROJECT/queries"
```

Here, `$request` is a variable that holds the JSON payload (including the query text).

The response is a JSON message that contains the schema of the result set and five rows, each of which is an array of values. Here's the schema in this case:

```
"schema": {
 "fields": [
   {
    "name": "start_station_name",
    "type": "STRING",
    "mode": "NULLABLE"
   },
   {
    "name": "duration",
    "type": "FLOAT",
    "mode": "NULLABLE"
```

---

4 See *05_devel/rest_query.sh* in the GitHub repository for this book.

```
    },
    {
      "name": "num_trips",
      "type": "INTEGER",
      "mode": "NULLABLE"
    }
  ]
},
```

Following is the first row:

```
{
    "f": [
      {
        "v": "Belgrove Street , King's Cross"
      },
      {
        "v": "1011.0766960393793"
      },
      {
        "v": "234458"
      }
    ]
},
```

The f stands for fields, and the v for values. Each row is an array of fields, and each field has a value. This means that the highest number of trips was at the station on Belgrove Street, where the average duration of trips was 1,011 sec and the total number of trips was 234,458.

Limitations

In the case we've just considered, the query happens to finish within the default time-out period (it's possible to specify a longer timeout), but what if the query takes longer? Let's simulate this by artificially lowering the timeout and disabling the cache:[5]

```
{
    "useLegacySql": false,
    "timeoutMs": 0,
    "useQueryCache": false,
    "query": \"${QUERY_TEXT}\"
}
```

Now the response no longer contains the rows of the result set. Instead, we get a promissory note in the form of a jobId:

```
{
    "kind": "bigquery#queryResponse",
```

---

5 See *04_devel/rest_query_async.sh* in the GitHub repository for this book.

```
  "jobReference": {
  "projectId": "cloud-training-demos",
  "jobId": "job_gv0Kq8nWzXIkuBwoxsKMcTJIVbX4",
  "location": "EU"
  },
  "jobComplete": false
}
```

We are now expected to get the status of the `jobId` using the REST API by sending a GET request, as shown here:

```
.../projects/<PROJECT>/jobs/<JOBID>
```

This continues until the response has `jobComplete` set to true. At that point, we can obtain the query results by sending a GET request, as follows:

```
.../projects/<PROJECT>/queries/<JOBID>
```

Sometimes the query results are too large to be sent in a single HTTP response. Instead, the results are provided to us in chunks. Recall, however, that REST is a stateless protocol and the server does not maintain session context. Therefore, the results are actually stored in a temporary table that is maintained for 24 hours. The client can page through this temporary table of results using a page token that serves as a bookmark for each call to get query results.

In addition to all this complexity, add in the possibility of network failure and the necessity of retries, and it becomes clear that the REST API is quite difficult to program against. Therefore, even though the REST API is accessible from any language that is capable of making calls to web services, we typically recommend using a higher-level API.

Google Cloud Client Library

The Google Cloud Client Library for BigQuery is the recommended option for accessing BigQuery programmatically. As of this writing, a client library is available for seven programming languages: Go, Java, Node.js, Python, Ruby, PHP, and C++. Each client library provides a good developer experience by following the convention and typical programming style of the programming language.

You can install the BigQuery client library using `pip` (or `easy_install`):

```
pip install google-cloud-bigquery
```

To use the library, first instantiate a client (this takes care of the authentication (*https://cloud.google.com/docs/authentication/production*) that was accomplished by using an access token when directly invoking the REST API):

```
from google.cloud import bigquery
bq = bigquery.Client(project=PROJECT)
```

The project passed into the `Client` is the globally unique name of the project that will be billed for operations carried out using the bq object.

 You can find a Python notebook with all of the code in this section at *https://github.com/GoogleCloudPlatform/bigquery-oreilly-book/blob/master/05_devel/bigquery_cloud_client.ipynb.* Use the notebook as a source of Python snippets to try out in your favorite Python environment.

The API documentation for the BigQuery client library is available at *https://googleapis.github.io/google-cloud-python/latest/bigquery/reference.html.* Because it is impossible to cover the full API, we strongly suggest that you have the documentation open in a browser tab as you read through the following section. As you read the Python snippets, see how you could discover the Python methods to invoke.

Dataset manipulation

To view information about a dataset using the BigQuery client library, use the `get_dataset` method:

```
dsinfo = bq.get_dataset('bigquery-public-data.london_bicycles')
```

If the project name is omitted, the project passed into the `Client` at the time of construction is assumed; let's take a look:

```
dsinfo = bq.get_dataset('ch04')
```

This returns an object with information about the dataset we created in the previous chapter.

Dataset information. Given the `dsinfo` object, it is possible to extract different attributes of the dataset. For example,

```
print(dsinfo.dataset_id)
print(dsinfo.created)
```

on the `ch04` object yields

```
ch04
2019-01-26 00:41:01.350000+00:00
```

whereas

```
print('{} created on {} in {}'.format(
    dsinfo.dataset_id, dsinfo.created, dsinfo.location))
```

for the `bigquery-public-data.london_bicycles` dataset yields the following:

```
london_bicycles created on 2017-05-25 13:26:18.055000+00:00 in EU
```

It is also possible to examine the access controls on the dataset using the dsinfo object. For example, we could find which roles are granted READER access to the lon don_bicycles dataset using this:

```
for access in dsinfo.access_entries:
    if access.role == 'READER':
        print(access)
```

This yields the following:

```
<AccessEntry: role=READER, specialGroup=allAuthenticatedUsers>
<AccessEntry: role=READER, domain=google.com>
<AccessEntry: role=READER, specialGroup=projectReaders>
```

It is because all authenticated users are granted access to the dataset (see the first line in the preceding example) that we have been able to query the dataset in previous chapters.

Creating a dataset. To create a dataset named ch05 if it doesn't already exist, use this:

```
dataset_id = "{}.ch05".format(PROJECT)
ds = bq.create_dataset(dataset_id, exists_ok=True)
```

By default, the dataset is created in the US. To create the dataset in another location—for example, the EU—create a local Dataset object (we're calling it dsinfo), set its location attribute, and then invoke create_dataset on the client object using this Dataset (instead of the dataset_id, as in the previous code snippet):

```
dataset_id = "{}.ch05eu".format(PROJECT)
dsinfo = bigquery.Dataset(dataset_id)
dsinfo.location = 'EU'
ds = bq.create_dataset(dsinfo, exists_ok=True)
```

Deleting a dataset. To delete a dataset named ch05 in the project passed into the Cli ent, do the following:

```
bq.delete_dataset('ch05', not_found_ok=True)
```

To delete a dataset in a different project, qualify the dataset name by the project name:

```
bq.delete_dataset('{}.ch05'.format(PROJECT), not_found_ok=True)
```

Modifying attributes of a dataset. To modify information about a dataset, modify the dsinfo object locally by setting the description attribute and then invoke update_dataset on the client object to update the BigQuery service:

```
dsinfo = bq.get_dataset("ch05")
print(dsinfo.description)
dsinfo.description = "Chapter 5 of BigQuery: The Definitive Guide"
```

```
dsinfo = bq.update_dataset(dsinfo, ['description'])
print(dsinfo.description)
```

The first `print` in the preceding snippet prints out `None` because the dataset `ch05` was created without any description. After the `update_dataset` call, the dataset in Big-Query sports a new description:

```
None
Chapter 5 of BigQuery: The Definitive Guide
```

Changing tags, access controls, and so on of a dataset works similarly. For example, to give one of our colleagues access to the `ch05` dataset, we could do the following:

```
dsinfo = bq.get_dataset("ch05")
entry = bigquery.AccessEntry(
    role="READER",
    entity_type="userByEmail",
    entity_id="xyz@google.com",
)
if entry not in dsinfo.access_entries:
  entries = list(dsinfo.access_entries)
  entries.append(entry)
  dsinfo.access_entries = entries
  dsinfo = bq.update_dataset(dsinfo, ["access_entries"]) # API request
else:
  print('{} already has access'.format(entry.entity_id))
print(dsinfo.access_entries)
```

In this code, we create an entry for a user, and if the user doesn't already have some sort of access to the dataset, we get the current set of access entries, append the new entry, and update the dataset with the new list.

Table management

To list the tables in a dataset, invoke the `list_tables` method on the client object:

```
tables = bq.list_tables("bigquery-public-data.london_bicycles")
for table in tables:
    print(table.table_id)
```

The result is the two tables in the `london_bicycles` dataset:

```
cycle_hire
cycle_stations
```

Obtaining table properties.   In the previous code snippet, we got the `table_id` from the table object. Besides the `table_id`, other attributes of the table are available: the number of rows, the descriptions, tags, the schema, and more.

The number of rows in the table is part of the table metadata and can be obtained from the table object itself. Unlike a full-fledged query with a COUNT(*), getting the number of rows in this manner does not incur BigQuery charges:

```
table = bq.get_table(
    "bigquery-public-data.london_bicycles.cycle_stations")
print('{} rows in {}'.format(table.num_rows,
    table.table_id))
```

This yields the following:

```
787 rows in cycle_stations
```

For example, we can search the schema for columns whose name contains a specific substring (count) using the table object:

```
table = bq.get_table(
        "bigquery-public-data.london_bicycles.cycle_stations")
for field in table.schema:
  if 'count' in field.name:
    print(field)
```

Here's the result:

```
SchemaField('bikes_count', 'INTEGER', 'NULLABLE', '', ())
SchemaField('docks_count', 'INTEGER', 'NULLABLE', '', ())
```

Of course, rather than hand-roll this sort of search, it would be better to use INFORMA TION_SCHEMA (covered in Chapter 8) or Data Catalog.

Deleting a table.   Deleting a table is similar to deleting a dataset, and if desired, you can ignore the error thrown if the table doesn't exist:

```
bq.delete_table('ch05.temp_table', not_found_ok=True)
```

Restoring Deleted Tables

Use BigQuery's "time travel" capability to restore deleted tables. For up to two days, you can restore a table if you accidentally delete it. For example, to restore the version of the table as it existed at a certain time within the past seven days, you can make a copy of it by specifying the timestamp:

```
bq --location=US cp ch05.temp_table@1418864998000
ch05.temp_table2
```

Here, 1418864998000 is the timestamp (the number of seconds since epoch).

Note, however, that the snapshots are lost if a table bearing the same ID in the dataset was created after the deletion time or if the encapsulating dataset was also deleted. This has implications on your workflow—you can save yourself a lot of grief if you minimize the chance of creating tables with the same name from different software

---

applications. For example, you could use organizational boundaries (e.g., "accounting") or the names of applications and workloads (e.g., "shipping") when naming datasets. You might also avoid creating tables from your applications; instead, create them externally before your applications start.

Creating an empty table. Creating an empty table is similar to creating a dataset, and if desired, you can ignore the exception thrown if the dataset already exists:

```
table_id = '{}.ch05.temp_table'.format(PROJECT)
table = bq.create_table(table_id, exists_ok=True)
```

Updating a table's schema. Of course, you don't usually want to create empty tables. You want to create an empty table with a schema and insert some rows into it. Because the schema is part of the attributes of the table, you can update the schema of the empty table similarly to the way you updated the access controls of the dataset. You get the table, modify the table object locally, and then update the table using the modified object to specify what aspects of the table object are being updated:

```
schema = [
  bigquery.SchemaField("chapter", "INTEGER", mode="REQUIRED"),
  bigquery.SchemaField("title", "STRING", mode="REQUIRED"),
]
table_id = '{}.ch05.temp_table'.format(PROJECT)
table = bq.get_table(table_id)
print(table.etag)
table.schema = schema
table = bq.update_table(table, ["schema"])
print(table.schema)
print(table.etag)
```

To prevent race conditions, BigQuery tags the table with each update. So when you get the table information using `get_table`, the table object includes an `etag`. When you upload a modified schema using `update_table`, this update succeeds only if your `etag` matches that of the server. The returned table object has the new `etag`. You can turn off this behavior and force an update by setting `table.etag` to `None`.

When a table is empty, you can change the schema to anything you want. But when there is data in the table, any schema changes must be compatible with the existing data in the table. You can add new fields (as long as they are `NULLABLE`), and you can relax constraints from `REQUIRED` to `NULLABLE`.

After this code is run, we can check in the BigQuery web UI that the newly created table has the correct schema, as depicted in Figure 5-2.

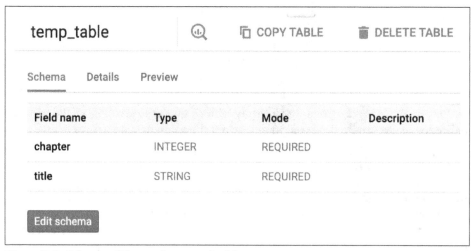

Figure 5-2. Schema of the newly created table

Inserting rows into a table. After you have a table with a schema, you can insert rows into the table using the client. The rows consist of Python tuples in the same order as defined in the schema:

```
rows = [
    (1, u'What is BigQuery?'),
    (2, u'Query essentials'),
]
errors = bq.insert_rows(table, rows)
```

The errors list will be empty if all rows were successfully inserted. If, however, you had passed in a noninteger value for the chapter field

```
rows = [
    ('3', u'Operating on data types'),
    ('wont work', u'This will fail'),
    ('4', u'Loading data into BigQuery'),
]
errors = bq.insert_rows(table, rows)
print(errors)
```

you will get an error whose reason is invalid on index=1 (the second row; this is 0-based), location=chapter:

```
{'index': 1, 'errors': [{'reason': 'invalid', 'debugInfo': '', 'message': 'Cannot
convert value to integer (bad value):wont work', 'location': 'chapter'}]}
```

Because BigQuery treats each user request as atomic, none of the three rows will be inserted. On the other rows, you will get an error whose reason is stopped:

```
{'index': 0, 'errors': [{'reason': 'stopped', 'debugInfo': '', 'message': '',
'location': ''}]}
```

In the BigQuery web UI, shown in Figure 5-3, the table details show that the inserted rows are in the streaming buffer, but the two inserted rows are not reflected in the table's number of rows.

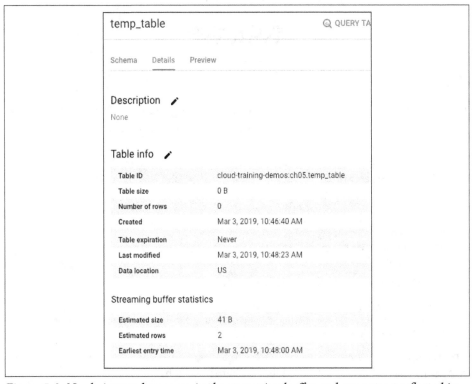

Figure 5-3. Newly inserted rows are in the streaming buffer and are not yet reflected in the number of rows shown in the "Table info" section

 Because inserting rows into the table is a streaming operation, the table metadata is not updated immediately—for example:

```
rows = [
  (1, u'What is BigQuery?'),
  (2, u'Query essentials'),
]
print(table.table_id, table.num_rows)
errors = bq.insert_rows(table, rows)
print(errors)
table = bq.get_table(table_id)
print(table.table_id, table.num_rows) # DELAYED
```

The table.num_rows in this code snippet will *not* show the updated row count. Moreover, streaming inserts, unlike load jobs, are not free.

Queries on the table will reflect the two rows in the streaming buffer:

```
SELECT DISTINCT(chapter) FROM ch05.temp_table
```

This shows that there are two chapters in the table:

Row	chapter
1	2
2	1

Creating an empty table with schema. Instead of creating a table and then updating this schema, a better idea is to provide the schema at the time of table creation:

```
schema = [
  bigquery.SchemaField("chapter", "INTEGER", mode="REQUIRED"),
  bigquery.SchemaField("title", "STRING", mode="REQUIRED"),
]
table_id = '{}.ch05.temp_table2'.format(PROJECT)
table = bigquery.Table(table_id, schema)
table = bq.create_table(table, exists_ok=True)
print('{} created on {}'.format(table.table_id, table.created))
print(table.schema)
```

The created table contains the desired schema:

```
temp_table2 created on 2019-03-03 19:30:18.324000+00:00
[SchemaField('chapter', 'INTEGER', 'REQUIRED', None, ()), SchemaField('title',
'STRING', 'REQUIRED', None, ())]
```

The table created is empty, and so we'd use this technique if we are going to do a streaming insert of rows into the table. What if, though, you already have the data in a file and you want simply to create a table and initialize it with data from that file? In that case, load jobs are much more convenient. Unlike streaming inserts, loads do not incur BigQuery charges.

The BigQuery Python client supports three methods of loading data: from a pandas DataFrame, from a URI, or from a local file. Let's look at these next.

Loading a pandas DataFrame. pandas (*https://pandas.pydata.org/*) is an open source library that provides data structures and data analysis tools for the Python programming language. The BigQuery Python library supports directly loading data from an in-memory pandas DataFrame. Because pandas DataFrames can be constructed from in-memory data structures and provide a wide variety of transformations, using pandas provides the most convenient way to load data from Python applications. For example, to create a DataFrame from an array of tuples, you can do the following:

```
import pandas as pd
  data = [
    (1, u'What is BigQuery?'),
```

```
    (2, u'Query essentials'),
]
df = pd.DataFrame(data, columns=['chapter', 'title'])
```

After you have created the DataFrame, you can load the data within it into a Big-Query table using the following:[6]

```
table_id = '{}.ch05.temp_table3'.format(PROJECT)
job = bq.load_table_from_dataframe(df, table_id)
job.result() # blocks and waits
print("Loaded {} rows into {}".format(job.output_rows,
                                       tblref.table_id))
```

Because load jobs can potentially be long running, the load_table_ function returns a job object that you can use either to poll, using the job.done() method, or to block and wait, using job.result().

If the table already exists, the load job will append to the existing table as long as the data you are loading matches the existing schema. If the table doesn't exist, a new table is created with schema that is inferred from the pandas DataFrame.[7] You can change this behavior by specifying a load configuration:

```
from google.cloud.bigquery.job \
      import LoadJobConfig, WriteDisposition, CreateDisposition
load_config = LoadJobConfig(
   create_disposition=CreateDisposition.CREATE_IF_NEEDED,
   write_disposition=WriteDisposition.WRITE_TRUNCATE)
job = bq.load_table_from_dataframe(df, table_id,
                                   job_config=load_config)
```

The combination of CreateDisposition and WriteDisposition controls the behavior of the load operation, as is shown in Table 5-2.

Table 5-2. Impact of CreateDisposition and WriteDisposition on the behavior of the load operation

CreateDisposition	WriteDisposition	Behavior
CREATE_NEVER	WRITE_APPEND	Appends to existing table.
	WRITE_EMPTY	Appends to table, but only if it is currently empty. Otherwise, a duplicate error is thrown.
	WRITE_TRUNCATE	Clears out any existing rows in the table, i.e., overwrites the data in the table.

---

6 This requires the pyarrow library. If you don't have it already, install it by using pip install pyarrow.

7 Because pandas, by default, alphabetizes the column names, your BigQuery table will have a schema that is alphabetized and not in the order in which the column names appear in the tuples.

CreateDisposition	WriteDisposition	Behavior
CREATE_IF_NEEDED	WRITE_APPEND	Creates new table based on schema of the input if necessary. Appends to existing or newly created table. This is the default behavior if job_config is not passed in.
	WRITE_EMPTY	Creates new table based on schema of the input if necessary. Requires that the table, if it already exists, be empty. Otherwise, a duplicate error is thrown.
	WRITE_TRUNCATE	Creates new table based on schema of the input if necessary. Clears out any existing rows in the table, i.e., overwrites the data in the table.

Loading from a URI. It is possible to load a BigQuery table directly from a file whose Google Cloud URI is known. In addition to Cloud Datastore backups and HTTP URLs referring to Cloud Bigtable, Google Cloud Storage wildcard patterns are also supported.[8] We can, therefore, load the college scorecard comma-separated values (CSV) file that we used in the previous chapter by using the following:

```
job_config = bigquery.LoadJobConfig()
job_config.autodetect = True
job_config.source_format = bigquery.SourceFormat.CSV
job_config.null_marker = 'NULL'
uri = "gs://bigquery-oreilly-book/college_scorecard.csv"
table_id = '{}.ch05.college_scorecard_gcs'.format(PROJECT)
job = bq.load_table_from_uri(uri, table_id, job_config=job_config)
```

You can set all of the options that we considered in Chapter 4 (on loading data) by using the JobConfig flags. Here, we are using autodetect, specifying that the file format is CSV and that the file uses a nonstandard null marker before loading the file from the URI specified.

Even though you can block for the job to finish as you did in the previous section, you can also poll the job every 0.1 seconds and get the table details only after the load job is done:

```
while not job.done():
    print('.', end='', flush=True)
    time.sleep(0.1)
print('Done')
table = bq.get_table(tblref)
print("Loaded {} rows into {}.".format(table.num_rows, table.table_id))
```

After a few dots to represent the wait state, you get back the number of rows loaded (7,175).

---

8 For the full set of support URIs, see *https://cloud.google.com/bigquery/docs/reference/rest/v2/jobs#configuration.load.sourceUris*.

Loading from a local file. To load from a local file, create a file object and use `load_table_from_file`:

```
with gzip.open('../04_load/college_scorecard.csv.gz') as fp:
    job = bq.load_table_from_file(fp, tblref, job_config=job_config)
```

In other respects, this is similar to loading from a URI.

Copying a table. You can copy a table from one dataset to another by using the `copy_table` method:

```
source_tbl = 'bigquery-public-data.london_bicycles.cycle_stations'
dest_tbl = '{}.ch05eu.cycle_stations_copy'.format(PROJECT)
job = bq.copy_table(source_tbl, dest_tbl, location='EU')
job.result() # blocks and waits
dest_table = bq.get_table(dest_tbl)
print(dest_table.num_rows)
```

Note that we are copying the London `cycle_stations` data to a dataset (ch05eu) that we created in the EU. Note also that we are making sure to copy tables only within the same region.

Extracting data from a table. We can export data from a table to a file in Google Cloud Storage using the `extract_table` method:

```
source_tbl = 'bigquery-public-data.london_bicycles.cycle_stations'
dest_uri = 'gs://{}/tmp/exported/cycle_stations'.format(BUCKET)
config = bigquery.job.ExtractJobConfig(
    destination_format =
        bigquery.job.DestinationFormat.NEWLINE_DELIMITED_JSON)
job = bq.extract_table(source_tbl, dest_uri,
                       location='EU', job_config=config)
job.result() # blocks and waits
```

If the table is sufficiently large, the output will be sharded into multiple files. As of this writing, extraction formats that are supported include CSV, Avro, and newline-delimited JSON. As with copying tables, make sure to export to a bucket in the same location as the dataset.[9] Of course, after you export a table, Google Cloud Storage charges will begin to accrue for the output files.

Browsing the rows of a table. In the BigQuery web UI, you have the ability to preview a table without incurring querying charges. The same capability is available via the REST API as `tabledata.list`, and consequently through the Python API.

---

9 To create a bucket in the EU region, use: `gsutil mb -l EU` gs://some-bucket-name.

To list an arbitrary five rows from the cycle_stations table,[10] you could do the following:

```
table_id = 'bigquery-public-data.london_bicycles.cycle_stations'
table = bq.get_table(table_id)
rows = bq.list_rows(table,
                    start_index=0,
                    max_results=5)
```

Omitting the start_index and max_results allows you to get all of the rows in the table:

```
rows = bq.list_rows(table)
```

Of course, the table needs to be small enough to fit into memory. If that is not the case, you can paginate through the entire table, processing the table in chunks:

```
page_size = 10000
row_iter = bq.list_rows(table,
                        page_size=page_size)
for page in row_iter.pages:
  rows = list(page)
  # do something with rows ...
  print(len(rows))
```

Instead of getting all of the fields, you can select the id field and any columns whose name includes the substring count by doing the following:

```
fields = [field for field in table.schema
          if 'count' in field.name or field.name == 'id']
rows = bq.list_rows(table,
                    start_index=300,
                    max_results=5,
                    selected_fields=fields)
```

You can then format the resulting rows to have a fixed width of 10 characters using the following:

```
fmt = '{!s:<10} ' * len(rows.schema)
print(fmt.format(*[field.name for field in rows.schema]))
for row in rows:
  print(fmt.format(*row))
```

---

10 Which five rows we get will be arbitrary because BigQuery does not guarantee ordering. The purpose of providing the start_index is so that we can get the "next page" of five rows by supplying start_index=5.

This produces the following result:

```
id          bikes_count docks_count
658         20          30
797         20          30
238         21          32
578         22          32
477         26          36
```

Querying

The major benefit of using the Google Cloud Client Library comes when querying. Much of the complexity regarding pagination, retries, and so on is handled transparently.

The first step, of course, is to create a string containing the SQL to be executed by BigQuery:

```
query = """
SELECT
  start_station_name
  , AVG(duration) as duration
  , COUNT(duration) as num_trips
FROM `bigquery-public-data`.london_bicycles.cycle_hire
GROUP BY start_station_name
ORDER BY num_trips DESC
LIMIT 10
"""
```

This query finds the 10 busiest stations in London, as measured by the total number of trips initiated at those stations, and reports each station name, the average duration of trips initiated at this station, and the total number of such trips.

Dry run. Before actually executing the query, it is possible to do a dry run to obtain an estimate of how much data will be processed by the query:[11]

```
config = bigquery.QueryJobConfig()
config.dry_run = True
job = bq.query(query, location='EU', job_config=config)
print("This query will process {} bytes."
            .format(job.total_bytes_processed))
```

When we ran the preceding code, it returned the following:

```
This query will process 903989528 bytes.
Your result might be somewhat different given that this table is refreshed with
new data as it is made available.
```

---

11 This is the same API used by the BigQuery web UI to show you the estimate.

The dry run does not incur charges. Use dry runs to check that query syntax is correct both during development and in your testing harness. For example, you can use dry runs to identify undeclared parameters and to validate the schema of the query result without actually running it. If you are building an application that sends queries to BigQuery, you can use the dry run feature to provide billing caps. We look at performance and cost optimization in more detail in Chapter 7.

Sometimes it is impossible to compute the bytes processed ahead of time without actually running the query. In such cases, the dry run returns either zero or an upper-bound estimate. This happens in two situations: when querying a federated table (for which the data is stored outside BigQuery; see Chapter 4) and when querying a clustered table (see Chapter 7). In the case of federated tables, the dry run will report 0 bytes, and in the case of clustered tables, BigQuery will attempt to calculate the worst-case scenario and report that number. In either case, though, when actually performing the query, you'll be billed only for the data that actually needs to be read.

Executing the query.   To execute the query, simply start to iterate over the job object. The job will be launched, and pages of results will be retrieved as you iterate over the job using the for loop:

```
job = bq.query(query, location='EU')
fmt = '{!s:<40} {:>10d} {:>10d}'
for row in job:
    fields = (row['start_station_name'],
            (int)(0.5 + row['duration']),
            row['num_trips'])
    print(fmt.format(*fields))
```

Given a row, it is possible to obtain the value for any of the columns in the result set using the aliased name of the column in the SELECT (look at how the column num_trips appears in the result set).

The formatted result of the query is as follows:

```
Belgrove Street, King's Cross              1011      234458
Hyde Park Corner, Hyde Park                2783      215629
Waterloo Station 3, Waterloo                866      201630
Black Lion Gate, Kensington Gardens        3588      161952
Albert Gate, Hyde Park                     2359      155647
Waterloo Station 1, Waterloo                992      145910
Wormwood Street, Liverpool Street           976      119447
Hop Exchange, The Borough                  1218      115135
Wellington Arch, Hyde Park                 2276      110260
Triangle Car Park, Hyde Park               2233      108347
```

Creating a pandas DataFrame. Earlier in this section, we saw how to load a BigQuery table from a pandas DataFrame. It is also possible to execute a query and get the results back as a pandas DataFrame, thus using BigQuery as a highly distributed and scalable intermediate step in a data science workflow:

```
query = """
SELECT
  start_station_name
  , AVG(duration) as duration
  , COUNT(duration) as num_trips
FROM `bigquery-public-data`.london_bicycles.cycle_hire
GROUP BY start_station_name
"""
df = bq.query(query, location='EU').to_dataframe()
print(df.describe())
```

This code uses the pandas describe() functionality to print out the distribution of the numeric columns in the result set:

```
          duration        num_trips
count   880.000000       880.000000
mean   1348.351153     27692.273864
std     434.057829     23733.621289
min       0.000000         1.000000
25%    1078.684974     13033.500000
50%    1255.889223     23658.500000
75%    1520.504055     35450.500000
max    4836.380090    234458.000000
```

Thus there are 880 stations in total, with an average of 27,692 trips starting at each station, although there is a station with only one trip and a station with 234,458 trips. The median station has supported 23,658 rides, and the majority of stations have had between 13,033 and 35,450 rides.

Parameterized queries. The queries do not need to be static strings. Instead, you can parameterize them, so that the query parameters are specified at the time the query job is created. Here is an example of a query that finds the total number of trips that were longer than a specific duration. The actual threshold, min_duration, will be specified at the time the query is run:

```
query2 = """
SELECT
  start_station_name
  , COUNT(duration) as num_trips
FROM `bigquery-public-data`.london_bicycles.cycle_hire
WHERE duration >= @min_duration
GROUP BY start_station_name
ORDER BY num_trips DESC
LIMIT 10
"""
```

The @ symbol identifies min_duration as a parameter to the query. A query can have any number of such named parameters.

Creating a query by doing string formatting is an extremely bad practice. String manipulation such as the following can make your data warehouse subject to SQL injection attacks:

```
query2 = """
SELECT
  start_station_name
  , COUNT(duration) as num_trips
FROM `bigquery-public-data`.london_bicycles.cycle_hire
WHERE duration >= {}
GROUP BY start_station_name
ORDER BY num_trips DESC
LIMIT 10
""".format(min_duration)
```

We strongly suggest that you use parameterized queries, especially when constructing queries that include user input.

When executing a query that has named parameters, you need to supply a job_con fig with those parameters:

```
config = bigquery.QueryJobConfig()
config.query_parameters = [
  bigquery.ScalarQueryParameter('min_duration', "INT64", 600)
]
job = bq.query(query2, location='EU', job_config=config)
```

Here, we are specifying that we want to retrieve the number of trips over 600 seconds in duration.

As before, iterating over the job will allow you to retrieve the rows, and each row functions like a dictionary of column names to values:

```
fmt = '{!s:<40} {:>10d}'
for row in job:
    fields = (row['start_station_name'],
              row['num_trips'])
    print(fmt.format(*fields))
```

Running this code yields the following:

```
Hyde Park Corner, Hyde Park                 203592
Belgrove Street, King's Cross               168110
Waterloo Station 3, Waterloo                148809
Albert Gate, Hyde Park                      145794
Black Lion Gate, Kensington Gardens         137930
Waterloo Station 1, Waterloo                106092
Wellington Arch, Hyde Park                  102770
Triangle Car Park, Hyde Park                 99368
```

```
Wormwood Street, Liverpool Street          82483
Palace Gate, Kensington Gardens            80342
```

In this section, we covered how to programmatically invoke BigQuery operations, whether they involve table or dataset manipulation, querying data, or streaming inserts. The programmatic APIs, especially the Google Cloud Client Library, are what you would use whenever you are building applications that need to access BigQuery.

However, in some specific instances, there are higher-level abstractions available. We cover these in the next section.

Accessing BigQuery from Data Science Tools

Notebooks have revolutionized the way that data science is carried out. They are an instance of *literate programming*, a programming paradigm introduced by the computer science legend Donald Knuth, wherein computer code is intermixed with headings, text, plots, and so on. Because of this, the notebook serves simultaneously as an executable program and as an interactive report.

Jupyter is the most popular of the notebook frameworks and works in a variety of languages, including Python. In Jupyter, the notebook is a web-based interactive document in which you can type and execute code. The output of the code is embedded directly in the document.

Notebooks on Google Cloud Platform

To create a notebook on Google Cloud Platform (GCP), launch a Deep Learning Virtual Machine and get the URL to Jupyter. You can do this from the AI Platform section of the GCP Cloud Console, or you can automate it by using the gcloud command-line tool:[12]

```
#!/bin/bash

gcloud beta notebooks instances create bqbook \
      --location=us-west1-a \
      --vm-image-family=tf-latest-cpu \
      --vm-image-project=deeplearning-platform-release \
      --machine-type=n1-standard-2
```

Access the URL (or from the AI Platform Notebooks section of the GCP Cloud Console, click the Open JupyterLab link), and you will be in Jupyter. Click the button to create a Python 3 notebook, and you will be able to try out the snippets of code.

The Cloud AI Platform Notebook already has the Google Cloud Client Library for BigQuery installed, but if you are in some other Jupyter environment, you can install

---

12 This is the script *05_devel/launch_notebook.sh* in the GitHub repository for this book.

the library and load the necessary extensions by running the following code in a code cell:

```
!pip install google-cloud-bigquery
%load_ext google.cloud.bigquery
```

In a Jupyter Notebook, any line preceded by an exclamation point (!) is run using the command-line shell, whereas any line preceded by a percent sign (%) invokes an extension, also called a magic. So in the preceding code snippet, the `pip install` is carried out on the command line, whereas the extension named `load_ext` is used to load the BigQuery Magics.

You can clone the repository corresponding to this book by clicking the Git icon (highlighted in Figure 5-4) and cloning *https://github.com/GoogleCloudPlatform/bigquery-oreilly-book*, as demonstrated in Figure 5-4.

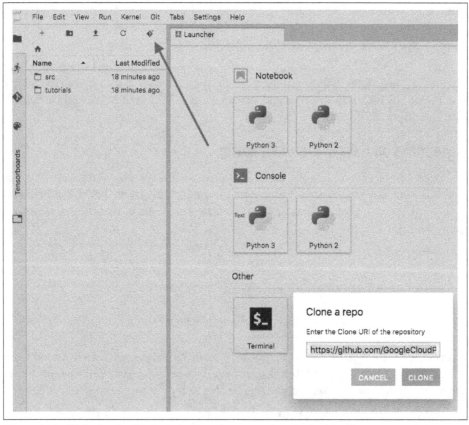

Figure 5-4. Click the the Git icon (where the arrow is pointing) to clone a repository

Browse to and open the *05_devel/magics.ipynb* notebook to try out the code in this section of the book. Change the PROJECT variable in the notebook to reflect your project. Then, on the menu at the top, select Run > Run All Cells.

Jupyter Magics

The BigQuery extensions for Jupyter make running queries within a notebook quite easy. For example, to run a query, you simply need to specify %%bigquery at the top of the cell:

```
%%bigquery --project $PROJECT
SELECT
  start_station_name
  , AVG(duration) as duration
  , COUNT(duration) as num_trips
FROM `bigquery-public-data`.london_bicycles.cycle_hire
GROUP BY start_station_name
ORDER BY num_trips DESC
LIMIT 5
```

Running a cell with this code executes the query and displays a nicely formatted table with the five desired rows, as shown in Figure 5-5.

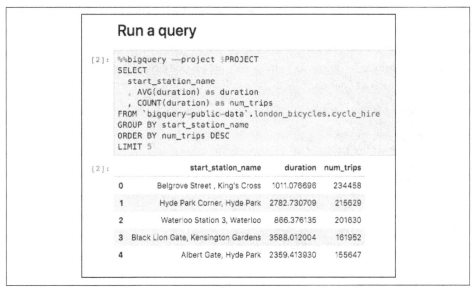

Figure 5-5. The result of a query, nicely formatted, is embedded into the document

Running a parameterized query

To run a parameterized query, specify --params in the magic, as depicted in Figure 5-6. The parameters themselves are a Python variable that is typically defined elsewhere in the notebook.

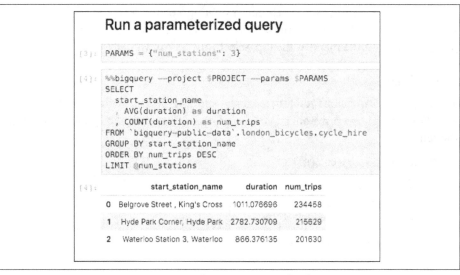

Figure 5-6. How to run a parameterized query in a notebook

In the preceding example, the number of stations is a parameter that is specified as a Python variable and used in the SQL query to limit the number of rows in the result.

Saving query results to pandas

Saving the results of a query to pandas involves specifying the name of the variable (e.g., df) by which the pandas DataFrame will be referenced:

```
%%bigquery df --project $PROJECT
SELECT
  start_station_name
  , AVG(duration) as duration
  , COUNT(duration) as num_trips
FROM `bigquery-public-data`.london_bicycles.cycle_hire
GROUP BY start_station_name
ORDER BY num_trips DESC
```

You can use the variable df like any other pandas DataFrame. For example, we could ask for statistics of the numeric columns in df by using:

```
df.describe()
```

We can also use the plotting commands available in pandas to draw a scatter plot of the average duration of trips and the number of trips across all the stations, as presented in Figure 5-7.

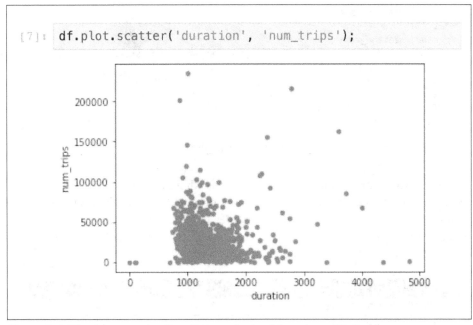

```
[7]:  df.plot.scatter('duration', 'num_trips');
```

Figure 5-7. Plotting a pandas DataFrame obtained by using a BigQuery query

Working with BigQuery, pandas, and Jupyter

We have introduced linkages between the Google Cloud Client Library for BigQuery and pandas in several sections of this book. Because pandas is the de facto standard for data analysis in Python, it might be helpful to bring together all of these capabilities and use them to illustrate a typical data science workflow.

Imagine that we are receiving anecdotes from our customer support team about bad bicycles at some stations. We'd like to send a crew out to spot-check a number of problematic stations. How do we choose which stations to spot-check? We could rely on stations from which we have received customer complaints, but we will tend to receive more complaints from busy stations simply because they have lots more customers.

We believe that if someone rents a bicycle for less than 10 minutes and returns the bicycle to the same station they rented it from, it is likely that the bicycle has a problem. Let's call this a bad trip (from the customer's viewpoint, it is). We could have our crew do a spot check of stations where bad trips have occurred more frequently.

To find the fraction of bad trips, we can query BigQuery using Jupyter Magics and save the result into a pandas DataFrame called badtrips using the following:

```
%%bigquery badtrips --project $PROJECT
```

```
WITH all_bad_trips AS (
SELECT
  start_station_name
  , COUNTIF(duration < 600 AND start_station_name = end_station_name) AS bad_trips
  , COUNT(*) as num_trips
FROM `bigquery-public-data`.london_bicycles.cycle_hire
WHERE EXTRACT(YEAR FROM start_date) = 2015
GROUP BY start_station_name
HAVING num_trips > 10
)
SELECT *, bad_trips / num_trips AS fraction_bad FROM all_bad_trips
ORDER BY fraction_bad DESC
```

The WITH expression counts the number of trips whose duration is less than 600 seconds and for which the starting and ending stations are the same. By grouping this by start_station_name, we get the total number of trips and bad trips at each station. The outer query computes the desired fraction and associates it with the station. This yields the following result (only the first few rows are shown):

start_station_name	bad_trips	num_trips	fraction_bad
Contact Centre, Southbury House	20	48	0.416667
Monier Road, Newham	1	25	0.040000
Aberfeldy Street, Poplar	35	955	0.036649
Ormonde Gate, Chelsea	315	8932	0.035266
Thornfield House, Poplar	28	947	0.029567
...			

It is clear that the station at the top of the table is quite odd. Just 48 trips originated from the Southbury House station, and 20 of those are bad! Nevertheless, we can confirm this by using pandas to look at the statistics of the DataFrame:

```
badtrips.describe()
```

This returns the following:

	bad_trips	num_trips	fraction_bad
count	823.000000	823.000000	823.000000
mean	75.074119	11869.755772	0.007636
std	70.512207	9906.268656	0.014739
min	0.000000	11.000000	0.000000
25%	41.000000	5903.000000	0.005002
50%	62.000000	9998.000000	0.006368
75%	91.500000	14852.500000	0.008383
max	967.000000	95740.000000	0.416667

Examining the results, we notice that `fraction_bad` ranges from 0 to 0.417 (look at the min and max), but it is not clear how relevant this ratio is because the stations also vary quite dramatically. For example, the number of trips ranges from 11 to 95,740.

We can look at a scatter plot to see if there is any clear trend:

```
badtrips.plot.scatter('num_trips', 'fraction_bad');
```

Figure 5-8 displays the result.

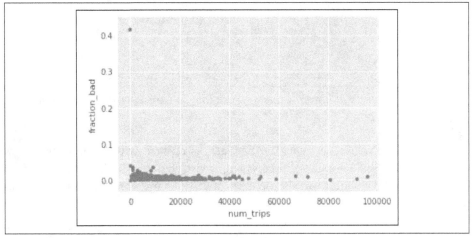

Figure 5-8. In this plot, it seems that higher values of `fraction_bad` are associated with stations with low `num_trips`

It appears from the graph that higher values of `fraction_bad` are associated with stations with low `num_trips`, but the trend is not clear because of the outlier 0.4 value. Let's zoom in a bit and add a line of best fit using the `seaborn` plotting package:

```
import seaborn as sns
ax = sns.regplot(badtrips['num_trips'],badtrips['fraction_bad']);
ax.set_ylim(0, 0.05);
```

As Figure 5-9 shows, this yields a clear depiction of the trend between the fraction of bad trips and how busy the station is.

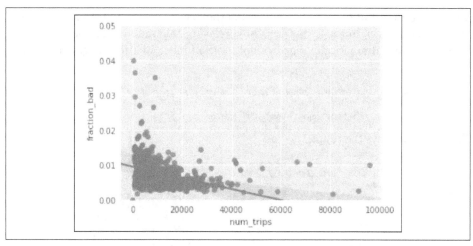

Figure 5-9. It is clear that higher values of `fraction_bad` *are associated with stations with low* `num_trips`

Because higher values of `fraction_bad` are associated with stations with low `num_trips`, we should not have our crew simply visit stations with high values of `frac` `tion_bad`. So, how should we choose a set of stations on which to conduct a spot check?

One approach could be to pick the five worst of the really busy stations, five of the next most busy, and so forth. We can do this by creating four different bands from the quantile of the stations by `num_trips` and then finding the five worst stations within each band. That's what this pandas snippet does:

```
stations_to_examine = []
for band in range(1,5):
  min_trips = badtrips['num_trips'].quantile(0.2*(band))
  max_trips = badtrips['num_trips'].quantile(0.2*(band+1))
  query = 'num_trips >= {} and num_trips < {}'.format(
                            min_trips, max_trips)
  print(query) # band
  stations = badtrips.query(query)
  stations = stations.sort_values(
                  by=['fraction_bad'], ascending=False)[:5]
  print(stations) # 5 worst
  stations_to_examine.append(stations)
  print()
```

The first band consists of the 20th to 40th percentile of stations by busyness:

```
num_trips >= 4826.4 and num_trips < 8511.8
                start_station_name  bad_trips   num_trips  fraction_bad
6           River Street, Clerkenwell        221        8279      0.026694
9   Courland Grove, Wandsworth Road        105        5369      0.019557
```

```
10        Stanley Grove, Battersea       92    4882    0.018845
12         Southern Grove, Bow          112    6152    0.018205
18   Richmond Way, Shepherd's Bush      126    8149    0.015462
```

The last band consists of the 80th to 100th percentile of stations by busyness:

```
num_trips >= 16509.2 and num_trips < 95740.0
                       start_station_name bad_trips num_trips fraction_bad
25  Queen's Gate, Kensington Gardens        396      27457      0.014423
74    Speakers' Corner 2, Hyde Park         468      41107      0.011385
76     Cumberland Gate, Hyde Park           303      26981      0.011230
77         Albert Gate, Hyde Park           729      66547      0.010955
82    Triangle Car Park, Hyde Park          454      41675      0.010894
```

Notice that in the first band, it takes a `fraction_bad` of 0.015 to make the list, while in the last band, a `fraction_bad` of 0.01 is sufficient. The smallness of these numbers might make you complacent, but this is a 50% difference.

We can then use pandas to concatenate the various bands and the BigQuery API to write these stations back to BigQuery:

```
stations_to_examine = pd.concat(stations_to_examine)
bq = bigquery.Client(project=PROJECT)
tblref = TableReference.from_string(
                '{}.ch05eu.bad_bikes'.format(PROJECT))
job = bq.load_table_from_dataframe(stations_to_examine, tblref)
job.result() # blocks and waits
```

We now have the stations to examine in a persistent storage, but we still need to get the data out to our crew. The best format for this is a map, and we can create it in Python if we know the latitude and longitude of our stations. We do, of course—the location of the stations is in the `cycle_stations` table:[13]

```
%%bigquery stations_to_examine --project $PROJECT
SELECT
  start_station_name AS station_name
  , num_trips
  , fraction_bad
  , latitude
  , longitude
FROM ch05eu.bad_bikes AS bad
JOIN `bigquery-public-data`.london_bicycles.cycle_stations AS s
ON bad.start_station_name = s.name
```

And here is the result (not all rows are shown):

---

13 This is the point of data warehousing: to bring enterprise data together into a centralized repository so that any enterprise data that an analyst might possibly need is only a join away.

station_name	num_trips	fraction_bad	latitude	longitude
Ormonde Gate, Chelsea	8932	0.035266	51.487964	-0.161765
Stanley Grove, Battersea	4882	0.018845	51.470475	-0.152130
Courland Grove, Wandsworth Road	5369	0.019557	51.472918	-0.132103
Southern Grove, Bow	6152	0.018205	51.523538	-0.030556
...				

With the location information in hand, we can plot a map using the `folium` package:

```
import folium
map_pts = folium.Map(location=[51.5, -0.15], zoom_start=12)
for idx, row in stations_to_examine.iterrows():
    folium.Marker( location=[row['latitude'], row['longitude']],
                popup=row['station_name'] ).add_to(map_pts)
```

This produces the beautiful interactive map shown in Figure 5-10, which our crew can use to check on the stations that we've identified.

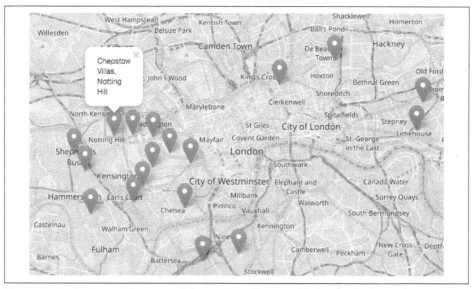

Figure 5-10. An interactive map of the stations that need to be checked

We were able to seamlessly integrate BigQuery, pandas, and Jupyter to accomplish a data analysis task. We used BigQuery to compute aggregations over millions of bicycle rides, pandas to carry out statistical tasks, and Python packages such as `folium` to visualize the results interactively.

Working with BigQuery from R

Python is one of the most popular languages for data science, but it shares that perch with R, a long-standing programming language and software environment for statistics and graphics.

To use BigQuery from R, install the library bigrquery from CRAN:

```
install.packages("bigrquery", dependencies=TRUE)
```

Here's a simple example of querying the bicycle dataset from R:

```
billing <- 'cloud-training-demos' # your project name
sql <- "
SELECT
  start_station_name
  , AVG(duration) as duration
    , COUNT(duration) as num_trips
  FROM `bigquery-public-data`.london_bicycles.cycle_hire
  GROUP BY start_station_name
  ORDER BY num_trips DESC
  LIMIT 5
"
tbl <- bq_project_query(billing, sql)
bq_table_download(tbl, max_results=100)
grid.tbl(tbl)
```

You use `bq_project_query` to create a BigQuery query, and you execute it by using `bq_table_download`.

You can also use R from a Jupyter notebook. The `conda` environment for Jupyter[14] has an R extension that you can load by running the following:

```
!conda install rpy2
%load_ext rpy2.ipython
```

To carry out a linear regression to predict the number of docks at a station based on its location, you can first populate an R DataFrame from BigQuery:

```
%%bigquery docks --project $PROJECT
SELECT
  docks_count, latitude, longitude
FROM `bigquery-public-data`.london_bicycles.cycle_stations
WHERE bikes_count > 0
```

Then Jupyter Magics for R can be performed just like the Jupyter Magics for Python. Thus, you can use the R magic to perform linear modeling (`lm`) on the docks DataFrame:

---

14 As of this writing, the PyTorch image for the Notebook Instance on GCP is built using conda.

```
%%R -i docks
mod <- lm(docks ~ latitude + longitude)
summary(mod)
```

Cloud Dataflow

We introduced Cloud Dataflow in Chapter 4 as a way to load data into BigQuery from MySQL. Cloud Dataflow is a managed service for executing pipelines written using Apache Beam. Dataflow is quite useful in data science because it provides a way to carry out transformations that would be difficult to perform in SQL. As of this writing, Beam pipelines can be written in Python, Java, and Go, with Java the most mature.

As an example of where this could be useful, consider the distribution of the length of bicycle rentals from an individual bicycle station shown in Figure 5-11.

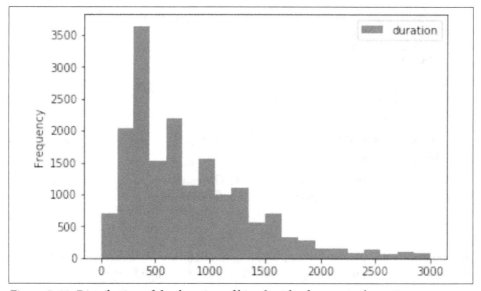

Figure 5-11. Distribution of the duration of bicycle rides from a single station

As Figure 5-11 demonstrates, because the bar at $x = 1000$ has $y = 1500$, there were approximately 1,500 rides that were around 1,000 seconds in duration.

Although the specific durations are available in the BigQuery table, it can be helpful to fit these values to a theoretical distribution so that we can carry out simulations and study the effect of pricing and availability changes more readily. In Python, given an array of duration values, it is quite straightforward to compute the parameters of a Gamma distribution (*https://en.wikipedia.org/wiki/Gamma_distribution*) fit using the scipy package:

```
from scipy import stats
ag,bg,cg = stats.gamma.fit(df['duration'])
```

Imagine that you want to go through all of the stations and compute the parameters of the Gamma distribution fit to the duration of rentals from each of those stations. Because this is not convenient in SQL but can easily be done in Python, we can write a Dataflow job to compute the Gamma fits in a distributed manner—that is, to parallelize the computation of Gamma fits on a cluster of machines.

The pipeline starts with a query[15] to pull the durations for each station, sends the resulting rows to the method compute_fit, and then writes the resulting rows to Big-Query, to the table station_stats:[16]

```
opts = beam.pipeline.PipelineOptions(flags = [], **options)
RUNNER = 'DataflowRunner'
query = """
    SELECT start_station_id, ARRAY_AGG(duration) AS duration_array
    FROM `bigquery-public-data.london_bicycles.cycle_hire`
    GROUP BY start_station_id
    """

with beam.Pipeline(RUNNER, options = opts) as p:
    (p
     | 'read_bq' >> beam.io.Read(beam.io.BigQuerySource(query=query))
     | 'compute_fit' >> beam.Map(compute_fit)
     | 'write_bq' >> beam.io.gcp.bigquery.WriteToBigQuery(
         'ch05eu.station_stats',
    schema='station_id:string,ag:FLOAT64,bg:FLOAT64,cg:FLOAT64')
    )
```

The compute_fit method is a Python function that takes in a dictionary corresponding to the input BigQuery row and returns a dictionary corresponding to the desired output row:

```
def compute_fit(row):
    from scipy import stats
    result = {}
    result['station_id'] = row['start_station_id']
    durations = row['duration_array']
    ag, bg, cg = stats.gamma.fit(durations)
    result['ag'] = ag
    result['bg'] = bg
    result['cg'] = cg
    return result
```

The fit values are then written to a destination table.

---

15 These queries are billed as part of the Dataflow job.

16 See *05_devel/statfit.ipynb* in the GitHub repository for this book.

After launching the Dataflow job, we can monitor it via the GCP Cloud Console, shown in Figure 5-12, and see the job autoscaling to process the stations in parallel.

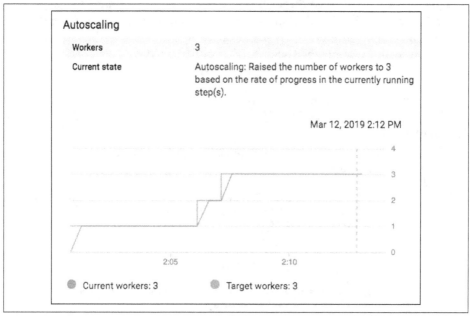

Figure 5-12. The Dataflow job is parallelized and run on a cluster whose size is auto-scaled based on the rate of progress in each step

When the Dataflow job finishes, we can query the table and obtain statistics of the stations and plot the parameters of the Gamma distribution (see the notebook on GitHub (*https://github.com/GoogleCloudPlatform/bigquery-oreilly-book/blob/master/05_devel/statfit.ipynb*) for the graphs).

JDBC/ODBC drivers

Because BigQuery is a warehouse for structured data, it can be convenient if database-agnostic APIs like Java Database Connectivity (JDBC) and Open Database Connectivity (ODBC) can be employed by a Java or .NET application to communicate with a BigQuery database driver. This is not recommended for new applications —use the client library instead. If, however, you have a legacy application that communicates with a database today and needs to be converted with minimal code changes to communicate with BigQuery, the use of a JDBC/ODBC driver might be warranted.

We strongly recommend the use of the client libraries (in the language of your choice) over the use of JDBC/ODBC drivers because the functionality exposed by the JDBC/ODBC driver is a subset of the full capabilities of BigQuery. Among the features missing are support for large-scale ingestion (i.e., many of the loading techniques described in the previous chapter), large-scale export (meaning data movement will be slow), and nested/repeated fields (preventing the use of many of the performance optimizations that we cover in Chapter 7). Designing new systems based on JDBC/ODBC drivers tends to lead to painful technical debt.

A Google partner provides ODBC and JDBC drivers capable of executing BigQuery Standard SQL queries.[17] To install the Java drivers, for example, you would download a ZIP file, unzip it, and place all of the Java Archive (JAR) files in the ZIP folder in the classpath of your Java application. Using the driver in a Java application typically involves modifying a configuration file that specifies the connection information. There are several options to configure the authentication and create a connection string that can be used within your Java application.

Incorporating BigQuery Data into Google Slides (in G Suite)

It is possible to use Google Apps Script (*https://developers.google.com/apps-script/advanced/bigquery*) to manage BigQuery projects, upload data, and execute queries. This is useful if you want to automate the population of Google Docs, Google Sheets, or Google Slides with BigQuery data.

As an example, let's look at creating a pair of slides with analysis of the London bicycles data. Begin by going to *https://script.google.com/create* to create a new script. Then, on the Resources menu, choose Advanced Google Services and flip on the bit for the BigQuery API (name the project if prompted).

The full Apps Script for this example is in the GitHub repository for this book (*https://github.com/GoogleCloudPlatform/bigquery-oreilly-book/blob/master/05_devel/bq_to_slides.gs*), so copy the script and paste it into the text editor. Then, at the top of the script, change the PROJECT_ID, choose the function createBigQueryPresenta tion, and then click the run button, as illustrated in Figure 5-13.

---

17 See *https://cloud.google.com/bigquery/partners/simba-drivers/* and *https://www.simba.com/drivers/bigquery-odbc-jdbc/*.

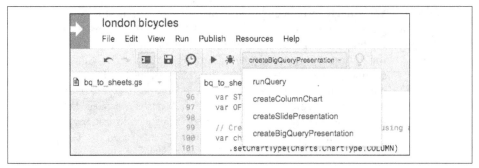

Figure 5-13. Use Google Apps Script to create a presentation from data in BigQuery

The resulting spreadsheet and slide deck will show up in Google Drive (you can also find their URLs by clicking View > Logs). The slide deck will look similar to that shown in Figure 5-14.

Figure 5-14. Slide deck created by the Google Apps Script

The function createBigQueryPresentation carried out the following code:

```
function createBigQueryPresentation() {
  var spreadsheet = runQuery();
  Logger.log('Results spreadsheet created: %s', spreadsheet.getUrl());
```

```
    var chart = createColumnChart(spreadsheet); // UPDATED
    var deck = createSlidePresentation(spreadsheet, chart); // NEW
    Logger.log('Results slide deck created: %s', deck.getUrl()); // NEW
}
```

Essentially, it calls three functions:

- runQuery to run a query and store the results in a Google Sheets spreadsheet

- createColumnChart to create a chart from the data in the spreadsheet

- createSlidePresentation to create the output Google Slides slide deck

The runQuery() method uses the Apps Scripts client library to invoke BigQuery and page through the results:

```
var queryResults = BigQuery.Jobs.query(request, PROJECT_ID);
var rows = queryResults.rows;
  while (queryResults.pageToken) {
      queryResults = BigQuery.Jobs.getQueryResults(PROJECT_ID, jobId, {
        pageToken: queryResults.pageToken
      });
      rows = rows.concat(queryResults.rows);
  }
```

Then it creates a spreadsheet and adds these rows to the sheet. The other two functions employ Apps Scripts code to draw graphs, create a slide deck, and add both types of data to the slide deck.

Bash Scripting with BigQuery

The bq command-line tool that is provided as part of the Google Cloud Software Development Kit (SDK (*https://cloud.google.com/sdk/*)) provides a convenient way to invoke BigQuery operations from the command line. The SDK is installed by default on Google Cloud virtual machines (VMs) and clusters. You can also download and install the SDK in your on-premises development and production environments.

You can use the bq tool to interact with the BigQuery service when writing Bash scripts or by calling out to the shell from many programming languages without the need to depend on the client library. Common uses of bq include creating and verifying the existence of datasets and tables, executing queries, loading data into tables, populating tables and views, and verifying the status of jobs. Let's look at each of these.

Creating Datasets and Tables

To create a dataset, use bq mk and specify the location of the dataset (e.g., US or EU). It is also possible to specify nondefault values for such things as the table expiration time. It is a best practice to provide a description for the dataset:

```
bq mk --location=US \
      --default_table_expiration 3600 \
      --description "Chapter 5 of BigQuery Book." \
      ch05
```

Checking whether a dataset exists

The bq mk in the preceding example fails if the dataset already exists. To create the dataset only if the dataset doesn't already exist, you need to list existing datasets using bq ls and check whether that list contains a dataset with the name you're looking for:[18]

```
#!/bin/bash
  bq_safe_mk() {
      dataset=$1
      exists=$(bq ls --dataset | grep -w $dataset)
      if [ -n "$exists" ]; then
          echo "Not creating $dataset since it already exists"
      else
          echo "Creating $dataset"
          bq mk $dataset
      fi
}
# this is how you call the function
bq_safe_mk ch05
```

Creating a dataset in a different project

The dataset ch05 is created in the default project (specified when you logged into the VM or when you ran gcloud auth using the Google Cloud SDK). To create a dataset in a different project, qualify the dataset name with the name of the project in which the dataset should be created:

```
bq mk --location=US \
      --default_table_expiration 3600 \
      --description "Chapter 5 of BigQuery Book." \
      projectname:ch05
```

---

18 This is, of course, subject to race conditions if someone else created the dataset between your check and actual creation.

Creating a table

Creating a table is similar to creating a dataset except that you must add `--table` to the `bq mk` command. The following creates a table named `ch05.rentals_last_hour` that expires in 3,600 seconds and that has two columns named `rental_id` (a string) and `duration` (a float):

```
bq mk --table \
    --expiration 3600 \
    --description "One hour of data" \
    --label persistence:volatile \
    ch05.rentals_last_hour rental_id:STRING,duration:FLOAT
```

You can use the label to tag tables with characteristics; Data Catalog supports the ability to search for tables that have a specific label—here, `persistence` is the key and `volatile` is the label.

Complex schema

For more complex schemas that cannot easily be expressed by a comma-separated string, specify a JSON file, as explained in Chapter 4:

```
bq mk --table \
    --expiration 3600 \
    --description "One hour of data" \
    --label persistence:volatile \
    ch05.rentals_last_hour schema.json
```

Copying datasets

The most efficient way to copy datasets is through the command-line tool. For example, this copies a table from the `ch04` dataset to the `ch05` dataset:

```
bq cp ch04.old_table ch05.new_table
```

> Copying tables can take a while, but your script might not be able to proceed until the job is complete. An easy way to wait for a job to complete is to use `bq wait`:
>
> ```
> bq wait --fail_on_error job_id
> ```
>
> This preceding code waits forever until the job completes, whereas the following waits a maximum of 600 seconds:
>
> ```
> bq wait --fail_on_error job_id 600
> ```
>
> If there is only one running job, you can omit the `job_id`.

To do a cross region copy, you can use the BigQuery Transfer Service.

First, create the destination dataset:

```
bq mk --location eu ch10eu
```

Then, create a transfer config whose data source is `cross_region_copy`:

```
bq mk --transfer_config --data_source=cross_region_copy \
    --params='{"source_dataset_id": "iowa_liquor_sales", \
               "source_project_id": "bigquery-public-data"}' \
    --target_dataset=ch10eu --display_name=liquor \
    --schedule_end_time="$(date -v +1H -u +%Y-%m-%dT%H:%M:%SZ)"
```

Because the data transfer service is meant for routine copies, this will repeat every 24 hours. In this example, we have set the end time to be 1-hour from now, so that the transfer happens only once.

Backing up and restoring datasets

BigQuery is fully managed and takes care of managing redundant backups in storage. It also supports "time-travel", the ability to query a snapshot as of a day ago. So, if an ETL job goes bad and you want to revert back to yesterday's data, you can simply do:

```
CREATE OR REPLACE TABLE dataset.table_restored
AS
SELECT *
FROM dataset.table
FOR SYSTEM TIME AS OF
    TIMESTAMP_ADD(CURRENT_TIMESTAMP(), INTERVAL -1 DAY)
```

However, time travel is restricted to 7 days. There are situations (playback, regulatory compliance, etc.) when you might need to restore a table as it existed 30 days ago or 1 year ago.

To back up a table, make sure to save its metadata (the schema and table definition as well as the data in the table. All three can be accomplished from the command-line using:

```
bq show --schema dataset.table. # schema.json
bq --format=json show dataset.table.  # tbldef.json
bq extract --destination_format=AVRO \
        dataset.table gs://.../data_*.avro # AVRO files
```

When restoring, you will need to use the table definition to find characteristics such as whether the table is time-partitioned, range-partitioned, or clustered and then invoke the command:

```
bq load --source_format=AVRO \
    --time_partitioning_expiration ... \
    --time_partitioning_field ... \
    --time_partitioning_type ... \
    --clustering_fields ... \
    --schema ... \
    todataset.table_name \
    gs://.../data_*.avro
```

For your convenience, we have put together a pair of Python programs for backing up and restoring BigQuery tables and datasets (*https://github.com/GoogleCloudPlat form/bigquery-oreilly-book/tree/master/blogs/bigquery_backup*). Get them from the GitHub repository of this book.

Loading and inserting data

We covered loading data into a destination table using bq load rather exhaustively in Chapter 4. For a refresher, see that chapter.

To insert rows into a table, write the rows as newline-delimited JSON and use bq insert:

```
bq insert ch05.rentals_last_hour data.json
```

In this example, the file data.json contains entries corresponding to the schema of the table being inserted into the following:

```
{"rental_id":"345ce4", "duration":240}
```

Extracting data

You can extract from a BigQuery table to one or more files on Cloud Storage by using bq extract:

```
bq extract --format=json ch05.bad_bikes gs://bad_bikes.json
```

Executing Queries

To execute a query, use bq query and specify the query:

```
bq query \
    --use_legacy_sql=false \
    'SELECT MAX(duration) FROM \
    `bigquery-public-data`.london_bicycles.cycle_hire'
```

You also can provide the query string via the standard input:

```
echo "SELECT MAX(duration) FROM \
`bigquery-public-data`.london_bicycles.cycle_hire" \
| bq query --use_legacy_sql=false
```

Providing the query in a single string and escaping quotes and so on can become quite cumbersome. For readability, use the ability of Bash to read a multiline string into a variable:[19]

```
#!/bin/bash
read -d '' QUERY_TEXT << EOF
```

---

19 See *05_devel/bq_query.sh* in the GitHub repository for this book.

```
SELECT
  start_station_name
  , AVG(duration) as duration
  , COUNT(duration) as num_trips
FROM \`bigquery-public-data\`.london_bicycles.cycle_hire
GROUP BY start_station_name
ORDER BY num_trips DESC
LIMIT 5
EOF
bq query --project_id=some_project --use_legacy_sql=false $QUERY_TEXT
```

In this code, we are reading into the variable QUERY_TEXT a multiline string that will be terminated by the word EOF. We can then pass that variable into bq query.

The preceding code is also an illustration of explicitly specifying the project that is to be billed for the query.

Remember to use --use_legacy_sql=false, because the default dialect used by bq is not the Standard SQL that we cover in this book!

Setting Flags in .bigqueryrc

If you tend to use the bq command-line tool interactively, it can be helpful to place common flags such as --location in $BIGQUERYRC/.bigqueryrc or in $HOME/.bigqueryrc if the environment variable $BIGQUERYRC is not defined. Here is an example of a .bigqueryrc file:

```
--location=EU
--project_id=some_project
[mk]
--expiration=3600
[query]
--use_legacy_sql=false
```

In this resource file, all BigQuery commands will be invoked with --location=EU and billed to some_project, whereas all bq mk will be invoked with --expiration=3600, and all bq query will be invoked with --use_legacy_sql=false. Explicitly specifying an --expiration on the command line will override the value from the resource file.

If you do have a BigQuery resource file, be aware that any scripts you write or invoke will work differently on machines where you have this resource file installed (typically development machines) versus machines where you don't have the resource file (typically production machines). This can lead to a great deal of confusion. In our experience, any gains in productivity caused by having the resource file are cancelled out by the increased debugging challenge when using the scripts on different machines. Your mileage may vary.

Previewing data

To preview a table, use bq `head`. Unlike a query of SELECT `*` followed by LIMIT, this is deterministic and doesn't incur BigQuery charges.

To view the first 10 rows, you can do the following:

```
bq head -n 10 ch05.bad_bikes
```

To view the next 10 rows, do this:

```
bq head -s 10 -n 10 ch05.bad_bikes
```

Note that the table is not actually ordered, and so you should treat this as a way to read an arbitrary set of rows.

Creating views

You can create views and materialized views from queries using bq `mk`. For example, this creates a view named `rental_duration` in the dataset ch05:

```
#!/bin/bash
read -d '' QUERY_TEXT << EOF
SELECT
  start_station_name
  , duration/60 AS duration_minutes
FROM \`bigquery-public-data\`.london_bicycles.cycle_hire
EOF
bq mk --view=$QUERY_TEXT ch05.rental_duration
```

Views in BigQuery can be queried just like tables, but they act like subqueries—querying a view will bring the full text of the view into the calling query. Materialized views save the query results of the view into a table that is then queried. BigQuery takes care of ensuring that the materialized view is up to date. We cover views and materialized views in more detail in Chapter 10. To create a materialized view, replace `--view` in the preceding snippet with `--materialized_view`.

BigQuery Objects

We looked at bq `ls --dataset` as a way to list the datasets in a project. As Table 5-3 demonstrates, there are other things you can list as well.

Table 5-3. Commands and subsequent lists

Command	What it lists
bq ls ch05	Tables in the dataset ch05
bq ls -p	All projects
bq ls -j some_project	All the jobs in the specified project
bq ls --dataset	All the datasets in the default project
bq ls --dataset some_project	All the datasets in the specified project

Command	What it lists
`bq ls --models`	Machine learning models

`bq ls --transfer_run \`
`    --filter='states:PENDING' \`
`    --run_attempt='LATEST' \`
`    projects/p/locations/l \`
`    /transferConfigs/c`
	Transfer runs filtered to show only pending ones

`bq ls --reservation_grant \`
`    --project_id=some_proj \`
`    --location='us'`
	Reservation grants for slots in the specified project

Showing details

Table 5-4 illustrates how you can look at the details of a BigQuery object using `bq show`.

Table 5-4. BigQuery commands and details shown

Command	Details of this object are shown
`bq show ch05`	The dataset `ch05`
`bq show -j some_job_id`	The specified job
`bq show --schema ch05.bad_bikes`	The schema of the table `ch05.bad_bikes`
`bq show --view ch05.some_view` `bq show --materialized_view ch05.some_view`	The specified view
`bq show --model ch05.some_model`	The specified model
`bq show --transfer_run \` `    projects/p/locations/l/transferConfigs/c/runs/r`	The transfer run

In particular, note that you can list jobs using `bq ls` and verify the status of jobs using `bq show`.

Updating

You can update the details of already created tables, datasets, and so on using `bq update`:

```
bq update --description "Bikes that need repair" ch05.bad_bikes
```

You can use `bq update` to update the query corresponding to a view or materialized view,

```
bq update \
    --view "SELECT ..."\
    ch05.rental_duration
```

and even the size of a reservation (we will look at slots and reservations in Chapter 6):

```
bq update --reservation --location=US \
          --project_id=some_project \
          --reservation_size=2000000000
```

Summary

In this chapter, we looked at three different forms of BigQuery client libraries:

- A REST API that can be accessed from programs written in any language that can communicate with a web server
- A Google API client that uses autogenerated language bindings in many programming languages
- A custom-built BigQuery client library that provides a convenient way to access BigQuery from a number of popular programming languages

Of these, the recommended approach is to use the BigQuery client library, provided one is available for your language of choice. If a BigQuery client library doesn't exist, use the Google API client. Only if you are working in an environment in which even the API client is not available should you interact with the REST API directly.

There are a couple of higher-level abstractions available that make programming against BigQuery easy in two commonly used environments: Jupyter notebooks and shell scripts. We delved into the support for BigQuery from Jupyter and pandas and illustrated how the combination of these tools provides a powerful and extensible environment for sophisticated data science workflows. We also touched on integration with R and with G Suite and covered many of the capabilities of the bq command-line tool. Finally, we covered Bash scripting with BigQuery.

Architecture of BigQuery

BigQuery aspires to scale to your datasets and run as fast as your business requires. The experience should seem like magic. The problem with things that appear to be "magic" is that when you encounter a problem, you don't know how to even begin fixing it.

This chapter delves into the inner workings of BigQuery. We cover its high-level architecture and the Dremel query engine and provide details on the storage metadata. We cover the details on how BigQuery handles security, availability, and disaster recovery in Chapter 10. At best, this chapter might just satisfy your curiosity. However, in case something doesn't behave the way you expect it to, this chapter can help you to understand more about what is actually going on and how you can fix or work around the problem.

High-Level Architecture

BigQuery is a large-scale distributed system with hundreds of thousands of execution tasks in dozens of interrelated microservices in several availability zones across every Google Cloud region. This section presents a simplified view of how the high-level pieces fit together. Describing all of the components in detail might require its own book, and we'd lose most of our readers by the time we got past the storage transcoder, and the rest would drop out long before we got to the stubby proxy (yes, that's a real thing, and no, it isn't as weird as it sounds).

Life of a Query Request

To understand how BigQuery is put together, let's step through what happens when you send a query request. We won't go into actual query execution yet; we save that for a later section. Instead, we'll just walk through the high-level components.

Figure 6-1 shows the simplified control flow when running a query. We discuss the detailed responsibilities of each block on the diagram later in the chapter.

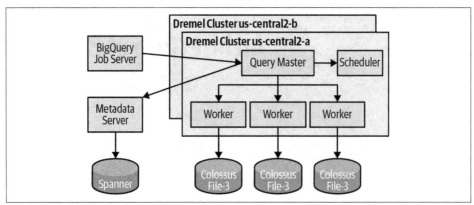

Figure 6-1. The simplified path that a query request takes through the BigQuery system

To begin, let's see what happens when you run the simplest of SQL queries: SELECT 17. This query doesn't even need to read any data; it just returns a single value.

Step 1: HTTP POST

The client sends an HTTP POST request to the BigQuery endpoint. Usually that request is wrapped up in a library or in a Java Database Connectivity (JDBC) driver, but at the basic level, anyone can run a query using curl or any other tool that lets you send raw HTTP requests (see Chapter 5).

Here is what the query request looks like on the wire:

```
POST /bigquery/v2/projects/bigquery-e2e/jobs HTTP/1.1
User-Agent: curl/7.30.0
Host: www.googleapis.com
Accept: */*
Authorization: Bearer <redacted>
Content-Type: application/json
Content-Length: 126
{'configuration': {'query': {'query': 'SELECT 17'}}}
```

There are a few important parts here: the first is the HTTP verb, which in this case is POST, because we're going to be modifying state by creating a query job. The second is the Authorization token. This is an OAuth2 token that identifies you. The last part is the JSON payload, which indicates that we're running a query, and the query text is SELECT 17. As you might imagine, there are lots of other options that you can send; check out the BigQuery API documentation (*https://cloud.google.com/bigquery/docs/reference/rest/*) to find out more.

Figure 6-2 shows a more detailed version of the path that this request takes through the system; the next few sections explore what each stage in the request does and why it is necessary.

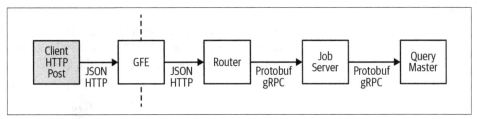

Figure 6-2. The detailed path a query request takes to start a query

Step 2: Routing

The HTTP POST request is routed through the magic of the internet[1] to the REST endpoint *http://www.googleapis.com/bigquery/v2/projects/bigquery-e2e/jobs*. This address is served by a Google Front-End (GFE) server, the same type of server that services Google Search and other Google products. In this case, the GFE needs to find the BigQuery backend that can service your request.

BigQuery is a global service. How does it know which region to route the request to? There are a number of hints that determine where to send the request. Part of the URL indicates which cloud project is responsible for paying for the request. Some cloud projects are set up with restrictions on where they are allowed to run queries. If your organization has configured your project to run only in Australia, your query will be routed to Australia. Some other projects are tied to a flat-rate reservation. If you have a reservation in a particular location, the request will be sent there.

If you don't have a reservation and you haven't specified which region to run in as part of the job name, the router must parse the query to determine what datasets are involved. Datasets are tied to locations, so BigQuery looks up the region of the dataset in order to route to that region. If you are extremely performance conscious or you want to control the location of the output results, you can specify the region to which you want to route the query as part of the query request by filling in the job reference field.

In our query example, however, we didn't provide the router any help at all, and there were no datasets involved. In this case, the router falls back to sending the request to the US.

The router transforms the JSON HTTP request to Protocol Buffers (*https://develop ers.google.com/protocol-buffers/*) (Protobufs), which is the platform- and language-

---

1 Many enterprise customers use direct peering so that the request never goes to the public internet.

neutral serialization format used for communication between virtually all Google services.

Step 3: Job Server

The BigQuery Job Server is responsible for keeping track of the state of a request. Because the network connection between the client and BigQuery server is considered fallible and some queries can take minutes or even hours to run, the Job Server is designed to operate asynchronously.

The Job Server performs authorization to ensure that the caller is allowed to run a query that is billed to the enclosing project of the job. This is important to prevent someone from being able to run up a bill on your account. Authorization of the actual tables is deferred until the query starts.

The Job Server is in charge of dispatching the request to the correct query server. Each project generally has a primary and a secondary availability zone. If the primary zone is not available, queries are routed to the secondary.

Project and Data Rebalancing

In BigQuery, any two tables in the same region can be joined together as long as the user has access to both tables. This provides a challenge for the backend, because if the two tables aren't located in the same physical location, running the query will be slow and costly (to Google, not the user) because it will need to move a lot of data over the network.

In the background, BigQuery continually solves a complex optimization problem: how to make sure that all tables that are joined together end up close to one another. Moreover, it also must understand the capacity of various compute and storage clusters, network topology, availability zones, and where the data currently exists.

If the background rebalancer decides that a project needs to move, it will start replicating the data to another availability zone or even another region (in the event the data is stored in a multiregional location—if you're storing data in a single-region location, it will never get moved anywhere else). In this way, data is always joinable, and clusters with finite capacity do not run out of room despite large increases in usage.

When backup or failover processes happen infrequently, they often don't work as expected when they're actually needed. A solution is to trigger such failover processes routinely, so that they can be counted on to be reliable. BigQuery triggers a *drain*, or failover, of a compute cluster on the order of once per week, in one region or another. Drains can happen for a number of different reasons, like a network switch failure, degradation of a dependent service, or unusually high queue length.

When a query computation cluster (i.e., zone) is drained, all projects that use it transition to their secondary clusters. Replication state is carefully tracked, so any newly loaded or rebalanced data that has not yet arrived in the secondary cluster will be read from any other location in which it can be found. In the rare event that no live copies of the data can be found, BigQuery will report an error rather than query over missing data.

Step 4: Query engine

Query execution is described in a later section, so we just go over the high-level parts here. Queries are routed to a Query Master, which is responsible for overall query execution. The Query Master contacts the metadata server to establish where the physical data resides and how it is partitioned. Partition pruning happens at this stage, so if the query doesn't read all of the partitions, only the metadata of the active partitions will be returned.

After the query server knows how much data is involved in the query and has a chance to put together a preliminary query plan, the Query Master requests slots from the scheduler. A slot is a thread of execution on a query worker shard; it generally represents half of a CPU core and about 1 GB of RAM. This amount is somewhat fuzzy, because slots can grow or shrink if they need more or fewer resources and as computers in a Google datacenter are upgraded.

The scheduler decides how to farm out work among the query shards. A request for slots returns the addresses of the shards that will run the query. The Query Master then sends the query request to each of the Dremel shards in parallel. See "Query Execution" on page 199 for more details on how query execution works.

Step 5: Returning the query results

After the query worker shards finish executing the query, the results are split into two parts. The first page or so of results is stored in Spanner (*https://ai.google/research/pubs/pub39966*), a distributed relational database, along with the query metadata. The Spanner data is located in the same region in which the query is running. The remaining data is written to Colossus,[2] Google's distributed filesystem. Queries that have small results do not need to touch the disk at all, so their results can be returned very quickly.

The BigQuery API is designed to be reconnectable. That is, it is designed to be able to run synchronously in the best case, but if it times out, the calling client should be able to reconnect. To make this possible, before timing out, the Job Server will return a job

---

2 See *https://cloud.google.com/files/storage_architecture_and_challenges.pdf*. Colossus is available to Google Cloud customers as Google Cloud Storage (see *https://cloud.google.com/storage/*).

ID to the client, and the client can look up that job to get the results. The BigQuery clients bq.py (the cloud client libraries) and the Open Database Connectivity (ODBC)/JDBC drivers encapsulate this protocol, so end users can reliably get query results.

BigQuery results are stored for 24 hours; they are functionally equivalent to a table and can be queried as if they were a table. Results are limited to 10 GB for normal SELECT queries. If you want to write more data than this, you can use CREATE TABLE AS SELECT or INSERT statements, which have no size limits.

BigQuery Upgrades

BigQuery can do in-place upgrades without any downtime. In fact, upgrades happen all the time, usually at least once per week. Upgrades are usually rolled out slowly over several days, starting with a single zone in a single region on the first day and then increasing in reach each subsequent day. The goal is to be able to catch any problems with as small of a "blast radius" as possible.

BigQuery can even update without failing queries. To start an upgrade, a portion of the shards are drained of work (i.e., they stop accepting new work). These shards are then upgraded in place. Shards are designed to be highly failure tolerant and generally cause no more than a small hiccup in the runtime of queries that they are running. As Query Masters complete their queries, they can also be upgraded. Because the failure of a Query Master can cause queries to restart, they take a long time to drain.

Job Servers can be updated fairly easily because they maintain their state in Spanner; when they restart, they can pick up where they left off. Finally, routers have very little state, so they can be updated almost at will. Schedulers have a single master per Dremel cluster, so to update them, their standbys are first updated, and then they go into failover mode.

Query Engine (Dremel)

Dremel was created in 2006 by an engineer who built a query engine because he grew tired of waiting for his MapReduce jobs to finish. Dremel became very popular in Google; at one point, 80% of Google employees were active users of Dremel, directly or indirectly.

The initial topology of Dremel was tree structured. Queries would enter at the root, branch out, and be sent to the leaves, which each operated on part of the query. Results and aggregations flowed back up the tree to the root. Even though Dremel no longer uses a fixed-tree structure, Dremel clusters are still often referred to as "trees."

This query can be simply computed via an execution tree:

```
SELECT
  COUNT(*)
    , start_station_name
FROM
  `bigquery-public-data`.london_bicycles.cycle_hire
GROUP BY 2
ORDER BY 1 DESC
LIMIT 10
```

The query does a simple scan and aggregate. The scan can be done at the leaves, the aggregation can be done higher up the tree, and the final combination at the root. If you didn't follow that, don't worry; we describe in detail how this actually works.

In 2010, Dremel architecture changed to build execution plans dynamically rather than have a single static topology. Although a tree works great for certain types of queries, namely scan-filter-aggregate queries like the one just shown, it does poorly on more complicated queries. If your query needs to do a JOIN operation or has nested subqueries, it will need multiple passes through the tree. Moreover, each pass through the tree operates over differently sized data and thus will need to scale differently.

For an example of a query that cannot be processed by a simple static tree, look at the following:

```
SELECT
  COUNT(*)
    , starts.start_station_id as point_a
    , ends.start_station_id as point_b
FROM
 `bigquery-public-data`.london_bicycles.cycle_hire starts,
 `bigquery-public-data`.london_bicycles.cycle_hire ends
WHERE
  starts.start_station_id = ends.end_station_id
  AND ends.start_station_id = starts.end_station_id
  AND starts.start_station_id <> ends.start_station_id
  AND starts.start_date = ends.start_date
GROUP BY 2, 3
ORDER BY 1 DESC
LIMIT 10
```

This query finds the London bike share stations that have the most trips going back and forth between them during a single day. Because this query does a join, it requires additional layers in the execution tree.

The current Dremel architecture, called Dremel X (because this is the 10th version), builds a dynamic query plan that can be any number of levels and can even change the plan while the query is running. Figure 6-3 shows the simplified control flow of a query in Dremel X. Note that although execution might still look like a tree, because of the shuffle step between each query stage, any number of levels can be added.

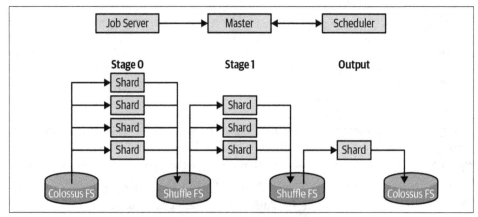

Figure 6-3. Dremel X data flow for a query with two execution stages and one output stage

Dremel Architecture

The query engine has three parts: the Query Master, the Scheduler, and the Worker Shard. The Query Master is responsible for query planning (determining what work to do), the Scheduler is responsible for assigning slots (identifying who is available to do the work), and the Worker Shards are responsible for executing the query (doing the work). This section goes into each of these three components in more detail.

Query Master

The Query Master is responsible for running the query. The first thing that it does is parse the query in order to extract two pieces of information: the tables involved in the query and the filters applied to each table. The Query Master then looks up the table metadata from the metadata server, which returns the file locations for the tables.

The filters are needed in order to do partition pruning. In BigQuery, if you partition a table by a column and then filter by that column, you can avoid scanning any data outside the filter. The other data is "pruned" away. To prune the partitions, all of the filters are passed to the metadata server when doing the request; the partition filters can be pushed all the way down to the underlying metadata database so that it returns only file locations for the partitions that match the filter.

One of the files returned by the metadata server is special: it is the meta-file. This meta-file shows locations of files within the table and how they map to field values. To extract this information, the Query Master runs another Dremel query against just the meta-file.

After the Query Master looks up the file information, it knows how much work is involved in running the query. This is important, because to schedule the query, the scheduler needs to know how many slots it needs to schedule.

Before the Query Master can schedule the query, however, it still needs to do one important thing: create a query plan. Query plans are dynamic in BigQuery, but the query starts with an initial plan that describes how the query can run; plans generally start simple and become more complex as needed. The query plan divides the query into stages, with each stage performing a set of operations. If you look at the execution details in the BigQuery web user interface (UI), shown in Figure 6-4, you can see an example query plan.

Figure 6-4. The query plan in the BigQuery web UI

After creating an initial query plan, the Query Master contacts the Scheduler to find some slots in which to run the query. The Scheduler allocates Worker Shards and returns their addresses to the Query Master. The Query Master then sends units of work (generally one file at a time) to the shards. Execution is done in parallel to the limit of slots returned by the Scheduler. If there aren't enough slots available, the Query Master will wait until some of the Worker Shards finish their current work and then ask the Scheduler for more. The Scheduler can increase or decrease the slots allocated to the query at any time.

After the Worker Shards begin to complete, the Query Master will go back to the Scheduler and ask for slots to run the second and subsequent stages of the query. When the final stage is done, the Query Master returns to the Job Server.

Scheduler

The BigQuery Scheduler is responsible for assigning *slots* to queries. A slot is a unit of work that generally corresponds to the processing of a single file (read stages) or *shuffle sink* for later stages. A shuffle sink is a temporary storage location for intermediate query results. A slot is a thread of execution on the Worker Shards. Many slots can be run in a single Worker Shard task.

A single query can use as few as one slot or millions of slots, depending on the amount of data it needs to process and how the data is laid out physically. A query that processes a petabyte of data might use 10 million total slots. Obviously, not all 10 million slots can be run at once, so the Scheduler will assign as many slots as is feasible, and the remaining slots will still be pending. If you look at the execution graph from a large query (Figure 6-5), you can see the pending slots are activated over time. The number of input units is the number of schedulable slots. The number of slots in use is the height of the "active" portion of the graph.

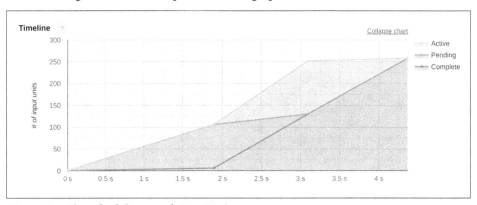

Figure 6-5. Slot scheduling graph in a BigQuery query

The Scheduler is the arbiter of who is allotted resources. As of this writing, an on-demand BigQuery user can use up to 2,000 slots just by running a query. However, these resources are not guaranteed; if not enough slots are available to give everyone who needs slots up to their 2,000 maximum, the Scheduler will reduce all on-demand users' slot allocation proportionally. Suppose that the on-demand pool is 100,000 slots and all slots are already being used by 50 different users. If a new user wants to run a query that needs 2,000 slots, the slot allocation for each of the existing users will be reduced by 39 slots (2,000/51) so that the new user can have the same 1,961 slots as everyone else.

The Scheduler is "fair" among users of the same priority, and among queries from the same project. If I run a query that uses 2,000 slots, and then run a second query while the first one is running, the first query will lose half of its slots, and each of my queries will continue with 1,000 slots. If the project's slots are reduced to 1,900 because of overall load on the system, each of those queries will then be allotted 950 slots instead.

The Scheduler can cancel running slots at any time to make way for a user with higher priority or to ensure fairness. Each unit of work in BigQuery is atomic and idempotent, so it can start, get killed, and run again. This property also helps when Worker Shards crash; if the Worker Shard doesn't respond fast enough, the work that is being done is simply rescheduled somewhere else, and the query proceeds normally, but perhaps it takes an extra few hundred milliseconds to complete. If, for some reason, more than one Worker Shard finishes the same work, the results from the shard that finishes second are discarded.

Some users of BigQuery purchase "reserved" slots. This means that they have right of first refusal for those slots. Those users are guaranteed to have that many slots whenever they need them. They pay a flat fee for access to those slots, and they can run as many (or as few) queries as they want using those slots. If they run queries that use more slots than are available in the reservation, portions of those queries are queued until resources become available.

A flat-rate user can divide their reservation into sub-reservations, and assign one or more projects to each of those sub-reservations. For instance, if you purchase 5,000 slots, you might decide to allocate project A to a sub-reservation for "BI," whereas you might assign project B to a sub-reservation for "ETL." Note that BI and ETL don't mean anything to BigQuery; they're merely designations that indicate to people at your organization what you use them for. You might decide to give 4,000 slots to BI because you want BI to handle lots of concurrent querying, and then give the remaining 1,000 slots to ETL. When all of the slots are in use, the BI users are limited to those 4,000 slots, whereas the ETL users are limited to 1,000 slots. If the current BI workloads are using up only 2,000 slots, the ETL users can use up the remaining 3,000 slots (and vice versa).

Worker Shard

The Worker Shard is responsible, not surprisingly, for actually getting the work done in a query. A Worker Shard is a task running in Borg,[3] Google's container management system that allows Dremel to run many thousands of parallel tasks in containers without having to worry about management of hardware or infrastructure. The Worker Shard itself is capable of running multiple tasks in parallel; each of these tasks represents a schedulable unit, which is the aforementioned slot.

---

3 See *https://ai.google/research/pubs/pub43438*. Borg was the inspiration behind Kubernetes, which is offered on Google Cloud via Kubernetes Engine (see *https://cloud.google.com/kubernetes-engine/*).

The Worker Shard exposes a Remote Procedure Call (RPC) interface to run a small portion of one stage of a query. The RPC interface instructs the Worker Shard as to exactly which part of the query to run and on which data. If you look at the execution plan in the BigQuery UI (Figure 6-4), you can see the SQL snippet that is executed on the shard. Most of that snippet will look like normal SQL, but the source and destination tables might not look familiar, especially if you look at a stage in the middle of a query.

The sources of a query are either files on Colossus representing the tables being queried or outputs of previous stages. In general, one input file is assigned to a single thread of execution (slot), and the Worker Shard does the portion of the query requested and then writes the result to the destination location.

The destination location is usually an in-memory filesystem. The exception is when the query requires writing out a lot of data and this is the final stage; in such a case, the destination will be Colossus. The in-memory filesystem provides short-term durable storage between stages of the query and allows the query to perform a shuffle between stages.

Shuffle

Shuffle is an important part of any distributed processing system. In the case of Big-Query, Shuffle allows data-dependent dataflows between stages by fanning out the data to a number of *sinks*. For example, Shuffle might write everything beginning with "A" to sink 1, and everything beginning with "B" to sink 2. Then, in the next stage, a single Worker Shard could read from sink 1 and know that it had access to all of the data that begins with "A," whereas a different Worker Shard could read from sink 2 and know it had access to all of the data that begins with "B."

The number of shards involved in a stage is largely dependent on the number of shuffle sinks that were written. So how many shuffle sinks should you use? This is somewhat of a black-magic step; BigQuery will dynamically change the number of shuffle sinks during a query depending on the size and shape of the output, as shown in Figure 6-6. This dynamic behavior is good for ensuring that queries can make forward progress and never run out of memory. That said, the better that BigQuery estimates sink count correctly at the outset, the faster the query will run.

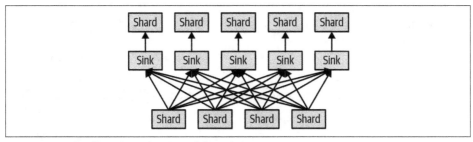

Figure 6-6. Shuffling four shards to five sinks

The in-memory filesystem is limited in size; if a query shuffles too much data in a single stage, it will begin to spill to disk. The latency of memory is several orders of magnitude faster than the latency of a disk. Any time the query needs to write shuffle results to disk, it can degrade performance pretty severely. You can recognize when a query had a shuffle that spilled to disk by looking at the query statistics in the query plan after the query completes, as depicted in Figure 6-7. Note that this is one area where there is significant development being done, so the penalty for spilling to disk will diminish over time. You can work around this problem by sharding the query into two (or more) queries and processing different ranges of the data in each one and then combining the results.

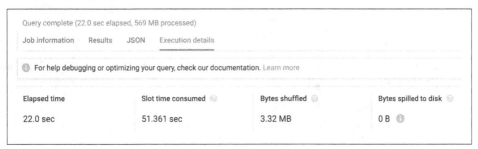

Figure 6-7. The "Execution details" window showing bytes shuffled and bytes spilled to disk

Query Execution

Now that we've introduced the components of the Dremel query engine, let's discuss how they coordinate to run a query. We'll begin with a very simple query and work our way to more complex ones.

Scan-filter-count query

The simplest useful query is a scan-filter-count query—that is, a query that reads a table, applies a filter, and then counts the results. Here is an example:

```
SELECT COUNT(*) as c
FROM `bigquery-public-data`.new_york_taxi_trips.tlc_yellow_trips_2017
WHERE passenger_count > 5
```

This query computes the number of Yellow Cab trips in New York City in 2017 for which the passenger count was more than five. When the query completes, we can click the "Execution details" tab to show the query plan, as illustrated in Figure 6-8.

Figure 6-8. *The query plan for a scan-filter-count query*

The execution plan tells us a lot, but we'll leave that for Chapter 7, in which we look at execution plans in more detail.

Notice in Figure 6-8 that there are two execution stages: S00 and S01. The first is input; this is a read phase, which reads from Colossus. The second is output, which is responsible for combining the final results and returning them to the user.

The Query Master looks at how much data is involved in the query and divides it into chunks (generally corresponding to a file). In this case, there are nine files. The Query Master then asks the scheduler for nine slots. Because nine slots are available, the scheduler returns information about nine different Worker Shards. Armed with this information, the Query Master sends requests to all nine Worker Shards in parallel.

How Do We Know How Many Slots Were Used?

When an input stage does a full aggregation (returning only one row), the number of total output rows in the stage is equal to the number of inputs to that stage. When the number of inputs is large, it will be larger than the number of schedulable slots. Therefore, assuming that each input gets its own slot won't be accurate (note that row count doesn't have any direct correspondence to the number of inputs). But for a

---

small query like this, there were almost certainly at least nine slots available, so we can see that the query used nine slots. To confirm this, you can examine the information from the query statistics via the bq command-line tool:

```
bq --format=prettyjson show -j <my_job_id> \
    | grep completedParallelInputs
```

This results in the following:

```
"completedParallelInputs": "9",
"completedParallelInputs": "1",
```

This confirms that the first stage had nine parallel inputs and that the second had one.

Note that you can also see when more slots would improve performance because you'll see a high wait time. If you're spending time waiting for slots, more slots will reduce the wait time and make your query run faster.

After the Worker Shards receive the request, stage 0 begins.

Stage 0.   In stage 0, each Worker Shard will need to read a file and retain only cab rides with more than five passengers. It then just needs to count up how many taxi rides are left. Because we're computing the results in parallel, each shard doesn't have enough information to compute the total result; it needs to send its partial result to the next stage.

If we expand the first stage, S00, as shown in Figure 6-9, we can see the work that was done.

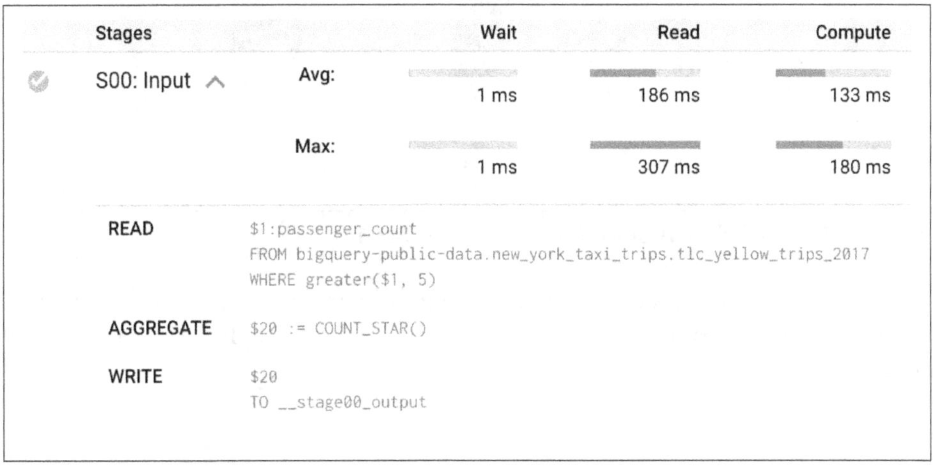

Stages		Wait	Read	Compute
⊘ S00: Input ⌃	Avg:	1 ms	186 ms	133 ms
	Max:	1 ms	307 ms	180 ms
READ	$1:passenger_count FROM bigquery-public-data.new_york_taxi_trips.tlc_yellow_trips_2017 WHERE greater($1, 5)			
AGGREGATE	$20 := COUNT_STAR()			
WRITE	$20 TO __stage00_output			

Figure 6-9. Work done in the first stage of a scan-filter-count query

The first two parts make sense; reading passenger count from the table, applying a filter, and then counting the results. The last part says "write the results to the `stage_00` output." This is an in-memory location that will be picked up in subsequent stages. `COUNT_STAR()` is an internal operator that counts the number of rows.

After computing these partial results and writing them to the designated output area, each shard returns to the Query Master.

Post–stage 0. After the first Worker Shard from stage 0 returns to the Query Master, the Query Master can schedule stage 1. This involves another round trip to the scheduler to request more slots; in this case, only a single slot is necessary because it will need only to compute the sum of nine values. The next step can start before stage 0 completes because it will keep reading from the output of `stage_00` until the file is closed. But in this case, it doesn't help much given that stage 1 doesn't have much work to do.

Stage 1. Stage 1's job is really simple; read nine inputs and compute the sum, as depicted in Figure 6-10.

	S01: Output ∧	Avg:				
				1 ms		0 ms
		Max:				
				1 ms		0 ms
	READ	$20				
		FROM __stage00_output				
	AGGREGATE	$10 := SUM_OF_COUNTS($20)				
	WRITE	$10				
		TO __stage01_output				

Figure 6-10. Work done in stage 1 of a scan-filter-count query

This is why stage 1 takes only one millisecond to complete. After stage 1 computes those nine values, reading from the in-memory file, it writes the results to the final output.

After stage 1 completes, the Query Master reads the result from the stage 1 output and returns it to the Job Server. The query has been completed, and the user is now one step closer to finding out that more than three million taxi rides carried more than five passengers in 2017.

After the Query Master returns to the Job Server, the Job Server can return the results to the client. Because the results are small, they are written to Spanner so that the client can retrieve them at will.

Scan-filter-aggregate query

The next most simple type of query is a scan-filter-aggregate query. This type of query can be executed in a single pass over the data. To show what happens at larger scale, we'll use a new table that contains one billion page-view logs from Wikipedia. Note that if you run these queries yourself, it might become expensive, so you probably just want to follow along here in the book as we show you. Here's the first query we run:

```
SELECT title, COUNT(title) as c
FROM `bigquery-samples.wikipedia_benchmark.Wiki1B`
WHERE title LIKE "G%o%o%g%l%e"
GROUP BY title
ORDER BY c DESC
```

This finds pages that have the letters "G," "o," "o," "g," "l," and "e," in that order, counts the number of views for each page, and returns them in order of popularity:

Row	title	c
1	Google	2904
2	Google_Chrome	1302
3	Google_Wave	623
4	Google_Translate	561
5	Google_AdSense	426

Stage 0. The first stage of this query sends the query to lots of parallel Worker Shards, each of which reads the title column and filters out things that don't match. It then does a partial aggregation. Figure 6-11 shows what the execution plan looks like.

Stages		Wait	Read	Compute	Write		Rows
S00: Input ∧	Avg:	1869 ms	1931 ms	2211 ms	8 ms	Input:	1,249,541,131
	Max:	2556 ms	3716 ms	2837 ms	219 ms	Output:	28,693

READ	`$1:title`
	`FROM bigquery-samples.wikipedia_benchmark.Wiki1B`
	`WHERE like($1, 'G%o%o%g%l%e')`

AGGREGATE	`GROUP BY $30 := $1` `$20 := COUNT($1)`

WRITE	`$30, $20`
	`TO __stage00_output`
	`BY HASH($30)`

Figure 6-11. Work done in the first stage of a scan-filter-aggregate query

The READ stage reads the title field (no other fields are needed) and applies the filter. The AGGREGATE step counts all the records per title (only the ones that make it through the filter). Note that the count isn't the total count: it is just the count of the number of times the title shows up in the current file being read.

The WRITE stage writes to `__stage00_output`, like the previous query, but this time it does something different: it adds a `BY HASH` directive, which instructs it to shuffle by the value. Shuffle is used to send the results to different buckets. These buckets are shared among Worker Shards, so all the shards that encounter a particular value will send their results to the same bucket. In this case we're shuffling by the title field, which means that every time "Google" shows up, it will go to the same bucket, and when "Goodnight Seattle" shows up, it will go to a different bucket. This routing is key to being able to compute the global results at scale.

What's a Hash?

The term *hash* comes up a lot when describing how BigQuery works. Although this term is generally familiar to computer scientists, it isn't as common elsewhere. Hashing is a technique that divides an unknown data distribution into a fixed number of buckets. If you think about trying to run a parallel distributed system, hashing would come in handy because it helps you to divide the work among the parallel Worker Shards. One of the key properties of a hash function is that things that are equal have the same hash and always end up in the same bucket.

Suppose that you have the property sales records for all of the houses in Seattle and you want to find out which houses sold most frequently in the past decade. This is a lot of work to compute on your own, so let's further suppose that you recruit nine of your friends to help you. You can begin by dividing up the records by year among you and your friends, each of you reading a year's worth of data and keeping track of how often the houses you saw had been sold.

But how do you combine records? Note that you can't just all share the most frequently sold houses that you see, because a house that was sold every year would show up only once for each of you, but it might be the one you're looking for. Meanwhile, a house that was sold three times in one year might never be sold again. Clearly combining is tricky. A hash function can come to the rescue.

You need to establish a way to divide the houses among yourselves, not just the source data. So every time the building at 601 N. 34th Street was sold, the same person looks at it. Then that person can just report their top sold houses and ignore all of the others.

To solve the distribution problem, we can apply a hash function to the address. The hash function we'll use here is a simple one: just add the digits in the address, and take the final digit. So 931 Crockett Avenue would add to 13, and taking the final digit, we'd have "3." 2444 Second Avenue would add to 14, and taking the final digit, we'd have "4." Thus, each of the 10 friends would pick a number from zero to nine, and they'd be assigned the houses that hash to that number. If we had another person join us to help out and needed 11 buckets instead of 10, we could have divided the number by 11 and taken the remainder (this is effectively what taking the last digit does, with 10 buckets). This operation is called *modulus*, which is a fancy name for dividing and taking the remainder.

Because some queries could have billions or trillions of different values (and you'll see this in the next query), instead of creating one bucket per value, we apply a mathematical hash function to the values (this is what BY HASH means) and use the output as the bucket name. This means that the same input value will always get the same output value, which is important so that we can process the results on a single Worker Shard. It also means that multiple different input values can be placed into the same bucket, which reduces the number of unique buckets.

The "rows" column in the query details shown in Figure 6-11 has some other interesting information. Unlike the previous query, we can't see how many slots are being used because each Worker Shard produces more than one row of output. The number of output rows is one row per each unique value seen, per Worker Shard. So if each Worker Shard sees 100 distinct values and there were 200 shards, this number would be 20,000 (100 * 200). In our case, the product of the slots used and values was 28,693.

Stage 1. The next stage reads from the shuffled output of stage 0 and does the final aggregation. Figure 6-12 presents the relevant part of the query details.

Figure 6-12. Work done in stage 1 of a scan-filter-aggregate query

Because the input data has been shuffled by the thing we are counting, we can do the final aggregation in parallel. That is, because all of the partial counts for titles matching "Google" were sent to the same bucket, we can compute the total count for "Google" by just reading values from the "Google" bucket. Another Worker Shard can compute the total for "Google_Chrome" by reading the "Google_Chrome" bucket.

There are 5,115 output rows, which is the number of total rows. We didn't apply a limit, so they all must be returned to the user.

Stage 2. Stage 2 is extremely simple: it just reads the 5,115 values and sorts them, as illustrated in Figure 6-13.

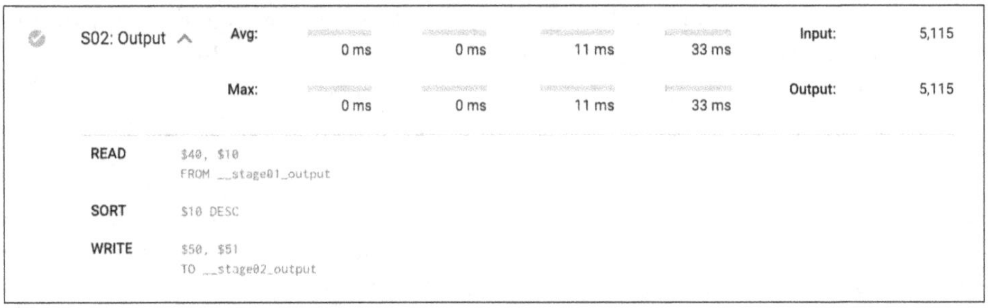

Figure 6-13. Work done in stage 2 of a scan-filter-aggregate query

The sort operation is done on a single Worker Shard unless there are very large numbers of values, in which case a distributed sort algorithm is used.

Scan-filter-aggregate query with high cardinality

What would happen if you tried to run the same query but didn't apply a filter? There are millions of different titles (the cardinality of the title column is high), so if we choose a number that is too small for the number of buckets to hash the values into, this could mean that a small number of Worker Shards would need to do a lot of work, and the query would take a long time.

Let's try running the same query again but without filtering by title; we're going to return data on all of the Wikipedia pages in descending order of popularity:

```
SELECT title, COUNT(title) as c
FROM `bigquery-samples.wikipedia_benchmark.Wiki1B`
GROUP BY title
ORDER BY c DESC
```

This query takes significantly longer, because it needs to compute a lot more counts, can't prefilter any data, and needs to return more than 280 million rows.

There are now 15 stages in the query details (0–9, A–E).

Stage 0. Stage 0 is identical to the previous case, except there is no filter, so it outputs 1,205,625,714 values. Stages 1 through 8 are new, though. Figure 6-14 shows what stage 1 looks like.

Figure 6-14. Work done in stage 1 of a scan-filter-aggregate query with high cardinality involves a repartition

The workers in stage 1 read from an input and then they don't write anything. What's happening is that the hash buckets are becoming too big, and they're being split. In essence, it means that BigQuery has picked a number of hash buckets that are too small, and then it needs to reshuffle the data into a larger number of buckets. This will allow later stages to avoid getting bogged down.

Distributed sort. We also see something new in stages B and C (these stages have a letter in their name because they are inserted into the original query plan after stage 0 due to the reshuffle), as demonstrated in Figure 6-15.

| | SOB: Compute ^ | Avg: | | | 1 ms | 0 ms | 658 ms | 7 ms | Input: | 280,512,407 |
| | | Max: | | | 3 ms | 0 ms | 953 ms | 43 ms | Output: | 5,384 |

READ $40, $10
FROM __stage09_output

WRITE $10
TO __stage0B_output

| | SOC: Sort+ ^ | Avg: | | | 6 ms | 0 ms | 11 ms | 5 ms | Input: | 5,384 |
| | | Max: | | | 6 ms | 0 ms | 11 ms | 5 ms | Output: | 1 |

READ $10
FROM __stage0B_output

AGGREGATE $57 := ARRAY_AGG($56)

SORT $10 DESC

Figure 6-15. Work done in stages B and C of a scan-filter-aggregate query with high cardinality

Remember, this query is going to return 280 million rows in sorted order. 280 million values are too many to sort on a single node.

Imagine someone has pulled out all of the pages of the dictionary, and you and a group of friends are tasked with reassembling them in sorted order. One way to do this is to give each person a range of letters to start with. Maybe you take A through C, and the next person takes D through G, and so on. Then you each could sift through the pages and pick only the pages that begin with a letter in your range. After everyone has collected their pages, you could each sort your small pile and then recombine at the end. This is one way to do a distributed sort.

The problem, however, is that you might not know the distribution of pages in advance. If one person got just the letter "X," they wouldn't have much work to do, because there are so few words that begin with that letter.

Stage B is computing the distribution, or *split points* for performing a distributed sort. We're sorting by page views (the computed count value). Based on the amount of data, a parallelization is picked (e.g., the number of "friends" who are going to help). In this case, we have 5,384 different Worker Shards (look on the second row, last column of Figure 6-15). BigQuery scans through the data and computes a rough approximation of where 1/5,384th of the data would be and then outputs those values. Stage C just takes those values and puts them into an array in a single row so that they can be used later.

Stage D is actually going to split the data; that's the equivalent of the friends searching through the pages, looking for things that match the range they are looking for. We read the split points from stage C, and then the final tallies from stage 9 (we skipped describing stage 9 because it looks like stages we've seen before). These final tally values are written to 5,384 buckets (note you can't see this here) that map to a range of the counts, as illustrated in Figure 6-16.

Figure 6-16. Work done in stage D of a scan-filter-aggregate query with high cardinality

Stage E is the one that finally writes the output. It does the distributed sort and writes the final results. Because each worker has already gathered the values that map to a nonoverlapping range, they can just sort the values locally and then emit them. The final results will be in different files, and the files will need to be read in a particular order that maps to the sort order of the overall results, as shown in Figure 6-17.

Figure 6-17. Work done in stage E of a scan-filter-aggregate query with high cardinality

Broadcast JOIN query

So far, the queries we've looked at have just operated on a single table. But what about joins? There are two types of joins in BigQuery; *broadcast* and *hash*. We've already seen some use of hashing for aggregation, but let's begin with broadcast joins, because they are simpler. Broadcast joins can be used when one of the tables is small: about 150 MB or less, as of this writing.

Broadcast joins take the small table and send the entire table to every worker. If there are 100 workers processing the larger table, the entire small table is sent to each of those 100 workers. This is a bit of a brute-force way to do the join, but the advantage is that it can be done with just a single pass through the large table and doesn't require a shuffle.

To see how this works, think about how joins operate. They use a key to match up rows in two or more tables, and they need to look at all of the matching values on both sides. This means that when key "123" shows up in the left side of the join, you need to match it with all of the rows corresponding to "123" on the right side of the join (or, if there are no rows, you need to know that, too). To do this matching, you need to get the rows from the left for a particular key in the same place as the rows from the right matching a key. Broadcast join does this by just sending one of the tables everywhere, so everything is colocated.

For this example, we use the GitHub sample dataset, which contains information about all GitHub commits in the history of that service. We use two tables that we join: the commits table, which contains information about every commit operation, and the languages table, which has information about the programming languages that are being used.

The query that we look at will pick out the GitHub contributions of the book's authors and rank them by numbers of bytes of code written in the repository per language. The query is as follows:

```
WITH
repo_commits AS (
  SELECT repos AS repo_name, author.name AS author
  FROM `bigquery-public-data.github_repos.commits` c, c.repo_name repos
  WHERE author.name IN ("Valliappa Lakshmanan", "Jordan Tigani")
  GROUP BY repos, author),
repo_languages AS (
  SELECT lang.name AS lang, lang.bytes AS lang_bytes, repos.repo_name AS repo_name
  FROM `bigquery-public-data.github_repos.languages` repos, repos.LANGUAGE AS lang
)

SELECT lang, author, SUM(lang_bytes) AS total_bytes
FROM repo_languages
JOIN repo_commits USING (repo_name)
GROUP BY lang, author
ORDER BY total_bytes DESC
```

The result is similar to the following:[4]

---

4 Jordan: For those who are interested in keeping score but don't want to run the query, Lak has a lot more bytes in GitHub than me. Lak: This is due primarily to the flatulent storage format of Jupyter Notebooks.

Row	lang	author	total_bytes
1	Jupyter Notebook	Valliappa Lakshmanan	78900202
2	Python	Valliappa Lakshmanan	33742613
	...		
8	Jupyter Notebook	Jordan Tigani	153243
9	Python	Jordan Tigani	134409
	...		

This query uses some reasonably advanced query techniques, such as flattening arrays via CROSS JOIN and WITH statements to make the query easier to read (see Chapter 8). The key part of the query is this:

```
SELECT lang, author, SUM(lang_bytes) AS total_bytes
FROM repo_languages
JOIN repo_commits USING (repo_name)
GROUP BY lang, author
ORDER BY total_bytes DESC
```

This part of the query joins the language table against the commits table on the repository name field.

If you look at the query plan for this query, it is mostly things we've already seen, with two new types of stages: *coalesce* and *join+*. The coalesce stage is very simple, as is evident in Figure 6-18.

	S03: Coalesce	^	Avg:					Input:	37
				1 ms	0 ms	5 ms	50 ms		
			Max:					Output:	37
				4 ms	0 ms	8 ms	59 ms		
	READ	FROM __stage01_output							

Figure 6-18. Coalesce stage of a broadcast join query

Coalesce is a dynamic stage that is added when BigQuery detects that one of the tables in a join is going to be small. The reason it is necessary is because we want to get all of the data for the table into a single node so that we can broadcast it. But previous stages might have taken a large table and filtered it down, turning it into a small table (as in the case with our query, when we filtered by commits by this book's authors). Coalesce doesn't change the number of rows; it just shuffles them into the same location.

The other new stage is the join+, illustrated in Figure 6-19.

S04: Join+ ∧	Avg:					Input:	3,348,733
		1 ms	935 ms	3400 ms	155 ms		
	Max:					Output:	17
		1 ms	935 ms	3400 ms	155 ms		

READ	`$1:repo_name, $2:language.name, $3:language.bytes`
	`FROM bigquery-public-data.github_repos.languages`
READ	`$70, $71`
	`FROM __stage03_output`
AGGREGATE	`GROUP BY $90 := $80, $91 := $82`
	`$30 := SUM($81)`
JOIN	`INNER HASH JOIN EACH WITH ALL ON $1 = $70`
WRITE	`$91, $30, $90`
	`TO __stage04_output`
	`BY HASH($90, $91)`

Figure 6-19. Join+ stage of a broadcast join query

This stage is called `join+` instead of `join` because it does a JOIN and an AGGRE-GATE all in one step. We see two READ statements, one to read for the left of the join and the other for the right. The left, in this case, is the languages table. The right is the coalesced broadcast table from the previous stage. As of this writing, the only way to identify a broadcast join is from the text "EACH WITH ALL". This means taking each row of the table on the left of the join and matching it with "ALL"—that is, the entire table on the right.

Hash join query

The second type of common join is a hash join. This, in general, is much more computationally expensive. Hash joins work by hashing both sides of the join so that rows containing the same keys end up in the same bucket. This is the same hash process that we saw in the aggregation queries, but we do it for both tables. Because the hash process routes all equivalent values to the same bucket, it means that a single worker can pick up each bucket and have all the information it needs to perform the join of the keys in the bucket.

To demonstrate the hash join, we use the same query as earlier, but we comment out the filter expression so that it will join the tables, in their entirety, against each other. Both tables will be too large to fit into memory, so we need to use a hash join instead of a broadcast join. Here is the updated query:

```
WITH
repo_commits AS (
  SELECT repos AS repo_name, author.name AS author
  FROM `bigquery-public-data.github_repos.commits` c, c.repo_name repos
  -- WHERE author.name IN ("Valliappa Lakshmanan", "Jordan Tigani")
  GROUP BY repos, author),
repo_languages AS (
  SELECT lang.name AS lang, lang.bytes AS lang_bytes, repos.repo_name AS repo_name
```

```
    FROM `bigquery-public-data.github_repos.languages` repos, repos.LANGUAGE AS lang
)

SELECT lang, author, SUM(lang_bytes) AS total_bytes
FROM repo_languages
JOIN repo_commits USING (repo_name)
GROUP BY lang, author
ORDER BY total_bytes DESC
LIMIT 100
```

The result is similar to the following:

Row	lang	author	total_bytes
1	C	Eric Dumazet	2917514359851
2	C	Russell King	2878666474184
3	C	Thomas Gleixner	2876903624978

The query plan for this query looks nearly identical to that of the broadcast join. There is no coalesce stage, and there are a couple more repartitioning stages while the query engine hones in on the number of buckets that it needs. There is also a subtle difference in the join+ stage, as shown in Figure 6-20.

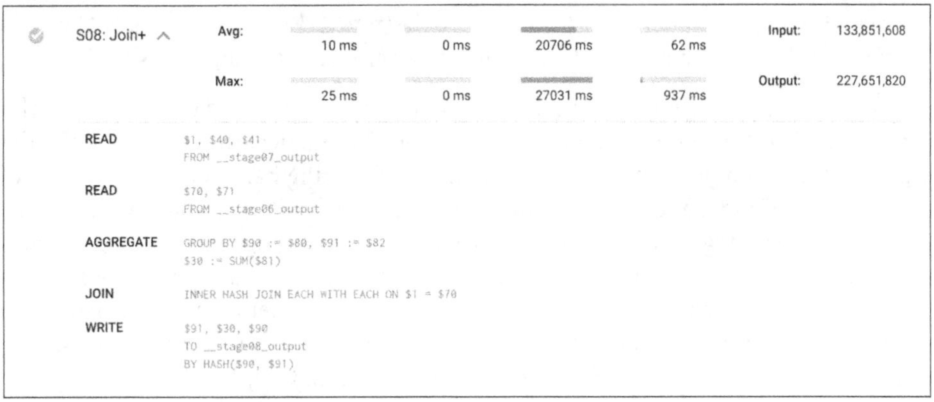

Figure 6-20. Join+ stage of a hash join query

Here we see that we're doing EACH WITH EACH, instead of EACH WITH ALL. This means that each row on the left is joined with each matching row on the right, which requires them to be previously colocated. If we look at the previous stages, we also see that the inputs were HASH shuffled, as discussed earlier in the section on scan-filter-aggregate queries.

Storage

One of the secrets to the success of any database management system is efficient storage. Many of the key features that allow BigQuery to be fast are derived from how it stores data. From the underlying storage hardware (using a massive distributed filesystem) to the file format (a custom column store), BigQuery's storage stack, which comprises both the metadata and the storage data, is optimized for speed of analysis.

Storage Data

BigQuery stores exabytes of data, distributed across millions of physical disks in dozens of regions. The primary goal of the lower layer storage system is to make all of this distributed data fast to access and ensure that any two tables can be joined against each other, which means they need to reside in the same place.

One of the secrets of large-scale analytics is that the biggest gains in performance can be realized through improvements in the storage system. This section describes how the BigQuery storage system works and what makes it fast.

When you load data to BigQuery, it's written to Capacitor files and stored on Colossus. Colossus encodes the data using *erasure encoding*, which means that it stays durable even if a large number of disks fail or are destroyed. Writing to a single Colossus cluster is sufficient to make the data durable to a very large number of 9's.[5]

However, to ensure the data is both durable and available, the data is replicated to another availability zone within the same region. In practice, this means a different building that has a different power system and networking hardware. The chances of multiple availability zones going offline at once is very small. But what happens if the entire metro area region is destroyed—perhaps by a rampaging Godzilla or, less probable than that, an earthquake or other natural disaster? If you use multiregional BigQuery locations (such as US or EU), BigQuery stores another copy of the data in an off-region replica; that way, the data is recoverable in the event of a major disaster. We discuss availability and disaster recovery in more detail in Chapter 10.

Physical storage: Colossus

BigQuery stores all of its data on Colossus, which we've mentioned is the distributed storage system used throughout Google. Colossus is an evolution of Google File System (GFS), which was a pioneering large-scale distributed storage system developed at Google. Colossus solves a number of scalability, flexibility, and reliability problems in GFS by creating a more flexible metadata system and getting rid of single points of failure.

---

5 That is, to a 99.999…% reliability.

Colossus operates a large number of disks in a large number of servers that combine to form the filesystem. If you have tens or hundreds of thousands of disks, dozens of those disks are going to fail every day. However, the goal is to not lose any data, ever (or at least within a few million years). The way to avoid losing any data when disks die is to write the data multiple times. When this is done in Colossus, it is called *encoding*.

The simplest type of encoding is called *replicated encoding*. In replicated encoding (see Figure 6-21), you just write more than one copy of the data. How many copies do you need? That depends on how safe you want to be. With two copies, you can lose data if the wrong two disks fail. Three copies are generally considered to be safe, as long as there is a good replacement policy. The chances of all three disks dying on the same day is something like once in 100 million years. Distributed storage reliability is determined by the rate at which things fail and the rate at which broken things are replaced. It is difficult to control how often things fail; but it is a lot easier to develop a process to replace things quickly. If you can replace disks quickly, you will expect to lose particular data once every 10 billion years or so. Of course, life is more complicated, and there are lots of disks, and you want to make sure that it is exceedingly rare that you lose data.

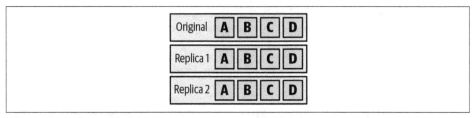

Figure 6-21. Replicated encoding, in which chunks of files are stored three times

Replicating files is expensive, however, because you need to store full copies of the data. To store less data, many distributed filesystems use something called *erasure encoding* or *Reed-Solomon encoding*. Erasure encoding stores mathematical functions of the data on other disks to trade off complexity for space, as illustrated in Figure 6-22. Depending on how you encode the data, you can achieve far better durability than replicated encoding, but store less than one full additional copy. There is a penalty, though, which is that if the primary copy isn't available, you might need to read a number of additional disks to recover the data.

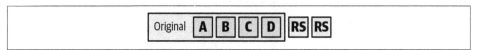

Figure 6-22. Erasure encoding, in which extra "encoded" data can be used to recover data in the event of a failure of any of the original chunks of data

BigQuery stores most data with erasure encoding and uses enough recovery blocks to make it orders of magnitude more durable than three-way replicated encoding. Replicated encoding is generally faster to read than erasure encoding. For replicated encoding, if you don't hear back from the first replica in a short amount of time, you can send a read request to one of the other copies. For erasure encoding, if you can't read from the primary copy, you can start a recovery read, but that can take several additional reads. If one of those is slow, you can recover the other chunks, but that again requires more reads.

Storage encoding has a major impact on BigQuery performance because tail latency is important. Disks die all the time; chances are, within BigQuery at any point in time, there are several failed disks, so reading from tables on them will require recovery reads. Note that there are several mechanisms that Colossus employs to minimize the slowdowns caused by recovery reads, such as caching the recovered data. Many Big-Query queries involve reading from hundreds of thousands of files or more; this means that every query will hit the long tail of latency from Colossus. It is a good thing that Colossus is so fast.

Storage format: Capacitor

The format in which data is stored is as important as the way the physical bytes are stored. BigQuery chose to create its own columnar storage format: Capacitor.

What Is a Column Store?

Traditionally, databases have stored data in row-oriented format; that is, they store one record after another in the file. If you have a number of records and you want to store them in a file, row-oriented is the most obvious way to do it. Row-oriented files have some nice properties, in that if they are fixed length, you can skip ahead by just adding a known offset. Record-oriented files are also convenient when you're reading an entire row at a time.

Figure 6-23 shows a record-oriented store; rows are written to the file one at a time.

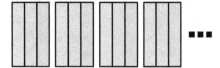

Figure 6-23. A record-oriented store with three columns

However, most queries don't actually read an entire row at once; they often read only a few columns per table. If you have a row-oriented file, you must read the entire row, even if you need only a single column. Moreover, row-oriented files generally aren't very compressible; if you want to reduce the amount of data that you want to read on

---

disk, one great way to do this is to compress it. Compression works by encoding repeated data in a smaller way. However, there is usually very little repeated data across a row. Imagine a table with "Customer Name," "Country," "Phone Number," and "Customer ID." A row in this table will have very little redundant information. A phone number doesn't tell you much about a country, and even less about a customer ID.

But what if you turned the problem 90 degrees? Instead of storing a *row at a time*, what if you stored a *column at a time*? A column containing country names might have only a few distinct values, and most of those might be the same. Customer IDs might all begin with "0000." And phone numbers will have common prefixes.

Figure 6-24 demonstrates a column-oriented store; each column is written to a different stream in the file.

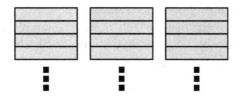

Figure 6-24. A columnar store with three columns

If you store columns separately, you also gain when you want to read only a few columns in a query; if there are 100 columns in the table, and you read only three, you thus need to read only 3% of the data. Most queries read a small fraction of the columns in the table, so reading a column at a time can dramatically improve performance.

One of the reasons that column stores didn't take off before distributed filesystems is the physical layout on disk. If you're reading two columns in a query, you need to iterate through those columns in sequence. To read in lockstep, you need to instruct the disk to read the first few rows of column A and then seek to where column B is stored to read the first few rows there, and then seek back to column A to read the next few rows. Seeks are expensive, and they thwart the common read-ahead algorithms used by disk hardware and operating systems.

A distributed filesystem helps a lot here; it generally will read in larger stripes and also enable you to read from multiple stripes in parallel because they're stored on different disks. For example, if you want to read column A and column G, you can fire off a read for column A, which will read from one disk, and then column G, which will read from a different disk, in parallel.

Capacitor is the second generation of format used within BigQuery; the first was a basic column store. Capacitor built on top of what was learned in the eight years of running a distributed query engine over exabytes of data. The format has evolved with the query engine, which helps improve performance even more—deep knowledge of the format can be embedded in the query engine, and vice versa. Consequently, Capacitor contains features and optimizations learned from a decade or so of operating very large-scale analysis systems at Google.

Parquet and Optimized Row Columnar (ORC) are two popular open source columnar storage formats; however, BigQuery chose not to use these under the hood. The reasons are not just the "Not Invented Here" syndrome; when Capacitor was created, Parquet was in its infancy and ORC had not been popularized. Moreover, there are a number of optimizations that tie the Capacitor storage format to BigQuery's Dremel query engine, and it is advantageous to be able to iterate quickly on the storage format and add features quickly.

One of the key features of Capacitor is *dictionary encoding*. That is, for fields that have relatively small cardinality (few distinct values), it stores a dictionary in the file header. For example, suppose that the table contains songs played by a jukebox; there is a reasonably small number of songs that can be played. The dictionary might look like the representation shown in Figure 6-25.

Dictionary

0	Hey Jude
1	Michelle
2	Here Comes the Sun

Figure 6-25. Dictionary encoding in Capacitor

Instead of storing the full title, Capacitor can just store the offset into the dictionary, which is much more compact. It would look like Figure 6-26, where the first column is the encoded song title, and the second column is another data field (perhaps the customer who requested that the song be played).

Data

0	xc*
1	c8!
1	8ec
0	7h!
2	a7c
1	c-%

Figure 6-26. Two columns in Capacitor, the first of which is dictionary encoded

There is another advantage to dictionary encoding that comes when you filter. Suppose that you were looking for rows in which the song titles contain the word "Sun."

This is a relatively expensive filter because it needs to be able to find the value anywhere in the string.

Normally, you'd compare each row of the table looking for values that matched the predicate. In Capacitor, however, we can just test the predicates against the dictionary and create a truth table with the results, as depicted in Figure 6-27.

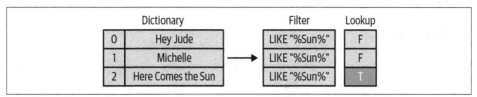

Figure 6-27. Dictionary encoding makes filters more efficient

Now, the lookup table is an array in which the values indicate whether the predicate is true. When scanning all of the rows, we can just index into the lookup table. For instance, if the encoded value was "1," we would look up the value at offset 1 in the lookup table and see that the predicate evaluates to false; on the other hand, "2" evaluates to true, so that's a row we'd want to keep.

To further save on space, Capacitor does *run-length encoding*. That is, if the value "2" appears five times in a row, rather than storing "2,2,2,2,2", you can store "2:5". For long runs of the same value, this can give significant compression.

But what if the rows are ordered such that there are no long runs of the same value multiple times? To solve this, Capacitor employs a clever trick—it simply reorders the rows to obtain a compact encoding. Rows in BigQuery are not ordered, and there is no guarantee or even expectation of which rows come after which other rows. Figure 6-28 illustrates an example.

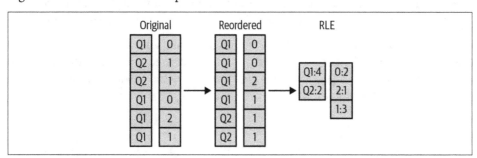

Figure 6-28. BigQuery reorders rows to obtain compact run-length encoding

Because computing the best ordering is an NP-hard problem,[6] BigQuery applies a set of heuristics that gives good compaction but runs in a short amount of time.

These examples are just two ways that Capacitor helps BigQuery improve performance.

Metadata

Metadata is data about the data that is stored. This makes it "meta." Metadata includes entities like schema, field sizes, statistics, and the locations of the physical data. Managing metadata effectively is almost as important as managing the physical data itself. In fact, many of the limits that BigQuery imposes, like the number of tables that can be referenced in a query or the number of fields that a table can have, are due to limits in the metadata system.

BigQuery table metadata has three layers, only two of which are directly visible to the user. The outer layer is the dataset, which is a collection of tables, models, routines, and so on with a single set of access control permissions (more on this in Chapter 10). The next layer is the table, which contains the schema and key statistics. The inner layer is the storage set, which contains data about how the data is physically stored. Storage sets are not a user-visible concept, and information about them is hidden from the user.

Storage sets

A storage set is an atomic unit of data, created in response to a load job, streaming extraction, or Data Manipulation Language (DML) query. Storage sets enable updates to BigQuery tables to be ACID compliant; that is, they are Atomic (they happen all at once or not at all), Consistent (after they commit, they are available everywhere), Idempotent (you don't need to worry about multiple commits if there is an error or a network partition), and Durable (after it is committed, the commit won't be lost).

The underlying physical storage for BigQuery is immutable. After a file is closed, it can never be changed again. Storage sets are likewise immutable; after they are committed, they are never changed again. Figure 6-29 illustrates what a table with three storage sets would look like.

---

6 An NP problem in computer science is a problem for which one can efficiently verify that a solution is correct, but finding the solution cannot be done efficiently. Computing the best ordering is an NP problem because you can efficiently determine whether a list is sorted or not—you need to traverse the list just once—but finding the best ordering belongs to a class of problems that are called NP-hard. If you discover a fast algorithm to solve any one NP-hard problem, this means that there will be fast algorithms to solve all NP-hard problems because they are, in some sense, equivalent. In practice, NP-hard problems are handled through heuristics because finding the single correct solution would be too inefficient.

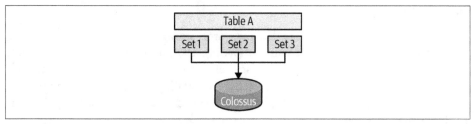

Figure 6-29. A table with three storage sets

Storage sets generally go through a life cycle during which they first are created in PENDING state, progress to COMMITTED, and finally move to GARBAGE. A PENDING storage set has data being actively written to it, and the data in that storage set is never visible to a user through any mechanism. After the data has been fully written, it progresses to COMMITTED, which makes it visible to queries against the table. When a storage set is no longer needed, it is marked GARBAGE, which means that it can be garbage collected after the requisite waiting period has elapsed.

Time travel

As of this writing, BigQuery supports time travel for seven days in the past, which means that you can read the state of the table at any point within that time window. This can be useful if you accidentally deleted something via DML or if you want to be able to run a repeatable query over a table that is changing.

To enable time travel, BigQuery keeps track of the timestamp at which storage set transitions happen. If you time travel back to before a storage set was committed, the storage set will be removed from consideration. If a storage set is marked GARBAGE and you time travel back to when it was COMMITTED, it will be revived in the context of that query.

Figure 6-30 shows a table with three storage sets, committed at times T1, T2, and T3, respectively. If you want to read the table at some time between T2 and T3, you will need only the first two storage sets.

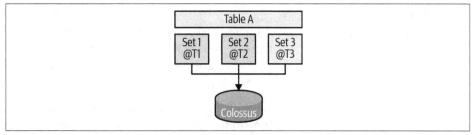

Figure 6-30. A table with three storage sets, committed at times T1, T2, and T3

Storage optimization

When you are writing or updating data over time, storage can often become fragmented. For example, suppose that you are loading 100 kb of data every two minutes. Each one of those 100 kb will get a storage set and its own file. After a month, you'll have 2 TB of data, which isn't a whole lot, but 21,000 files and storage sets can become inefficient for querying because BigQuery will spend a lot of time opening files and reading storage set metadata.

The storage optimizer helps arrange data into the optimal shape for querying. It does this by periodically rewriting files. Files can be written first in a format that is fast to write (write-optimized storage) and later in a format that is fast to query (read-optimized storage). The storage system can be said to be *generational*, meaning that data is written into multiple generations, each one being older and more optimized.

Figure 6-31 shows a table with the first generation of data being optimized and rewritten to Generation 1.

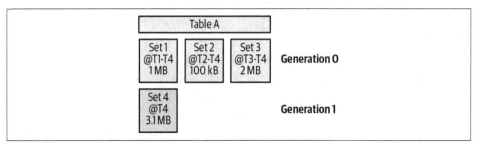

Figure 6-31. Generation 0 of data being optimized and rewritten to Generation 1

The optimized storage set (Set 4) contains the exact same data from Sets 1, 2, and 3. When Set 4 commits, it marks the first three storage sets as garbage but doesn't remove them immediately. This fact is important for time travel because users might want to read the table as of a time when only the earlier storage sets were around; thus, BigQuery needs to keep track of that metadata.

Partitioning

Partitioning in BigQuery allows you to divide large logical tables into smaller partitions and query over only the parts that you need. Say, for example, that you want to query only the data from May 3, 2019; if you have your table partitioned by date, you can efficiently read just that data using the partitioned table.

Under the hood, a partition is essentially a lightweight table. Data for one partition is stored in a physically separate location from other partitions, and partitions have a full set of metadata. This lets you treat partitions as if they were tables for a lot of cases. For example, you can call the REST API endpoint for `tables.delete()` on a partition to delete it. If you set a partition expiration duration, it will cause date-based partitions to expire after a certain period of time, as if they were tables.

Partitions have an advantage over multiple tables in that you can efficiently query across them. For example, if you query over a date range, you can use a normal filter over the date field and scan only the data that you need. This makes it easier to manage than lots of logical tables and allows more efficient access. Partition filters can generally be pushed down to the metadata database layer (Spanner) so that it can save on reading unnecessary metadata, not just unnecessary data.

Partitions are designed for low-cardinality (i.e., low number of distinct values) fields —generally, less than a few thousand. If you overpartition your tables, you will create a lot of metadata. Although this doesn't hurt cases for which you filter by a small number of partitions, if you ever need to read the entire table, it will be inefficient because you need to read all of the metadata. If you need higher cardinality, you should use clustering. One way of reducing the number of partitions is to create coarser-grained partitions, such as monthly partitions. You can do this by creating a separate field that truncates the event date to the month level and partitions by that field.

To represent partitions in the metadata, BigQuery uses storage sets that are marked with the partition ID. This makes it easy to filter based on partitions; to read only the partition matching a certain date, BigQuery can apply the filter at the metadata layer without even needing to open the physical data. Storage sets also have field size information, which is how a dry run can determine how much data would be scanned without actually running a query.

Figure 6-32 shows our table with three storage sets. Each storage set in this case represents a different partition.

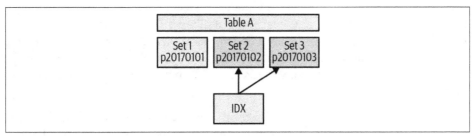

Figure 6-32. Three storage sets representing three different partitions

Suppose that the partitioning field is `eventDate` and we were running a query that included the filter `WHERE eventDate >= '20170102'`. This should match only the two storage sets `20170102` and `20170103`. There is a Spanner database index (IDX in Figure 6-32) that helps us find only the storage sets within that range. This means that we consider the table to contain only those two storage sets for the purpose of the query, which means the query will scan less data and usually run faster.

Clustering

Clustering is a feature that stores the data in semisorted format based on a key that is built up from columns in your data. Data files get nonoverlapping ranges of the key space. This allows for efficient lookups and range scans because the query engine needs to open only files that have the key, and it can do a binary search to find the files at the beginning and end of the range.

Figure 6-33 shows how you can use clustering.

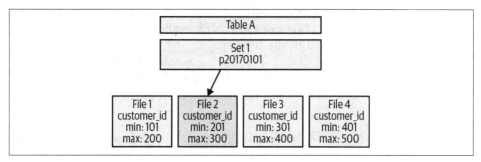

Figure 6-33. A storage set with clustering based on the `customer_id` *field*

The table is clustered by the `customer_id` field, and the data in the files is sorted such that files have nonoverlapping ranges for `customer_id`. File 1 has customer IDs 101 through 200, File 2 has customer IDs 201 through 300, and so on.

Suppose that the query to be executed is `SELECT … WHERE customer_id = 275`. Because we know the files are in ascending order of `customer_id`, we can just look at the file headers and realize that `customer_id` 275 is in File 2. We can do a binary search to find the starting file, and we don't need to look at other files after we have found the correct one, because the entire range we were looking for is in the same file. Because the table was clustered, we need to read only a single file instead of all of them.

The data files have headers that contain the `min` and `max` values of all of the field. Virtually all column stores have this feature (including open source ones like Parquet and ORC). The advantage here is that it allows you to check whether a value is in the table just by looking at the header. Moreover, the file headers are cached, so often the exact files needed can be determined without doing disk I/O at all.

When the data is sorted across files, each file has a narrow range of keys. For example, File 1 has values `aa-ac`, File 2 will have values `ad-ag`, File 3 has values `ah-ap`, and so on. if you wanted to find value `ae`, you would open up the header for File 1, see that the value you were looking for wasn't there, and then open File 2, where you would see that the value you were looking for was completely contained in that range. So you could use that file and wouldn't even need to look further. This means that the query engine needs to scan only one file; this will be faster and less expensive than scanning all of the files.

Note that the data is not sorted within the file, just across files. Data in Capacitor files (more on this shortly) is reordered to improve compression ratios, and sorting the data would make it slower to read. But sorting the data within the file wouldn't help much, because you'd end up having to read the same number of blocks from the disk.

Reclustering. The tricky part of clustering is maintaining the clusters when the data is changing. For the previous example, what if someone adds two rows with keys ab and ao? Those would go right in the ranges of File 1 and File 3, respectively. But files are immutable, and you probably don't want to create files with only a single row each. So BigQuery will write these two new rows in a single file in a new storage set. Now, when the table is being queried, both storage sets need to be inspected, and you'll end up having to do redundant work. If data is being changed over time, you'll end up with a lot of storage sets, and they can all have overlapping ranges. At some point, you'll essentially need to scan all of the files in order to find a single value.

The solution to this fragmentation is reclustering. Periodically, in the background, BigQuery will recluster tables. BigQuery maintains a *clustering ratio*, which is the fraction of the data that is completely clustered. If that fraction dips too low, it will rewrite the data in sorted format. This will be done in a new storage set, to preserve the ability to time travel back to previous table states. Reclustering happens automatically without any user intervention, and it happens using "system resources," not resources that users must pay for.

Figure 6-34 shows reclustering in action.

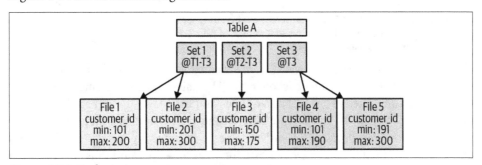

Figure 6-34. Reclustering creates a new storage set

There are two storage sets, and each one has an overlapping cluster range; the first storage set has two files ranging from key value 101 to 300. The second storage set, which committed at a later time (T2), has a smaller key range, from 150 to 175, but it overlaps with the files from Storage Set 1.

The reclustering event comes at T3, and it makes a copy of all of the data in files 1, 2, and 3 and then reclusters the data. It marks the earlier storage sets garbage as of T3 and commits the new copy at T3. After this completes, further queries will see the nicely clustered data in Storage Set 3.

Partitioning Versus Clustering

Partitioning can be thought of as dividing your table into a lot of subtables based on data in a column. Clustering, on the other hand, is like sorting your tables on a particular set of columns. The differences can be subtle, but clustering works better when you have a large number of distinct values. For example, if you have a million customers and often do queries that look up a single customer, clustering by customer ID will make those lookups very fast. If partitioned by `customer_id`, lookups would be fast, but the amount of metadata needed to keep track of all of the partitions would mean that queries across all users would slow down.

Partitioning is often used in conjunction with clustering; you can partition by the low-cardinality field (e.g., event date) and cluster by the high-cardinality one (e.g., customer ID). This lets you operate over a date-range slice of the table as if it were itself a table, but it also lets you find records from a particular customer without having to scan all of the data in the partition.

Performance optimizations with clustered tables.   Clustering also enables a number of query optimizations. For example, one optimization will push constraints across from one side of the join to another. Suppose that you're doing a query that looks like this:

```
SELECT orders.order_id
FROM retail.orders AS orders JOIN retail.customers
ON orders.customer_id = customers.customer_id
WHERE customers.customer_name = 'Jordan Tigani'
```

This will find all of the orders by a customer named "Jordan Tigani." Let's assume that the orders table is clustered by `customer_id`. The naive way to implement this would be to execute the filter of the customer tables and broadcast the remainder to every shard, and then scan the full orders table to find orders that had the matching customer ID. However, because the orders table is clustered by `customer_id`, we just need to look at the files that have the matching `customer_id`, and thus we don't need to scan the full table. This reduces cost and improves performance significantly.

Another thing to note is that clustering doesn't just work when you filter by the field that is clustered; it also works when you are filtering by fields that are correlated to the clustered fields. Imagine, for example, that you have your orders table clustered

---

by order_id, and orders are roughly in sequential order. If you do a query that filters by a narrow range of transaction dates, those transaction dates will be in a small number of files; BigQuery will need to scan only the files with those transaction dates, even though you're not filtering by order_id. This optimization doesn't just apply to performance; it also will reduce the cost of the query if you're operating in on-demand mode. In general, anything that BigQuery can do to reduce the amount of data that needs to be scanned will reduce cost when operating over clustered tables.

DML

DML is a set of special SQL statements that let you modify tables (see Chapter 8). They come in four flavors: INSERT, DELETE, UPDATE, and MERGE.

INSERT operations, which add rows to a table, are simple because they are basically the same as loading more data to the table. When an INSERT operation runs, files representing the new data are written to Colossus, and a new storage set is added to the metadata. The new storage set has a commit timestamp with the time the data was ingested.

DELETE operations, which remove rows from a table, are more complicated, however. BigQuery uses immutable files and metadata (storage sets). Suppose that you want to delete a single row (DELETE … WHERE customer_id = 1234), and furthermore, imagine that row existed in file C in Storage Set 3.

Because files are immutable in BigQuery, to delete a single row, it can't just delete the row from the middle of file C. Instead, BigQuery will make a copy of the file without the row; let's call this C2. BigQuery will then mark the old storage set GARBAGE because it isn't in use any more. The rewritten file will need a storage set, Storage Set 4. However, that won't be enough, because the new storage set will need to contain everything else that was in Storage Set 3. The new storage set will point at the old files from Storage Set 3, with the exception of file C, which had the now-deleted row. Figure 6-35 demonstrates how all of this would transpire.

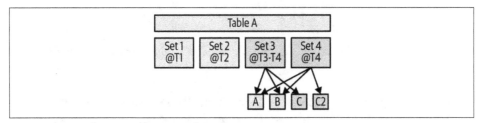

Figure 6-35. Delete operations involve creating an entire new storage set to point to a combination of files from the old storage set and new files without the deleted record

If this sounds like a lot of work to delete a single row, you're absolutely right. It is for this reason that the best practice is to batch your updates and apply as many of them as you can at once.

UPDATE is usually implemented as an atomic combination of an INSERT and a DELETE operation. That is, instead of actually modifying data, you delete the old records and add new ones. This allows the underlying files to be immutable and just changes which rows or files are live. MERGE is basically a very fancy UPDATE statement that lets you do a combination of read, modify, and write operations at the same time. Therefore, UPDATE and MERGE operations are very similar to a DELETE operation from an architecture standpoint; UPDATE will just write in new additional data that has the new value of the rows that were updated. Likewise, MERGE will write out more merged data.

Meta-File

One of the ways BigQuery can achieve good performance when doing partition pruning is via a meta-file. As we discussed earlier in the chapter, this is a file that contains metadata about all of the data files that make up the table. It contains minimum and maximum constraints for all fields as well as the location of each data file. This file is stored in the same format as the BigQuery data files, which means that it can be queried just like any other BigQuery file. This is important because it means that in order to determine which files need to be read, the query engine doesn't need to look at all of the file headers. It just reads this one file, and then it can pare down to the exact files that are actually needed in the query.

Figure 6-36 shows an example of a meta-file.

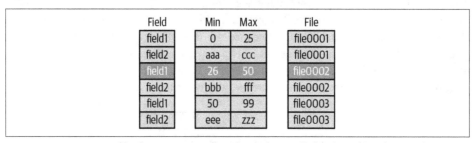

Figure 6-36. A meta-file that contains metadata about all the data files that make up a table

If we're querying from the table with the predicate WHERE field1 = 30, we can first send a query to this file and then send the result back that the only file we need is file0002. Armed with that information, we don't need to open any other files to satisfy the query.

Summary

In this chapter, we delved into the inner workings of BigQuery to demystify the service and provide the basis to understand what is happening when your query is being executed.

Starting with high-level architecture, we followed the life of a query from the time the query is received by the GFE server and routed to the appropriate BigQuery Job Server and handled by the Dremel query server. We examined the stages of different types of queries from the simplest scan-filter-count query to more complex scan-filter-aggregate queries, even those with high cardinalities that might require repartitions. We also explored the two ways in which joins are implemented—broadcast joins for small tables and hash joins for larger ones—and how to recognize from the query plan which join mechanism is being used.

We also discussed the way data is stored, the advantages of BigQuery's columnar format, dictionary encoding, and how the use of storage sets makes time travel possible. Finally, we looked at how partitioning and clustering are implemented, and why they improve query performance.

Optimizing Performance and Cost

Performance tuning of BigQuery is usually carried out because we want to reduce query execution times or cost, or both. In this chapter, we look at a number of performance optimizations that might work for your use case.

Principles of Performance

Donald Knuth, the legendary computer scientist, made the famous observation that premature optimization is the root of all evil. Yet Knuth's full quote is more balanced:[1]

> We *should* forget about small efficiencies, say about 97% of the time: premature optimization is the root of all evil. Yet we should not pass up our opportunities in that critical 3%. A good programmer will not be lulled into complacency by such reasoning, he will be wise to look carefully at the critical code; but only *after* that code has been identified.

Following Knuth, we would like to caution that performance tuning should be carried out only at the end of the development stage, and only if it is observed that typical queries take too long. It is far better to have flexible table schema and elegant, readable, and maintainable queries than to obfuscate your table layouts and queries in search of a tiny bit of added performance. However, there will be instances for which you do need to improve the performance of your queries, perhaps because they are carried out so often that small improvements are meaningful. Another aspect to consider is that knowledge of performance trade-offs can help you in deciding between alternative designs.

---

1 This quote is from his 1974 article "Structured Programming with go to Statements." You can download a PDF of the article from *http://citeseerx.ist.psu.edu/viewdoc/summary?doi=10.1.1.103.6084*.

Key Drivers of Performance

In this chapter, we do two things. In the first part, we show you how to measure the performance of queries so that you can identify the critical, optimizable parts of your program. Then we draw on the experience of BigQuery users and our knowledge of BigQuery's architecture to identify the types of things that tend to fall into Knuth's critical 3%. This way, we can design table schema and queries with an awareness of where performance bottlenecks are likely to occur, thereby helping us make optimal choices during the design phase.

To optimize the performance of queries in BigQuery, it helps to understand the key drivers of query speed, which is the focus of the second part of this chapter. The time taken for a query to complete depends on how much data is read from storage, how that data is organized, how many stages your query requires, how parallelizable those stages are, how much data is processed at each stage, and how computationally expensive each of the stages is.

In general, a simple query that reads three columns will take 50% more time than a query that reads only two columns, because the three-column query needs to read 50% more data.[2] A query that requires a group-by will tend to be slower than a query that doesn't, because the group-by operation adds an extra stage to the query.

Controlling Cost

The cost of a query depends on your pricing plan. There are two types of BigQuery pricing plans. The first type is on-demand pricing, in which your employer pays ours (Google) based on the amount of data processed by your queries. If you are on a flat-rate plan, your business gets a certain number of *slots*[3] (e.g., 500 slots), and you can run as many queries you want without incurring any additional costs.

In an on-demand (per query) pricing plan, the cost of a query is proportional to the amount of data processed by the query. To reduce cost in an on-demand pricing model, your queries should process less data. In general, reducing the amount of data scanned will also improve query speed. The third part of this chapter—optimizing how data is stored and accessed—should be of help there.

---

2 The difference can be difficult to measure precisely because BigQuery is a service, and network overhead to reach the service and the load on the service tends to vary. You might need to run the query many times to get a good estimate of the speed.

3 A slot is a unit of computational capacity required to execute SQL queries. BigQuery automatically calculates how many slots are required by each query. See Chapter 6 for more details.

If you are using a flat-rate reservation, the net cost of your query is quite aligned with the time taken for the query to complete.[4] You can indirectly reduce costs in a flat-rate model by hogging the slot reservations for less time—that is, by increasing your query speeds, as discussed in the second part of this chapter.

Estimating per-query cost

If you are on an on-demand pricing plan, you can obtain a cost estimate for a query before submitting it to the service. The BigQuery web user interface (UI) validates queries and provides an estimate of the amount of data that will be processed. You can see the number of bytes the query will process before you run the query by clicking the Query Validator. If you are using the bq command-line client, specify --dry_run to take a look at the query plan and the amount of data processed before invoking the query for real. Dry runs are free. Knowing the amount of data that will be processed by the query, you can use the Google Cloud Platform (GCP) Pricing Calculator (*https://cloud.google.com/products/calculator/*) to estimate the cost of the query in dollars. Tools such as BigQuery Mate (*https://oreil.ly/dGMCK*) and super-Query (*https://web.superquery.io*) provide a price estimate directly but might not have access to information about negotiated discounts. As of this writing, the cost is five dollars per terabyte (for US and EU multiregions) after the free tier usage of one free terabyte per month is exceeded. Note that BigQuery needs to read only the columns that are referenced in your queries, and partitioning and clustering can further reduce the amount of data that needs to be scanned (and hence the cost).

 To experiment with BigQuery, you can use the BigQuery sandbox. This is subject to the same limits as the free tier (10 GB of active storage and 1 TB of processed query data per month), but you can access it without a credit card being required.[5]

When invoking a query, you can specify the --maximum_bytes_billed parameter to put a limit on the amount of data that a query can process. If the bytes scanned in the query exceeds the maximum bytes that can be billed, the query will fail without incurring a charge. You can also manage costs by requesting a custom quota from the GCP Cloud Console (*https://console.cloud.google.com/iam-admin/quotas*) for a limit on the amount of query data processed per day. You can set this limit at a per-project or per-user level.

---

4 Nonparallelizable operations might not add to the cost, because the remaining slots can presumably address other workloads.

5 See *https://cloud.google.com/bigquery/docs/sandbox* for further details.

Finding the most expensive queries

When trying to control costs, it can be helpful to create a short list of queries to focus on. You can do this by querying the INFORMATION_SCHEMA associated with a project to find the most expensive queries:

```
SELECT
    job_id
    , query
    , user_email
    , total_bytes_processed
    , total_slot_ms
FROM `some-project`.INFORMATION_SCHEMA.JOBS_BY_PROJECT
WHERE EXTRACT(YEAR FROM creation_time) = 2019
ORDER BY total_bytes_processed DESC
LIMIT 5
```

The preceding query lists the five most expensive queries in 2019 in some project based on total_bytes_processed. If you are on flat-rate pricing, you might choose to order the queries based on total_slot_ms instead.

Measuring and Troubleshooting

To tune the performance of queries, it is important to ascertain all of the following aspects of a query so that you know what to focus on:

- How much data is read from storage and how that data is organized
- How many stages your query requires and how parallelizable those stages are
- How much data is processed at each stage and how computationally expensive each stage is

As you can see, each of these requires one aspect that can be measured (e.g., how much data is read) and something that needs to be understood (e.g., the performance implications of how that data is organized).

In this section, we look at how we can measure the performance of a query, peruse BigQuery logs, and examine query explanations. Having done this, we can use our understanding of BigQuery architecture (Chapter 6) and performance characteristics (later sections in this chapter) to potentially improve performance. In the later sections of this chapter, we present queries and their performance characteristics without spelling out the measurement steps that might lead you to apply those performance improvements.

Measuring Query Speed Using REST API

Because BigQuery has a REST API, it is possible to use any web service measurement tool to measure how long a query takes to execute. If your organization already uses one of these tools, it is quite straightforward to use them to measure the performance of a query.

Occasionally, you will need to measure performance of a query from a server where these rich clients are not installed. On such bare-bones machines, the simplest way to measure query time is to use the Unix tools `time` and `curl`. As explained in Chapter 5, we can read in the query text and request JSON into Bash variables:[6]

```
read -d '' QUERY_TEXT << EOF
SELECT
  start_station_name
  , AVG(duration) as duration
  , COUNT(duration) as num_trips
FROM \`bigquery-public-data\`.london_bicycles.cycle_hire
GROUP BY start_station_name
ORDER BY num_trips DESC
LIMIT 5
EOF

read -d '' request << EOF
{
  "useLegacySql": false,
  "useQueryCache": false,
  "query": \"${QUERY_TEXT}\"
}
EOF
request=$(echo "$request" | tr '\n' ' ')
```

One key point to note from the preceding code snippet is that we need to turn the query cache off so that all the necessary processing is carried out on the server side each time we invoke the query.

Chapter 5 also discusses how to use the `gcloud` command-line tool to get the access token and project ID that we require to invoke the REST API:

```
access_token=$(gcloud auth application-default print-access-token)
PROJECT=$(gcloud config get-value project)
```

Finally, we invoke the query repeatedly and compute the total time taken so that we can compute the average query performance and not be at the mercy of occasional network hiccups:

---

6 See *07_perf/time_query.sh* in the GitHub repository for this book (*https://github.com/GoogleCloudPlatform/bigquery-oreilly-book*).

```
NUM_TIMES=10
time for i in $(seq 1 $NUM_TIMES); do
echo -en "\r ... $i / $NUM_NUMTIMES ..."
curl --silent \
    -H "Authorization: Bearer $access_token" \
    -H "Content-Type: application/json" \
    -X POST \
    -d "$request" \
    "https://www.googleapis.com/bigquery/v2/projects/$PROJECT/queries" > /dev/null
done
```

When we did this, we got the following result:

```
Real    0m16.875s
User    0m0.265s
Sys     0m0.109s
```

The total time to run the query 10 times was 16.875 seconds, indicating that the query took 1.7 seconds on average. Note that this includes the roundtrip time to the server and time spent fetching results; it is not purely the query processing time.

We can estimate what this roundtrip time is by turning the query cache on:

```
read -d '' request << EOF
{
  "useLegacySql": false,
  "useQueryCache": true,
  "query": \"${QUERY_TEXT}\"
}
EOF
```

When we repeat the time query again, we get the following:

```
Real    0m6.760s
user    0m0.264s
sys     0m0.114s
```

Because the query is cached, the new numbers are almost all due to network latency. This indicates that the actual query processing time is (16.875 – 6.760)/10, or about 1 second.

Measuring Query Speed Using BigQuery Workload Tester

Although using a web service measurement tool or Unix low-level tools is possible and desirable on bare-bones systems, we recommend that you use the BigQuery Workload Tester (*https://github.com/GoogleCloudPlatform/pontem/tree/dev/BigQuery WorkloadTester*) for measuring the speed of BigQuery queries in your development environment. Unlike a vanilla web service measurement tool, the Workload Tester is able to net out the roundtrip network time (over which you have little control) and report the query processing time (which is what you want to optimize) without having to repeat the queries. It can measure the time taken for individual queries and for workloads (queries that need to be executed serially), and it can invoke the queries in parallel if you want concurrency testing.

The Workload Tester requires Gradle (*https://gradle.org/*), an open source build tool. Thus, to install the Workload Tester, you first need to install Gradle. Cloud Shell provides a quick way to try out the Workload Tester. On it and other Debian-based Linux systems, you can install Gradle using the following command:

```
sudo apt-get -y install gradle
```

On macOS, you can use this:

```
brew install gradle
```

For other operating systems, see the Gradle installation instructions (*https://gradle.org/install/*).

Then clone the GitHub repository containing the Workload Tester, and build it from source:[7]

```
git clone https://github.com/GoogleCloudPlatform/pontem.git
cd pontem/BigQueryWorkloadTester
gradle clean :BigQueryWorkloadTester:build
```

Let's measure the speed of a query to find the average duration of bicycle trips in London. As with our script in the previous section, we could have simply embedded the query in a Bash variable, but it is helpful to have a record of queries measured, so we will write the query text to a file:[8]

```
cat <<EOF| tr '\n' ' ' > queries/busystations.sql
SELECT
  start_station_name
  , AVG(duration) as duration
  , COUNT(duration) as num_trips
FROM \`bigquery-public-data\`.london_bicycles.cycle_hire
GROUP BY start_station_name
ORDER BY num_trips DESC
LIMIT 5
EOF
```

We then create a configuration file for each workload for which the workload consists of a set of queries or query files:

```
cat <<EOF>./config.yaml
concurrencyLevel: 1
isRatioBasedBenchmark: true
benchmarkRatios: [1.0, 2.0]
outputFileFolder: $OUTDIR
```

---

7 See *07_perf/install_workload_tester.sh* in the GitHub repository for this book.

8 See *07_perf/time_bqwt.sh* in the GitHub repository for this book.

```
workloads:
- name: "Busy stations"
  projectId: $PROJECT
  queryFiles:
     - queries/busystations.sql
  outputFileName: busystations.json
EOF
```

In this configuration, we set the base concurrency level to 1, meaning that we send only one query at a time. We do, however, also specify a set of benchmark ratios to measure query times at concurrency levels between 1.0 and 2.0 times the base concurrency level (i.e., 1 and 2 concurrent queries). To try concurrency levels of 1, 2, 5, 10, 15, and 20, use the following:

```
concurrencyLevel: 10
isRatioBasedBenchmark: true
benchmarkRatios: [0.1, 0.25, 0.5, 1.0, 1.5, 2.0]
```

Then we launch the measurement tool by using this:

```
gradle clean :BigQueryWorkloadTester:run
```

The result is a file that contains both the total elapsed time (including roundtrip) and the actual processing time for each of the queries that were run. In our case, the first query (with concurrency level of 1) had a query processing time of 1,111 milliseconds (1.111 seconds), whereas the second and third queries (which ran simultaneously because of the concurrency level of 2) had processing times of 1.108 seconds and 1.026 seconds. In other words, BigQuery provided nearly the same performance whether it was handling one query or two.

Troubleshooting Workloads Using Cloud Logging

Aside from measuring the speed of individual queries, it can be helpful to gauge the performance of entire workflows using the BigQuery logs. You can do this from the GCP web console, in the Cloud Logging section. For example, you can look at warnings (and more severe errors) issued by BigQuery for queries and operations on the dataset from Chapter 5 by selecting the ch05 dataset and Warning from the drop-down menus, as shown in Figure 7-1.

Figure 7-1. Use Cloud Logging to look at log messages emanating from BigQuery

This ability to view all BigQuery error messages from a project in a centralized loca‐
tion can be helpful, especially if the queries emanate from scripts and dashboards that
don't display BigQuery error messages. Indeed, it is possible (provided you have the
necessary permissions) to look at the logs and piece together the set of operations that
are being carried out by a workload to determine whether unnecessary operations are
being performed. For example, look at the subset of the operations on the dataset
ch05eu, shown in Figure 7-2, and read it from the bottom to the top.

▸	🔳	2019-03-12 09:59:11.079 PDT	Bigquery	DeleteDataset	ch05eu	vlakshmanan@google
▸	🔳	2019-03-12 09:58:44.440 PDT	Bigquery	DeleteTable	ch05eu:cycle_stations_copy	
▸	🔳	2019-03-12 09:58:36.189 PDT	Bigquery	DeleteTable	ch05eu:bad_bikes	vlakshmana
▸	🔳	2019-03-04 18:05:04.403 PST	Bigquery	InsertJob	ch05eu:bad_bikes	vlakshmanan@
▸	🔳	2019-03-03 21:55:54.661 PST	Bigquery	DeleteDataset	ch05eu	663413318684-compu
▸	🔳	2019-03-03 16:41:05.594 PST	Bigquery	InsertJob	ch05eu:cycle_stations_copy v1	
▸	🔳	2019-03-03 16:26:49.334 PST	Bigquery	InsertDataset	ch05eu	vlakshmanan@google

*Figure 7-2. It is possible to use Cloud Logging to piece together the set of operations car‐
ried out by a workload*

In this case, it appears that a dataset named ch05eu was created, and a table named
cycle_stations_copy was added to it. Then an attempt was made to delete the
ch05eu dataset, but it failed because the dataset was not empty. A new table named
bad_bikes was added. After this, the bad_bikes table was deleted, and the cycle_sta
tions_copy table was also deleted. Finally, the dataset itself was deleted.

We can examine the details of each of the jobs—for example, let's look at the first insert job that created the cycle_stations_copy. The details include the schema of the created table, as illustrated in Figure 7-3.

```
▼  🗋   2019-03-03 16:41:05.594 PST  Bigquery  InsertJob  ch05eu:cycle_stations_copy

   ▼ {
        insertId: "hrcuqle2g4g5"
        logName: "projects/cloud-training-demos/logs/cloudaudit.googleapis.com%2Fa
      ▼ protoPayload: {
          @type: "type.googleapis.com/google.cloud.audit.AuditLog"
        ▶ authenticationInfo: {…}
        ▶ authorizationInfo: [1]
        ▼ metadata: {
            @type: "type.googleapis.com/google.cloud.audit.BigQueryAuditMetadata"
          ▼ tableCreation: {
              jobName: "projects/cloud-training-demos/jobs/3051c867-ad0c-413d-a6d6
              reason: "JOB"
            ▼ table: {
                schemaJson: "{
                "fields": [{
                    "name": "id",
                    "type": "INTEGER",
                    "mode": "NULLABLE"
                },{
                    "name": "install date".
```

Figure 7-3. Examine the details of an insert job to ascertain the schema of the table being created

Given these details and knowledge of the context, it might be the case that the cycle_stations_copy table did not use any of the fields in bad_bikes. Perhaps the entire set of operations around bad_bikes was unnecessary and can be removed from the workflow.

Reading Query Plan Information

In addition to measuring query speed and examining the logs, you can diagnose query performance by looking at information available about the query plan. The query plan information lists the stages into which the query is broken down and provides information about the data processed in each of the execution steps that make up each stage. The query plan information is available in JSON form from the job information and visually in the BigQuery web UI.

In BigQuery, the execution graph of an SQL statement is broken up into query stages, where each stage consists of units of work that are executed in parallel by many workers. The stages communicate via a distributed shuffle architecture (see Chapter 6), and so most stages start by reading the output of previous stages and end by writing to the input of subsequent stages. Keep in mind that it is not necessary for a previous stage to complete before a subsequent stage starts—stages can start with the data at hand. So stages do not execute sequentially.

 You should keep in mind that the query plan is dynamic given that the exact data size and computational cost of intermediate stages is not known before the stage in question is executed. If the actual size is very different from the anticipated size, new stages might be introduced so as to repartition the data and improve data distribution among the workers. Because of the dynamic nature of the query plan, when exploring query performance, look at the query plan information after the query is complete.

Obtaining query plan information from the job details

The information listed about each stage of a completed query in the job information includes the timestamps at which the stage was started and finished, the total number of records read and written, and the number of bytes written across all workers in order to process this query. For example, try executing the following query:

```
SELECT
  start_station_name,
  AVG(duration) AS duration,
  COUNT(duration) AS num_trips
FROM
  `bigquery-public-data`.london_bicycles.cycle_hire
GROUP BY
  start_station_name
ORDER BY
  num_trips DESC
LIMIT
  5
```

Now you can list the job details by invoking the REST API:[9]

```
JOBID=8adbf3fd-e310-44bb-9c6e-88254958ccac   # CHANGE
access_token=$(gcloud auth application-default print-access-token)
PROJECT=$(gcloud config get-value project)
curl --silent \
    -H "Authorization: Bearer $access_token" \
    -X GET \
    "https://www.googleapis.com/bigquery/v2/projects/$PROJECT/jobs/$JOBID"
```

---

9 This is *07_perf/get_job_details.sh* in the GitHub repository for this book. You can get the required job ID from the "Query history" in the BigQuery web UI. If your query was run outside the US and EU, you also need to specify the job location in a job resource object (sorry!). You can also get the job details by using bq ls -j.

For example, the data about the first stage includes the following information about the time spent waiting for data, the ratio of I/O to compute in the query, and data read, shuffled, and written out:

```
"waitRatioAvg": 0.058558558558558557,
"readRatioAvg": 0.070270270270270274,
"computeRatioAvg": 0.860360360360360034
...
"shuffleOutputBytes": "356596",
"shuffleOutputBytesSpilled": "0",
"recordsRead": "24369201",
"recordsWritten": "6138",
"parallelInputs": "7",
```

Because this is primarily an input stage, we care primarily about read and shuffle performance—because this stage kept the processor busy 86% of the time and no data needed to be spilled to disk, it appears that bottlenecks (if any) in this query are not related to I/O. If this query is slow, we'll need to look elsewhere, perhaps at reasons for the relatively low number of parallelization (7); in this case, this low count is fine because the input data of 24 million records is rather small and quite capable of being processed in seven chunks.

Visualizing the query plan information

Much of the information about the query plan in the job details is represented visually in the BigQuery web UI. Open the query and click the "Execution details" tab to see a depiction of the query plan. This includes the overall timing as well as a breakdown of this timing at the level of the steps that make up each stage of the query.

As Figure 7-4 shows, the "Execution details" tab provides key information about query performance.

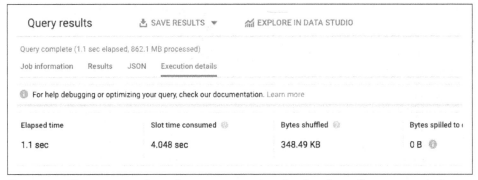

Figure 7-4. Key measures from the query execution details tab; performance optimization will typically focus on reducing the slot time and/or bytes shuffled

The overall timing depicted in Figure 7-5 indicates seven parallel inputs being active in the first 0.6 seconds, and then two more units being activated.

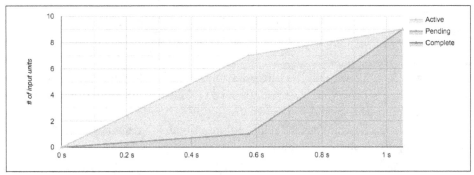

Figure 7-5. Timing data from the query plan information

Further details of the stages and steps are provided visually as well, as illustrated in Figure 7-6.

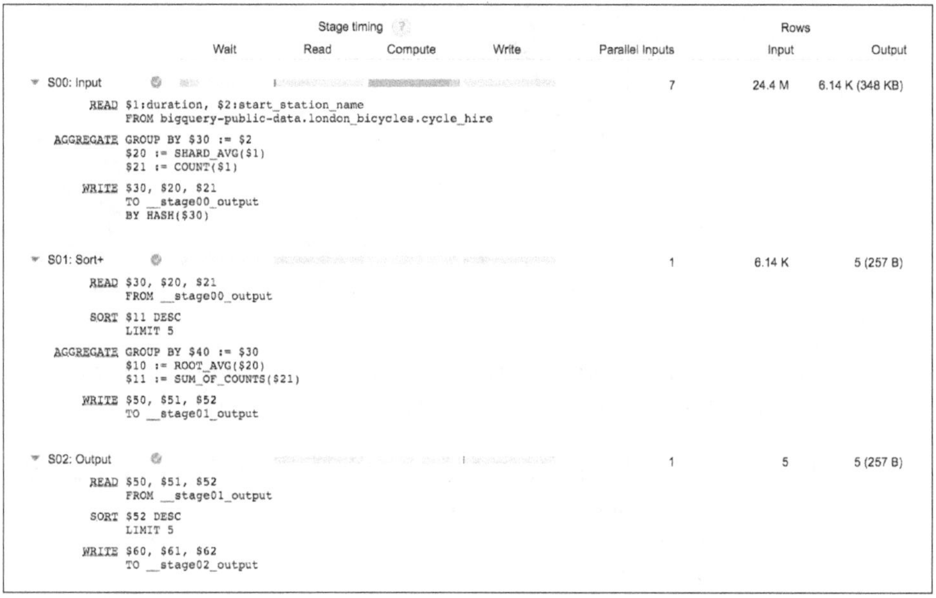
Stage timing
Wait
Read
Compute
Write
Parallel Inputs
Rows
Input
Output
S00: Input
7
24.4 M
6.14 K (348 KB)
READ $1:duration, $2:start_station_name
FROM bigquery-public-data.london_bicycles.cycle_hire
AGGREGATE GROUP BY $30 := $2
$20 := SHARD_AVG($1)
$21 := COUNT($1)
WRITE $30, $20, $21
TO __stage00_output
BY HASH($30)
S01: Sort+
1
6.14 K
5 (257 B)
READ $30, $20, $21
FROM __stage00_output
SORT $11 DESC
LIMIT 5
AGGREGATE GROUP BY $40 := $30
$10 := ROOT_AVG($20)
$11 := SUM_OF_COUNTS($21)
WRITE $50, $51, $52
TO __stage01_output
S02: Output
1
5
5 (257 B)
READ $50, $51, $52
FROM __stage01_output
SORT $52 DESC
LIMIT 5
WRITE $60, $61, $62
TO __stage02_output

Figure 7-6. Stages and steps from the query plan information

From Figure 7-6, we see that the query has three stages. The first stage (`S00`) is the input stage, the second (`S01`) consists of sorting, and the third (`S02`) is the output stage. The timing of each stage is shown visually as well in Figure 7-6. The ratios that were available numerically in the JSON response to the job details request are depicted in the color bars shown in Figure 7-7.[10]

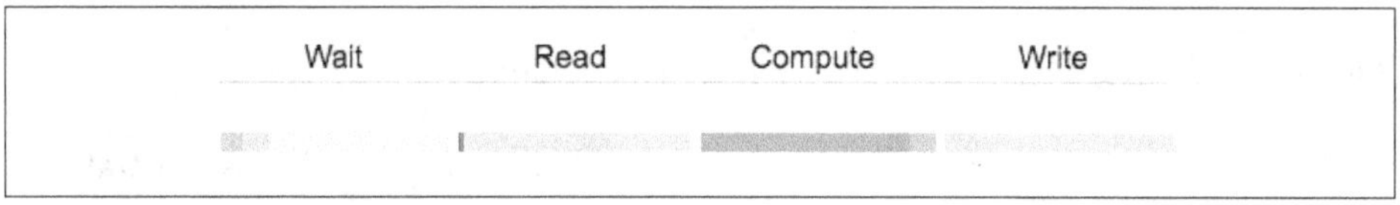
Wait
Read
Compute
Write

Figure 7-7. Stage timing from the query plan information

The dark colors indicate the average time spent waiting, reading, computing, or writing. Here, most of the time is spent performing computation, and a little bit of time is spent waiting. The wait stage is somewhat variable (the intermediate color indicates the maximum wait, and the difference between the average and the maximum is an indicator of variability)—here, the maximum wait time is nearly double the average wait time. Reading, on the other hand, is quite consistent, whereas the writing overhead is negligible.

10 If you are reading this in a format that renders the diagram in grayscale, please try out the query and look at the query details in the BigQuery web UI.

Zooming in on the input stage, shown in Figure 7-8, we see that it consists of three steps: reading two columns (`duration` and `start_station_name`, referred to as $1 and $2) from the BigQuery table, aggregating, and writing the output.

	Wait	Read	Compute	Write	Parallel Inputs	Input	Output
S00: Input					7	24.4 M	6.14 K (348 KB)

```
      READ  $1:duration, $2:start_station_name
            FROM bigquery-public-data.london_bicycles.cycle_hire
 AGGREGATE  GROUP BY $30 := $2
            $20 := SHARD_AVG($1)
            $21 := COUNT($1)
     WRITE  $30, $20, $21
            TO __stage00_output
            BY HASH($30)
```

Figure 7-8. The steps that form the first stage

The aggregation step consists of three operations: grouping by `start_station_name` (recall that $2 refers to this input column), finding the average `duration` ($1) within each shard, and maintaining the count of non-null durations. The writing stage writes the groups ($30), average duration ($20), and count of duration ($21) to an intermediate output, distributing the output by the hash of the station name. In case more than one worker is needed in the next stage, the hash of the station name controls which workers process which parts of the `stage_00` output.

Looking back again at Figure 7-6, you can see that the first stage is carried out in parallel over seven workers, while the remaining two stages are carried out on a single worker. The input stage reads in 24.4 million rows and writes out around 6,140 rows, which totals 348 KB. These rows are sorted by the second stage, and five rows are written to the third stage. When we have a stage with only one worker, we should ensure that the memory load on that worker is well within the bounds of what a single worker can handle (we cover ways to do so later in this chapter)—348 KB definitely qualifies, and so this query should not pose any performance issues due to limits on the resources available to a single worker.

Another option to visualize the BigQuery query plan is to use the BigQuery Visualizer (*https://oreil.ly/Unw_c*) at *https://bqvisualiser.appspot.com/*, as shown in Figure 7-9.

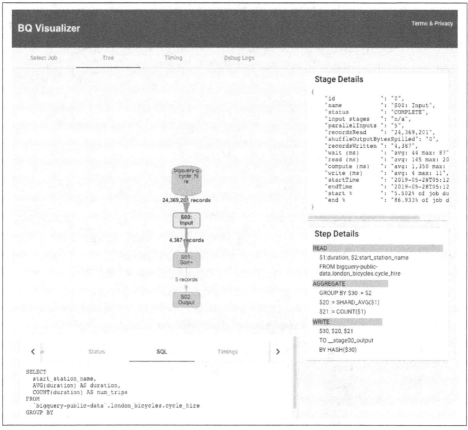

Figure 7-9. Visualizing a BigQuery job using the BigQuery Visualizer

The visualizer becomes especially useful for complex queries with tens of stages, which can be difficult to comprehend from just the synopsis available in the Big-Query web UI.

Increasing Query Speed

As discussed in the previous section, you should carry out the following steps to measure query speed and identify potential problems:

1. Measure the overall workload time using the BigQuery Workload Tester.

2. Examine the logs to ensure that the workload is not performing any unexpected operations.

3. Examine the query plan information of the queries that form the workload to identify bottlenecks or unnecessary stages.

Once you have identified that a problem exists and have determined that there are no obvious errors in the workflow, it is time to consider how to improve speed on the critical parts of the workload. In this section, we provide a few possible ways to improve query speed, including the following:

- Minimizing I/O
- Caching the results of previous queries
- Performing efficient joins
- Avoiding overwhelming a worker
- Using approximate aggregation functions

Minimizing I/O

As we noted earlier, a query that computes the sum of three columns will be slower than a query that computes the sum of two columns, but most of the performance difference will be due to reading more data, not the extra addition. Therefore, a query that computes the mean of a column will be nearly as fast as a query whose aggregation method is to compute the variance of the data (even though computing variance requires BigQuery to keep track of both the sum and the sum of the squares), because most of the overhead of simple queries is caused by I/O, not by computation.

Be purposeful in SELECT

Because BigQuery uses columnar file formats, the fewer the columns that are read in a SELECT, the less the amount of data that needs to be read. In particular, doing a SELECT * reads every column of every row in the table, making it quite slow and expensive. The exception is when you use a SELECT * in a subquery and then reference only a few fields in an outer query; the BigQuery optimizer will be smart enough to read only the columns that are absolutely required.

Explicitly list the columns that you want to see in the final result. For example, it is much more efficient to find the bike_id responsible for the longest duration trip in the dataset by doing the following:

```
SELECT
  bike_id
  , duration
FROM
  `bigquery-public-data`.london_bicycles.cycle_hire
ORDER BY duration DESC
LIMIT 1
```

A less efficient method is this:

```
SELECT
  *
FROM
  `bigquery-public-data`.london_bicycles.cycle_hire
ORDER BY duration DESC
LIMIT 1
```

The first query took us 1.8 seconds and cost 372 MB, whereas the second one took us 5.5 seconds (three times slower) and cost 2.59 GB (seven times costlier).

 Unless you are reading from a clustered table, applying a LIMIT clause does not affect the amount of data you are billed for reading. When reading clustered tables, reductions in the number of bytes scanned will be passed along to you as savings (although they will be less predictable). To preview a table, use the preview button on the web UI instead of doing a SELECT * with a LIMIT. The preview does not incur charges, whereas a SELECT * incurs the same charge as a table scan.

If you require nearly all of the columns in a table, consider using SELECT * EXCEPT so as to avoid reading the ones you don't require (see Chapter 2).

Reducing data being read

When tuning a query, it is important to start with the data that is being read and consider whether it is possible to reduce it. Suppose that you want to find the typical duration of the most common one-way rentals; you could do the following:

```
SELECT
  MIN(start_station_name) AS start_station_name
  , MIN(end_station_name) AS end_station_name
  , APPROX_QUANTILES(duration, 10)[OFFSET(5)] AS typical_duration
  , COUNT(duration) AS num_trips
FROM
  `bigquery-public-data`.london_bicycles.cycle_hire
WHERE
  start_station_id != end_station_id
GROUP BY
  start_station_id, end_station_id
ORDER BY num_trips DESC
LIMIT 10
```

This takes 14.7 seconds when we run it, and it yields the following:

Row	start_station_name	end_station_name	typical_duration	num_trips
1	Black Lion Gate, Kensington Gardens	Hyde Park Corner, Hyde Park	1,500	12,000

Row	start_station_name	end_station_name	typical_duration	num_trips
2	Black Lion Gate, Kensington Gardens	Palace Gate, Kensington Gardens	780	11,833
3	Hyde Park Corner, Hyde Park	Albert Gate, Hyde Park	1,920	11,745
4	Hyde Park Corner, Hyde Park	Triangle Car Park, Hyde Park	1,380	10,923
5	Hyde Park Corner, Hyde Park	Black Lion Gate, Kensington Gardens	1,680	10,652

The details of the query indicate that the sorting (for the approximate quantiles for every station pair) requires a repartition of the outputs of the input stage, but most of the time is spent during computation, as demonstrated in Figure 7-10.

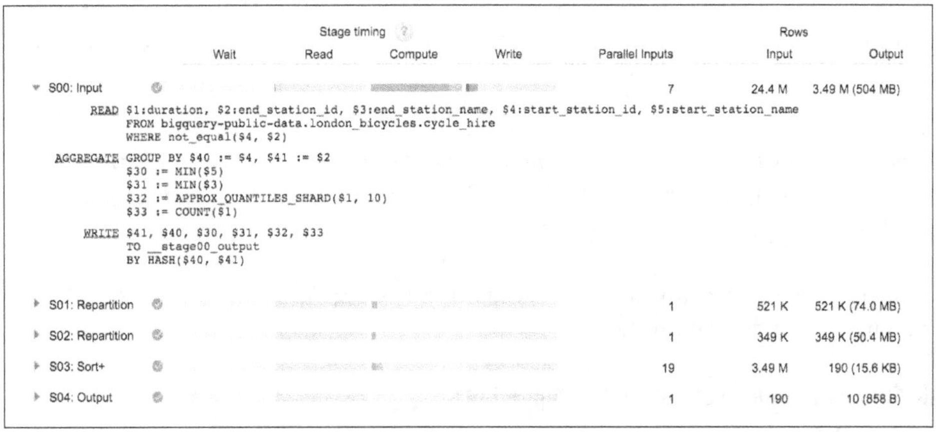

Figure 7-10. This query requires two repartition stages, but most of the time is spent in computation

Nevertheless, we can reduce the I/O overhead of the query if we do the filtering and grouping using the station name rather than the station ID, because we will need to read fewer columns:

```
SELECT
  start_station_name
  , end_station_name
  , APPROX_QUANTILES(duration, 10)[OFFSET(5)] AS typical_duration
  , COUNT(duration) AS num_trips
FROM
  `bigquery-public-data`.london_bicycles.cycle_hire
WHERE
  start_station_name != end_station_name
GROUP BY
  start_station_name, end_station_name
ORDER BY num_trips DESC
LIMIT 10
```

This query avoids the need to read the two ID columns and finishes in 9.6 seconds, a 30% increase in speed. This increase is caused by the downstream effects of reading less data: the query requires one less repartition, and fewer workers (10, versus 19 earlier) for the sort, as shown in Figure 7-11.

	Stage timing ?					Rows	
	Wait	Read	Compute	Write	Parallel Inputs	Input	Output
▼ S00: Input ⊘					7	24.4 M	2.85 M (380 MB)

```
    READ $1:duration, $2:end_station_name, $3:start_station_name
         FROM bigquery-public-data.london_bicycles.cycle_hire
         WHERE not_equal($3, $2)
AGGREGATE GROUP BY $40 := $3, $41 := $2
         $30 := APPROX_QUANTILES_SHARD($1, 10)
         $31 := COUNT($1)
    WRITE $41, $40, $30, $31
         TO __stage00_output
         BY HASH($40, $41)
```

▶ S01: Repartition ⊘					1	509 K	509 K (70.0 MB)
▶ S02: Sort+ ⊘					10	2.85 M	100 (8.36 KB)
▶ S03: Output ⊘					1	100	10 (858 B)

Figure 7-11. By taking advantage of the 1:1 relationship between station_id *and* station_name, *we are able to read fewer columns, remove one stage, and use fewer workers for the sort*

The query result remains the same because there is a 1:1 relationship between the station name and the station ID.

Reducing the number of expensive computations

Suppose that you want to find the total distance traveled by each bicycle in the dataset. A naive way to do this would be to find the distance traveled in each trip undertaken by each bicycle and sum up the distances:

```
WITH trip_distance AS (
  SELECT
    bike_id
    , ST_Distance(ST_GeogPoint(s.longitude, s.latitude),
                  ST_GeogPoint(e.longitude, e.latitude)) AS distance
  FROM
    `bigquery-public-data`.london_bicycles.cycle_hire,
    `bigquery-public-data`.london_bicycles.cycle_stations s,
    `bigquery-public-data`.london_bicycles.cycle_stations e
  WHERE
    start_station_id = s.id
    AND end_station_id = e.id
)

SELECT
  bike_id
  , SUM(distance)/1000 AS total_distance
FROM trip_distance
```

```
GROUP BY bike_id
ORDER BY total_distance DESC
LIMIT 5
```

This query takes 7.1 seconds (44 seconds of slot time) and shuffles 1.69 MB. The result is that some bicycles have been ridden nearly 6,000 kilometers:

Row	bike_id	total_distance
1	12925	5990.988493972133
2	12757	5919.736998793672
3	12496	5883.1268196056335
4	12841	5870.757769474104
5	13071	5853.763514457338

Computing the distance is a pretty expensive operation, and we can avoid joining the cycle_stations table against the cycle_hire table if we precompute the distances between all pairs of stations:

```
WITH stations AS (
  SELECT
    s.id AS start_id
    , e.id AS end_id
    , ST_Distance(ST_GeogPoint(s.longitude, s.latitude),
                  ST_GeogPoint(e.longitude, e.latitude)) AS distance
  FROM
    `bigquery-public-data`.london_bicycles.cycle_stations s,
    `bigquery-public-data`.london_bicycles.cycle_stations e
),
```

The rest of the query is quite similar, except that the join is against the table of precomputed distances:

```
trip_distance AS (
  SELECT
    bike_id
    , distance
  FROM
    `bigquery-public-data`.london_bicycles.cycle_hire,
    stations
  WHERE
    start_station_id = start_id
    AND end_station_id = end_id
)

SELECT
  bike_id
  , SUM(distance)/1000 AS total_distance
FROM trip_distance
GROUP BY bike_id
```

```
ORDER BY total_distance DESC
LIMIT 5
```

Now the query takes only 31.5 seconds of slot time (a 30% increase in speed) in spite of having to shuffle more data (33.44 MB) between nodes.

Caching computations using materialized views

BigQuery materialized views are precomputed views that periodically (and automatically) cache the results of a query in a BigQuery table for increased performance and efficiency. A materialized view may be a subset of the rows and/or columns of a table or join result, or may be a summary using an aggregate function. So when a query is re-run and a materialized view exists, the query doesn't need to rescan all the tables again, but can quickly report the answer from the materialized view. This significantly improves performance and cuts down cost because the amount of data scanned is much smaller.

In return for the additional costs for storing the materialized view tables and keeping them up to date, we can avoid rescanning the entire base table.

Imagine that we have a dashboard that displays the average duration of one-way rentals and the dashboard allows users to select different weeks to explore. The query that the dashboard runs is:

```
WITH oneway AS (
  SELECT EXTRACT(date from start_date) AS rental_date,
  duration, start_station_name, end_station_name
  FROM
  ch07eu.cycle_hire
  WHERE start_station_name != end_station_name
)

SELECT
  rental_date, AVG(duration) AS avg_duration,
  start_station_name, end_station_name
FROM oneway
WHERE rental_date BETWEEN '2015-01-01' AND '2015-01-07'
GROUP BY rental_date, start_station_name, end_station_name
```

Temporary beta limitation

At the time we are writing this (May 2020), materialized views are in beta and one restriction is that they have to be created in the same dataset as the base table. That's why you see that the dataset being queried is named ch07eu—it's a copy of the London bicycles cycle_hire table. This restriction may be gone by the time you are reading this, and if so, replace the FROM item in the queries in this section by the BigQuery public dataset.

The above query processes 1.7 GB each time the user selects a different rental_date period to explore because it has to re-scan the entire table to recompute the aggregates. Instead, we could create a materialized view for all dates:

```
CREATE OR REPLACE MATERIALIZED VIEW ch07eu.oneway_rentals
AS

WITH oneway AS (
  SELECT EXTRACT(date from start_date) AS rental_date,
  duration, start_station_name, end_station_name
  FROM
  ch07eu.cycle_hire
  WHERE start_station_name != end_station_name
)

SELECT
  rental_date, AVG(duration) AS avg_duration,
  start_station_name, end_station_name
FROM oneway
GROUP BY rental_date, start_station_name, end_station_name
```

Then, querying for a time period needs to scan only 1.3 GB:

```
SELECT
  rental_date, avg_duration,
  start_station_name, end_station_name
FROM ch07eu.oneway_rentals
WHERE rental_date BETWEEN '2015-01-01' AND  '2015-01-07'
```

BigQuery materialized views are zero maintenance, always fresh, and self-tuning. All incremental data changes from the base tables are automatically added to the materialized views. Materialized views are always consistent with the base table (including BigQuery streaming tables). Materialized views unite their data with the delta changes in the base table and return any new data in real time. If a query or part of a query against the source table can instead be resolved by querying the materialized views, BigQuery will rewrite (reroute) the query to use the materialized view for better performance and efficiency.

Caching the Results of Previous Queries

The BigQuery service automatically caches query results in a temporary table. If the identical query is submitted within approximately 24 hours, the results are served from this temporary table without any recomputation. Cached results are extremely fast and do not incur charges.

There are, however, a few caveats to be aware of. Query caching is based on exact string comparison. So even whitespaces can cause a cache miss. Queries are never cached if they exhibit nondeterministic behavior (for example, they use CURRENT_TIMESTAMP or RAND), if the table or view being queried has changed (even if the columns/rows of interest to the query are unchanged), if the table is associated with a streaming buffer (even if there are no new rows), if the query uses Data Manipulation Language (DML) statements, or if it queries external data sources.

 We recommend against reading directly from the cached temporary tables, because cached tables can expire—if the results of a query can serve as inputs to other queries, we recommend the use of tables or materialized views, as discussed in the next section.

Caching intermediate results

It is possible to improve overall performance at the expense of increased I/O by taking advantage of temporary tables and materialized views. For example, suppose that you have a number of queries that start out by finding the typical duration of trips between a pair of stations:

```
WITH typical_trip AS (
SELECT
  start_station_name
  , end_station_name
  , APPROX_QUANTILES(duration, 10)[OFFSET(5)] AS typical_duration
  , COUNT(duration) AS num_trips
FROM
  `bigquery-public-data`.london_bicycles.cycle_hire
GROUP BY
  start_station_name, end_station_name
)
```

The WITH clause (also called a common table expression) improves readability but does not improve query speed or cost because results are not cached. The same applies to views and subqueries as well. If you find yourself using a WITH clause, a view, or a subquery often, one way to potentially improve performance is to store the result in a table (or materialized view):[11]

```
CREATE OR REPLACE TABLE ch07eu.typical_trip AS
SELECT
  start_station_name
  , end_station_name
  , APPROX_QUANTILES(duration, 10)[OFFSET(5)] AS typical_duration
  , COUNT(duration) AS num_trips
FROM
  `bigquery-public-data`.london_bicycles.cycle_hire
GROUP BY
  start_station_name, end_station_name
```

---

11 You will need to measure this, of course. In some cases, the extra overhead involved in reading the table of intermediate results will make this more expensive than simply recomputing the results of a WITH clause.

Let's use the WITH clause to find days when bicycle trips are much longer than usual:

```
SELECT
    EXTRACT (DATE FROM start_date) AS trip_date
    , APPROX_QUANTILES(duration / typical_duration, 10)[OFFSET(5)] AS ratio
    , COUNT(*) AS num_trips_on_day
FROM
    `bigquery-public-data`.london_bicycles.cycle_hire AS hire
JOIN typical_trip AS trip
ON
    hire.start_station_name = trip.start_station_name
    AND hire.end_station_name = trip.end_station_name
    AND num_trips > 10
GROUP BY trip_date
HAVING num_trips_on_day > 10
ORDER BY ratio DESC
LIMIT 10
```

This takes 19.1 seconds and processes 1.68 GB. Now, let's use the table:

```
SELECT
    EXTRACT (DATE FROM start_date) AS trip_date
    , APPROX_QUANTILES(duration / typical_duration, 10)[OFFSET(5)] AS ratio
    , COUNT(*) AS num_trips_on_day
FROM
    `bigquery-public-data`.london_bicycles.cycle_hire AS hire
JOIN ch07eu.typical_trip AS trip
ON
    hire.start_station_name = trip.start_station_name
    AND hire.end_station_name = trip.end_station_name
    AND num_trips > 10
GROUP BY trip_date
HAVING num_trips_on_day > 10
ORDER BY ratio DESC
LIMIT 10
```

This takes 10.3 seconds (a 50% increase in speed because the computation is avoided) and processes 1.72 GB (a slight increase in cost because the new table is now being read). Both queries return the same result, that trips on Christmas take longer than usual:

Row	trip_date	ratio	num_trips_on_day
1	2016-12-25	1.6	34477
2	2015-12-25	1.5263157894736843	20871
3	2015-08-01	1.25	41200
4	2016-07-30	1.2272727272727273	43524
5	2015-08-02	1.2222222222222223	41243

The table ch07eu.typical_trip is not refreshed when new data is added to the cycle_hire table. One way to solve this problem of stale data is to use a materialized view or to schedule queries to update the table periodically. You should measure the cost of such updates to see whether the improvement in query performance makes up for the extra cost of keeping the intermediate table up to date.

Are Materialized Views/Tables Always More Efficient?

In the main text, we showed you many instances where materializing the result of a WITH statement is faster because the output of the WITH statement is used multiple times in the query.

However, it is not the case that materialized views or tables will always reduce computation cost. For example, suppose that you were to use a WITH clause to abstract away an expensive regular expression (regex) function, but the main expression always has a restrictive filter (here, of trips longer than 84,000 seconds):

```
WITH trip AS (
SELECT
  REGEXP_REPLACE(start_station_name,
      r"^# ([a-zA-Z0-9\s]+$)", "FROM: \\1") AS start_station_name
  , REGEXP_REPLACE(end_station_name,
      r"^# ([a-zA-Z0-9\s]+$)", "TO: \\1") ASend_station_name
  , duration
FROM
  `bigquery-public-data`.london_bicycles.cycle_hire
)
SELECT * FROM trip
WHERE duration > 84000
```

The BigQuery optimizer that looked at the entire query would be able to limit the number of times the regex is invoked. However, if the WITH clause trip were to be materialized into a table or view, the regex function would need to be called for every row.

Accelerating queries with BI Engine

If there are tables that you access frequently in Business Intelligence (BI) settings, such as dashboards with aggregations and filters, one way to speed up your queries is to employ BI Engine. It will automatically store relevant pieces of data in memory (either actual columns from the table or derived results) and will use a specialized query processor tuned for working with mostly in-memory data. You can use the Big-Query Admin Console to reserve the amount of memory (up to a current maximum of 10 GB) that BigQuery should use for its cache, as depicted in Figure 7-12.

Figure 7-12. Reserve memory for caching table data by setting up a BI Engine reservation

Make sure to reserve this memory in the same region as the dataset you are querying. Then BigQuery will start to cache tables, parts of tables, and aggregations in memory and serve results faster.

A primary use case for BI Engine is for tables that are accessed from dashboard tools such as Google Data Studio. By providing memory allocation for a BI Engine reservation, you can make dashboards that rely on a BigQuery backend much more responsive.

Performing Efficient Joins

Joining two tables requires data coordination and is subject to limitations imposed by the communication bandwidth between slots. If it is possible to avoid a join, or to reduce the amount of data being joined, do so.

Denormalization

One way to improve the read performance and avoid joins is to give up on storing data efficiently and instead add redundant copies of data. This is called *denormalization*. Thus, instead of storing the bicycle station latitudes and longitudes separately from the cycle hire information, we could create a denormalized table:

```
CREATE OR REPLACE TABLE ch07eu.london_bicycles_denorm AS
SELECT
  start_station_id
  , s.latitude AS start_latitude
  , s.longitude AS start_longitude
  , end_station_id
  , e.latitude AS end_latitude
  , e.longitude AS end_longitude
```

```
FROM
  `bigquery-public-data`.london_bicycles.cycle_hire as h
JOIN
  `bigquery-public-data`.london_bicycles.cycle_stations as s
ON
  h.start_station_id = s.id
JOIN
  `bigquery-public-data`.london_bicycles.cycle_stations as e
ON
  h.end_station_id = e.id
```

Then all subsequent queries will not need to carry out the join because the table will contain the necessary location information for all trips:

Row	start_station_id	start_latitude	start_longitude	end_station_id	end_latitude	end_longitude
1	439	51.5338	-0.118677	680	51.47768469	-0.170329317
2	597	51.473471	-0.20782	622	51.50748124	-0.205535908
3	187	51.49247977	-0.178433004	187	51.49247977	-0.178433004
4	15	51.51772703	-0.127854211	358	51.516226	-0.124826
5	638	51.46663393	-0.169821175	151	51.51213691	-0.201554966

In this case, you are trading off storage and reading more data for the computational expense of a join. It is quite possible that the cost of reading more data from disk will outweigh the cost of the join—you should measure whether denormalization brings performance benefits.

Avoiding self-joins of large tables

Self-joins happen when a table is joined with itself. Although BigQuery supports self-joins, they can lead to performance degradation if the table being joined with itself is very large. In many cases, you can avoid the self-join by taking advantage of SQL features such as aggregation and window functions.

Let's look at an example. One of the BigQuery public datasets is the dataset of baby names published by the US Social Security Administration. It is possible to query the dataset to find the most common male names for the year 2015 in the state of Massachusetts:

```
SELECT
  name
  , number AS num_babies
FROM `bigquery-public-data`.usa_names.usa_1910_current
WHERE gender = 'M' AND year = 2015 AND state = 'MA'
ORDER BY num_babies DESC
LIMIT 5
```

Here's the result of that query:

Row	name	num_babies
1	Benjamin	456
2	William	445
3	Noah	403
4	Mason	365
5	James	354

Similarly, the most common female names (`gender = 'F'`) for the year 2015 in Massachusetts were as follows:

Row	name	num_babies
1	Olivia	430
2	Emma	402
3	Sophia	373
4	Isabella	350
5	Charlotte	344

What are the most common names assigned to both male and female babies in the country over all the years in the dataset? A naive way to solve this problem involves reading the input table twice and doing a self-join:

```
WITH male_babies AS (
SELECT
  name
  , number AS num_babies
FROM `bigquery-public-data`.usa_names.usa_1910_current
WHERE gender = 'M'
),
female_babies AS (
SELECT
  name
  , number AS num_babies
FROM `bigquery-public-data`.usa_names.usa_1910_current
WHERE gender = 'F'
),
both_genders AS (
SELECT
  name
  , SUM(m.num_babies) + SUM(f.num_babies) AS num_babies
  , SUM(m.num_babies) / (SUM(m.num_babies) + SUM(f.num_babies)) AS frac_male
FROM male_babies AS m
JOIN female_babies AS f
USING (name)
GROUP BY name
)

SELECT * FROM both_genders
```

```
WHERE frac_male BETWEEN 0.3 and 0.7
ORDER BY num_babies DESC
LIMIT 5
```

This took 74 seconds and yielded the following:

Row	name	num_babies	frac_male
1	Jordan	982149616	0.6705115608373867
2	Willie	940460442	0.5722103705452823
3	Lee	820214744	0.689061146650151
4	Jessie	759150003	0.5139710590240227
5	Marion	592706454	0.32969114589732473

To add insult to injury, the answer is also wrong: as much as we like the name Jordan, the entire US population is only around 330 million, so there cannot have been 982 million babies with that name. The self-join unfortunately joins across state and year boundaries.[12]

A faster, more elegant (and correct!) solution is to recast the query to read the input only once and avoid the self-join completely. This took only 2.4 seconds—a 30-times increase in speed:

```
WITH all_babies AS (
SELECT
  name
  , SUM(IF(gender = 'M', number, 0)) AS male_babies
  , SUM(IF(gender = 'F', number, 0)) AS female_babies
FROM `bigquery-public-data.usa_names.usa_1910_current`
GROUP BY name
),

both_genders AS (
SELECT
  name
  , (male_babies + female_babies) AS num_babies
  , SAFE_DIVIDE(male_babies, male_babies + female_babies) AS frac_male
FROM all_babies
WHERE male_babies > 0 AND female_babies > 0
)

SELECT * FROM both_genders
WHERE frac_male BETWEEN 0.3 and 0.7
```

---

12 You can verify that this is the key reason for the incorrect value for num_babies by adding state and year to the USING clause (and making sure to add the two fields to the first two selects). Then the number of babies is in the correct ballpark (e.g., 2,018,162 for Jessie, whereas the correct answer is 229,263). The answer is still incorrect because rows with NULLs for these fields are ignored by the join (NULL is never equal to anything else).

```
ORDER BY num_babies desc
limit 5
```

Here's the result, in case you're curious:

Row	name	num_babies	frac_male
1	Jessie	229263	0.4327213723976394
2	Riley	187762	0.46760792918694943
3	Casey	181176	0.5916456925862145
4	Jackie	161428	0.4624042916966078
5	Johnnie	136208	0.6842549629977681

Reducing the data being joined

It is possible to carry out the previous query with an efficient join as long as we reduce the amount of data being joined by grouping the data by name and gender early on:

```
with all_names AS (
  SELECT name, gender, SUM(number) AS num_babies
  FROM `bigquery-public-data`.usa_names.usa_1910_current
  GROUP BY name, gender
),

male_names AS (
  SELECT name, num_babies
  FROM all_names
  WHERE gender = 'M'
),

female_names AS (
  SELECT name, num_babies
  FROM all_names
  WHERE gender = 'F'
),

ratio AS (
  SELECT
    name
    , (f.num_babies + m.num_babies) AS num_babies
    , m.num_babies / (f.num_babies + m.num_babies) AS frac_male
  FROM male_names AS m
  JOIN female_names AS f
  USING (name)
)

SELECT * from ratio
WHERE frac_male BETWEEN 0.3 and 0.7
ORDER BY num_babies DESC
LIMIT 5
```

The early grouping serves to trim the data early in the query, before the query performs a JOIN. That way, shuffling and other complex operations execute only on the much smaller data and remain quite efficient. This query finished in two seconds and returned the correct result.

Using a window function instead of self-join

Suppose that you want to find the duration between a bike being dropped off and it being rented again; in other words, the duration that a bicycle stays at the station. This is an example of a dependent relationship between rows. It might appear that the only way to solve this is to join the table with itself, matching the end_date of one trip against the start_date of the next.

You can, however, avoid a self-join by using a window function (we cover window functions in Chapter 8):

```
SELECT
  bike_id
  , start_date
  , end_date
  , TIMESTAMP_DIFF(
      start_date,
      LAG(end_date) OVER (PARTITION BY bike_id ORDER BY start_date),
      SECOND) AS time_at_station
FROM `bigquery-public-data`.london_bicycles.cycle_hire
LIMIT 5
```

Here's the result of that query:

Row	bike_id	start_date	end_date	time_at_station
1	2	2015-01-05 15:59:00 UTC	2015-01-05 16:17:00 UTC	*null*
2	2	2015-01-07 01:31:00 UTC	2015-01-07 01:50:00 UTC	119640
3	2	2015-01-21 07:56:00 UTC	2015-01-21 08:12:00 UTC	1231560
4	2	2015-01-21 16:15:00 UTC	2015-01-21 16:31:00 UTC	28980
5	2	2015-01-21 16:57:00 UTC	2015-01-21 17:23:00 UTC	1560

Notice that the first row has a null for time_at_station because we don't have a timestamp for the previous dropoff. After that, the time_at_station tracks the difference between the previous dropoff and the current pickup.

Using this, we can compute the average time that a bicycle is unused at each station and rank stations by that measure:

```
WITH unused AS (
SELECT
  bike_id
  , start_station_name
  , start_date
```

```
  , end_date
  , TIMESTAMP_DIFF(start_date, LAG(end_date) OVER (PARTITION BY bike_id ORDER BY
start_date), SECOND) AS time_at_station
FROM `bigquery-public-data`.london_bicycles.cycle_hire
)

SELECT
  start_station_name
  , AVG(time_at_station) AS unused_seconds
FROM unused
GROUP BY start_station_name
ORDER BY unused_seconds ASC
LIMIT 5
```

From this query, we learn that bicycles turn over the fastest at the following stations:

Row	start_station_name	unused_seconds
1	LSP1	1500.0
2	Wormwood Street, Liverpool Street	4605.427372968633
3	Hyde Park Corner, Hyde Park	5369.884926322234
4	Speakers' Corner 1, Hyde Park	6203.571977906734
5	Albert Gate, Hyde Park	6258.720194303267

Joining with precomputed values

Sometimes it can be helpful to precompute functions on smaller tables and then join with the precomputed values rather than repeat an expensive calculation each time.

For example, suppose that you want to find the pair of stations between which our customers ride bicycles at the fastest pace. To compute the pace[13] (minutes per kilometer) at which they ride, we need to divide the duration of the ride by the distance between stations.

We could create a denormalized table with distances between stations and then compute the average pace:

```
with denormalized_table AS (
  SELECT
    start_station_name
    , end_station_name
    , ST_DISTANCE(ST_GeogPoint(s1.longitude, s1.latitude),
                  ST_GeogPoint(s2.longitude, s2.latitude)) AS distance
    , duration
  FROM
    `bigquery-public-data`.london_bicycles.cycle_hire AS h
  JOIN
```

---

13 In bicycling and running, pace is the inverse of speed.

```
      `bigquery-public-data`.london_bicycles.cycle_stations AS s1
    ON h.start_station_id = s1.id
      JOIN
        `bigquery-public-data`.london_bicycles.cycle_stations AS s2
    ON h.end_station_id = s2.id
  ),

  durations AS (
    SELECT
      start_station_name
      , end_station_name
      , MIN(distance) AS distance
      , AVG(duration) AS duration
      , COUNT(*) AS num_rides
    FROM
      denormalized_table
    WHERE
      duration > 0 AND distance > 0
    GROUP BY start_station_name, end_station_name
    HAVING num_rides > 100
  )

  SELECT
      start_station_name
      , end_station_name
      , distance
      , duration
      , duration/distance AS pace
  FROM durations
  ORDER BY pace ASC
  LIMIT 5
```

This query invokes the geospatial function `ST_DISTANCE` once for each row in the cycle_hire table (24 million times), takes 16.1 seconds, and processes 1.86 GB.

Alternatively, we can use the `cycle_stations` table to precompute the distance between every pair of stations (this is a self-join) and then join it with the reduced-size table of average duration between stations:

```
with distances AS (
  SELECT
    a.id AS start_station_id
    , a.name AS start_station_name
    , b.id AS end_station_id
    , b.name AS end_station_name
    , ST_DISTANCE(ST_GeogPoint(a.longitude, a.latitude),
              ST_GeogPoint(b.longitude, b.latitude)) AS distance
  FROM
    `bigquery-public-data`.london_bicycles.cycle_stations a
  CROSS JOIN
    `bigquery-public-data`.london_bicycles.cycle_stations b
  WHERE a.id != b.id
```

```
  ),

  durations AS (
    SELECT
      start_station_id
      , end_station_id
      , AVG(duration) AS duration
      , COUNT(*) AS num_rides
    FROM
      `bigquery-public-data`.london_bicycles.cycle_hire
    WHERE
      duration > 0
    GROUP BY start_station_id, end_station_id
    HAVING num_rides > 100
  )

SELECT
    start_station_name
    , end_station_name
    , distance
    , duration
    , duration/distance AS pace
FROM distances
JOIN durations
USING (start_station_id, end_station_id)
ORDER BY pace ASC
LIMIT 5
```

The recast query with the more efficient joins takes only 5.4 seconds, an increase in speed of three times, and processes 554 MB, a reduction in cost of nearly four times.

JOIN versus denormalization

What if we were to store the distance traveled in each trip in a denormalized table?

```
CREATE OR REPLACE TABLE ch07eu.cycle_hire AS
SELECT
  start_station_name
  , end_station_name
  , ST_DISTANCE(ST_GeogPoint(s1.longitude, s1.latitude),
                ST_GeogPoint(s2.longitude, s2.latitude)) AS distance
  , duration
FROM
  `bigquery-public-data`.london_bicycles.cycle_hire AS h
JOIN
  `bigquery-public-data`.london_bicycles.cycle_stations AS s1
ON h.start_station_id = s1.id
JOIN
  `bigquery-public-data`.london_bicycles.cycle_stations AS s2
ON h.end_station_id = s2.id
```

Querying this table returns results in 8.7 seconds and processes 1.6 GB—in other words, it's 60% slower and about three times more expensivethan the previous query. In this instance, therefore, joining with a smaller table turns out to be more efficient than querying a larger, denormalized table. However, this is the sort of thing that you need to measure for your particular use case. You will see later how you can efficiently store data at differing levels of granularity in a single denormalized table with nested and repeated fields.

Avoiding Overwhelming a Worker

Some operations (e.g., ordering) need to be carried out on a single worker. Having to sort too much data can overwhelm a worker's memory and result in a "resources exceeded" error. Avoid overwhelming the worker with too much data. As the hardware in Google datacenters is upgraded, what "too much" means in this context expands over time. Currently, this is on the order of one gigabyte.

Limiting large sorts

Suppose that you want to go through the bike rentals and number them 1, 2, 3, and so on, in the order that the rentals ended. We could do that by using the ROW_NUMBER() function (we cover window functions in Chapter 8):

```
SELECT
  rental_id
  , ROW_NUMBER() OVER(ORDER BY end_date) AS rental_number
FROM `bigquery-public-data`.london_bicycles.cycle_hire
ORDER BY rental_number ASC
LIMIT 5
```

Here's the result:

Row	rental_id	rental_number
1	40346512	1
2	40346508	2
3	40346519	3
4	40346510	4
5	40346520	5

However, this query takes 29.9 seconds to process just 372 MB because it needs to sort the entirety of the london_bicycles dataset on a single worker. Had we processed a larger dataset, it would have overwhelmed that worker.

In such cases, we might want to consider whether it is possible to limit the large sorts and distribute them. Indeed, it is possible to extract the date from the rentals and then sort trips within each day:

```
WITH rentals_on_day AS (
SELECT
  rental_id
  , end_date
  , EXTRACT(DATE FROM end_date) AS rental_date
FROM `bigquery-public-data.london_bicycles.cycle_hire`
)

SELECT
  rental_id
  , rental_date
  , ROW_NUMBER() OVER(PARTITION BY rental_date ORDER BY end_date) AS
rental_number_on_day
FROM rentals_on_day
ORDER BY rental_date ASC, rental_number_on_day ASC
LIMIT 5
```

This takes 8.9 seconds (an increase in speed of three times) because the sorting can be done on just a single day of data at a time. It yields the rental number on a day-by-day basis:

Row	rental_id	rental_date	rental_number_on_day
1	40346512	2015-01-04	1
2	40346508	2015-01-04	2
3	40346519	2015-01-04	3
4	40346510	2015-01-04	4
5	40346520	2015-01-04	5

Data skew

The same problem of overwhelming a worker (in this case, overwhelming the memory of the worker) can happen during an ARRAY_AGG with GROUP BY if one of the keys is much more common than the others.[14]

Because there are more than three million GitHub repositories and the commits are well distributed among them, this query succeeds:

```
SELECT
  repo_name
  , ARRAY_AGG(STRUCT(author, committer, subject, message, trailer, difference,
encoding) ORDER BY author.date.seconds)
FROM `bigquery-public-data.github_repos.commits`, UNNEST(repo_name) AS repo_name
GROUP BY repo_name
```

---

14 This is a current limitation of the BigQuery dynamic execution runtime; it might be eased in the future.

However, most of the people using GitHub live in only a few time zones, so grouping by the time zone fails—we are asking a single worker to sort a significant fraction of 750 GB:

```
SELECT
  author.tz_offset, ARRAY_AGG(STRUCT(author, committer, subject, message,
trailer, difference, encoding) ORDER BY author.date.seconds)
FROM `bigquery-public-data.github_repos.commits`
GROUP BY author.tz_offset
```

One solution is to add a `LIMIT` to the `ORDER BY`:

```
SELECT
  author.tz_offset, ARRAY_AGG(STRUCT(author, committer, subject, message,
trailer, difference, encoding) ORDER BY author.date.seconds LIMIT 1000)
FROM `bigquery-public-data.github_repos.commits`
GROUP BY author.tz_offset
```

If you do require sorting all of the data, use more granular keys (i.e., distribute the group's data over more workers) and then aggregate the results corresponding to the desired key. For example, instead of grouping only by the time zone, it is possible to group by time zone *and* repo_name and then aggregate across repositories to get the actual answer for each time zone:

```
SELECT
  repo_name, author.tz_offset
  , ARRAY_AGG(STRUCT(author, committer, subject, message, trailer, difference,
encoding) ORDER BY author.date.seconds)
FROM `bigquery-public-data.github_repos.commits`, UNNEST(repo_name) AS repo_name
GROUP BY repo_name, author.tz_offset
```

Optimizing user-defined functions

Invoking a JavaScript user-defined function (UDF) requires a V8 subprocess to be launched, and this degrades performance. JavaScript UDFs are computationally expensive and have access to limited memory, so reducing the amount of data processed by the UDF can help improve performance.

Although BigQuery supports UDFs in JavaScript, opt to write your UDFs using SQL wherever possible; SQL is distributed and optimized by BigQuery natively. If you are writing a UDF in SQL, there is no performance difference between embedding the SQL function directly in the query or using temporary and permanent functions. The reason to use an SQL UDF is for reusability, composability, and readability.

Using Approximate Aggregation Functions

BigQuery provides fast, low-memory approximations of aggregate functions. Instead of using COUNT(DISTINCT …), we can use APPROX_COUNT_DISTINCT on large data streams when a small statistical uncertainty in the result is tolerable.

Approximate count

For example, you can find the number of unique GitHub repositories by using:

```
SELECT
  COUNT(DISTINCT repo_name) AS num_repos
FROM `bigquery-public-data`.github_repos.commits, UNNEST(repo_name) AS repo_name
```

This query takes 7.1 seconds to compute the correct result of 3,348,576. On the other hand, the following query takes 3.2 seconds (an increase in speed of two times) and returns an approximate result of 3,400,927, which overestimates the correct answer by 1.5%:

```
SELECT
  APPROX_COUNT_DISTINCT(repo_name) AS num_repos
FROM `bigquery-public-data`.github_repos.commits, UNNEST(repo_name) AS repo_name
```

On smaller datasets, however, there might be no advantage. Let's look at an example that finds the total number of unique bicycles in the london_bicycles dataset:

```
SELECT
  COUNT(DISTINCT bike_id) AS num_bikes
FROM `bigquery-public-data`.london_bicycles.cycle_hire
```

This takes 0.9 seconds and returns the correct result of 13,705. Using the approximate counterpart takes 1.6 seconds (which is slower than the exact query) and returns an approximate result of 13,699:

```
SELECT
  APPROX_COUNT_DISTINCT(bike_id) AS num_bikes
 FROM `bigquery-public-data`.london_bicycles.cycle_hire
```

> The approximate algorithm is much more efficient than the exact algorithm only on large datasets and is recommended in use cases for which errors of approximately 1% are tolerable. Before using the approximate function, always measure on your use case!

Approximate top

Other available approximate functions include APPROX_QUANTILES to compute percentiles, APPROX_TOP_COUNT to find the top elements, and APPROX_TOP_SUM to compute top elements based on the sum of an element.

Here's an example of using `APPROX_TOP_COUNT` to find the five most frequently rented bicycles:

```
SELECT
  APPROX_TOP_COUNT(bike_id, 5) AS num_bikes
FROM `bigquery-public-data`.london_bicycles.cycle_hire
```

This yields the following:

Row	num_bikes.value	num_bikes.count
1	12925	2922
	12841	2489
	13071	2474
	12926	2467
	12991	2444

Note that the result is a single row and consists of an array of values so that ordering is preserved.

> If your queries are taking too long, you can use `APPROX_TOP_COUNT` to check whether data skew is the reason. If so, consider the tips earlier in the chapter on dealing with data skew by carrying out the operation at a more granular level or using `LIMIT` to reduce the data being processed.

To find the top five stations based on duration of bicycle rentals, you can use `APPROX_TOP_SUM`:

```
SELECT
  APPROX_TOP_SUM(start_station_name, duration, 5) AS num_bikes
FROM `bigquery-public-data`.london_bicycles.cycle_hire
WHERE duration > 0
```

Here is the result of that query:

Row	num_bikes.value	num_bikes.sum
1	Hyde Park Corner, Hyde Park	600037440
	Black Lion Gate, Kensington Gardens	581085720
	Albert Gate, Hyde Park	367235700
	Speakers' Corner 1, Hyde Park	318485820
	Speakers' Corner 2, Hyde Park	268442640

HLL functions

In addition to the just-described `APPROX_*` functions (which carry out the entire approximate aggregation algorithm), BigQuery also supports the HyperLogLog++

(HLL++) algorithm (*https://research.google.com/pubs/pub40671.html*), which allows you to break down the count-distinct problem into three separate operations:

1. Initialize a set, called an HLL sketch, by adding new elements to it by using `HLL_COUNT.INIT`

2. Find the cardinality (count) of an HLL sketch by using `HLL_COUNT.EXTRACT`

3. Merge two HLL sketches into a single sketch by using `HLL_COUNT.MERGE_PARTIAL`

In addition, `HLL_COUNT.MERGE` combines steps 2 and 3, computing the count from a set of HLL sketches.

For example, here's a query that finds the count of distinct stations in the London bicycles table regardless of whether a trip started or ended at the station:

```
WITH sketch AS (
SELECT
    HLL_COUNT.INIT(start_station_name) AS hll_start
    , HLL_COUNT.INIT(end_station_name) AS hll_end
FROM `bigquery-public-data`.london_bicycles.cycle_hire
)

SELECT
  HLL_COUNT.MERGE(hll_start) AS distinct_start
  , HLL_COUNT.MERGE(hll_end) AS distinct_end
  , HLL_COUNT.MERGE(hll_both) AS distinct_station
FROM sketch, UNNEST([hll_start, hll_end]) AS hll_both
```

This returns the following:

Row	distinct_start	distinct_end	distinct_station
1	880	882	882

Of course, you also can achieve this by using `APPROX_COUNT_DISTINCT` directly:

```
SELECT
    APPROX_COUNT_DISTINCT(start_station_name) AS distinct_start
    , APPROX_COUNT_DISTINCT(end_station_name) AS distinct_end
    , APPROX_COUNT_DISTINCT(both_stations) AS distinct_station
FROM
    `bigquery-public-data`.london_bicycles.cycle_hire
    , UNNEST([start_station_name, end_station_name]) AS both_stations
```

This yields the same result and is much simpler to read and understand. Mostly, therefore, you would use the `APPROX_` variants.

One reason to use the HLL functions might be that you need to employ manual aggregation or prevent storage of specific columns. Suppose that your data has the schema `user_id`, `date`, `product`, `country`, and you need to compute the number of distinct users. However, the column `user_id` is personally identifying, and so you would prefer to not store it indefinitely. In such a case, you can compute a manual aggregation using `HLL_COUNT.INIT`, as follows:

```
INSERT INTO approx_distinct_users_agg AS
SELECT date, product, country, HLL_COUNT.INIT(user_id) AS sketch
GROUP BY date, product, country, sketch
```

Now you don't need to store `user_id`; you only need to store the sketch. Whenever you need to compute any higher-level aggregation, you can do the following:

```
SELECT date, HLL_COUNT.MERGE(sketch)
FROM approx_distinct_users_agg
GROUP BY date
```

Optimizing How Data Is Stored and Accessed

In the previous section, we discussed how to improve query performance, but we limited ourselves to methods that do not change the layout of the table, where it is stored, or how it is accessed. In this section, we look at how addressing these factors can have a dramatic impact on query performance. Obviously, you will want to keep these tips in mind as you design your tables, because changing the schema of a table tends to break existing queries.

Minimizing Network Overhead

BigQuery is a regional service that is globally accessible. If you are querying a dataset that resides in the EU region, for example, the query will run on computational resources that are located in an EU datacenter. If you store the results of the query into a destination table, that table must be in a dataset that is also in the EU. You can, however, invoke the BigQuery REST API (i.e., invoke the query) from anywhere in the world, even from machines outside of GCP.

When working with other GCP resources such as Google Cloud Storage or Cloud Pub/Sub, the best performance will be obtained if you also locate them in the same region as the dataset. Thus, for example, if you are invoking a query from a Compute Engine instance or a Cloud Dataproc cluster, network overhead will be minimized if the instance or cluster is also located in the same region as the dataset being queried.

If you're invoking BigQuery from outside GCP, consider the network topology and try to minimize the number of hops between the client machine and the GCP datacenter in which the dataset resides.

Compressed, partial responses

When invoking the REST API directly, you can minimize network overhead by accepting compressed, partial responses. To accept compressed responses, you can specify in the HTTP header that you will accept gzip and make sure that the string "gzip" appears in the name of the user-agent—for example:

```
Accept-Encoding: gzip
User-Agent: programName (gzip)
```

Then the responses are compressed using gzip.

By default, responses from BigQuery contain all of the fields promised in the documentation. However, if we know what part of the response we are interested in, we can ask BigQuery to send back only that bit of the response, thus lowering the network overhead. For example, earlier in this chapter, we looked at how to get back the complete job details using the Jobs API. If you are interested in only a subset of the full response (for example, only the steps in the query plan), you can specify the field(s) of interest to limit the size of the response:[15]

```
JOBSURL="https://www.googleapis.com/bigquery/v2/projects/$PROJECT/jobs"
FIELDS="statistics(query(queryPlan(steps)))"
curl --silent \
    -H "Authorization: Bearer $access_token" \
    -H "Accept-Encoding: gzip" \
    -H "User-Agent: get_job_details (gzip)" \
    -X GET \
    "${JOBSURL}/${JOBID}?fields=${FIELDS}" \
| zcat
```

Note that we are also specifying that we accept gzip encoding.

Batching multiple requests

When using the REST API, it is possible to batch multiple BigQuery API calls by using the `multipart/mixed` content type and nesting HTTP requests in each of the parts. The body of each part specifies the HTTP operation (GET, PUT, etc.), path portion of the URL, headers, and body. The server's response is a single HTTP response with a `multipart/mixed` content type, with the parts being responses (in order) to the requests that form the batched request. Even though the responses are in order, the server might execute the calls in any order. Thus you should treat the batched request as a parallel execution.

Here's an example of sending a batched request to get some query plan details of the last five queries in our project. You first use the BigQuery command-line tool to get the five most recent successful jobs:[16]

```
# The 5 most recent successful jobs
JOBS=$(bq ls -j -n 50 | grep SUCCESS | head -5 | awk '{print $1}')
```

---

15 This is *07_perf/get_job_details_compressed.sh* in the GitHub repository for this book.

16 This is *07_perf/get_recent_jobs.sh* in the GitHub repository for this book.

The request goes to the batch endpoint for BigQuery:

```
BATCHURL="https://www.googleapis.com/batch/bigquery/v2"
JOBSPATH="/projects/$PROJECT/jobs"
FIELDS="statistics(query(queryPlan(steps)))"
```

Using the URL path, you can form the individual requests:

```
request=""
for JOBID in $JOBS; do
read -d '' part << EOF

--batch_part_starts_here
GET ${JOBSPATH}/${JOBID}?fields=${FIELDS}

EOF
request=$(echo "$request"; echo "$part")
done
```

Then you can send the request to the batch endpoint as a multipart request:

```
curl --silent \
    -H "Authorization: Bearer $access_token" \
    -H "Content-Type: multipart/mixed; boundary=batch_part_starts_here" \
    -X POST \
    -d "$request" \
    "${BATCHURL}"
```

Bulk reads using BigQuery Storage API

In Chapter 5, we discussed using the BigQuery REST API and associated client libraries to list table data and get query results. The REST API provides the data in record-oriented, paginated views that are more conducive to relatively small result sets. Yet, with the advent of machine learning and distributed Extract, Transform, and Load (ETL) tools, external tools now require fast, efficient bulk access to BigQuery's managed storage. Such bulk read access is provided by the BigQuery Storage API via Remote Procedure Call (RPC)–based protocol. With the BigQuery Storage API, structured data is sent over the wire in a binary serialization format that maps more closely to the columnar format in which the data is stored. This allows for additional parallelism among multiple consumers for a set of results.

It is unlikely that you will use the BigQuery Storage API directly[17] if you are an end user. Instead, you will take advantage of tools such as Cloud Dataflow, Cloud Dataproc, TensorFlow, AutoML, and others that employ the Storage API to read directly from BigQuery's managed storage instead of going through the BigQuery API.

---

17 You can if you want to, however; see *https://cloud.google.com/bigquery/docs/reference/storage/samples*. The endpoint for the BigQuery Storage API is different from that of the BigQuery REST API—it's *bigquerystorage.googleapis.com*.

Because the Storage API directly accesses stored data, permission to access the Big-Query Storage API is distinct from the existing BigQuery API. The BigQuery Storage API must be enabled independently of enabling BigQuery.

The BigQuery Storage API provides several benefits to tools that read directly from BigQuery's managed storage. For example, consumers can read disjoint a set of rows from a table using multiple streams (enabling distributed reads from different workers in Cloud Dataproc, for example), dynamically shard these streams (thus reducing tail latency, which can be a significant problem for MapReduce jobs), select a subset of columns to read (enabling machine learning frameworks to read only the features used by the model), filter column values (reducing the data transmitted over the network), and still ensure snapshot consistency (i.e., read data as of a specific point in time).

In Chapter 5, we looked at using the Jupyter Magics `%%bigquery` to load the result of queries into pandas DataFrames. However, those datasets were relatively small—on the order of a dozen to a few hundred rows. What if you want to load the entire `london_bicycles` dataset (24 million rows) into a pandas DataFrame? In that case, it is possible to specify an option on the Magics to load the data into the pandas Data-Frame using the Storage API rather than the BigQuery API. You will need to first install the Storage API Python client library with Avro and pandas support. You can do this within Jupyter by using the following:

```
%pip install google-cloud-bigquery-storage[fastavro,pandas]
```

Then use the `%%bigquery` Magics as before, but add the Storage API option:

```
%%bigquery df --use_bqstorage_api --project $PROJECT
SELECT
  start_station_name
  , end_station_name
  , start_date
  , duration
FROM `bigquery-public-data`.london_bicycles.cycle_hire
```

Note that we are taking advantage of the ability of the Storage API to provide direct access to individual columns; it is not necessary to read the entire BigQuery table into the pandas DataFrame. If it so happens that the amount of data returned by the query is comfortably small, the Magics falls back automatically to the BigQuery API. Therefore, there is no harm in always using this flag in your notebook cells. To turn `--use_bqstorage_api` on by default in all the Magics cells within a notebook session, you can set a context flag:

```
import google.cloud.bigquery.magics
google.cloud.bigquery.magics.context.use_bqstorage_api = True
```

Choosing an Efficient Storage Format

Query performance depends on where the table data is stored, and in what format. In general, the fastest performance is obtained if you store data in such a way that queries need to do very little seeking or type conversion.

Internal versus external data sources

Even though BigQuery supports querying directly from external sources such as Google Cloud Storage, Cloud Bigtable, and Google Sheets, the fastest query performance will be obtained if you use native tables.

We recommend that you use BigQuery as your analytics data warehouse for all your structured and semi-structured data. Use external data sources for staging (Google Cloud Storage), real-time ingest (Cloud Pub/Sub, Cloud Bigtable), or transactional updates (Cloud SQL, Cloud Spanner). Then, as described in Chapter 4, set up a periodic data pipeline to load the data from these external sources into BigQuery.

If your use case is such that you need to query the data from Google Cloud Storage, store it in a compressed, columnar format (e.g., Parquet) if you can. Use row-based formats such as JSON or comma-separated values (CSV) only as a last resort.

Setting up life cycle management on staging buckets

If you are loading data into BigQuery by staging it in Google Cloud Storage first, consider deleting the Google Cloud Storage data after the data is loaded. If you are performing ETL on the data to load it into BigQuery (so that the data in BigQuery is heavily transformed or is only a subset), you might want to retain the raw data in Google Cloud Storage. In such cases, reduce costs by creating life cycle rules on buckets, to downgrade the Google Cloud Storage storage class.

To enable life cycle management on a bucket so that data in multiregional or standard classes older than 30 days is moved to Nearline Storage, and Nearline data older than 90 days is moved to Coldline Storage:

```
gsutil lifecycle set lifecycle.yaml gs://some_bucket/
```

In this example, the file *lifecycle.yaml* contains this content:

```
{
"lifecycle": {
  "rule": [
  {
     "action": {
       "type": "SetStorageClass",
       "storageClass": "NEARLINE"
     },
     "condition": {
       "age": 30,
```

```
        "matchesStorageClass": ["MULTI_REGIONAL", "STANDARD"]
      }
    },
    {
      "action": {
        "type": "SetStorageClass",
        "storageClass": "COLDLINE"
      },
      "condition": {
        "age": 90,
        "matchesStorageClass": ["NEARLINE"]
      }
    }
  ]}}
```

You can use life cycle management not just to change an object's class but also to delete objects older than a certain threshold.[18]

Storing data as arrays of structs

One of the BigQuery public datasets is a dataset of cyclonic storms (hurricanes, typhoons, cyclones, etc.) as observed and measured by various meteorological agencies around the world. Cyclonic storms can last up to a few weeks, and observations are carried out once every three hours or so. Suppose that you want to query this dataset to find all of the storms in 2018, the maximum wind speed attained by each storm over its lifetime, and the time and location of the storm when this maximum wind speed was reached. This query pulls out the necessary information from the public dataset:

```
SELECT
  sid, number, basin, name,
  ARRAY_AGG(STRUCT(iso_time, usa_latitude, usa_longitude, usa_wind) ORDER BY
usa_wind DESC LIMIT 1)[OFFSET(0)].*
FROM
  `bigquery-public-data`.noaa_hurricanes.hurricanes
WHERE
  season = '2018'
GROUP BY
  sid, number, basin, name
ORDER BY number ASC
```

We are extracting the storm ID (sid), the storm number within the season, the basin, and the name of the storm (if named) and then finding the array of observations made of this storm, ranking the observations in descending order of wind speed, and

---

18 For more details, see *https://cloud.google.com/storage/docs/managing-lifecycles#change_an_objects_storage_class*.

taking the highest wind speed observed for each storm. The storms themselves are ordered by number. The result consists of 88 rows, and looks something like this:

Row	sid	number	basin	name	iso_time	usa_latitude	usa_longitude	usa_wind
1	2018002N09123	1	WP	BOLAVEN	2018-01-02 18:00:00 UTC	9.7	117.2	29
2	2018003S15053	2	SI	AVA	2018-01-05 06:00:00 UTC	-17.9	50.0	93
3	2018006S13092	3	SI	IRVING	2018-01-07 18:00:00 UTC	-15.8	83.0	89
4	2018010S18123	4	SI	JOYCE	2018-01-11 18:00:00 UTC	-18.7	121.6	54

The query processed 41.7 MB and took 1.4 seconds. The first row is of a storm named Bolaven that reached a maximum wind speed of 29 kph on January 2, 2018, at 18:00 UTC.

Because observations are carried out by multiple meteorological agencies, it is possible to standardize this data using nested fields and store the structs in BigQuery, as follows:[19]

```
CREATE OR REPLACE TABLE ch07.hurricanes_nested AS

SELECT sid, season, number, basin, name, iso_time, nature, usa_sshs,
       STRUCT(usa_latitude AS latitude, usa_longitude AS longitude, usa_wind AS
wind, usa_pressure AS pressure) AS usa,
       STRUCT(tokyo_latitude AS latitude, tokyo_longitude AS longitude,
           tokyo_wind AS wind, tokyo_pressure AS pressure) AS tokyo,
       ... AS cma,
       ... AS hko,
       ... AS newdelhi,
       ... AS reunion,
       ... bom,
       ... AS wellington,
       ... nadi
FROM `bigquery-public-data`.noaa_hurricanes.hurricanes
```

Querying this table is similar to querying the original table, except that field names change a bit (usa.latitude instead of usa_latitude):

---

19 You can find all queries in this section in *07_perf/hurricanes.sql* in the GitHub repository for this book.

```
SELECT
  sid, number, basin, name,
  ARRAY_AGG(STRUCT(iso_time, usa.latitude, usa.longitude, usa.wind) ORDER BY
usa.wind DESC LIMIT 1)[OFFSET(0)].*
FROM
  ch07.hurricanes_nested
WHERE
  season = '2018'
GROUP BY
  sid, number, basin, name
ORDER BY number ASC
```

The query processes the same amount of data and takes the same time as the original query on the public dataset. Using nested fields (i.e., structs) does not change the query speed or cost, although it might make your query more readable.

Because there are multiple observations of the same storm over its life cycle, we can change the storage to have a single row per storm and store an array of observations for each storm:

```
CREATE OR REPLACE TABLE ch07.hurricanes_nested_track AS

SELECT sid, season, number, basin, name,
 ARRAY_AGG(
   STRUCT(
       iso_time,
       nature,
       usa_sshs,
       STRUCT(usa_latitude AS latitude, usa_longitude AS longitude, usa_wind AS
wind, usa_pressure AS pressure) AS usa,
       STRUCT(tokyo_latitude AS latitude, tokyo_longitude AS longitude,
           tokyo_wind AS wind, tokyo_pressure AS pressure) AS tokyo,
       ... AS cma,
       ... AS hko,
       ... AS newdelhi,
       ... AS reunion,
       ... bom,
       ... AS wellington,
       ... nadi
   ) ORDER BY iso_time ASC ) AS obs
FROM `bigquery-public-data`.noaa_hurricanes.hurricanes
GROUP BY sid, season, number, basin, name
```

Notice that we are now storing sid, season, and so on as scalar columns because they do not change over the lifetime of the storm. The remaining data that changes for each observation is stored as an array of structs. Here's how querying this table now looks:[20]

---

20 Chapter 2 covers SQL syntax for working with arrays.

```
SELECT
  number, name, basin,
  (SELECT AS STRUCT iso_time, usa.latitude, usa.longitude, usa.wind
        FROM UNNEST(obs) ORDER BY usa.wind DESC LIMIT 1).*
FROM ch07.hurricanes_nested_track
WHERE season = '2018'
ORDER BY number ASC
```

The result is the same, but this time the query processes only 14.7 MB (a reduction in cost of three times) and finishes in one second (a 30% improvement in speed). Why does this improvement in performance happen? When we store the data as an array, the number of rows in the table reduces dramatically (from 682,000 to 14,000),[21] because there is now only one row per storm instead of one row per observation time. Then when we filter the rows by checking for season, BigQuery is able to discard many related observations simultaneously, as shown in Figure 7-13.

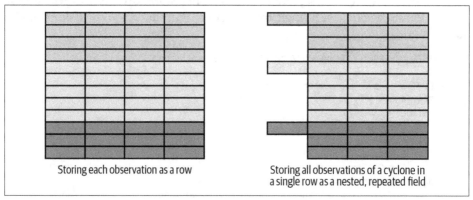

Storing each observation as a row   Storing all observations of a cyclone in
                                       a single row as a nested, repeated field

Figure 7-13. Nested and repeated fields can speed up query performance by allowing BigQuery to discard many related observations simultaneously

Another benefit is that we no longer need to duplicate rows of data when we have unequal levels of granularity within the same table. You can store both the granular-level individual hurricane latitude and longitude data as well as the high-level hurricane ID, name, and season data in the same table. And because BigQuery stores table data as highly compressed individual columns, you can query and process the high-level data without the cost of operating over the rows of granular data—it is now stored as an array of values per hurricane.

For example, if you simply want to query the number of storms by year, you could query just the columns you want from the details:

---

21 Because the hurricanes dataset is continually refreshed, the row numbers might be larger when you are reading this.

```
WITH hurricane_detail AS (

SELECT sid, season, number, basin, name,
 ARRAY_AGG(
   STRUCT(
       iso_time,
       nature,
       usa_sshs,
       STRUCT(usa_latitude AS latitude, usa_longitude AS longitude, usa_wind AS
wind, usa_pressure AS pressure) AS usa,
       STRUCT(tokyo_latitude AS latitude, tokyo_longitude AS longitude, tokyo_wind
AS wind, tokyo_pressure AS pressure) AS tokyo
   ) ORDER BY iso_time ASC ) AS obs
FROM `bigquery-public-data`.noaa_hurricanes.hurricanes
GROUP BY sid, season, number, basin, name
)

SELECT
  COUNT(sid) AS count_of_storms,
  season
FROM hurricane_detail
GROUP BY season
ORDER BY season DESC
```

The preceding query processes 27 MB instead of the 56 MB it would have had to process had we not used nested, repeated fields.

Nested fields by themselves do not improve performance, although they can improve readability by essentially prejoining other related tables into a single location. Nested, repeated fields, on the other hand, are extremely advantageous from a performance standpoint. Consider using nested, repeated fields in your schema, because they have the potential to provide you a significant boost in speed and lower query costs whenever you have queries that filter on a column that is not nested or repeated (season, in our case).

A key drawback to nested, repeated fields is that you cannot easily stream to this table if the streaming updates involve adding elements to existing arrays—it is no longer as simple as appending a row to the table: you now need to mutate the existing row. Of course, because the hurricane data is updated with new observations, this drawback would be quite significant, and it explains why the public dataset of hurricanes does not use nested, repeated fields.

On the other hand, the public dataset of GitHub commits (bigquery-public-data.github_repos.commits) uses a nested, repeated field (repo_name) to store the list of repositories affected by a commit. This doesn't change over time. So using a nested, repeated field for repo_name provides a speedup to queries that filter on any other field.

Practicing with Arrays

In our experience, nested, repeated fields require a bit of practice and familiarity. The Google Analytics sample dataset[22] in BigQuery is ideal for this purpose. The easiest way to identify nested data in a schema is by looking for RECORD in the *Type column*, which indicates a STRUCT data type, and by looking for REPEATED in the *Mode column*, as you can see here:

Field name	Type	Mode
visitorId	INTEGER	NULLABLE
visitStartTime	INTEGER	NULLABLE
date	STRING	NULLABLE
totals	**RECORD**	NULLABLE
totals. visits	INTEGER	NULLABLE
totals. hits	INTEGER	NULLABLE
hits	**RECORD**	**REPEATED**
hits. hitNumber	INTEGER	NULLABLE
hits. time	INTEGER	NULLABLE

In this sample schema, TOTALS is a STRUCT (but not repeated), and HITS is a STRUCT that is REPEATED. This makes sense because Google Analytics tracks visitor session data at the aggregate level (one session value for totals.hits) and at the detail level (individual hits.time values for every page and image accessed on your site). Storing data at this differing level of granularity, without duplicating visitorId across rows, is possible only with ARRAYs.

After data is stored in a repeated format with arrays, you will need to UNNEST the data in your queries, as shown here:[23]

```
SELECT DISTINCT
  visitId
  , totals.pageviews
  , totals.timeOnsite
  , trafficSource.source
  , device.browser
  , device.isMobile
  , h.page.pageTitle
FROM
  `bigquery-public-
data`.google_analytics_sample.ga_sessions_20170801,
```

---

22 The dataset is bigquery-public-data.google_analytics_sample.ga_sessions_20170801.

23 This is in *07_perf/google_analytics.sql* in the GitHub repository for this book.

```
  UNNEST(hits) AS h
WHERE
  totals.timeOnSite IS NOT NULL AND h.page.pageTitle =
'Shopping Cart'
ORDER BY pageviews DESC
LIMIT 10
```

Unnesting an array breaks it apart from [1,2,3,4,5] into individual rows, like so:

```
[1,
 2
 3
 4
 5]
```

Now you can run normal SQL operations like a WHERE clause to filter all of the page
hits where the title was Shopping Cart. Try it out!

Storing data as geography types

Within the BigQuery public dataset of utility data is a table of polygon boundaries of
US zip codes (available in bigquery-public-data.utility_us.zipcode_area) and
another table of polygon boundaries of US cities (bigquery-public-
data.utility_us.us_cities_area). The US zip code geometry column (zip
code_geom) is a string,[24] whereas the city geometry column (city_geom) is a
geography type.

From these two tables, it is possible to get a list of all the zip codes for Santa Fe, New
Mexico:[25]

```
SELECT name, zipcode
FROM `bigquery-public-data`.utility_us.zipcode_area
JOIN `bigquery-public-data`.utility_us.us_cities_area
ON ST_INTERSECTS(ST_GeogFromText(zipcode_geom), city_geom)
WHERE name LIKE '%Santa Fe%'
```

The query took 51.9 seconds and processed 305.5 MB to produce the following:

Row	name	zipcode
1	Santa Fe, NM	87505
2	Santa Fe, NM	87501
3	Santa Fe, NM	87507

---

24 This is actually a deprecated dataset for reasons that will become apparent in this section. The more up-to-
    date data is bigquery-public-data.geo_us_boundaries.us_zip_codes—that dataset does use geography
    types.

25 Chapter 4 covers geographic types and GIS functions.

Row	name	zipcode
4	Eldorado at Santa Fe, NM	87508
5	Santa Fe, NM	87508
6	Santa Fe, NM	87506

Why did the query take so long? This is not because ST_INTERSECTS is expensive; it is mainly because the ST_GeogFromText function needs to compute the S2 cells[26] and build a GEOGRAPHY type corresponding to each zip code.

We can change the zip code table to do this computation beforehand and store the geometry as a GEOGRAPHY type:

```
CREATE OR REPLACE TABLE ch07.zipcode_area AS
SELECT
  * REPLACE(ST_GeogFromText(zipcode_geom) AS zipcode_geom)
FROM
  `bigquery-public-data`.utility_us.zipcode_area
```

 SELECT * REPLACE (see the previous snippet) is a convenient way to replace a column from a SELECT * statement.

The new dataset is 131.8 MB, which is somewhat larger than the 116.5 MB of the original table. However, the trade-off is that queries against the table can take advantage of S2 coverings and become much faster. Thus, the following query finishes in 5.3 seconds (a speed increase of 10 times) and processes 320.8 MB (a slight increase in cost if you are using on-demand pricing):

```
SELECT name, zipcode
FROM ch07.zipcode_area
JOIN `bigquery-public-data`.utility_us.us_cities_area
ON ST_INTERSECTS(zipcode_geom, city_geom)
WHERE name LIKE '%Santa Fe%'
```

The performance advantages of storing geographic data as GEOGRAPHY types instead of as strings or primitives are very compelling. This is why the utility_us dataset is deprecated (it's still publicly accessible so as to not break already written queries). We recommend that you use the table bigquery-public-data.geo_us_boundaries.us_zip_codes, which uses GEOGRAPHY types and is kept up to date.

---

26 See *https://oreil.ly/PkIsx*.

Partitioning Tables to Reduce Scan Size

Imagine that you frequently query the london_bicycles dataset by year:

```
SELECT
  start_station_name
  , AVG(duration) AS avg_duration
FROM `bigquery-public-data`.london_bicycles.cycle_hire
WHERE EXTRACT(YEAR from start_date) = 2015
GROUP BY start_station_name
ORDER BY avg_duration DESC
LIMIT 5
```

This takes 2.8 seconds and processes 1 GB to return the stations responsible for the longest trips in 2015:

Row	start_station_name	avg_duration
1	Mechanical Workshop Penton	105420.0
2	Contact Centre, Southbury House	5303.75
3	Stewart's Road, Nine Elms	4836.380090497735
4	Black Lion Gate, Kensington Gardens	4788.747908066496
5	Speakers' Corner 2, Hyde Park	4610.192911183014

The query, however, must read through the entire table to find rows from 2015. In this section, we look at various ways to cut down on the size of the data being processed.

Antipattern: Table suffixes and wildcards

If filtering by year is very common, one way to cut down on the data being read is to store the data in multiple tables, with the name of each table suffixed by the year. This way, querying the data for 2015 does not require traversing rows corresponding to all the years but can instead just read the cycle_hire_2015 table.

Let's go ahead and create such a table using the following:

```
CREATE OR REPLACE TABLE ch07eu.cycle_hire_2015 AS (
  SELECT * FROM `bigquery-public-data`.london_bicycles.cycle_hire
  WHERE EXTRACT(YEAR from start_date) = 2015
)
```

Now let's create it with a year-sharded table. The query finishes in one second (a speed increase of three times) and needs to process only 345 MB (a cost saving of three times):

```
SELECT
  start_station_name
  , AVG(duration) AS avg_duration
 FROM ch07eu.cycle_hire_2015
```

```
  GROUP BY start_station_name
  ORDER BY avg_duration DESC
  LIMIT 5
```

 Use partitioned tables and template tables (covered next) instead of manually splitting your data across multiple tables.

It is possible to use wildcards and table suffixes to search for multiple years:

```
SELECT
  start_station_name
  , AVG(duration) AS avg_duration
FROM `ch07eu.cycle_hire_*`
WHERE _TABLE_SUFFIX BETWEEN '2015' AND '2016'
GROUP BY start_station_name
ORDER BY avg_duration DESC
LIMIT 5
```

Partitioned tables

Partitioned tables allow you to store all of your related data in a single logical table but also efficiently query a subset of that data. If, for example, you store the last year's worth of data but usually query only the last week, partitioning by time allows you to run queries that will need to scan only the last seven days' worth of partitions. This can save orders of magnitude in query cost, slot utilization, and time.

The year-named tables discussed in the previous section are inefficient: BigQuery needs to maintain a copy of the schema and metadata for each of the sharded tables and verify permissions on each of the queried tables. Also, a single query cannot query more than 1,000 tables, and this might make querying the entire dataset difficult if your tables are sharded by date rather than by year (1,000 tables is not even three years of data if the tables are date-sharded). Furthermore, streaming into date-sharded tables can lead to the need for clock and time zone synchronization among multiple clients. The recommended best practice, therefore, is to use partitioned tables.

 Partitioning and clustering are the most effective ways to reduce your query cost and improve performance. When in doubt, you should partition and cluster your tables; this enables a number of performance optimizations that are not available to unpartitioned or unclustered tables.

A partitioned table is a special table that is divided into partitions, with the partitions managed by BigQuery. We can create a partitioned version of the London cycle_hire dataset using the following:

```
CREATE OR REPLACE TABLE ch07eu.cycle_hire_partitioned
    PARTITION BY DATE(start_date) AS
SELECT * FROM `bigquery-public-data`.london_bicycles.cycle_hire
```

 You can keep storage costs in check by specifying an expiration time for a partition and asking BigQuery to ensure that users are always using a partition filter (and not querying the entire table by mistake):

```
CREATE OR REPLACE TABLE ch07eu.cycle_hire_partitioned
    PARTITION BY DATE(start_date)
    OPTIONS(partition_expiration_days=1000,
            require_partition_filter=true) AS
SELECT * FROM `bigquery-public-
data`.london_bicycles.cycle_hire
```

If you forget to set this option at the time of creating the table, you can always add it after the fact:

```
ALTER TABLE ch07eu.cycle_hire_partitioned
SET OPTIONS(require_partition_filter=true)
```

Then, to find the stations with the longest average rentals in 2015, query the partitioned table, making sure to use the partition column (start_date) in the filter clause:

```
SELECT
  start_station_name
  , AVG(duration) AS avg_duration
FROM ch07eu.cycle_hire_partitioned
WHERE start_date BETWEEN '2015-01-01' AND '2015-12-31'
GROUP BY start_station_name
ORDER BY avg_duration DESC
LIMIT 5
```

The query takes one second and processes only 419.4 MB, a little more than the year-sharded table (because of the need to read the start_date column), but it is still a saving over having to read the full dataset. Note, however, that there are disadvantages to formulating the query as follows:

```
SELECT
  start_station_name
  , AVG(duration) AS avg_duration
FROM ch07eu.cycle_hire_partitioned
WHERE EXTRACT(YEAR FROM start_date) = 2015
GROUP BY start_station_name
ORDER BY avg_duration DESC
LIMIT 5
```

This will end up processing 1 GB and will not yield any savings on the amount of data processed. To obtain the benefits of partitioning, the BigQuery runtime must be able to statically determine the partition filters.

It is possible to ask BigQuery to automatically partition the table based on ingestion time rather than a date/time column. To do so, use _PARTITIONTIME or _PARTITIONDATE as the partitioning column. These are pseudocolumns that refer to the ingestion time and do not actually exist in your dataset. You can, however, use these pseudocolumns in your queries to restrict the rows being scanned.

If you are streaming to an ingestion-time-partitioned table, data in the streaming buffer is held in the __UNPARTITIONED__ partition. To query data in the __UNPARTITIONED__ partition, look for NULL values in the _PARTITIONTIME pseudocolumn.

Besides partitioning by date, it is possible to partition by hour and by any integer-valued column. For example, to partition by the bike_id in increments of 5 between 0 and 1000, we would do:

```
bq mk --range_partitioning=bike_id,0,1000,5 \
    ch07eu.partition_cycle_hire  schema.json
```

New data written to an integer range partitioned table will automatically be partitioned. This includes writing to the table via load jobs, queries, and streaming. As your dataset changes over time, BigQuery will automatically re-partition the table.

Reducing number of partitions

At the time of writing, the maximum number of partitions in a single table is 4000. If you are partitioning by date, you will run out of partitions after 10 years.

If you are partitioning by hour, you will run out of partitions in a few months if you will receive data at all hours of the day. On the other hand, if you will receive data only between 9 a.m. and 5 p.m., only 8 partitions will be used and you have enough partitions for more than one year.

The fact that the number of partitions depends on usage provides the mitigation mechanism. We suggest routinely collapsing multiple partitions in older data into a single partition. You can do this by truncating the timestamp used as the partitioning column. For example, to collapse daily partitions into monthly partitions for data older than 2015, you could do:

```
IF(ts < '2015-01-01 00:00:00',
    TIMESTAMP_TRUNC(ts, MONTH), TIMESTAMP_TRUNC(ts, DAY))
    AS partition_ts
```

It is possible to use table decorators to quickly access specific segments of the table. For example, to get all the bicycle rides in the first partition (0-5 ID range), we can add the $0 suffix to the table name:

```
bq query 'SELECT * FROM ch07eu.partition_cycle_hire$0'
```

We recommend against doing this, though. It is better to just write queries naturally with a `WHERE` clause on the `bike_id` and allow BigQuery to optimize the query to read only a single partition.

Clustering Tables Based on High-Cardinality Keys

Clustering, like partitioning, is a way to instruct BigQuery to store data in a way that can allow less data to be read at query time. Whereas a partitioned table behaves similarly to a number of independent tables (one per partition), clustered tables are stored in a sorted format as a single table. This ordering allows unlimited unique values to be stored without any performance penalty, and it also means that when a filter is applied, BigQuery can skip opening any file that doesn't contain the range of values being requested.

Clustering can be done on any primitive nonrepeated columns (`INT64`, `BOOL`, `NUMERIC`, `STRING`, `DATE`, `GEOGRAPHY`, and `TIMESTAMP`). Usually, you'd cluster on columns that have a very high number of distinct values, like `customerId` if you have millions of customers. If you have columns that aren't as high in cardinality but are frequently used together, you can cluster by more than one column at a time. When you cluster by multiple columns, you can filter by any prefix of the clustering columns and realize the benefits of clustering.

If most of the queries on our bicycles dataset use `start_station_name` and `end_station_name`, we could optimize the storage to take advantage of this commonality in our queries by creating the table as follows:

```
CREATE OR REPLACE TABLE ch07eu.cycle_hire_clustered
  PARTITION BY DATE(start_date)
  CLUSTER BY start_station_name, end_station_name
AS (
 SELECT * FROM `bigquery-public-data`.london_bicycles.cycle_hire
)
```

Then queries that use the clustering columns in order could experience a significant benefit—for example:

```
SELECT
  start_station_name
  , end_station_name
  , AVG(duration) AS duration
FROM ch07eu.cycle_hire_clustered
```

```
WHERE
  start_station_name LIKE '%Kennington%'
  AND end_station_name LIKE '%Hyde%'
GROUP BY start_station_name, end_station_name
```

But in this case, the entire table is only 1.5 GB and fits into a single block, thus there is no improvement.

To see the benefits of clustering, we must use a larger table. Our colleague Felipe Hoffa has conveniently created a clustered table of 2.20 TB of Wikipedia views, where the clustering was as follows:

```
CLUSTER BY wiki, title
```

As long as we use `wiki` (and, optionally, `title`) in our queries, we will gain the benefits of clustering. For example, we can search English Wikipedia for the number of page views in June 2017 for articles whose titles contained the term "Liberia":

```
SELECT title, SUM(views) AS views
FROM `fh-bigquery.wikipedia_v3.pageviews_2017`
WHERE DATE(datehour) BETWEEN '2017-06-01' AND '2017-06-30'
AND wiki = 'en'
AND title LIKE '%Liberia%'
GROUP BY title
```

This query took 4.8 seconds elapsed and processed 38.6 GB. Had the table not been clustered (only partitioned),[27] the query would have taken 25.9 seconds (five times slower) and processed 180.2 GB (five times costlier). On the other hand, a query that doesn't first filter by wiki will not experience any benefits.

Clustering by the partitioning column

Partitioned tables are partitioned by date (whether it is a column or it is by ingestion time). If you need hour-level partitioning, one option is to use date-based partitioning and then cluster by hour along with whatever other attributes are appropriate.

So a common pattern is to cluster by the same column as you partition by. For example, if you partition by `event_time`, a timestamp at which your log events occur, this will let you do very fast and efficient queries over arbitrary time periods that are smaller than the day boundary used in the partitioning. You could, for instance, query over only the last 10 minutes of data, and you wouldn't need to scan anything older than that.

In a partitioned table, each partition consists of a single day of data, and BigQuery maintains the metadata necessary to ensure that queries, load jobs, and Data Defini-

---

27 Try it using fh-bigquery.wikipedia_v2.pageviews_2017.

tion Language (DDL)/DML statements all take advantage and maintain the integrity of the partitions.

Reclustering

In a clustered table, BigQuery sorts the data based on the values in the clustering columns and organizes them into storage blocks that are optimally sized for efficient scanning and discarding of unnecessary data. However, unlike with partitioning, BigQuery does not maintain the sorting of data within clusters as data is streamed to it. BigQuery will recluster the data periodically in order to maintain efficient data pruning and scan speed. You can see how efficiently clustered the table is by looking at the clustering_ratio of the table (1.0 is completely optimal).

Updating a table using DML forces a recluster of the partition being updated. For example, assume that you periodically receive a table of corrections (which consist of cycle hires that were somehow missed in the previous updates). Using a MERGE statement such as the following will cause a recluster of any partitions that are updated:

```
MERGE ch07eu.cycle_hire_clustered all_hires
USING ch07eu.cycle_hire_corrections some_month
ON all_hires.start_station_name = some_month.start_station_name
WHEN MATCHED
  AND all_hires._PARTITIONTIME = DATE(some_month.start_date) THEN
  INSERT (rental_id, duration, ...)
  VALUES (rental_id, duration, ...)
```

 If you don't want to wait until BigQuery gets around to reclustering the table into which you have streamed updates, you can take advantage of the ability of DML statements to force a recluster. For example, you can apply a no-op UPDATE to the partitions of interest (perhaps those written in the past 24 hours):

```
UPDATE ch07eu.cycle_hire_clustered
SET start_station_id = 300
WHERE start_station_id = 300
AND start_date > TIMESTAMP_SUB(CURRENT_TIMESTAMP(),
INTERVAL 1 DAY)
```

Table 7-1 summarizes the differences between partitioning and clustering and might help you choose between partitioning a table based on a column and clustering the table by that column.

Table 7-1. Partitioning versus clustering

	Partitioning	Clustering
Distinct values	Less than 10,000	Unlimited
Data management	Like a table (can expire, delete, etc.)	DML only
Dry run cost	Precise	Upper bound
Final cost	Precise	Block level (difficult to predict)
Maintenance	None (exact partitioning happens immediately)	Background (impact might be delayed until background clustering occurs)

Side benefits of clustering

Remember that we mentioned that running `SELECT * ... LIMIT 10` in BigQuery is an antipattern because it ends up billing you for the full scan of the table. For clustered tables, this is not true. When you're reading from a clustered table, BigQuery will pass along any optimizations that can be done to prevent reading data. So if you do `SELECT * ... LIMIT 10` on a clustered table, the execution engine will be able to stop reading data as soon as 10 rows have been returned. Because of how the query engine employs a number of parallel workers, any of which could happen to finish first, the amount of data that is scanned is not deterministic. On the plus side, you will end up with queries that cost you much less on large tables.

A surprising side effect of the "early stop" cost reduction is that you can get performance benefits even if you don't filter on the clustering columns—if you filter by columns that are correlated to your clustering columns, BigQuery might be able to read less data!

Suppose that you have a table with two columns: `zip_code` and `state`. You cluster based on `zip_code`, which means that the data is sorted by `zip_code` when it is stored on disk. In the United States, there is a correlation between `state` and `zip_code` because zip code ranges are assigned geographically (`00000` in the Northeast and `99999` in the Northwest). If you run a query that filters by `state`, even though you're not filtering by the clustering column, BigQuery skips any data block that doesn't have that state, and you'll end up paying less for the query.

When a table is clustered, it allows BigQuery to apply a number of performance optimizations that are not possible with nonclustered tables. One of these optimizations is designed for *star schemas*, which let you filter based on constraints in a dimension table. For example, suppose that you have a fact table containing `orders`, which is clustered by `customer_id`, and a dimension table containing `customers`, and you run the following query:

```
SELECT o.*
FROM orders o
```

```
JOIN customers c USING (customer_id)
WHERE c.name = "Changying Bao"
```

Ordinarily, this query would need to scan the full `orders` table in order to execute the join. But because the orders table is clustered by the column that is being used for the join, the righthand side of the join—querying customers and finding the matching customer IDs—is done first. Then the second part of the query just needs to look up the clustering column that matches the `customer_id`. From a bytes-scanned perspective, it is as if BigQuery ran the following queries in parallel:

```
// First look up the customer id.
// This scans only the small dimension table
SET id = SELECT customer_id FROM customers
WHERE c.name = "Changying Bao"
// Next look up the customer from the orders table.
// This will filter by the cluster column,
// and so only needs to read a small amount of data.
SELECT * FROM orders WHERE customer_id=$id ;
```

In short, clustering is highly recommended if you want to reduce query costs and improve performance.

Cost Optimization

BigQuery is designed to minimize the time taken to derive insights from data. Consequently, we can carry out ad hoc, interactive analytics on large datasets and stream in updates to those datasets in near real time. Sometimes, though, you might be less time sensitive. Perhaps all you need are nightly reports. In such cases, you might be willing to have your queries be queued up and executed when possible, and this might be sufficient for the reports to reflect data as of an hour ago.

The practices recommended in this section can be helpful in controlling cost but our recommendations are based on standard pricing models at the time of writing. Pricing is subject to change. We recommend that you verify whether your business has negotiated any pricing discounts. For example, Google sometimes takes on the storage costs associated with public datasets created by non-profits. You should verify pricing before putting any of the practices discussed in this section into effect.

Batch Queries

You can submit a set of queries, called *batch queries*, to the service, and they will be queued on your behalf and started when idle resources are available. At the time they were introduced, in 2012 (*https://developers.googleblog.com/2012/08/now-in-bigquery-batch-queries-and.html*), batch queries provided a pricing benefit. However, as of this writing, both interactive and batch queries cost the same. If you use flat-rate pricing, both batch queries and interactive queries share your allocated slots.

Because batch queries are not less expensive and use the same reservations and slots as interactive resources, the primary reason that you might want to employ batch queries is that they don't count toward your concurrent rate limit and can make scheduling hundreds of queries easier.

There are a number of rate limits that affect interactive (i.e., nonbatch) queries. For example, you might be able to have at most 100 queries running concurrently,[28] with concurrent byte limits and "large query" limits. If those limits are reached, the query will fail immediately. This is because BigQuery assumes that an interactive query is something the user needs to run immediately. When you use batch queries, on the other hand, if you ever reach a rate limit, the queries will be queued and retried later. There are still similar rate limits, but they operate separately from interactive rate limits, so your batch queries won't affect your interactive ones.

One example might be that you have periodic queries that you run daily or hourly to build dashboards. Maybe you have 500 queries that you want to run. If you try to run them all at once as interactive, some will fail because of concurrent rate limits. Additionally, you don't necessarily want these queries to interfere with other queries you are running manually from the BigQuery web UI. So you can run the dashboard queries at batch priority, and the other queries will run normally as interactive.

To use batch queries, provide the `--batch` flag to the `bq` command-line tool or specify the job priority in the console or REST API to be `BATCH`, not `INTERACTIVE`. If Big-Query hasn't started the query within 24 hours, BigQuery changes the job priority to interactive. However, the typical wait time before a query starts is on the order of minutes, unless you are submitting more queries than your quota of concurrent requests. Then queries will be run after earlier ones complete.

Optimizing Storage Cost

Reduce the cost of storing data by reducing the time it is stored, by editing it infrequently, and by taking advantage of federated queries.

BigQuery charges for storage based on the amount of data stored in your tables per second. To optimize the storage cost of data, consider whether there is a period beyond which the data will not be needed. that is not needed long-term. If so, make sure to specify an expiration time stamp for that data. You can also specify a default expiration for newly created tables in a dataset and can alter the `expiration_time stamp` of existing tables using `ALTER TABLE`. Expiration timestamps can be set at the partition level. This is particularly useful if your tables are partitioned hourly or daily by ingestion time.

---

28 This is the default, but you can request these quotas to be increased. These soft quotas also keep changing. It was 50 when we first wrote the book, and 100 in May 2020. See *https://cloud.google.com/bigquery/quotas*.

The storage cost is lower for data stored in tables or partitions that have not been modified for 90 days. This lower price for longer-term storage is automatic and does not come with any reduction in performance, durability, availability or any other functionality. Design your schema in such a way that editing older data using DML operations is not necessary in order to keep it up-to-date. One way is to add time-stamps to each row, and have queries get the version of the data with the latest time-stamp. Also, avoid actions such as streaming, copying, or DDL that will bring your data back to active storage and reset the 90-day timer. Instead, consider loading the new batch of data to a new table partition.

The storage cost is based on the uncompressed data size but loading data into Big-Query is free. Google Cloud Storage, however, charges for compressed data. There-fore, for infrequently queried or highly compressible data, it might be more cost-effective to use federated queries. Take into account, however, that queries that run on external sources will be slower than queries executed on same data stored on Big-Query, since data stored on BigQuery is optimized for better query performance. Further, with clustering and partitioning, queries on BigQuery native storage may be less expensive as well. Because of this, the crossover point varies by dataset, and so you will have to measure the different in query costs between BigQuery native and federation and the difference in storage costs between uncompressed and compressed storage.

Avoid storing duplicate copies of your data. Store your data either in Google Cloud Storage or in BigQuery, not in both. For example, for storing archives for legal rea-sons, exporting BigQuery data into the Coldline class of Cloud Storage might be very cost-effective. In such cases, remove the data from BigQuery.

Query Cost Control

Set up cost controls (hard limits on the bytes processed by BigQuery) to catch acci-dental human errors. This is particularly important if you are on on-demand pricing but is beneficial even on flat-rate pricing to avoid legitimate users being slowed down by erroneous queries.

Administrators (project owners, editors, and anyone with the `serviceusage.quo tas.update` permission) can set cost controls at the user level and at the project level. They can manage costs by requesting a custom quota that specifies a limit on the amount of query data processed per day. This is done from the IAM quotas section (*http://console.cloud.google.com/iam-admin/quotas*) of the Google Cloud Console.

If you are sending queries through a tool, you can also specify maximum bytes billed at the level of an individual query. You can also carry out a query dry-run and have the user confirm the query cost if the query will cost above a certain threshold.

We recommend that most users start with on-demand pricing coupled with tight cost controls. Once your BigQuery monthly bill hits the minimum flat-rate price (*https://cloud.google.com/bigquery/pricing*) (currently $10,000 for 500 slots), start to check your monthly slot utilization using Cloud Monitoring. Flat-rate pricing might allow you to have a stable monthly cost for unlimited data processed rather than paying a variable on-demand rate based on the bytes processed by queries. Of course, queries beyond the flat rate limit will run slower—hence the importance of checking the slot utilization pattern to see whether slot usage happens in a spiky way or is more spread out.

While most users will use either flat-rate pricing or on-demand pricing, BigQuery offers a third alternative: flex slots. Use flex slots assigned to separate projects for unusual activity without having to modify the per-user or per-project quotas associated with daily, interactive work. Large organizations will typically have a hybrid of flat-rate pricing (for routine, predictable workloads such as reporting), on-demand pricing with tight cost controls (for exploration-heavy workloads such as those of data science teams and new projects), and flex slots (for one-off activity and foreseeable spikes).

File Loads

If you care about minimizing the "time to insight" or wish to have the simplest possible data pipeline, we strongly encourage you to use streaming inserts into BigQuery via Cloud Pub/Sub and Cloud Dataflow. This architecture provides ingest speeds on the order of 100,000 rows per second, even on small Cloud Dataflow clusters. You can horizontally scale the Dataflow cluster by adding more machines and achieve several million rows per second of ingest performance without having to tweak any knobs.[29]

Streaming ingests incur charges, whereas load jobs are free. In some scenarios, you might be willing to trade off a few minutes' latency for reduced ingestion costs. In that case, consider using file loads instead of streaming inserts. You can do that from Apache Beam's `BigQueryIO` using the following:

```
BigQueryIO.writeTableRows()
            .to("project-id:dataset-id.table-id")
            .withCreateDisposition(
              BigQueryIO.Write.CreateDisposition.CREATE_IF_NEEDED)
            .withMethod(Method.FILE_LOADS)
            .withTriggeringFrequency(Duration.standardSeconds(600))
            .withNumFileShards(10)
```

---

[29] Because streaming ingests are charged for, you might have to ask for a quota increase. Check the default quotas at *https://cloud.google.com/bigquery/quotas#streaming_inserts* and request additional streaming quota from the GCP console.

```
            .withSchema(new TableSchema()...)
            .withoutValidation())
```

The previous code snippet writes to BigQuery every 10 minutes using file loads, thus avoiding the streaming ingestion charge. File loads can scale to 300,000 rows per second on medium-sized Dataflow clusters. However, you should be aware that computing and finalizing windows does take time, and so there will be a latency on the order of a few minutes. Because of per-table and per-project load quotas, and because failures and retries count against quota, we recommend that you do file loads no more frequently than every five minutes.

Summary

In this chapter, we looked at ways to control costs, by using the `dry_run` feature and by setting up limits on the number of bytes billed. Then we examined ways to measure query speed using the REST API or a custom measurement tool.

We also covered several methods for increasing query speed. To minimize the I/O overhead, we recommended ways to reduce the data being read. We also looked at different entities that could be cached, from previous query results to intermediate results and entire tables in memory. We also looked at ways to do joins efficiently, by avoiding self-joins, reducing the data being joined, and taking advantage of precomputed values. By limiting large sorts, safeguarding against data skew, and optimizing user-defined functions, we can minimize the chances of slots getting overwhelmed. Finally, we recommended the use of approximate aggregation functions, including count and top functions.

Finally, we looked at ways of optimizing data storage and speeding up data access. We suggested that our applications be refactored to accept compressed, partial responses, send requests in batches, and perform bulk reads using the Storage API. We discovered that storing data as arrays of structs and as geography types brings performance advantages. We also looked at different ways of reducing the size of data being scanned, namely through partitioning and clustering.

Checklist

We'd like to end this chapter the way we began, by recommending that, although these performance improvements can be significant, you should verify that they apply to your workflow. Follow this checklist if your query is running slow:

If you observe that:	Possible solutions
Self-join is being used	Use aggregate functions to avoid self-joins of large tables
	Use window (analytic) functions to compute self-dependent relationships
DML is being used	Batch your DML (INSERT, UPDATE, DELETE) statements

If you observe that:	Possible solutions
Join is slow	Reduce data being joined
	Perhaps denormalize the data
	Use nested, repeated fields instead
Queries are being invoked repeatedly	Take advantage of query caching
	Materialize previous results to tables
Workers are overwhelmed	Limit large sorts in window functions
	Check for data skew
	Optimize user-defined functions
Count, top, distinct are being used	Consider using approximate functions
I/O stage is slow	Minimize network overhead
	Perhaps use a join to reduce table size
	Choose efficient storage format
	Partition tables
	Cluster tables

Advanced Queries

In Chapters 2 and 3, we covered the essentials of the Standard SQL queries and data types supported in BigQuery. A parser and analyzer for the dialect of Standard SQL supported by BigQuery has been open sourced as ZetaSQL (*https://github.com/google/zetasql*). The ZetaSQL parser and analyzer is used to provide consistent behavior, type checking, implicit casting, name resolution, and more across all the Google Cloud Platform (GCP) products that support SQL (e.g., Cloud Spanner and Cloud Dataflow). However, these query engines might not support all of the features in the ZetaSQL language. For example, BigQuery does not, as of this writing, support multi-statement transactions. As of this writing, Cloud Dataflow does not support geographic queries, but if it ever does, the GIS SQL queries and geography types in Cloud Dataflow will be similar to those of BigQuery.

In this chapter, we look at features, data types, and functions of ZetaSQL supported by BigQuery that go beyond the Standard SQL or that might be unfamiliar to many data analysts. We begin by discussing the syntax of features like parameterized queries and user-defined functions that support reusability. Then we delve into the SQL syntax involving arrays, windows, table metadata, and data definition and manipulation. We cover how scripting and stored procedures are supported in BigQuery, and we end the chapter by covering Geographic Information Systems, statistical, and encryption functions.

Reusable Queries

BigQuery supports a number of features that allow queries and parts of a query to be reused. We can parameterize queries and extract commonly used code into functions, subqueries, or `WITH` clauses. Let's look at each of these in turn.

Parameterized Queries

Parameterized queries allow us to define a query in terms of parameters that are specified at the time of execution. This can allow the same query to be used in different contexts while avoiding the need to use string formatting to create the runtime query.[1]

As of this writing, invoking parameterized queries is not supported by the BigQuery web user interface (UI). In Chapter 4, we looked at running parameterized queries using the REST API and from a Jupyter Magics. To mix things up, in this chapter we demonstrate parameterized queries using the Python Cloud Client API.

Named parameters

Getting back to our London bike rental queries, suppose that we often want to look for the number of rentals from individual stations whose duration was within a specific range, but the station and duration thresholds tend to vary. We can define a parameterized query to provide this functionality, with the station name and duration threshold as parameters to the query:[2]

```
query = """
    SELECT
      start_station_name
      , AVG(duration) as avg_duration
    FROM
      `bigquery-public-data`.london_bicycles.cycle_hire
    WHERE
      start_station_name LIKE CONCAT('%', @STATION, '%')
      AND duration BETWEEN @MIN_DURATION AND @MAX_DURATION
    GROUP BY start_station_name
"""
```

The query has named parameters marked by an @ symbol, but note the way that the parameter is used within LIKE. Had we simply written '%@STATION%', BigQuery would have treated the @ symbol literally because of the enclosing single quotes. Hence, the parameter is formed using @ and then concatenated with strings containing the wildcard % symbol.

At execution time, the named parameters are replaced by query parameters, each of which is defined in terms of its name, its SQL data type, and its runtime value (this is Python, given that we are using the Python Cloud Client API for BigQuery):

---

1 As explained in Chapter 5, creating a query by doing string formatting can make your data warehouse subject to SQL injection attacks.

2 See *08_advqueries/param_named.py* in the GitHub repository for this book (*https://github.com/GoogleCloud Platform/bigquery-oreilly-book*).

```
query_params = [
    bigquery.ScalarQueryParameter(
        "STATION", "STRING", station_name),
    bigquery.ScalarQueryParameter(
        "MIN_DURATION", "FLOAT64", min_duration),
    bigquery.ScalarQueryParameter(
        "MAX_DURATION", "FLOAT64", max_duration),
]
```

To execute the query, we create a query job, pass in the query parameters, run the query, and parse the results as normal:

```
job_config = bigquery.QueryJobConfig()
job_config.query_parameters = query_params
query_job = client.query(
    query,
    location="EU",
    job_config=job_config,
)
for row in query_job:
    print("{}: \t{}".format(
        row.start_station_name, row.avg_duration))
```

The preceding code can be wrapped in a Python function that accepts the parameters as inputs:

```
def print_query_results(client,
                        station_name,
                        min_duration=0,
                        max_duration=84000):
```

The function can now be invoked multiple times with different parameters:

```
client = bigquery.Client()
print_query_results(client, 'Kennington', 300)
print_query_results(client, 'Hyde Park', 600, 6000)
```

This renders the following:

```
Kennington between 300 and 84000
Kennington Oval, Oval: 1269.0798128928543
Doddington Grove, Kennington:    1243.7377963737788
Kennington Road Post Office, Oval:       1360.2854550952536
Kennington Lane Rail Bridge, Vauxhall: 991.4344845855808
Cleaver Street, Kennington:      1075.6050140700947
Kennington Cross, Kennington:    996.2538654101008
Kennington Road, Vauxhall:       1228.6673653660118
Cotton Garden Estate, Kennington:        996.7003600110778
Kennington Lane Tesco, Vauxhall:         929.6523615439942
Kennington Station, Kennington:          1238.4088412072647


Hyde Park between 600 and 6000
Bayswater Road, Hyde Park:       1614.2670577732417
Wellington Arch, Hyde Park:      1828.9651324965134
```

```
Hyde Park Corner, Hyde Park:    2120.4145144213744
Cumberland Gate, Hyde Park:     1899.3282223532708
Speakers' Corner 1, Hyde Park: 2070.2458069837776
Triangle Car Park, Hyde Park:   1815.661582196573
Albert Gate, Hyde Pafrk:         1897.9349474341027
Knightsbridge, Hyde Park:       1963.0815096317635
Serpentine Car Park, Hyde Park:       1688.0595490490423
Park Lane, Hyde Park:  2055.451932776309
Speakers' Corner 2, Hyde Park: 2093.6202531645563
```

In many SQL engines, parameterized queries (or prepared statements) are precompiled and can offer improved performance. In BigQuery, this is not the case. As the previous code snippet indicates, the query and the job configuration containing the query parameters are both passed into the BigQuery service at the same time (in the client.query call). The performance of a parameterized query will, therefore, be quite similar to that of a static one in which the parameter values are hardcoded.

There are, however, benefits to using parameters in BigQuery. One of those benefits is security and prevention against *SQL injection attacks*. If you generate a query and filter by a user-specified value, you need to make sure the user-specified value doesn't have any special characters. It can be very difficult to ensure that generated queries are "safe" when they include user-specified identifiers. An easy way to safeguard the queries is to use parameters; this makes certain that no matter the values provided in the parameter, no SQL injection attacks can occur.

Named timestamp parameters

In the previous query, the query parameters were strings and floats. Timestamps work the same way, as long as we make sure to pass in the corresponding Python (or Go or whichever client language we are using) data type. In the case of Python, we'd use datetime.datetime. Thus, to find the average duration of trips within an hour centered around a specific time, you would first import the necessary Python libraries:

```
from google.cloud import bigquery
from datetime import datetime
from datetime import timedelta
import pytz
```

Next, compute the parameter values:

```
def print_query_results(client, mid_time):
    start_time = mid_time - timedelta(minutes=30)
    end_time = mid_time + timedelta(minutes=30)
```

Then set up the query in terms of these parameters:

```
query = """
    SELECT
      AVG(duration) as avg_duration
    FROM
      `bigquery-public-data`.london_bicycles.cycle_hire
    WHERE
      start_date BETWEEN @START_TIME AND @END_TIME
"""
query_params = [
    bigquery.ScalarQueryParameter(
        "START_TIME", "TIMESTAMP", start_time),
    bigquery.ScalarQueryParameter(
        "END_TIME", "TIMESTAMP", end_time),
]
job_config = bigquery.QueryJobConfig()
job_config.query_parameters = query_params
query_job = client.query(
    query,
    location="EU",
    job_config=job_config,
)
for row in query_job:
    print(row.avg_duration)
print("_____")
```

You can invoke the function by passing in a `datetime` object corresponding to Christmas Day 2015:

```
client = bigquery.Client()
print_query_results(client,
        datetime(2015, 12, 25, 15, 0, tzinfo=pytz.UTC))
```

This informs us that the average duration of trips started between 2:30 p.m. and 3:30 p.m. on Christmas 2015 was 3658.5000000000005 seconds.

 Any scheduled query, when invoked, automatically receives two parameters: @run_time, which is a TIMESTAMP; and @run_date, which is a DATE. So any scheduled query can be parameterized by these two parameters.

Positional parameters

Even though it is possible to use positional parameters in BigQuery, we strongly encourage the use of named parameters in queries because they enhance readability, both of the queries and of the invoking code.[3] To use positional parameters, specify the parameters using ? and make sure to pass the parameters in order:[4]

```
def print_query_results(client, params):
    query = """
        SELECT
          start_station_name
          , AVG(duration) as avg_duration
        FROM
          `bigquery-public-data`.london_bicycles.cycle_hire
        WHERE
          start_station_name LIKE CONCAT('%', ?, '%')
          AND duration BETWEEN ? AND ?
        GROUP BY start_station_name
    """
    query_params = [
        bigquery.ScalarQueryParameter(
            None, "STRING", params[0]),
        bigquery.ScalarQueryParameter(
            None, "FLOAT64", params[1]),
        bigquery.ScalarQueryParameter(
            None, "FLOAT64", params[2]),
    ]
```

Array and struct parameters

The examples so far have used *scalar query parameters*. BigQuery also supports *array parameters*. Imagine that we have a UI that shows the number of trips from stations, which the user can select interactively—this would require the set of station IDs selected by the user to be provided to the query as an array.

You can find the number of trips emanating from each of the stations listed in an array parameter @STATIONS by using the array functions IN and UNNEST:[5]

```
query = """
    SELECT
      start_station_id
      , COUNT(*) as num_trips
    FROM
      `bigquery-public-data`.london_bicycles.cycle_hire
    WHERE
      start_station_id IN UNNEST(@STATIONS)
      AND duration BETWEEN @MIN_DURATION AND @MAX_DURATION
    GROUP BY start_station_id
```

---

3 The reason positional parameters are supported is that Open Database Connectivity and Java Database Connectivity drivers expect that query engines denote parameters with a question mark.

4 See *08_advqueries/param_positional.py* in the GitHub repository for this book.

5 See *08_advqueries/param_array.py* in the GitHub repository for this book.

```
"""
query_params = [
    bigquery.ArrayQueryParameter(
        'STATIONS', "INT64", ids),
    bigquery.ScalarQueryParameter(
        'MIN_DURATION', "FLOAT64", min_duration),
    bigquery.ScalarQueryParameter(
        'MAX_DURATION', "FLOAT64", max_duration),
]
```

Now pass in a Python array of IDs as the `stations` parameter:

```
print_query_results(client, [270, 235, 62, 149], 300, 600)
```

This yields the number of trips for each of the IDs passed in:

```
270:    26400
149:    4143
235:    8337
62:     5954
```

It is possible to pass in a struct to a query by constructing a struct parameter as follows:

```
bigquery.StructQueryParameter(
        "bicycle_trip",
        bigquery.ScalarQueryParameter("start_station_id", "INT64", 62),
        bigquery.ScalarQueryParameter("end_station_id", "INT64", 421),
    )
```

Note that you cannot parameterize table or column names or other parts of the query itself. If you run a parameterized query with `--dry_run` and do not pass in the required parameters, the response includes the inferred type of all parameters.

SQL User-Defined Functions

In addition to reusing entire queries by parameterizing them, it is possible to foster more granular reuse. For example, we can reuse a set of operations within an SQL query by refactoring those operations into a user-defined function (UDF).

Suppose that you want to find the number of overnight rentals by day of the week (an overnight rental is one in which the starting timestamp and ending timestamp fall on different days). Such a query will require frequent date manipulation; it can be convenient to define these common manipulations as temporary SQL UDFs:

```
CREATE TEMPORARY FUNCTION dayOfWeek(x TIMESTAMP) AS
(
  ['Sun','Mon', 'Tue', 'Wed', 'Thu', 'Fri', 'Sat']
      [ORDINAL(EXTRACT(DAYOFWEEK from x))]
);
CREATE TEMPORARY FUNCTION getDate(x TIMESTAMP) AS
(
```

```
    EXTRACT(DATE FROM x)
);
```

After you have defined these functions, you can take advantage of them by using the WITH clause to find overnight trips:

```
WITH overnight_trips AS (
  SELECT
    duration
    , dayOfWeek(start_date) AS start_day
  FROM
    `bigquery-public-data`.london_bicycles.cycle_hire
  WHERE
    getDate(start_date) != getDate(end_date)
)
```

To find the number of overnight rentals by day of the week, you can group the result of the preceding common table expression by day of week:

```
SELECT
  start_day
  , COUNT(*) AS num_overnight_rentals
  , AVG(duration)/3600 AS avg_duration_hours
FROM
  overnight_trips
GROUP BY
  start_day
ORDER BY num_overnight_rentals DESC
```

The result indicates that the highest number of overnight rentals happen on Saturday and Friday, and the fewest overnight rentals happen early in the workweek:

Row	start_day	num_overnight_rentals	avg_duration_hours
1	Sat	28095	9.13462063237824
2	Fri	23746	8.772040203262295
3	Thu	18153	9.792348372169885
4	Sun	16648	13.834484622777499
5	Wed	15571	10.848297047930972
6	Mon	12507	10.729399536259686
7	Tue	12461	9.430337319102266

Persistent UDFs

Because the functions in the previous sections were defined as temporary functions, we can use them only within the same BigQuery query. To reuse them in other queries, you'd need to copy and paste the definitions. Naturally, this is quite error prone.

If you have a function that you want to reuse across queries, it is preferable to save the function in a dataset and then refer to it from any number of queries (you need to create a dataset named ch08eu in the EU region before trying out this query):

```
CREATE OR REPLACE FUNCTION ch08eu.dayOfWeek(x TIMESTAMP) AS
(
 ['Sun','Mon', 'Tue', 'Wed', 'Thu', 'Fri', 'Sat']
   [ORDINAL(EXTRACT(DAYOFWEEK from x))]
);
```

Just as with tables, choose between CREATE FUNCTION, CREATE OR REPLACE FUNCTION, or CREATE FUNCTION IF NOT EXISTS depending on how you want the save operation of the function to behave if the function already exists: fail, replace the existing function, or be a no-op,[6] respectively. As with tables, you can DROP FUNCTION to remove a function from a dataset. And as with tables, this capability can be accessed from not just from SQL but also from the REST API, the bq command-line tool, or various client libraries.

After a function has been saved in a dataset, you can use it in a query by making sure to reference the project and dataset in which the function can be found (as with table names in queries, the default is to use the currently active project):

```
WITH overnight_trips AS (
    SELECT
      duration
      , ch08eu.dayOfWeek(start_date) AS start_day
    FROM
      `bigquery-public-data`.london_bicycles.cycle_hire
    ...
```

You can view the function definition from the BigQuery web UI, as shown in Figure 8-1.

Figure 8-1. Click a persistent function in the BigQuery web UI to view/edit its definition

---

6 A no-op, short for "no operation," is a statement that does nothing. See *https://en.wikipedia.org/wiki/NOP_(code)*.

The permissions for accessing UDFs are stored on the dataset level, similar to tables, and behave similarly. For example, the `bigquery.routines.list` permission allows holders to list the functions in a dataset, and the `bigquery.routines.[create/get/update/delete]` permission allows them to create, invoke, update, or delete the function.

Public UDFs

In particular, it is possible to define useful UDFs in a dataset that is shared with `allAuthenticatedUsers` to essentially extend the capability of BigQuery. For example, although BigQuery has an `AVG` function, it doesn't have a built-in `MEDIAN` function. Our colleagues Elliott Brossard and Felipe Hoffa defined an SQL UDF to compute the median, taking care to correctly handle computing the median of both odd-length and even-length arrays:[7]

```
CREATE OR REPLACE FUNCTION fhoffa.x.median (arr ANY TYPE) AS ((
  SELECT IF (MOD(ARRAY_LENGTH(arr), 2) = 0,
      ( arr[OFFSET(DIV(ARRAY_LENGTH(arr), 2) - 1)] +
        arr[OFFSET(DIV(ARRAY_LENGTH(arr), 2))]     ) / 2,
      arr[OFFSET(DIV(ARRAY_LENGTH(arr), 2))]
  )
  FROM (SELECT ARRAY_AGG(x ORDER BY x) AS arr FROM UNNEST(arr) AS x)
));
```

Because the dataset x in the `fhoffa` project is public, you can find the stations with the longest median duration of trips:

```
SELECT
  start_station_name
  , COUNT(*) AS num_trips
  , fhoffa.x.median(ARRAY_AGG(tripduration)) AS typical_duration
FROM `bigquery-public-data`.new_york_citibike.citibike_trips
GROUP BY start_station_name
HAVING num_trips > 1000
ORDER BY typical_duration DESC
LIMIT 5
```

Let's take a look at the result:

Row	start_station_name	num_trips	typical_duration
1	Mobile 01	1039	1697.0
2	Soissons Landing	18484	1525.0
3	Yankee Ferry Terminal	18013	1496.0

---

7 An array with an odd number of elements has a single element in the middle and equal numbers of elements on either side. If the array has an even number of elements, however, there are two elements in the middle, and the median is defined as the average of these two middle elements.

Row	start_station_name	num_trips	typical_duration
4	Central Park North & Adam Clayton Powell Blvd	54465	1419.0
5	Broadway & Moylan Pl	6121	1413.0

Why did we use New York and not London to illustrate the use of the median function? All the datasets in a query must be in the same location; because `fhoffa.x` is in the United States, we need to pick a US bikeshare dataset. The London database would not have worked.

A collection of such community-developed, open source UDFs is available at *https:// github.com/GoogleCloudPlatform/bigquery-utils* and synced to the public dataset `bqutil.fn`. Elliott and Felipe's median function is part of this repository and dataset, so this also works (try it):

```
SELECT
  start_station_name
  , COUNT(*) AS num_trips
  , bqutil.fn.median(ARRAY_AGG(tripduration)) AS typical_duration
FROM `bigquery-public-data`.new_york_citibike.citibike_trips
GROUP BY start_station_name
HAVING num_trips > 1000
ORDER BY typical_duration DESC
LIMIT 5
```

Even if you don't have a use case for public UDFs, you can foster reuse by placing useful UDFs within a dataset that is shared within your company.

Reusing Parts of Queries

Suppose that you want to find days with the highest number of unusually long round-trip rentals. We could define "unusually long" as rides of more than twice the average duration such trips take. The query then requires three steps:

1. Find roundtrip rentals.

2. Compute the average duration of roundtrip rentals at each London bicycle station.

3. Find days with rides longer than twice the average duration.

Correlated subquery

We can write the necessary query "inside-out," as follows:

```
SELECT
  start_date,
  COUNT(*) AS num_long_trips
FROM -- "first from"
  (SELECT
```

```
            start_station_name
          , duration
          , EXTRACT(DATE from start_date) AS start_date
        FROM
          `bigquery-public-data`.london_bicycles.cycle_hire
        WHERE
          start_station_name = end_station_name) AS roundtrips
  WHERE -- "outer where"
      duration > 2*(
        SELECT
          AVG(duration) as avg_duration
        FROM
          `bigquery-public-data`.london_bicycles.cycle_hire
        WHERE
          start_station_name = end_station_name
          AND roundtrips.start_station_name = start_station_name
    )
  GROUP BY start_date
  ORDER BY num_long_trips DESC
  LIMIT 5
```

The first FROM clause consists of a subquery that pulls the necessary columns from the London bicycles dataset and extracts the date from the timestamp field. The outer WHERE clause consists of a check against twice the average duration where the average duration itself is computed using a subquery.

The second subquery is an example of a correlated subquery—a subquery that uses values (in this case, start_station_name, duration, and end_station_name) from the outer query. Here, the second subquery needs to compute the average duration of trips that start and end at this station.

WITH clause

The WITH clause makes it possible to reuse table expressions and make queries more readable. You can rewrite the query in the previous section using two WITH clauses:

```
WITH roundtrips AS (
SELECT
  start_station_name
  , duration
  , EXTRACT(DATE from start_date) AS start_date
FROM
  `bigquery-public-data`.london_bicycles.cycle_hire
WHERE
    start_station_name = end_station_name
),
station_avg AS (
SELECT
  start_station_name
  , AVG(duration) as avg_duration
FROM
```

```
    roundtrips
  GROUP BY start_station_name
  )
```

These two, in turn, simplify the third computation:

```
SELECT
  start_date,
  COUNT(*) AS num_long_trips
FROM
  roundtrips
JOIN station_avg USING(start_station_name)
WHERE duration > 2*avg_duration
GROUP BY start_date
ORDER BY num_long_trips DESC
LIMIT 5
```

Note how roundtrips is reused in the station_avg WITH clause as well as in the main query. We would like to caution you, however, that reusing WITH clauses is limited to readability—the actual data is not necessarily cached or reused. Indeed, examining the query execution plan, you can see that both stage 0 and stage 4 begin with a READ from the bigquery-public-data dataset and that in the first case, only three columns are needed, whereas in the second case, four columns are needed, as depicted in Figure 8-2.

The result includes two Christmas Days:

Row	start_date	num_long_trips	a)
1	2016-12-25	740	b)
2	2016-05-08	714	c)
3	2017-04-09	667	d)
4	2015-08-01	663	e)
5	2015-12-25	660	f)

A WITH clause allows reuse only within a query. To reuse the result set in multiple queries, we can use an intermediate table or create a materialized view. This has the potential to trade off an additional storage cost for faster and less-expensive computation, but this is something that you should measure—many times. The WITH clause will be faster especially if the intermediate table is larger than the original. For more details on this, see Chapter 7.

Stages		Wait	Read
✓ S00: Input ∧	Avg:	51 ms	144 ms
	Max:	113 ms	262 ms

READ	$10:duration, $12:start_station_name, $11:end_station_name FROM bigquery-public-data.london_bicycles.cycle_hire WHERE equal($12, $11)
AGGREGATE	GROUP BY $70 := $12 $60 := SHARD_AVG($10)
WRITE	$70, $60 TO __stage00_output BY HASH($70)

Stages		Wait	Read
✓ S01: Aggregate ∨	Avg:	1 ms	0 ms
	Max:	1 ms	0 ms
✓ S03: Coalesce ∨	Avg:	0 ms	0 ms
	Max:	2 ms	0 ms
✓ S04: Join+ ∧	Avg:	0 ms	236 ms
	Max:	1 ms	318 ms

READ	$1:duration, $3:start_date, $4:start_station_name, $2:end_station_name FROM bigquery-public-data.london_bicycles.cycle_hire WHERE equal($4, $2)
READ	$50, $80 FROM __stage03_output

Figure 8-2. The query execution plan shows that the data is read twice

Defining constants

It is possible to use a WITH clause to hold constants and provide a single place where they can be changed. For example, we could look for stations that have the greatest number of trips longer than a certain duration by using the following:

```
WITH params AS (
  SELECT 600 AS DURATION_THRESH
)
SELECT
  start_station_name
  , COUNT(duration) as num_trips
FROM
```

```
  `bigquery-public-data`.london_bicycles.cycle_hire
  , params
WHERE duration >= DURATION_THRESH
GROUP BY start_station_name
ORDER BY num_trips DESC
LIMIT 5
```

By defining the duration threshold as part of the WITH clause, we are able to provide a convenient place to capture all the "magic" numbers used in the query and give them readable names. Note that the FROM clause in the preceding query includes parameters so that the constant DURATION_THRESH can be used in the query.

Another way to express constants is to use scripting syntax and declare them as variables. We cover this later in this chapter.

Advanced SQL

In this section, we look at SQL syntax that tends to vary quite a bit between different SQL engines (see "Ambiguities in Standard SQL" on page 313) but is nevertheless worth having in our toolkit. Arrays and window functions can greatly enhance query performance. Table metadata allows for reflection[8] and some neat solutions to common problems. Data Definition Language and Data Manipulation Language allow many database maintenance operations to be carried out in SQL itself, thus allowing us to use the same development, review, test, or Continuous Integration/Continuous Deployment (CI/CD) frameworks that we use for our SQL queries for database maintenance.

Ambiguities in Standard SQL

The topics covered in this chapter tend to be areas not covered or left vague in Standard SQL. Take arrays, for example. PostgreSQL supports array syntax of the following form:

```
SELECT pay_by_quarter[3] FROM sal_emp;
```

Whereas BigQuery in this case would require us to clarify our intention with UNNEST by specifying the following:

```
SELECT pay_by_quarter[ORDINAL(3)] FROM sal_emp, UNNEST(pay_by_quarter)
```

The PostgreSQL approach looks cleaner, but ambiguity crops up in more complex cases. For example, suppose that SELECT author, book.title FROM ds.all_books worked in BigQuery to do a correlated cross-join of nested, repeated fields, so that

---

8 In this context, reflection refers to the ability of an SQL query to modify its own structure and behavior at runtime based on the schema of a table.

this above query would return author: STRING, book.title: STRING, one for each row. This seems awfully convenient, but when we have multiple nested, repeated fields, we'd have a problem. For example, assuming that each chapter has a title, what's the query engine to do with the following:

```
SELECT author, book.title, book.chapter.title
FROM ds.all_books
```

The user might want book.chapter.title to be an array, or they might want it all fully flattened. Maintaining a restriction that there is no expression other than a JOIN that changes the number of rows in the output and requiring a comma-join with UNN EST to access arrays removes this sort of ambiguity.

Working with Arrays

Arrays in BigQuery are ordered lists containing values of the same data type. You will find arrays being used whenever there is a need for ordering, or storing repeated values in a single row, or both.

Storing data as arrays can reduce storage overhead and, depending on cardinality, greatly speed up queries that do not require the repeated fields. Because of this, you should make it a point to understand and become familiar with arrays.

Using arrays to preserve ordering

As an example of the need to preserve ordering, consider that we need to carry out quite a bit of analysis on the 100 most frequently rented bicycles:

```
SELECT
  bike_id,
  COUNT(*) AS num_trips
FROM
  `bigquery-public-data`.london_bicycles.cycle_hire
GROUP BY
  bike_id
ORDER BY
  num_trips DESC
LIMIT
  100
```

The query returns 100 rows; here are the first three of them:

Row	bike_id	num_trips
1	12925	2922

Row	bike_id	num_trips
2	12841	2871
3	13071	2860

We could save these 100 rows to a table for later analysis from other queries or from outside BigQuery, but rows read from the table are not guaranteed to be ordered.[9] What if downstream analysis requires the data in order? One solution is to use a materialized view. Another solution is to store the result into a single row by aggregating the result into an array and moving the ORDER BY and LIMIT into the ARRAY_AGG:

```
WITH numtrips AS (
  SELECT
    bike_id AS id,
    COUNT(*) AS num_trips
  FROM
    `bigquery-public-data`.london_bicycles.cycle_hire
  GROUP BY
    bike_id
)

SELECT
  ARRAY_AGG(STRUCT(id,num_trips)
            ORDER BY num_trips DESC LIMIT 100)
        AS bike
FROM
  numtrips
```

This returns a single row, as shown here:

Row	bike.id	bike.num_trips
1	12925	2922
	12841	2871
	13071	2860

If you save this to a table, the list of most rented bicycles is stored in order and will be returned in order when read from downstream applications. Of course, this now puts the burden on the downstream analyst to be comfortable with arrays and unnesting.

As this example illustrates, you can maintain a one-to-one relationship between columns by creating an array of structs. Think of an array of structs, then, as a minitable that is stored in a single row. BigQuery does not support arrays of arrays, but you can create arrays of structs, each of which can contain arrays.

---

9 Actually, a result of 100 rows of a two-column table is small enough that it fits into a single shard and would likely be returned in order, but the general principle that you cannot rely on the order of rows read to be valid.

Using arrays to store repeated fields

Another reason to use arrays is if you need to store repeated fields even if you don't care about ordering. For example, there is a BigQuery dataset that contains US tax filings by charities. The vast majority of charities file taxes only once each year, but sometimes organizations file multiple returns in the same year. It can be helpful to store these filings by an organization in a single row:

```
SELECT
  ein
  , ARRAY_AGG(STRUCT(elf, tax_pd, subseccd)) AS filing
FROM `bigquery-public-data`.irs_990.irs_990_2015
WHERE ein BETWEEN '390' AND '399'
GROUP BY ein
LIMIT 3
```

This returns the following:

Row	ein	filing.elf	filing.tax_pd	filing.subseccd
1	390123480	E	201412	8
		E	201312	8
2	390233059	E	201412	12
3	390201015	E	201412	8

Note that the first organization happens to have filed two returns in 2015 (for years 2014 and 2013), whereas the others filed only once.

Arrays Enforce Data Integrity

Changing the schema of the table to use arrays provides a way to enforce best practice and avoid wrong logic in queries. The original schema where each filing is on a separate row can lead to logical errors when the analyst forgets that organizations do sometimes file multiple returns in the same year. For example, suppose that you want to find charities that do not file electronically (elf would be 'E' in that case), in which case it can be tempting to simply do this:

```
SELECT
  ein
FROM `bigquery-public-data`.irs_990.irs_990_2015
WHERE elf != 'E'
```

However, because some charities file multiple times, it is possible that they file some of these returns electronically and the others non-electronically. This is, indeed, the case, as you can verify by using the following:

```
SELECT
  ein
  , COUNTIF(elf = 'E', 1, 0) AS num_elf
```

```
  , COUNTIF(elf = 'E', 0, 1) AS num_not_elf
FROM `bigquery-public-data`.irs_990.irs_990_2015
GROUP BY ein
HAVING num_elf > 0 AND num_not_elf > 0
ORDER BY num_elf DESC
LIMIT 3
```

This query shows that there are several charities that filed both electronically and nonelectronically:

ow	ein	num_elf	num_not_elf
1	271157077	3	1
2	030555726	3	1
3	363977636	3	3

Had the schema of the table stored the filing as an array, it would be much more diffi-cult for analysts to make this mistake—the analyst looking for charities that do not file electronically would have known that the filing is an array and so would have done this:

```
SELECT
  ein
FROM
  [TABLENAME]
WHERE
  'E' NOT IN (SELECT elf FROM UNNEST(filing))
LIMIT 5
```

 Because the table does not store the filings as an array, try out the query by first converting it to the desired schema using a WITH clause and using filings as the table name in the main query:

```
WITH filings AS (
SELECT
  ein
  , ARRAY_AGG(STRUCT(elf, tax_pd, subseccd)) AS filing
FROM `bigquery-public-data`.irs_990.irs_990_2015
GROUP BY ein
)
```

The UNNEST function flattens the array and must be in a FROM clause. Note the use of the correlated subquery to pull out the elf field from the filing array of structs and the use of IN to check whether a value is in the array.

Another way to check whether 'E' exists in the array of structs is to use EXISTS:

```
SELECT
  ein
FROM
  [TABLENAME]
WHERE
  EXISTS (SELECT elf FROM UNNEST(filing) WHERE elf != 'E')
LIMIT 5
```

You can verify that the results obtained this way ('520910763', '237048405', '410519270', '592515700', and '420655796') are correct by using:

```
SELECT
  ein
  , SUM(IF(elf = 'E', 1, 0)) AS num_elf
  , SUM(IF(elf = 'E', 0, 1)) AS num_not_elf
FROM `bigquery-public-data`.irs_990.irs_990_2015
WHERE ein in UNNEST(
  ['520910763', '237048405', '410519270', '592515700',
  '420655796'])
GROUP BY ein
ORDER BY num_elf DESC
```

As expected, num_elf is zero for all of these ein.

Using arrays for generating data

Another reason to use arrays is if you need to generate data. Suppose that you need to have your lawn mowed in the summer every 10 days and that you have three minions who will do the job for you. You want to assign the minions to take turns doing the job.

You can begin by generating the list of summer days:

```
SELECT
  GENERATE_DATE_ARRAY('2019-06-23', '2019-08-22', INTERVAL 10 DAY) AS summer
```

Here is the result for this query:

Row	summer
1	2019-06-23
	2019-07-03
	2019-07-13
	2019-07-23
	2019-08-02
	2019-08-12
	2019-08-22

This is all in the same row. To create a multirow table with each day on its own row, you use UNNEST (carefully note the way we use the table days and the array summer in the FROM clause—UNNEST in BigQuery can be used only with a FROM clause):

```
WITH days AS (
  SELECT
    GENERATE_DATE_ARRAY('2019-06-23', '2019-08-22', INTERVAL 10 DAY) AS summer
)
SELECT summer_day
FROM days, UNNEST(summer) AS summer_day
```

This yields the summer days, one in each row:

Row	summer_day
1	2019-06-23
2	2019-07-03
3	2019-07-13
4	2019-07-23
5	2019-08-02
6	2019-08-12
7	2019-08-22

The comma in the preceding query does a correlated CROSS JOIN[10] and therefore excludes rows that have empty or NULL arrays. To include them, replace the comma with a LEFT JOIN:

```
FROM days LEFT JOIN UNNEST(summer) AS summer_day
```

We can hardcode the list of minions, as shown here:

```
SELECT ['Lak', 'Jordan', 'Graham'] AS minions
```

However, we need to assign the minions to each of the summer days in turn. To do that, we can generate a dayno array and use the modulo (or remainder) as the offset into the minions array:

```
WITH days AS (
  SELECT
    GENERATE_DATE_ARRAY('2019-06-23', '2019-08-22',
                        INTERVAL 10 DAY) AS summer,
    ['Lak', 'Jordan', 'Graham'] AS minions
```

---

10 This is a correlated cross join: the UNNEST operator references the column of ARRAYs from each row in the source table, which appears previously in the FROM clause. For each row in the source table, UNNEST flattens the ARRAY from that row into a set of rows containing the ARRAY elements, and then the CROSS JOIN joins this new set of rows with the single row from the source table. Because these cross joins in UNNEST are correlated to just the elements in the array, the performance impact is minimal.

```
    )
SELECT
    summer[ORDINAL(dayno)] AS summer_day
    , minions[OFFSET(MOD(dayno,
                        ARRAY_LENGTH(minions)))]
        AS minion
FROM
    days, UNNEST(GENERATE_ARRAY(1,ARRAY_LENGTH(summer),1)) dayno
ORDER BY summer_day ASC
```

The query yields the summer days and who's assigned to mow the lawn each day:

Row	summer_day	minion
1	2019-06-23	Jordan
2	2019-07-03	Graham
3	2019-07-13	Lak
4	2019-07-23	Jordan
5	2019-08-02	Graham
6	2019-08-12	Lak
7	2019-08-22	Jordan

Note that the indexing uses ORDINAL to configure a 1-based index and OFFSET to index the array with a 0-based value. We also used ARRAY_LENGTH to get the length of the summer array.

Array functions

If you have two arrays, you can concatenate them using ARRAY_CONCAT:

```
SELECT
  ARRAY_CONCAT(
    GENERATE_DATE_ARRAY('2019-03-23', '2019-06-22', INTERVAL 20 DAY)
    , GENERATE_DATE_ARRAY('2019-08-23', '2019-11-22', INTERVAL 20 DAY)
  ) AS shoulder_season
```

For debugging purposes, it can be helpful to print out an array of strings as a STRING. You do that using ARRAY_TO_STRING:

```
SELECT
ARRAY_TO_STRING(['A', 'B', NULL, 'D'], '*', 'na') AS arr
```

This returns the following:

Row	arr
1	A*B*na*D

The second parameter to `ARRAY_TO_STRING` is the separator, and the third string is how `NULL` elements are recorded (by default, they are skipped).

> For debugging purposes, it can be helpful to print out an array as a string. Although `ARRAY_TO_STRING` works with arrays of `STRING`, `TO_JSON_STRING` works with arrays of any type. For example, to get a readable print out of an array of dates, you can do this:
>
> ```
> SELECT
> TO_JSON_STRING(
> GENERATE_DATE_ARRAY('2019-06-23', '2019-08-22',
>                     INTERVAL 10 DAY)) AS json
> ```
>
> This prints out the array, converting the dates to JSON format:
>
> | Row | json |
> | --- | --- |
> | 1 | ["2019-06-23","2019-07-03","2019-07-13","2019-07-23", "2019-08-02","2019-08-12","2019-08-22"] |
>
> The JSON format of the resulting output is more obvious if the array is of structs:
>
> ```
> SELECT
> TO_JSON_STRING([
>     STRUCT(1 AS a, 'bbb' AS b),
>     STRUCT(2 AS a, 'ccc' AS b)
> ]) AS json
> ```
>
> Following is the result:
>
> | Row | json |
> | --- | --- |
> | 1 | [{"a":1,"b":"bbb"},{"a":2,"b":"ccc"}] |

Table 8-1 presents a summary of array functions, assuming that `minions` is an array of strings.

Table 8-1. Summary of array functions

Function	What it does	Example usage
GENERATE_ARRAY GENERATE_DATE_ ARRAY	Creates array	SELECT **GENERATE_ARRAY**(10, 20, 3)
OFFSET ORDINAL	Accesses array elements	SELECT minions[**OFFSET**(0)] FROM ... SELECT minions[**ORDINAL**(1)] FROM ...
ARRAY_LENGTH	Returns length of array	SELECT **ARRAY_LENGTH**(minions)

Function	What it does	Example usage

UNNEST	Flattens an array; this needs to be in a FROM clause	`WITH workers AS (`
		`    SELECT ['Lak', 'Jordan', 'Graham']`
		`        AS minions`
		`)`
		`SELECT m`
		`FROM workers, UNNEST(minions) AS m`

IN	Checks whether a value is present in an array	`WITH workers AS (`
		`    SELECT ['Lak', 'Jordan', 'Graham']`
		`        AS minions`
		`)`
		`SELECT 'Lak' IN UNNEST(minions)`
		`FROM workers`

EXISTS	Checks whether an array is non-empty	`WITH workers AS (`
		`    SELECT ['Lak', 'Jordan', 'Graham'] AS min`
		`ions`
		`    UNION ALL SELECT [] AS minions`
		`)`
		
		`SELECT`
		`    EXISTS (SELECT * FROM`
		`                UNNEST(minions))`
		`FROM workers`

ARRAY_AGG	Aggregates grouped items into an array	`SELECT` `  ein` `  , ARRAY_AGG(elf) AS elf` `FROM ` + "`bigquery-public-" + ` `data`.irs_990.irs_990_2015` `GROUP BY ein` `LIMIT 3`

ARRAY_CONCAT	Concatenates two arrays of the same type	`SELECT`
		`  ARRAY_CONCAT( ['A', 'B', 'C'],`
		`                ['D', 'E', 'F'])`

ARRAY_TO_STRING TO_JSON_STRING	Converts arrays to a string format	`SELECT TO_JSON_STRING([`
		`  STRUCT(1 AS a, 'bbb' AS b),`
		`  STRUCT(2 AS a, 'ccc' AS b)`
		`])`

Window Functions

An *analytic window function* (sometimes abbreviated as *analytic function* and other times as *window function*) computes aggregate analytics (such as SUM, COUNT, etc.) over a group of rows (called the window). There are three types of analytic functions: aggregate analytic functions, navigation functions, and numbering functions.

Aggregate analytic functions

Aggregate functions operate on the entire table and return a single aggregate value. For example, this query returns the longest trip duration and two other aggregate statistics over the full `london_bicycles` dataset:

```
SELECT
  MAX(duration) AS longest_duration
  , COUNT(*) AS num_trips
  , AVG(duration) AS average_duration
FROM
  `bigquery-public-data`.london_bicycles.cycle_hire
```

The result is a single row:

Row	longest_duration	num_trips	average_duration
1	2674020	24369201	1332.2942381245884

On the other hand, an aggregate analytic function returns an aggregate statistic for each row, where the aggregate is computed on rows "around" the row for which the result is being computed. For example, the following query computes moving average of duration of the 100 trips leading up to this one:

```
SELECT
  AVG(duration)
    OVER(ORDER BY start_date ASC
          ROWS BETWEEN 100 PRECEDING AND 1 PRECEDING)
  AS average_duration
FROM
  `bigquery-public-data`.london_bicycles.cycle_hire
LIMIT 5
```

Unlike the aggregate function `AVG(duration)`, the average is not computed over the full table because we have defined a window using the `OVER` clause. The window itself consists of the 100 rows before this one, for which the order is specified by the `start_date` column. This query yields an `average_duration` for each row, with the first row having `null` because there is no preceding row to put into the window:

Row	average_duration
1	null
2	360.0
3	510.0
4	380.0
5	390.0

Had we desired to compute the average length of the 50 trips before to 50 trips after, we would have specified the following:

```
ROWS BETWEEN 50 PRECEDING AND 50 FOLLOWING
```

To compute the average of rows from the start of the dataset to the current row (inclusive), here's what we would have specified:

```
ROWS BETWEEN UNBOUNDED PRECEDING AND CURRENT ROW
```

If we leave out the FOLLOWING, the bound defaults to the current row, so that ROWS 50 PRECEDING is the same as ROWS BETWEEN 50 PRECEDING AND CURRENT ROW.

What if you want the average duration of the previous 100 trips, but you want to restrict the window to trips that start from the same station as this row? In that case, you add a PARTITION BY to the OVER() clause:

```
SELECT
  AVG(duration)
    OVER(PARTITION BY start_station_id
        ORDER BY start_date ASC
        ROWS BETWEEN 100 PRECEDING AND 1 PRECEDING)
      AS average_duration
FROM
  `bigquery-public-data`.london_bicycles.cycle_hire
LIMIT 5
```

If you want to compute the moving average over the past hour, you use RANGE and specify an integer offset from the quantity you are ordering by:

```
SELECT
  AVG(duration)
    OVER(PARTITION BY start_station_id
        ORDER BY UNIX_SECONDS(start_date) ASC
        RANGE BETWEEN 3600 PRECEDING AND CURRENT ROW)
      AS average_duration
FROM
  `bigquery-public-data`.london_bicycles.cycle_hire
LIMIT 5
```

Note that you are now ordering by UNIX_SECONDS(start_date) and not just start_date so that we can look for rows whose UNIX_SECONDS(start_date) lies between 3,600 seconds ago and the present.

Navigation functions

The aggregate analytic functions compute an aggregate statistic over all of the rows in the window. Thus, AVG(duration) computes the average duration in the window and MAX(duration) computes the maximum duration in the window. But what if you want a single value denoted by the location of the row? Navigation functions are useful in that context.

For example, suppose that you want to find the "next" rental of a bike. In the OVER() clause, you would need to partition by bike_id, order by start_date, and window between the current row and the one following it. Over that window, you'd use LAST_VALUE to find the start_date of the last row in the window, because that would correspond to the next time the bike is rented:

```
SELECT
  start_date
  , end_date
  , LAST_VALUE(start_date)
      OVER(PARTITION BY bike_id
          ORDER BY start_date ASC
          ROWS BETWEEN CURRENT ROW AND 1 FOLLOWING)
      AS next_rental_start
FROM
  `bigquery-public-data`.london_bicycles.cycle_hire
LIMIT 5
```

This query yields the following:

Row	start_date	end_date	next_rental_start
1	2015-01-06 20:01:00 UTC	2015-01-06 20:13:00 UTC	2015-01-07 08:03:00 UTC
2	2015-01-07 08:03:00 UTC	2015-01-07 08:22:00 UTC	2015-01-07 10:06:00 UTC
3	2015-01-07 10:06:00 UTC	2015-01-07 10:14:00 UTC	2015-01-07 13:03:00 UTC
4	2015-01-07 13:03:00 UTC	2015-01-07 13:09:00 UTC	2015-01-07 14:46:00 UTC
5	2015-01-07 14:46:00 UTC	2015-01-07 15:00:00 UTC	2015-01-07 17:35:00 UTC

We can avoid explicitly specifying the window frame by using the LEAD function instead:

```
SELECT
  start_date
  , end_date
  , LEAD(start_date, 1)
      OVER(PARTITION BY bike_id
          ORDER BY start_date ASC )
      AS next_rental_start
FROM
  `bigquery-public-data`.london_bicycles.cycle_hire
LIMIT 5
```

The second parameter to the LEAD function is the number of rows to lag by. The default is 1, so we could have omitted it here.

The counterparts to LAST_VALUE and LEAD are FIRST_VALUE and LAG. As a generalization, we can use the NTH_VALUE function to get the value at any position in the window.

Numbering functions

Numbering functions provide the position of the current row in the window if the rows in the window were to be ordered in some way. For example, you can find the five longest trips that started at each of the stations in the london_bicycles dataset by creating windows that are partitioned by start_station_id, ordering the windows by duration, and then computing the rank of each trip:

```
SELECT
  start_station_id
, duration
, RANK()
      OVER(PARTITION BY start_station_id ORDER BY duration DESC)
      AS nth_longest
FROM
  `bigquery-public-data`.london_bicycles.cycle_hire
LIMIT 5
```

RANK is an analytic window function. Using it as we did in the preceding query yields the rank of each trip among all the trips that started at the same station:

Row	start_station_id	duration	nth_longest
1	13	1448640	1
2	13	346080	2
3	13	225420	3
4	13	165000	4
5	13	92700	5

By placing the preceding SELECT into a WITH clause, grouping by start_station_id, and using ARRAY_AGG, you can get the three longest trips at each station:

```
WITH longest_trips AS (
 SELECT
     start_station_id
   , duration
   , RANK()
       OVER(PARTITION BY start_station_id ORDER BY duration DESC)
       AS nth_longest
  FROM
      `bigquery-public-data`.london_bicycles.cycle_hire
)

SELECT
  start_station_id
, ARRAY_AGG(duration ORDER BY nth_longest LIMIT 3) AS durations
FROM
  longest_trips
GROUP BY start_station_id
LIMIT 5
```

Here's the result:

Row	start_station_id	durations
1	10	243300
		101700
		93840
2	17	737280
		247920
		197460
3	34	1017180
		588900
		560700
4	43	244740
		193980
		176580
5	60	1303260
		596520
		319140

Besides RANK(), BigQuery also supports DENSE_RANK() and ROW_NUMBER(). The difference between the three is how they deal with ties. The following quick example illustrates this:

```
WITH example AS (
  SELECT 'A' AS name, 32 AS age
  UNION ALL SELECT 'B', 32
  UNION ALL SELECT 'C', 33
  UNION ALL SELECT 'D', 33
  UNION ALL SELECT 'E', 34
)

SELECT
  name
  , age
  , RANK() OVER(ORDER BY age) AS rank
  , DENSE_RANK() OVER(ORDER BY age) AS dense_rank
  , ROW_NUMBER() OVER(ORDER BY age) AS row_number
FROM example
```

The result shows that RANK() skips numbers if there is a tie, DENSE_RANK() assigns a rank at least once, and ROW_NUMBER() assigns each row a unique number:

Row	name	age	rank	dense_rank	row_number
1	A	32	1	1	1
2	B	32	1	1	2

Row	name	age	rank	dense_rank	row_number
3	C	33	3	2	3
4	D	33	3	2	4
5	E	34	5	3	5

Table Metadata

So far, we have looked at how to query the data within a table. However, there is information about the data called *metadata*. This might include information such as what columns are present, when the table was created, who owns the table, who can access it, and so on. In this section, we look at how to access such table metadata.

Building queries dynamically

Recall that, earlier in this chapter, we suggested that a better way to organize the IRS filing data to reduce logic errors would be to store the filings made in a year as an array:

```
SELECT
  ein
  , ARRAY_AGG(STRUCT(elf, tax_pd, subseccd)) AS filing
FROM `bigquery-public-data`.irs_990.irs_990_2015
GROUP BY ein
```

Our example showed just three of the columns—elf, tax_pd, and subseccd—because it would have been too painful to type out all the column names. One way to generate the required statement with all the columns in the table is to use INFORMA TION_SCHEMA (*https://cloud.google.com/bigquery/docs/information-schema-tables*). This is a special table that is part of all datasets and contains metadata about all the tables in that dataset.

To retrieve the column names in the irs_990_2015 table in the irs_990 dataset, you could do this:

```
SELECT column_name
FROM `bigquery-public-data`.irs_990.INFORMATION_SCHEMA.COLUMNS
WHERE table_name = 'irs_990_2015'
```

This returns a result set with 246 columns, the first few of which we show here:

Row	column_name
1	ein
2	elf
3	tax_pd
4	subseccd
5	s501c3or4947a1cd

From here, we can use CONCAT to generate the necessary query text:

```
WITH columns AS (
  SELECT column_name
  FROM `bigquery-public-data`.irs_990.INFORMATION_SCHEMA.COLUMNS
  WHERE table_name = 'irs_990_2015' AND column_name != 'ein'
)

SELECT CONCAT(
  'SELECT ein, ARRAY_AGG(STRUCT(',
  ARRAY_TO_STRING(ARRAY(SELECT column_name FROM columns), ',\n   '),
  '\n) FROM `bigquery-public-data`.irs_990.irs_990_2015\n',
  'GROUP BY ein')
```

This returns the query to be run:

```
SELECT ein, ARRAY_AGG(STRUCT(ein,
   elf,
    tax_pd,
    subseccd,
  ...
    othrinc509,
    totsupp509
) FROM `bigquery-public-data`.irs_990.irs_990_2015
GROUP BY ein
```

Later in this section, we look at scripting and dynamic SQL. So, you can go beyond simply printing out the text of the query—you can even execute it!

Labels and tags

Information schemas, covered in the previous section, provide information about tables related to the column names and data types, creation time, and more of the tables. Labels are used to add custom metadata to resources (datasets, tables, views, etc.), such as which application created them (e.g., component:salesportal), which team owns them (e.g., team:emeasales), which environment they are used in (e.g., environment:production), and what stage of the life cycle they are in (e.g., state:validated). Each label is a key/value pair (e.g., environment is a key, and its value could be one of development, staging, test, or production). A label whose value is empty is called a tag, but you can work with it similarly.

The keys and values are totally arbitrary as far as BigQuery is concerned; it is up to your data governance team to define the keys and values that will be present on tables in your organization. The purpose of assigning labels to resources is so that you can search for resources by label in order to apply policies consistently across all resources with the same label.

For example, let's add a label to the `ch08eu` dataset using the `bq` command-line tool (it's also possible to do so using the GCP console, through `ALTER TABLE SET OPTIONS`, and through the various client libraries):

```
bq update --set_label costcenter:abc342 ch08eu
```

You can change the value by calling `--set_label` again with the updated value:

```
bq update --set_label costcenter:def456 ch08eu
```

It is also possible to assign a label to a query itself:

```
bq query --label costcenter:def456 --nouse_legacy_sql 'SELECT ...'
```

> Do not include sensitive or confidential data in labels—the labels themselves might be visible to roles that do not have access to the resources being labeled.

After you have labeled your datasets or tables, it is possible to search from them by label. For example, you can do the following (you can search using the REST API or the various client libraries):

```
bq ls --filter 'labels.costcenter:def456'
This returns the following:
  datasetId
  -----------
  ch08eu
```

Time travel

For up to seven days, you can query the historical state of a table. For example, to query a table as it existed six hours ago, you can use `SYSTEM_TIME`:

```
SELECT
  *
FROM `bigquery-public-data`.london_bicycles.cycle_stations
FOR SYSTEM_TIME AS OF
    TIMESTAMP_SUB(CURRENT_TIMESTAMP(), INTERVAL 6 HOUR)
```

Note that you cannot reference a single table at more than a single point in time. If you need to find differences between different time-versions of a table, copy over one of the versions (using Data Definition Language; see the next section) into a new table and then do the join.

> Use the time travel functionality if you need to run a repeatable query over a table that is fed data via a stream.

Data Definition Language and Data Manipulation Language

Data Definition Language (DDL) statements are SQL statements for creating, altering, and deleting tables and views. The Data Manipulation Language (DML) enables you to update, insert, and delete data from tables.

DDL

We have already looked at creating a table or view from a query statement. For example, to create a table consisting only of stations that have "Hyde" in their name, you could run this query:

```
CREATE OR REPLACE TABLE ch08eu.hydepark_stations AS
SELECT
  * EXCEPT(longitude, latitude)
  , ST_GeogPoint(longitude, latitude) AS location
FROM `bigquery-public-data`.london_bicycles.cycle_stations
WHERE name LIKE '%Hyde%'
```

Options list.   Chapter 7 looks at adding partitioning and clustering specifications at table creation time. At creation time, we can also use the options list to set an expiration timestamp, labels, and so on:

```
CREATE OR REPLACE TABLE ch08eu.hydepark_stations
OPTIONS(
  expiration_timestamp=TIMESTAMP "2020-01-01 00:00:00 UTC",
  description="Stations with Hyde Park in the name",
  labels=[("cost_center", "abc123")]
) AS
SELECT
  * EXCEPT(longitude, latitude)
  , ST_GeogPoint(longitude, latitude) AS location
FROM `bigquery-public-data.london_bicycles.cycle_stations`
WHERE name LIKE '%Hyde%'
```

Empty table.   To create an empty table, specify the column names and their types:

```
CREATE OR REPLACE TABLE ch08eu.hydepark_rides
(
  start_time TIMESTAMP,
  duration INT64,
  start_station_id INT64,
  start_station_name STRING,
  end_station_id INT64,
  end_station_name STRING
)
PARTITION BY DATE(start_time)
CLUSTER BY start_station_id
```

Changing options. You can change some of these options after the table is created—for example:

```
ALTER TABLE ch08eu.hydepark_rides
SET OPTIONS(
  expiration_timestamp=TIMESTAMP "2021-01-01 00:00:00 UTC",
  require_partition_filter=True,
  labels=[("cost_center", "def456")]
)
```

DML

BigQuery is primarily a data warehouse into which you will typically load or stream data and not modify it. However, BigQuery does provide the ability to modify data: DML lets you insert, update, delete, and merge data into tables.

 BigQuery is an analytical database, not an online transaction processing (OLTP) database. As such, it is not designed for very-high-frequency DML updates. If you find that you have a lot of data that you want to update, consider performing the updates in batches. One approach is to create a staging table with the updates that you want to apply, and then you can run a single UPDATE or MERGE statement to perform all of those changes in a single operation.

Insert SELECT. This query extracts data from the cycle_hires table and inserts it into our hydepark_rides table (which, in the previous section, we created as a partitioned table):

```
INSERT ch08eu.hydepark_rides
SELECT
  start_date AS start_time
  , duration
  , start_station_id
  , start_station_name
  , end_station_id
  , end_station_name
FROM
  `bigquery-public-data`.london_bicycles.cycle_hire
WHERE
  start_station_name LIKE '%Hyde%'
```

This statement adds 1.01 million rows to the table that we can query, as follows:

```
WITH rides_in_year AS (
SELECT
  EXTRACT(MONTH from start_time) AS month
  , duration
FROM ch08eu.hydepark_rides
WHERE
```

```
  DATE(start_time) BETWEEN '2016-01-01' AND '2016-12-31'
  AND start_station_id = 300
  AND end_station_id = 303
)

SELECT
  month
  , AVG(duration)/60 as avg_duration_minutes
FROM rides_in_year
GROUP BY month
ORDER BY avg_duration_minutes DESC
LIMIT 5
```

In this query, note the presence of the partitioning column start_time and the clustering column start_station_id in the WHERE clause. The partitioning column is required because we altered the table to enforce require_partition_filter=True, and we gain query efficiency because the table was created with CLUSTER BY start_station_id. This query processed 12 MB of data (as opposed to 740 MB if we had queried a nonclustered table). The use of a partitioned table, therefore, reduces query costs whether we have a reservation or are paying on-demand.

Insert VALUES. It is possible to INSERT a couple of rides after the table has been loaded:

```
INSERT ch08eu.hydepark_rides (
  start_time
  , duration
  , start_station_id
  , start_station_name
  , end_station_id
  , end_station_name
)
VALUES
('2016-02-18 17:21:00 UTC', 720, 300,
'Serpentine Car Park, Hyde Park', 303, 'Albert Gate, Hyde Park'),
('2016-02-18 16:30:00 UTC', 1320, 300,
'Serpentine Car Park, Hyde Park', 303, 'Albert Gate, Hyde Park')
```

Even though it is optional, best practice is to specify the column names in the INSERT, as we have done in the preceding example.

If you didn't care about readability, you could write the insert statement this way:

```
INSERT ch08eu.hydepark_rides
VALUES
('2016-02-18 17:21:00 UTC', 720, 300,
'Serpentine ... Park', 303, 'Albert Gate, Hyde Park'),
('2016-02-18 16:30:00 UTC', 1320, 300,
'Serpentine ... Park', 303, 'Albert Gate, Hyde Park')
```

Insert VALUES with subquery SELECT. Doing an insert the way we just did is dangerous because of the likelihood that we get the name of the stations wrong (is it `'Albert Gate, Hyde Park'` or `'Hyde Park: Albert Gate'`?). Far safer is to use a subselect query on the stations table instead of hardcoding the string:

```
  ...
  VALUES
    ('2016-02-18 17:21:00 UTC', 720,
      300, (SELECT name FROM `bigquery-public-data`.london_bicycles.cycle_stations
    WHERE id = 300),
      303, (SELECT name FROM `bigquery-public-data`.london_bicycles.cycle_stations
    WHERE id = 303)),
  ...
```

It is not possible to use a table name in an SQL function, so you cannot reduce the repetition by moving the subselect into a function:

```
CREATE TEMPORARY FUNCTION stationName(stationId INT64) AS(
  (SELECT name FROM
    `bigquery-public-data`.london_bicycles.cycle_stations
    WHERE id = stationId)
);
```

As of this writing, stored procedures are not supported in BigQuery, but it is on the road map. By the time you are reading this, you might be able to define a stored procedure and invoke it from the INSERT.

Deleting rows. If we discover a bug in our Extract, Transform, and Load (ETL) pipeline that was introduced in December 2016, causing the pipeline to mistakenly load zero-duration rides into the table, we can delete those rows by using DML:

```
DELETE ch08eu.hydepark_rides
WHERE
  start_time > '2016-12-01' AND
  (duration IS NULL OR duration = 0)
```

Beyond errors like these, where we erroneously inserted rows, there are other reasons that we might need to delete rows from our data warehouse. For example, the "right to be forgotten" rule requires companies to delete all user information in some circumstances. That is possible using the DELETE statement:[11]

```
DELETE ch08eu.hydepark_rides
WHERE
  userId = 3452123
```

Rather than doing this query one update at a time, it is better to batch these updates into a MERGE statement (which we look at shortly).

---

11 Because there is no userId column in our table, this query won't work.

Updating row values. Suppose that that the durations in our table from one of the stations came in as minutes, but we failed to convert the values into seconds before saving them. We can update the table to fix the issue:

```
UPDATE ch08eu.hydepark_rides
SET duration = duration * 60
WHERE
  start_time > '2016-12-01' AND
  start_station_id = 303
```

If one of the columns is an array, and a new entry needs to be added to the array, you can do so with an update as well. Assuming that stations have a `maintenance` column, you can obtain the existing maintenance schedule and add a new event to it:[12]

```
UPDATE ch08eu.stations_table
SET maintenance = ARRAY_CONCAT(maintenance,
  ARRAY_STRUCT<time TIMESTAMP, employeeID STRING>[
      (CURRENT_TIME(), emp303)
  ])
)
WHERE id = 303
```

When using DML statements, consider whether there is a better way to accomplish the necessary task. For example, if the use case is to update the maintenance events every time the station undergoes maintenance, it would be preferable to write the events to a separate table and perhaps join it with the stations table when needed in a query.

MERGE statement. A `MERGE` statement is an atomic combination of `INSERT`, `UPDATE`, and `DELETE` operations that runs (and succeeds or fails) as a single statement. Records from the source table (could be a subquery) are inserted into the target table, and for every row, a set of operations is carried out. It is possible to define a different set of operations in three scenarios: when the rows are `MATCHED`, `NOT MATCHED BY TARGET`, or `NOT MATCHED BY SOURCE`.

For example, the following query merges records from the public dataset of `london_bicycles` to the table in our `ch08eu` dataset and carries out different operations in different scenarios:

```
MERGE ch08eu.hydepark_stations T
USING
  (SELECT *
   FROM `bigquery-public-data`.london_bicycles.cycle_stations
   WHERE name LIKE '%Hyde%') S
ON T.id = S.id
```

---

12 Because our current `stations_table` does not have this column, the query won't work.

```
WHEN MATCHED THEN
    UPDATE
    SET bikes_count = S.bikes_count
WHEN NOT MATCHED BY TARGET THEN
    INSERT(id, installed, locked, name, bikes_count)
    VALUES(id, installed, locked,name, bikes_count)
WHEN NOT MATCHED BY SOURCE THEN
    DELETE
```

This query merges rows from the subquery on the public dataset table (the source table) into `ch08eu.hydepark_stations` (the destination table) with records joined by the `id` column. When a row matches, the `bikes_count` in the destination table is set to the value of `bikes_count` in the source table (other columns are left as-is). If the ID is present in the source but not in the destination, a row is inserted into the table. If the ID is present in the destination but is no longer in the source, the row in the target is deleted. This merge statement happens atomically.

Beyond SQL

So far in this book, we have covered SQL queries. Even though SQL is quite powerful, there are operations that are simpler to do in a proper procedural language. For this purpose, you can use JavaScript UDFs.

Many database systems support a method of stringing together SQL statements in some sort of procedural language. Even though you could orchestrate sets of SQL statements using the BigQuery client libraries, it can sometimes be more convenient to have the entire set of operations carried out on the server, thus simplifying failure handling, rollback, and data transfer. This is what scripting and stored procedures provide.

JavaScript UDFs

If possible, it is often preferable to write UDFs in SQL. BigQuery can optimize SQL, distribute it, and run it efficiently. This is not the case for UDFs in JavaScript; there are restrictions on the size of JavaScript code, the size of outputs, and the number of JavaScript functions in a query. JavaScript UDFs are more general purpose than SQL UDFs, but be aware that they have additional overhead because they are executed using the V8 engine in a sandboxed process.

That said, there are situations for which we need to carry out complex calculations that are difficult[13] to write in SQL. In such cases, JavaScript UDFs, even with all these restrictions, provide a convenient alternative. For example, perhaps your pricing function is quite complicated, but you have the code for `computePrice()` already

---

13 We said difficult. We *did not* say impossible. Please don't send us your SQL implementation of this function.

implemented in JavaScript to support a website. You can define that function and save it in your dataset (temporary JavaScript functions are also supported):

```
CREATE OR REPLACE FUNCTION ch08eu.computePrice(dur INT64)
RETURNS INT64
LANGUAGE js AS """
  function factorial(n) {
     return (n > 1) ? n * factorial(n - 1) : 1;
  }
  var nhours = 1 + Math.floor(dur/3600.0);
  var f = factorial(nhours);
  var discount = 0.8/(1+Math.pow(Math.E, -f));
  return 3 + Math.floor(dur * (1-discount) * 0.0023)
""";

SELECT
  duration, ch08eu.computePrice(duration) AS price
FROM
  `bigquery-public-data`.london_bicycles.cycle_hire
LIMIT 5
```

Note the key differences between a JavaScript UDF and an SQL UDF: you specify that the language is js and enclose the entire function within triple quotes. The function body can include other JavaScript functions (for example, ours includes the implementation of the factorial function). Here's the result of this query:

Row	duration	price
1	3180	6
2	7380	6
3	2040	4
4	2280	5
5	2340	5

It might be the case that there is an existing library function in JavaScript that you want to reuse. You can invoke a function in an external JavaScript package as long as you make sure to download it and store it in Google Cloud Storage. If, for example, the preceding factorial function is defined in a file named *mathfn.js*, you can store it in Google Cloud Storage and refer to it in the OPTIONS of the function:

```
CREATE TEMPORARY FUNCTION computePrice(dur INT64)
RETURNS INT64
LANGUAGE js AS """
  var nhours = 1 + Math.floor(dur/3600.0);
  var f = factorial(nhours);
  var discount = 0.8/(1+Math.pow(Math.E, -f));
  return 3 + Math.floor(dur * (1-discount) * 0.0023)
"""
OPTIONS (
  library=["gs://somebucket/path/to/mathfn.js",
```

```
                "gs://somebucket/path/to/someother.js"]
    );
```

JavaScript UDFs run on a single worker and are limited to what can be carried out on that single worker.[14] As of this writing, asynchronous JavaScript functions are not supported.

Scripting

We can write a BigQuery script consisting of multiple statements and send it to Big-Query in one request. The script can save results into variables and use loops to execute the same query multiple times.

A sequence of statements

One of the simplest reasons to write a script is to run a set of queries, one after the other. Let's say that you want to create an intermediate table, join against it, and then drop the table. You can accomplish this with scripting by simply writing the statements one after the other:[15]

```
CREATE OR REPLACE TABLE ch08eu.typical_trip AS
  SELECT
      start_station_name
    , end_station_name
    , APPROX_QUANTILES(duration, 10)[OFFSET(5)] AS typical_duration
    , COUNT(*) AS num_trips
  FROM
      `bigquery-public-data`.london_bicycles.cycle_hire
  GROUP BY
    start_station_name, end_station_name
;

CREATE OR REPLACE TABLE ch08eu.unusual_days AS
  SELECT
      EXTRACT (DATE FROM start_date) AS trip_date
    , APPROX_QUANTILES(duration / typical_duration, 10)[OFFSET(5)] AS ratio
    , COUNT(*) AS num_trips_on_day
  FROM
      `bigquery-public-data`.london_bicycles.cycle_hire AS hire
    , ch08eu.typical_trip AS trip
  WHERE
      hire.start_station_name = trip.start_station_name
      AND hire.end_station_name = trip.end_station_name
      AND num_trips > 10
```

---

14 For more advice on using JavaScript UDFs, see *https://cloud.google.com/bigquery/docs/reference/standard-sql/user-defined-functions#best-practices-for-javascript-udfs*.

15 For the complete script, see *https://github.com/GoogleCloudPlatform/bigquery-oreilly-book/blob/master/08_advqueries/script_seq.sql*.

```
    GROUP BY trip_date
    HAVING num_trips_on_day > 10
    ORDER BY ratio DESC
;

  DROP TABLE ch08eu.typical_trip;
```

Perhaps the only unusual thing about the script is that we are being careful to put a semicolon after every individual statement. You can submit this script as a single request.

 Many use cases that seem to require a script can be solved by using WITH clauses, joins, correlated subqueries, or GROUP BY. Before you decide to write a script, carefully consider whether you can solve the problem by using a single query. The single query will probably be more efficient.

For example, the previous script can be quite easily accomplished using a WITH clause. The WITH clause is often faster as well. Even seemingly more complex use cases can be accomplished with a single query. For example, suppose that you have a query to find the number of rentals of over 30 minutes for each bike_id in the lon don_bicycles dataset. If you want to repeat this analysis for thresholds of 60, 120, ..., 300 minutes, it might seem that you need a loop to execute this statement multiple times. However, you can get the result with a single query by joining against an array of thresholds and grouping the result by both bike_id and threshold.

Don't go overboard with scripts.

Temporary tables

Instead of creating a table and dropping it, you can simplify the previous script by using a temporary table:[16]

```
CREATE TEMPORARY TABLE typical_trip AS
  SELECT
      start_station_name
    , end_station_name
    , APPROX_QUANTILES(duration, 10)[OFFSET(5)] AS typical_duration
    , COUNT(*) AS num_trips
  FROM
      `bigquery-public-data`.london_bicycles.cycle_hire
```

---

16 For the complete script, see *https://github.com/GoogleCloudPlatform/bigquery-oreilly-book/blob/master/ 08_advqueries/script_seq.sql*.

```
    GROUP BY
        start_station_name, end_station_name
    ;

    CREATE OR REPLACE TABLE ch08eu.unusual_days AS
      SELECT
          EXTRACT (DATE FROM start_date) AS trip_date
          , APPROX_QUANTILES(duration / typical_duration, 10)[OFFSET(5)] AS ratio
          , COUNT(*) AS num_trips_on_day
      FROM
          `bigquery-public-data`.london_bicycles.cycle_hire AS hire
          , typical_trip AS trip
      WHERE
          hire.start_station_name = trip.start_station_name
          AND hire.end_station_name = trip.end_station_name
          AND num_trips > 10
      GROUP BY trip_date
      HAVING num_trips_on_day > 10
      ORDER BY ratio DESC
    ;
```

Temporary tables exist for the lifetime of a script and are automatically cleaned up when the script completes. Note also that, unlike permanent tables, temporary tables are not associated with a dataset.

Anatomy of a simple script

To look at a more full-fledged example of a script, let's write a script to find the return stations for the longest duration rentals from stations in Hyde Park. Most scripts begin with a declaration part in which we define the variables that are used in the script:[17]

```
-- Variables
DECLARE PATTERN STRING DEFAULT '%Hyde%';
DECLARE stations ARRAY<STRING>;
DECLARE MIN_TRIPS_THRESH INT64 DEFAULT 100;
```

Here, we have declared the pattern we will be searching for, and an array to hold the stations that match this pattern. The third variable is a threshold that we will use later in the script. Note the data types of the variables. The pattern is a string and the threshold is an integer. By giving them default values, we allow for the ability to use them as named constants in the script.

Variables can be any type supported by BigQuery. For example, the `stations` variable is an array of strings, which is one way to store the result of a query (we could have also used a temporary table):

---

17 The full script is available at *https://github.com/GoogleCloudPlatform/bigquery-oreilly-book/blob/master/ 08_advqueries/script_temptbl.sql*.

```
SET stations = (
  SELECT
      ARRAY_AGG(name)
  FROM
      `bigquery-public-data`.london_bicycles.cycle_stations
  WHERE
      name LIKE PATTERN
);
```

Note that the variable `stations` is being `SET` in the preceding code (to an array), and the variable `PATTERN` is being used. Because `stations` is an array, the `SELECT` calls `ARRAY_AGG` to aggregate the name column across all the rows. Using the `stations` array in the rest of the script will be like using any array (use `UNNEST`, etc.).

You can now find the end station for the longest duration rentals:

```
SELECT
  start_station_name
  , end_station_name
  , AVG(duration) AS avg_duration
  , COUNT(duration) AS num_trips
FROM
  `bigquery-public-data`.london_bicycles.cycle_hire
  , UNNEST(stations) AS station
WHERE
  start_station_name = station
GROUP BY start_station_name, end_station_name
HAVING num_trips > MIN_TRIPS_THRESH
ORDER BY avg_duration DESC
LIMIT 5
```

The average over a small number of trips will be heavily influenced by outliers. Because of that, look for trips that have been made enough times in the dataset that the average will be acceptable. The `HAVING` clause in this query filters on station pairs with at least 100 trips:

Row	start_station_name	end_station_name	avg_duration	num_trips
1	Hyde Park Corner, Hyde Park	Abbey Orchard Street, Westminster	10718.507462686563	268
2	Wellington Arch, Hyde Park	Imperial College, Knightsbridge	10062.04724409449	127
3	Hyde Park Corner, Hyde Park	Westminster University, Marylebone	9726.05042016807	119
4	Park Lane, Hyde Park	Westbourne Grove, Bayswater	9712.5	104
5	Albert Gate, Hyde Park	Paddington Green Police Station, Paddington	9182.72727272727	132

Looping

Scripting also supports control flows through `IF` conditions and a variety of looping primitives. The threshold of 100 was chosen quite arbitrarily. What happens if you change it? It can be convenient to try a whole bunch of thresholds and examine the results, so you can change the MIN_TRIPS_THRESH in a loop and put the SELECT statement within that loop:[18]

```
WHILE MIN_TRIPS_THRESH < 1000 DO
  SELECT … ;
  SET MIN_TRIPS_THRESH = MIN_TRIPS_THRESH * 2;
END WHILE
```

Now when you run the script, you see three sets of results, the last of which is as follows:

Row	start_station_name	end_station_name	avg_duration	num_trips
1	Bayswater Road, Hyde Park	Bayswater Road, Hyde Park	4289.155172413791	3480
2	Hyde Park Corner, Hyde Park	Wellington Arch, Hyde Park	3817.0747740345105	2434
3	Knightsbridge, Hyde Park	Hyde Park Corner, Hyde Park	3582.595834591005	3313
4	Park Lane, Hyde Park	Park Lane, Hyde Park	3524.174474450833	12701
5	Hyde Park Corner, Hyde Park	Knightsbridge, Hyde Park	3479.189736664417	1481

More primitive loop constructs are also supported. For example, the WHILE loop in the previous example could be implemented as follows:

```
LOOP
  IF MIN_TRIPS_THRESH >= 1000 THEN
      BREAK;
  END IF;

  SELECT MIN_TRIPS_THRESH;
  SET MIN_TRIPS_THRESH = MIN_TRIPS_THRESH * 2;
END LOOP;
```

Note the use of LOOP—it works similarly to a WHILE loop with an always-true condition. You can break out of a loop by using BREAK, as shown in the preceding example, and skip the rest of the iteration using CONTINUE.[19]

Exceptions

Wrap a set of statements within a BEGIN ... EXCEPTION block to handle exceptions. To simply obtain the stack trace:

```
BEGIN
  DECLARE stations ARRAY<INT64>;
```

---

18 The full script is available at *https://github.com/GoogleCloudPlatform/bigquery-oreilly-book/blob/master/ 08_advqueries/script_loop.sql.*

19 The BREAK and CONTINUE keywords behave similarly to how they work in C-based languages (such as Python, C#, or Java). The Matlab documentation has good explanations for BREAK (*https://www.mathworks.com/help/ matlab/ref/break.html*) and CONTINUE (*https://www.mathworks.com/help/matlab/ref/continue.html*).

```
  SET stations = (
    SELECT
        ARRAY_AGG(CAST(name AS INT64)) names
    FROM
        `bigquery-public-data`.london_bicycles.cycle_stations
    WHERE
        name LIKE '%Kings%'
  );
EXCEPTION WHEN ERROR THEN
  SELECT
    @@error.message,
    @@error.stack_trace;
END;
```

Notice that we are attempting to cast the station names to integers. Without the exception handling, the script fails. With the exception handling, though, the script succeeds and the result is:

Row	f0_	f1_.line	f1_.column	f1_.filename	f1_.location
1	Query error: Bad int64 value: Kings Gate House, Westminster at [3:17]	3	2	null	null

It is possible to raise an exception using the RAISE keyword:

```
BEGIN
 DECLARE stations ARRAY<STRING>;
 SET stations = (
   SELECT
       ARRAY_AGG(name) names
   FROM
       `bigquery-public-data`.london_bicycles.cycle_stations
   WHERE
       name LIKE '%Kings%'
 );
 IF ARRAY_LENGTH(stations) = 0 THEN
   RAISE USING MESSAGE = "No stations matched";
 END IF;
EXCEPTION WHEN ERROR THEN
  SELECT
    @@error.message,
    @@error.stack_trace;
END;
```

If the pattern is Kings, the script populates stations with an array of length 4. If the pattern is Manhattan, the exception is raised and the @@error.message is what was specified as the MESSAGE when the exception was raised.

System variables

BigQuery provides a few system variables (*https://cloud.google.com/bigquery/docs/reference/standard-sql/scripting#system_variables*) that can be referenced in any script. These include @@project_id, @@script.slot_ms and @@current_job_id.

Particularly useful is the ability to change the default timezone for the time commands in a script from UTC to a timezone that is meaningful to the person reading the report:

```
SET @@time_zone = "America/New_York";
SELECT FORMAT_TIMESTAMP("%c", TIMESTAMP "2008-12-25 15:30:00 UTC");
```

This prints the time (15:30) in a timezone that is five hours behind UTC:

Row	f0_
1	Thu Dec 25 10:30:00 2008

Dynamic SQL

It is possible to create a string dynamically within a script and execute it using EXE CUTE IMMEDIATE. This feature was announced in May 2020 at a program celebrating the 10th anniversary of BigQuery's launch at Google I/O. This was also a time when most of us were in quarantine due to the SARS-COV-2 virus. A public dataset, published by Johns Hopkins University, tracked the number of confirmed cases in regions around the world.

We can query that Johns Hopkins dataset as follows:

```
SELECT
 *
FROM `bigquery-public-data`.covid19_jhu_csse.confirmed_cases
WHERE country_region LIKE 'Canada'
```

When we do that, though, we see that there is a column for every date, a pretty unusual data structure, but it allows us to illustrate the benefits of creating a string dynamically and executing it as a SQL statement.

We can use INFORMATION_SCHEMA to get the list of columns and find the last three days using:

```
SELECT
   column_name,
     parse_date('_%m_%d_%y', column_name) AS date
FROM
   `bigquery-public-data`.covid19_jhu_csse.INFORMATION_SCHEMA.COLUMNS
WHERE
     table_name = 'confirmed_cases' AND
     STARTS_WITH(column_name, '_')
ORDER BY date DESC LIMIT 3
```

At the time of writing, this yielded:

Row	column_name	date
1	_5_18_20	2020-05-18
2	_5_17_20	2020-05-17
3	_5_16_20	2020-05-16

To run a dynamic SQL statement, we can use the FORMAT string function and pass the created string to EXECUTE IMMEDIATE:

```
DECLARE col_0 STRING;
SET col_0 = '_5_18_20';
EXECUTE IMMEDIATE format("""
  SELECT
     country_region, province_state,
     %s AS cases_day0
  FROM `bigquery-public-data`.covid19_jhu_csse.confirmed_cases
  WHERE country_region LIKE 'Canada'
  ORDER BY cases_day0 DESC
""", col_0);
```

Note that we specify %s in the format string in order to pass in col_0.

Combining these two ideas, we can put together a script to pull the data for all Canadian provinces over the most recent 3 days:

```
DECLARE columns ARRAY<STRUCT<column_name STRING, date DATE>>;
SET columns = (
  WITH all_date_columns AS (
    SELECT column_name,
           parse_date('_%m_%d_%y', column_name) AS date
    FROM
 `bigquery-public-data`.covid19_jhu_csse.INFORMATION_SCHEMA.COLUMNS
    WHERE table_name = 'confirmed_cases'
          AND STARTS_WITH(column_name, '_')
  )
  SELECT ARRAY_AGG(STRUCT(column_name, date)
                   ORDER BY date DESC LIMIT 3) AS columns
  FROM all_date_columns
);
EXECUTE IMMEDIATE format("""
  SELECT
     country_region, province_state,
     %s AS cases_day0, '%t' AS date_day0,
     %s AS cases_day1, '%t' AS date_day1,
     %s AS cases_day2, '%t' AS date_day2
  FROM `bigquery-public-data`.covid19_jhu_csse.confirmed_cases
  WHERE country_region LIKE 'Canada'
  ORDER BY cases_day0 DESC
""",
columns[OFFSET(0)].column_name, columns[OFFSET(0)].date,
```

```
  columns[OFFSET(1)].column_name, columns[OFFSET(1)].date,
  columns[OFFSET(2)].column_name, columns[OFFSET(2)].date
);
```

The first few rows of the result are:

Row	country_region	province_state	cases_day0	date_day0	cases_day1	date_day1	cases_day2	date_day2
1	Canada	Quebec	43636	2020-05-18	42928	2020-05-17	42192	2020-05-16
2	Canada	Ontario	24286	2020-05-18	23974	2020-05-17	23645	2020-05-16

Instead of using String format, we can do named variables as follows:

```
EXECUTE IMMEDIATE """
  SELECT country_region, province_state, _5_18_20 AS cases
  FROM `bigquery-public-data`.covid19_jhu_csse.confirmed_cases
  WHERE country_region LIKE @country
  ORDER BY cases DESC LIMIT 3
"""
USING 'Canada' AS country;
```

We can also do positional variables using question marks:

```
EXECUTE IMMEDIATE """
  SELECT country_region, province_state, _5_18_20 AS cases
  FROM `bigquery-public-data`.covid19_jhu_csse.confirmed_cases
  WHERE country_region LIKE ?
  ORDER BY cases DESC LIMIT ?
"""
USING 'Canada', 3;
```

The USING clause is tricky in some situations. For example, the following doesn't work:

```
EXECUTE IMMEDIATE """
  SELECT country_region, province_state, ? AS cases -- PROBLEM!!!
  FROM `bigquery-public-data`.covid19_jhu_csse.confirmed_cases
  WHERE country_region LIKE ?
  ORDER BY cases DESC LIMIT ?
"""
USING '_5_18_20', 'Canada', 3; -- DOESNT WORK!!!!
```

That's because the first parameter gets interpreted as a string literal ('_5_18_20' AS cases). Therefore, you can't pass in a column name through USING. Hence, we recommend using String FORMAT() or CONCAT() to create the query to execute immediately.

Stored procedures

After you have written a script, you can save it into a dataset, similar to the way you save UDFs. Such a saved script is called a *stored procedure*. Here's an example of defining a procedure:[20]

```
CREATE OR REPLACE PROCEDURE ch08eu.sp_unusual_trips()
BEGIN

-- Script starts here
CREATE TEMPORARY TABLE typical_trip AS
  SELECT
      start_station_name
    , end_station_name
    , APPROX_QUANTILES(duration, 10)[OFFSET(5)] AS typical_duration
    , COUNT(*) AS num_trips
  FROM
    `bigquery-public-data`.london_bicycles.cycle_hire
  GROUP BY
    start_station_name, end_station_name
;

CREATE OR REPLACE TABLE ch08eu.unusual_days AS
  SELECT
      EXTRACT (DATE FROM start_date) AS trip_date
    , APPROX_QUANTILES(duration / typical_duration, 10)[OFFSET(5)] AS ratio
    , COUNT(*) AS num_trips_on_day
  FROM
    `bigquery-public-data`.london_bicycles.cycle_hire AS hire
    , typical_trip AS trip
  WHERE
    hire.start_station_name = trip.start_station_name
    AND hire.end_station_name = trip.end_station_name
    AND num_trips > 10
  GROUP BY trip_date
  HAVING num_trips_on_day > 10
  ORDER BY ratio DESC
;
-- Script ends here

END;
```

After you've defined it, you can invoke a stored procedure as follows (note the parentheses):

```
CALL ch08eu.sp_unusual_trips();
```

---

20 See *08_advqueries/stored_procedure_def.sql* in the GitHub repository for this book.

Parameters to stored procedures

Stored procedures are akin to UDFs in that they can take input parameters and return output parameters.[21] For example, let's modify the script to be parameterized by the MIN_TRIPS_THRESH and return the result instead of storing into a table:[22]

```
CREATE OR REPLACE PROCEDURE ch08eu.sp_most_unusual(
    IN MIN_TRIPS_THRESH INT64,
    OUT result ARRAY<STRUCT<trip_date DATE, ratio FLOAT64, num_trips_on_day INT64>>)

BEGIN
  CREATE TEMPORARY TABLE typical_trip AS
    SELECT
        start_station_name
      , end_station_name
      , APPROX_QUANTILES(duration, 10)[OFFSET(5)] AS typical_duration
      , COUNT(*) AS num_trips
    FROM
      `bigquery-public-data`.london_bicycles.cycle_hire
    GROUP BY
      start_station_name, end_station_name
;

SET result = (
    WITH unusual_trips AS (
      SELECT
        EXTRACT (DATE FROM start_date) AS trip_date
      , APPROX_QUANTILES(duration / typical_duration, 10)[OFFSET(5)] AS ratio
      , COUNT(*) AS num_trips_on_day
      FROM
        `bigquery-public-data`.london_bicycles.cycle_hire AS hire
      , typical_trip AS trip
      WHERE
        hire.start_station_name = trip.start_station_name
        AND hire.end_station_name = trip.end_station_name
        AND num_trips > MIN_TRIPS_THRESH
      GROUP BY trip_date
      HAVING num_trips_on_day > MIN_TRIPS_THRESH
    )
    SELECT
    ARRAY_AGG(STRUCT(trip_date, ratio, num_trips_on_day)
     ORDER BY ratio DESC LIMIT 3)
    FROM unusual_trips
  );

END;
```

---

21 Parameters can function as both inputs and outputs; these are marked INOUT.

22 See *08_advqueries/stored_procedure_inout.sql* in the GitHub repository for this book.

When calling the procedure, pass in the required parameters, declaring any variables as needed:

```
DECLARE y ARRAY<STRUCT<trip_date DATE, ratio FLOAT64, num_trips_on_day INT64>>;
CALL ch08eu.sp_most_unusual(10, y);
SELECT y;
```

The following shows the result:

Row	y.trip_date	y.ratio	y.num_trips_on_day
1	2016-12-25	1.6111111111111112	34477
	2015-12-25	1.5161290322580645	20871
	2015-08-01	1.25	41200

Advanced Functions

In this section, we cover some advanced functions that are part of the BigQuery toolkit: functions for analysis with geographic types, for statistics, and for hashing and unique number generation. We examine machine learning in the next chapter.

BigQuery Geographic Information Systems

How many of the tables in your data warehouse have location information in them? Perhaps you record the latitude and longitude of your vehicles or packages over time, or perhaps you have the addresses of your customers and suppliers. Maybe you recorded customer transactions, and you could join it against another table that has store locations.

Not only is location information very common, but many business decisions also revolve around location. Identifying which neighborhoods and cities to focus on with a promotional offer is a common analysis task in marketing departments. Logistics and just-in-time manufacturing companies need to track the location of millions of small packages in their supply chain. Therefore, geospatial analysis is quite common in data analytics. Our colleague Chad Jennings ran a search over GitHub recently[23] and found that 9% of all *.sql* files there carry out spatial queries, using a very conservative way to estimate what constitutes a spatial query. BigQuery makes analyzing and visualizing geospatial data very easy and highly performant.

Traditionally, systems that allowed for analyzing geographic data were rather unique and were termed Geographic Information Systems (GIS). Now, of course, a general-purpose analytics tool like BigQuery supports the types of analysis that required

---

23 There is a public dataset in BigQuery of all the files in GitHub.

those custom tools. So the geospatial capabilities are also often referred to as *GIS features*.

Geographic types

GIS functions operate on geographic types. BigQuery supports points, lines, and polygons on the Earth's surface on the WGS84 reference ellipsoid.[24] For example, we can create a geographic type given the longitude and latitude of some London bicycle stations using ST_GeogPoint (note that longitude comes first):

```
SELECT
  name
  , ST_GeogPoint(longitude, latitude) AS location
FROM
  `bigquery-public-data`.london_bicycles.cycle_stations
WHERE
  id BETWEEN 300 and 305
```

In the result set, the location column is a Point type, and in the text depiction, it is shown in Well Known Text (*https://www.opengeospatial.org/standards/wkt-crs*) (WKT), a standard format for representing geographies as strings:

Row	name	location
1	Marylebone Lane, Marylebone	POINT(-0.148105415 51.51475963)
2	Serpentine Car Park, Hyde Park	POINT(-0.17306032 51.505014)
3	Albert Gate, Hyde Park	POINT(-0.158456089 51.50295379)
4	Kennington Lane Tesco, Vauxhall	POINT(-0.115853961 51.48677988)
5	Putney Pier, Wandsworth	POINT(-0.216573 51.466907)

When loading geospatial data from other systems, you'll find that the geographic data tends to come in either as WKT or as GeoJSON, another standard string format for representing geographies. If your exporting system provides a choice, choose Geo-JSON over WKT because there is no ambiguity in GeoJSON as to whether the polygon of interest is the "interior" one or the "exterior" one[25] (they both have the same

---

24 Because the Earth is not a perfect sphere but a lumpy mass, there are many possible approximations of the shape of the Earth, and different ellipsoidal approximations tend to be more accurate in different parts of the world. The Global Positioning System (GPS) uses WGS84; thus, nearly all the location coordinates you are likely to encounter will be with respect to WGS84.

25 When parsing WKT, there is ambiguity over which polygon is meant. By default, BigQuery assumes that the smaller polygon is the one that is intended. The ST_GeogFromText supports a parameter called oriented, which, if set to TRUE, will assume that the polygon of interest is being traversed counterclockwise.

coordinates) or whether the edges need to be tessellated.[26] If the geospatial data is in some other format, such as Shapefiles, use the open source tool `ogr2ogr` to convert the data into GeoJSON before loading into BigQuery.[27]

As discussed in Chapter 7, GIS queries in BigQuery are much more efficient if geographic data is stored as geography types rather than as primitives (e.g., longitude and latitude) or as strings.

If you have a dataset in which the data is held as primitives or strings, convert them into geographic types in your Extract, Load, and Transform (ELT) or ETL pipeline:

```
CREATE OR REPLACE TABLE ch08eu.cycle_stations AS
SELECT
  *, ST_GeogPoint(longitude, latitude) AS location
FROM
  `bigquery-public-
data`.london_bicycles.cycle_stations
```

To convert strings in the WKT or GeoJSON format to geographic types, use the function `ST_GeogFromText` or `ST_GeogFromGeoJSON`, respectively.

Handling geographic projections

BigQuery GIS uses the WGS84 coordinate system and can load new-line delimited GeoJSON directly. However, there are hundreds of GIS file types and projections. Loading them into BigQuery requires transforming the data type and its projection into WGS84. We recommend FME (*https://console.cloud.google.com/market place/details/safe-software-public/fme-platform-2020*), a data integration platform that is designed to import a wide variety of spatial formats, validate the geographies, and materialize them as BigQuery tables.

To convert geographies to strings in the WKT or GeoJSON format, use the function `ST_AsText` or `ST_AsGeoJSON`, respectively:

```
SELECT
  name
  , ST_AsGeoJSON(location) AS location_string
FROM
```

---

26 *Tessellation* refers to making sure that the polygons completely fill the plane with no overlaps and no gaps—all the polygons associated with the districts in a state must completely fill the state, for example. This is not a problem in GeoJSON, because the district edges will already be on a plane, but for WKT, BigQuery must tessellate the provided coordinates, and so points might be moved by up to 10 meters.

27 For details, see *https://oreil.ly/jZVpC*.

```
    ch08eu.cycle_stations
WHERE
    id BETWEEN 300 and 305
```

This yields the following:

Row	name	location_string
1	Marylebone Lane, Marylebone	{ "type": "Point", "coordinates": [-0.148105415, 51.51475963] }
2	Serpentine Car Park, Hyde Park	{ "type": "Point", "coordinates": [-0.17306032, 51.505014] }
3	Albert Gate, Hyde Park	{ "type": "Point", "coordinates": [-0.158456089, 51.50295379] }
4	Kennington Lane Tesco, Vauxhall	{ "type": "Point", "coordinates": [-0.115853961, 51.48677988] }
5	Putney Pier, Wandsworth	{ "type": "Point", "coordinates": [-0.216573, 51.466907] }

Creating Polygons

Suppose that you have a trip from station 300 to station 305, then to station 302, and finally back to station 300. You can use ST_MakeLine and ST_MakePolygon to represent one trip segment or the entire round trip, respectively:

```
WITH stations AS (
SELECT
    (SELECT location FROM ch08eu.cycle_stations WHERE id = 300)
        AS loc300,
    (SELECT location FROM ch08eu.cycle_stations WHERE id = 302)
        AS loc302,
    (SELECT location FROM ch08eu.cycle_stations WHERE id = 305)
        AS loc305
)

SELECT
    ST_MakeLine(loc300, loc305) AS seg1
    , ST_MakePolygon(ST_MakeLine(
        [loc300, loc305, loc302])) AS poly
FROM
    stations
```

Here is the result:

Row	seg1	poly
1	LINESTRING(-0.17306032 51.505014, -0.115853961 51.48677988)	POLYGON((-0.216573 51.466907, -0.115853961 51.48677988, -0.17306032 51.505014, -0.216573 51.466907))

Note from the way the polygon is constructed that a line can have multiple segments —a polygon is closed, whereas a line can be open.

Geographic Data in Machine Learning

Most machine learning frameworks that operate on structured data can deal only with numeric or categorical variables. Using state or country names might not provide the granularity you need, and so you might want to use the precise location. Do not convert geographic locations to WKT or GeoJSON for the purpose of providing the geographic location as a categorical input: it is preferable to use a geohash instead, because the character representation in the hash conveys geographic proximity.

As an example, let's look at how the first few letters of the geohash of the center point of nearby zip codes is the same across the state of Alaska:

```
SELECT
  state_code
, zip_code
, ST_GeoHash(internal_point, 2) AS ziphash_2
, ST_GeoHash(internal_point, 5) AS ziphash_5
, ST_GeoHash(internal_point, 10) AS ziphash_10
FROM
  `bigquery-public-
data`.geo_us_boundaries.us_zip_codes
WHERE
  state_code = 'AK'
ORDER BY ziphash_10 ASC
LIMIT 5
```

This returns the following:

Row	state_code	zip_code	ziphash_2	ziphash_5	ziphash_10
1	AK	99546	b1	b14qu	b14queqr8k
2	AK	99547	b1	b1k15	b1k158vcqn
3	AK	99638	b1	b1rug	b1rugtepv7
4	AK	99685	b3	b39d7	b39d7x4cgz
5	AK	99692	b3	b39dd	b39dd3d7xf

Both 99546 (Adak) and 99638 (Nikolski) are in the Aleutian Islands chain, and this spatial proximity is captured by the fact that the first two letters of the geohash are the same (b1). Even more proximate are the fourth and fifth zip codes in the example result set: 99692 (Dutch Harbor) is essentially surrounded by 99685 (*https://www.unitedstateszipcodes.org/99685*) (Unalaska), and the spatial proximity is captured by the fact that the first four letters of the geohash are the same (b39d) for the two zip codes. Note that the spatial proximity in both these instances is not captured by the numeric values of the zip codes.

Thus a good way to incorporate a geographic point in BigQuery into machine learning models is to provide the first few characters of the point's geohash. How many characters you choose to use reflects the resolution at which you want to represent the location. Do this at multiresolution; that is, provide the first character, the first two characters, and the first three characters as three separate categorical inputs to the model.

GIS predicate functions

BigQuery supports a number of spatial *predicate functions*. You can use these functions in WHERE clauses and in JOINs. For example, you can look for the zip codes best served by the New York Citibike system by looking for the number of stations within one kilometer (1,000 meters) of each zip code:

```
SELECT
    z.zip_code
    , COUNT(*) AS num_stations
FROM
    `bigquery-public-data`.new_york.citibike_stations AS s,
    `bigquery-public-data`.geo_us_boundaries.us_zip_codes AS z
WHERE
    ST_DWithin(
        z.zcta_geom,
        ST_GeogPoint(s.longitude, s.latitude),
        1000) -- 1km
GROUP BY z.zip_code
ORDER BY num_stations DESC
LIMIT 5
```

The key function being used is ST_DWithin (or distance within). This what the result looks like:

Row	zip_code	num_stations
1	11201	116
2	11217	112
3	10003	112
4	11238	103
5	10011	95

Similarly, we can check whether geometries intersect, contain, or are covered by another geometry using ST_Intersects, ST_Contains, or ST_CoveredBy. There are other spatial predicate functions (*https://cloud.google.com/bigquery/docs/reference/ standard-sql/geography_functions*) as well.

GIS Measures

One of the most useful GIS functions is ST_Distance, with which you can compute the distance between two geographies. For example, to compute the distance between Seattle and Miami, you can do the following:

```
WITH seattle AS (
  SELECT ANY_VALUE(internal_point) as loc
  FROM `bigquery-public-data`.geo_us_boundaries.us_zip_codes
  WHERE city = 'Seattle' and state_code = 'WA'
),
miami AS (
  SELECT ANY_VALUE(internal_point) as loc
  FROM `bigquery-public-data`.geo_us_boundaries.us_zip_codes
  WHERE city = 'Miami city' and state_code = 'FL'
)

SELECT
  ST_Distance(seattle.loc, miami.loc)/1000 AS dist
FROM seattle, miami
```

The result, when we ran it, was 4,364 kilometers. Your result might be slightly different because of the use of ANY_VALUE to select any of the zip codes in the two cities.

 To adhere to the privacy policies in place at your organization, you will often need to coarsen, or lower, the resolution of location data. ST_SnapToGrid allows you to round off locations. For example, ST_SnapToGrid(pt, 0.01) rounds off the latitude and longitude of pt to the second decimal place. This function also works for polygons and lines and does the right things (for example, clips off line segments that do not make sense once the vertices are rounded off).

Geometry transformations and aggregations

BigQuery also provides a variety of functions to compute the union, intersection, and more of geography types.

The query in the previous section picked any zip code in the city and used only the center of the polygon. A much better way is to combine all of the zip code polygons for each city into a single geometry using ST_UNION and compute the distance between these two geometries:

```
WITH seattle AS (
  SELECT ST_UNION(ARRAY_AGG(zcta_geom)) as loc
  FROM `bigquery-public-data`.geo_us_boundaries.us_zip_codes
  WHERE city = 'Seattle' and state_code = 'WA'
),
miami AS (
  SELECT ST_UNION(ARRAY_AGG(zcta_geom)) as loc
  FROM `bigquery-public-data`.geo_us_boundaries.us_zip_codes
  WHERE city = 'Miami city' and state_code = 'FL'
)

SELECT
```

```
  ST_Distance(seattle.loc, miami.loc)/1000 AS dist
FROM seattle, miami
```

The result is 4,356 kilometers, and this time, the result is deterministic: it is the distance from the most southeast corner of Seattle to the most northwest corner of Miami.

Computing the union of an aggregate is a common enough need that BigQuery provides a shortcut function ST_UNION_AGG that you could have used:

```
WITH seattle AS (
  SELECT ST_UNION_AGG(zcta_geom) as loc
  FROM `bigquery-public-data`.geo_us_boundaries.us_zip_codes
  WHERE city = 'Seattle' and state_code = 'WA'
)
```

To compute the centroid of an aggregate of geometries, use ST_CENTROID_AGG. Thus, this would be distance between the geometric city centers of Seattle and Miami:

```
WITH seattle AS (
  SELECT ST_CENTROID_AGG(zcta_geom) as loc
  FROM `bigquery-public-data`.geo_us_boundaries.us_zip_codes
  WHERE city = 'Seattle' and state_code = 'WA'
),
miami AS (
  SELECT ST_CENTROID_AGG(zcta_geom) as loc
  FROM `bigquery-public-data`.geo_us_boundaries.us_zip_codes
  WHERE city = 'Miami city' and state_code = 'FL'
)

SELECT
  ST_Distance(seattle.loc, miami.loc)/1000 AS dist
FROM seattle, miami
```

This returns 4,363 kilometers.

To visualize geospatial data, use BigQuery Geo Viz or a Jupyter Notebook (discussed in Chapter 5).

Useful Statistical Functions

BigQuery supports the computation of statistics over petabyte-scale datasets. We can compute the mean, standard deviation, and percentiles over a column as well as the Pearson correlation between a pair of columns.

Statistics

For example, here is a query to find bulk statistics on the duration column over the london_bicycles dataset:

```
SELECT
  MIN(duration) AS min_dur
  , MAX(duration) AS max_dur
  , COUNT(duration) AS num_dur
  , AVG(duration) AS avg_dur
  , SUM(duration) AS total_dur
  , STDDEV(duration) AS stddev_dur
  , VARIANCE(duration) AS variance_dur
FROM
  `bigquery-public-data`.london_bicycles.cycle_hire
```

The result is as follows:

Row	min_dur	max_dur	num_dur	avg_dur	total_dur	stddev_dur	variance_dur
1	-3540	2674020	24369201	1332.29	32466946080	9827.99	9.66E7

Of course, the minimum (–3,540?) and maximum (2,674,020 seconds = 31 days!) durations almost definitely represent invalid observations. As such, the mean duration is not to be trusted, because it includes these outlier values.

Quantiles

A safer central tendency to use on columns with significant outliers is the median. You can get that in BigQuery using APPROX_QUANTILES. You can specify the number of quantiles, so let's use 3:

```
SELECT
  APPROX_QUANTILES(duration, 3)
FROM
  `bigquery-public-data`.london_bicycles.cycle_hire
```

This returns the following:

Row	f0_
1	-3540
	600
	1080
	2674020

Why are there four numbers? Because we asked for three bins, and we need four boundaries to get three bins: (–3540, 600), (600, 1,080), and (1,080, 2,674,020). So –3,540 is the minimum duration and 2,674,020 is the maximum duration. One-third of the data is at or below 600 seconds. The top third of rentals are 1,080 seconds or longer. The middle third is between 600 and 1,080 seconds.

To find the median, or midpoint of the distribution, we can ask for exactly two bins:

```
SELECT
  APPROX_QUANTILES(duration, 2)
FROM
  `bigquery-public-data`.london_bicycles.cycle_hire
```

Here's what this query returns:

Row	f0_
1	-3540
	840
	2674020

From this table, the median is approximately 840 seconds.[28] Of course, we can do a finer-grained quantization and pick, say, the 95th percentile[29] of durations:

```
SELECT
  APPROX_QUANTILES(duration, 100)[OFFSET(95)]
FROM
  `bigquery-public-data`.london_bicycles.cycle_hire
```

This is what the query returns:

Row	f0_
1	3000

Based on that query, 95% of rentals last less than 3,000 seconds.

Correlation

Is there a correlation between stations that are close to the London city center and the duration of trips at those stations? To answer this question, let's create a column that captures the distance of a station from the city center and another that capture the median duration of rentals, and then compute the correlation:

```
WITH distances AS (
  SELECT
      id
    , ST_Distance(location, ST_GeogPoint(-0.12574, 51.50853)) AS distance
  FROM
      ch08eu.cycle_stations
),
durations AS (
  SELECT
      start_station_id AS id
```

---

28 Note that the median we got is the approximate quantile. The expected error is ±1%.

29 The 95th and 99th percentiles are often used to model "worst case" scenarios.

```
     , APPROX_QUANTILES(duration, 2)[OFFSET(1)] AS median_duration
  FROM
      `bigquery-public-data`.london_bicycles.cycle_hire
  GROUP BY start_station_id
)

SELECT CORR(distance, median_duration) AS pearson
FROM distances
JOIN durations
USING(id)
```

The result, 0.14, indicates that there is pretty much no correlation between distance from the city center and rental duration. A correlation coefficient of 1.0 indicates strong proportionality, and –1.0 an inverse relationship. Two variables that are linearly independent of each other will have a correlation coefficient of zero.

Hash Algorithms

A common requirement in many analysis tasks is to devise a short string that will uniquely represent a row. For example, you might need to quickly identify duplicate rows without going to the expense of comparing each and every column. There are two ways to do this: one is to compute a fingerprint of a row's values, and the other is to assign a universally unique identifier (UUID) to a row at the time of creation. Although there is no guarantee that the same fingerprint will not arise for two completely separate sets of values, the probability is very small. Similarly, there is no guarantee that the same UUID will not be generated by some other system somewhere else. Nevertheless, the likelihood of this happening is very small.

So even though you would not use fingerprinting or UUID for cryptography or money management, you could use it to safeguard against counting the same bicycle ride twice. There is a small theoretical probability that some customer gets a free ride, but no customer will be double-charged.[30] Of course, if you do have cryptographic needs, BigQuery has support for popular encryption algorithms (MD5 and SHA).

Fingerprint function

To compute the fingerprint, BigQuery uses the FARM fingerprint algorithm (*https:// github.com/google/farmhash*), an open source hash-computation algorithm with implementations in multiple programming languages (so that, if necessary, you can compute the same fingerprint in other systems off the same data). The function takes a STRING as input and returns an INT64.

---

30 And the computational costs you save by not having to compare each and every field or to build a truly unique and globally consistent infrastructure (like Cloud Spanner!) outweigh the cost of that occasional free bicycle ride.

We know that a bicycle rental can be uniquely identified by the bike_id, start time of the rental, and the station it was rented from. Instead of comparing all three values each time we want to check whether two rows correspond to the same rental, we can simply compare the two rows' fingerprints (provided we have already computed them, of course). Thus, to compute the fingerprint of a cycle hire, we can do this:

```
WITH identifier AS (
  SELECT
    CONCAT(
      CAST(bike_id AS STRING), '***',
      CAST(start_date AS STRING), '***',
      CAST(start_station_id AS STRING)
    ) AS rowid
  FROM `bigquery-public-data.london_bicycles.cycle_hire`
  LIMIT 10
)

SELECT
  rowid, FARM_FINGERPRINT(rowid) AS fingerprint
FROM identifier
```

This returns the following:

Row	rowid	fingerprint
1	8168***2016-09-15 10:09:00+00***176	6524654244988303787
2	7218***2016-06-08 18:49:00+00***114	-4994312061947208007
3	3648***2015-07-23 13:21:00+00***304	3924490378672877823
4	9403***2017-03-14 18:43:00+00***574	-1509385442790305242
5	10704***2016-08-16 20:58:00+00***223	-8271736518219415928
6	6048***2017-03-31 08:25:00+00***632	6083880842645302266
7	14039***2017-03-06 19:29:00+00***529	-5809138520111495006
8	7956***2015-07-27 09:55:00+00***14	-4999466933100478693
9	5744***2015-01-27 09:40:00+00***341	-8567341349676429749
10	13088***2016-08-06 22:50:00+00***29	6415473001431984902

Repeatable Sampling for Machine Learning

One common use of the fingerprint algorithm is to create a repeatable hash of rows in a dataset for machine learning. This can be used to split a dataset into test and train. For example, if you want to split rentals by stations and days, you could compute the hash of those two fields and use them to split the dataset:

```
WITH datasets AS (
  SELECT
    CONCAT(
      CAST(start_station_id AS STRING),
      CAST(EXTRACT(DATE FROM start_date) AS STRING))
```

```
  AS key,
    *
  FROM `bigquery-public-
data.london_bicycles.cycle_hire`
    LIMIT 100
)

SELECT
  IF(MOD(ABS(FARM_FINGERPRINT(key)), 10) < 8, 'train', 'test') AS ds,
  * EXCEPT(key)
FROM datasets
LIMIT 10
```

Here's what this returns (there are more columns, but only a few are shown; note, though, that the first column identifies rows as either train or test):

Row	ds	rental_id	duration	bike_id	end_station_id	end_station_name
1	train	63022577	600	8930	55	Finsbury Circus, Liverpool Street
2	test	41340757	540	9260	58	New Inn Yard, Shoreditch
3	train	47466877	2040	11137	210	Hinde Street, Marylebone
4	test	53171329	5760	7033	733	Park Lane, Mayfair
5	train	42268703	900	7005	248	Triangle Car Park, Hyde Park

MD5 and SHA

BigQuery also supports popular hashing algorithms. These are one-way hashes and can be useful for tokenizing Personally Identifiable Information (PII), although it should be noted that some hash algorithms are more secure than others, and you should make an informed choice about which algorithm to use for your data (we cover encryption in Chapter 10):

```
SELECT
  name
  , MD5(name) AS md5_
  , SHA256(name) AS sha256_
  , SHA512(name) AS sha512_
FROM UNNEST(['Joe Customer', 'Jane Employee']) AS name
```

This returns the following:

Row	name	md5_	sha256_	sha512_
1	Joe Customer	9JFfot7XXNa9 IFXrZYpkIQ==	ITPGdZjjJNgvrYfvHRP2HX ofhTntHalPMAn5tdA4AY8=	ysAXoRHTb+ENWL9jB2pCD1 arBasmuush7KJVa3sKWMbz1v zyUKHUS5CDI9jBNR3yxBDwRFL SQbHwPLklBuLptQ==
2	Jane Employee	g6HbGfBF02V JLdJoXs8tXQ==	wXJxfwK/hP4dgjQuz IcPOLVZEryACurXmL7qM cnC3tE=	N9tGIXX6AibvHpDNaZciAMHSYK/9/ nA9886fVkcPwykLONRIpilM 7zE25yUZy6RSEPvKM+sdM +IcsgG82qtj2Q==

UUID

To generate a universally unique string consisting of 32 hexadecimal digits that is unlikely to be generated for the same purpose on another system, use UUID:

```
SELECT GENERATE_UUID() AS uuid;
```

When we ran it, we got the following (you will get a different string, of course):

Row	uuid
1	5ae248e9-5872-410f-862f-8a27bb527b53

Random number generator

BigQuery also provides a random number generator, which can be useful if your analysis requires shuffling or adding noise to variables. To generate a uniformly distributed random number in the range 0 to 1, use:

```
SELECT RAND()
```

Summary

In this chapter, we looked at ways to foster reuse of SQL. Queries can be parameterized either with named parameters or with positional parameters, and those parameters can be passed in at execution time. It is possible to extract commonly used SQL code into functions that can be either temporary (available only to the current query) or persisted in a dataset and used by anyone with read access to the dataset. Other ways to improve reuse and readability are to use the WITH clause and correlated subqueries.

We also delved deeper into arrays, discussing situations in which they can be used: to preserve ordering, to store repeated fields, or to generate data. We also discussed window functions that are computed on a subset of a table either for computing moving averages, for navigation ("next three rows"), and for numbering (to find the first, last, etc.).

We covered examples of using table metadata to build queries dynamically and extensively covered the use of DDL and DML. We also discussed BigQuery support for scripting, whether it is for simply executing a sequence of statements or for more complex needs such as looping.

Finally, we discussed BigQuery GIS, how to create geography types, and how to calculate GIS predicates and transform existing geographies through the use of ST_Union, and more. Finally, we ended with illustrations of statistical functions and hash algorithms.

Machine Learning in BigQuery

Artificial intelligence (AI) is the domain of computer science focused on building computational systems that are capable of acting autonomously. Over the years, many different subfields have arisen in AI, but an approach that has proven successful in recent years has been the idea of using large datasets to train general-purpose models (such as decision trees and neural networks) that can solve complex problems with great accuracy.

Teaching a computer based on examples is called *supervised machine learning*, and it can be carried out in BigQuery with the data remaining in place. In this chapter, we look at how to solve a wide variety of machine learning problems using BigQuery ML. Even though machine learning can be carried out in BigQuery, being able to use powerful, industry-standard machine learning frameworks such as TensorFlow on the data in BigQuery can give us access to a much wider variety of machine learning models and components. Hence, in this chapter we also look at the connections that exist between BigQuery and full-fledged machine learning frameworks.

What Is Machine Learning?

If we have collected historical data (and what is a data warehouse for, if not precisely this?), and the historical data contains the correct answers (called the "*label*"), we can train machine learning models on this data to predict the outcome for cases where the label is not yet known. For example, if we have a historical dataset of actual sales figures, we can train machine learning models to predict sales in the future. As with data analytics, machine learning in BigQuery is also carried out in SQL.

Formulating a Machine Learning Problem

For example, suppose that your business operates several hundred movie theaters all over the country, and you want to predict how many movie tickets will sell for a particular showtime at a particular theater—this sort of prediction is useful if you are trying to determine how to schedule movies. If you have data about the movies that have been run in the past, our machine learning problem might be formulated as follows: use data about the movies in our historical dataset to learn the number of tickets sold for each showtime in each theater. Then apply that machine learning model to a candidate movie to determine how much demand there will be for this movie at a specific showtime.

The attributes of the movie that you will use as inputs to the machine learning model are called the *features* of the model. The label is what you want to learn how to predict, and in this case, the label is the number of tickets sold. Following are some examples of features that you might want to include in your model:

- Motion picture content rating[1] (for example, PG-13 means that parental guidance is recommended for children younger than 13)
- Is the showtime on a workday or on a weekend/holiday?
- At what time of day is the show (afternoon, evening, or night)?
- Movie genre (comedy, thriller, etc.)
- How long ago was the movie released (in days)?
- Average critics' rating of the movie (scale of 1 to 10)
- Total box office receipts for the previous movie by this director, if applicable
- Total box office receipts for the previous movie by the lead actor, if applicable
- Theater location
- Theater type (e.g., multiplex, drive-in, mall, etc.)

Note that the title of the movie, as is, is not a good input to the machine learning model.[2] Though *Tinker Tailor Soldier Spy*, a 2011 movie, might be part of our training dataset, we will typically not be interested in predicting the performance of that exact movie (for one, it has already run in our theater). Instead, our interest will be in

---

1 See *https://en.wikipedia.org/wiki/Motion_picture_content_rating_system*.

2 The individual words of the movie title might be more appropriate, as long as we take care to apply common Natural Language Processing techniques such as tokenization, stemming, and word embedding. Calculated features about the title of the movie might also prove useful; for example, the length of the title might have some predictive power, or whether the title has the word "spy" in it.

predicting the performance of, say, *Deep Water Horizon*, another thriller with similar critical reviews that was released in 2016.

Hence, the machine learning model needs to be based on features of the movie (things that describe the movie), not things that uniquely identify it. This way, our model might guess that *Deep Water Horizon*, if run at similar timings to *Tinker Tailor Soldier Spy*, will perform similarly because the movies are in the same genre, and because the critics' rating of the movies are similar.

The first four features (rating, type of showtime, showtime, genre) are categorical features, by which we mean that they take one of a finite number of possible values. In BigQuery, any feature that is a string is considered a categorical feature. If the database representation of categorical features happens to be some other type (for example, the showtime might be a number such as 1430 or a timestamp), you should cast it as a string in your query. The next four features (time since release, critics' ratings, box office receipts for director and lead actor) are numeric features, by which we mean that they are numbers with meaningful magnitudes. The last two features (theater type and location) will need to be represented in special ways; we discuss choices later in this chapter.

The label, or the correct answer for the prediction problem, is given by the number of tickets sold historically. During the training of the machine learning model, BigQuery is shown the input features and corresponding labels and creates the model that captures this information (see Figure 9-1). Then, during prediction, the trained machine learning model can be applied on a new set of input features to gain an estimate of how many tickets we can expect to sell if we schedule the movie at a specific time and location.

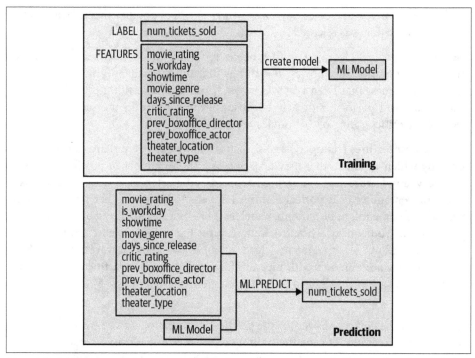

Figure 9-1. During training, the model is shown features and their corresponding labels. Then the trained model can be used for prediction. Given a set of features, the model predicts a value for the label.

Types of Machine Learning Problems

We tend to use different machine learning models and techniques depending on the nature of the input features and the labels. In this subsection, we'll provide brief definitions of the types of problems. We cover the solutions to these problems in greater detail in the rest of this chapter.

Regression

In the example in the previous section, we wanted to predict the number of tickets that would be sold for a particular showing of a movie. In that case, the label is a number, and so the type of machine learning problem it represents is called *regression*.

Classification

If the label is a categorical variable, the type of machine learning problem is called *classification*. The output of a classification model is the probability that a row belongs to a label value. For example, if you were to train a machine learning model to predict whether a show will sell out, you would be using a classification model, and the output of the model would be the probability that a show sells out.

Many classification problems have two classes: the show sells out or it doesn't, a customer buys the item or they don't, the flight is late or it isn't. These are called *binary classification problems*. In such cases, the label column should be True or False, or it should be 1 or 0. The prediction from the model will be the probability that the label is True. We typically threshold the probability at 0.5 to determine the most likely class.

A classification problem can have multiple classes. For example, revisiting our bike rental scenario, you might want to predict the station at which a bicycle will be returned, and because there are hundreds of possible values for this categorical label, this is a multiclass classification problem. The output of such a machine learning model will be a set of probabilities, one for each station in the network, and the sum of these probabilities will be 1.0. In a multiclass problem, we typically care about the top three or top five predictions, not about the actual value of the probability.

Recommender

The special case of multiclass classification for which the task is to recommend the "next" product based on ratings or past purchases is called a *recommender system*. Although a recommendation problem could be solved in the standard way that all multiclass classification problems are, special machine learning model types have been built for these problems, and it is preferable to use these more specific model types. Recommender systems are also the preferable way to address customer targeting problems—to find customers who will like a product or promotional offer.

Time series prediction

The special case of regression where the input is a time series of numbers, and for which the task is to predict a future value based within the same series is called a *time series prediction* problem. Powerful methods exist that are capable of predicting time series values taking into account seasonality, trends, and natural variations.

Clustering

If we don't have a label at all, we cannot do supervised learning. We could find natural groupings within the data; this type of ML problem is called *clustering*. We might employ clustering of customer features to perform customer segmentation, for example. Otherwise, we can use the Cloud Data Labeling Service to annotate our training dataset with human labelers as a precursor to carrying out supervised learning.

Unstructured data

In the discussion so far, we have assumed that our data consists of structured or semi-structured data. If some of the input features are unstructured (e.g., images or natural language text), consider using a preexisting model such as Cloud Vision API or Cloud Natural Language to process the unstructured data in question, and use the output of these APIs as numeric or categorical inputs to the machine learning model. For example, you could use the Natural Language API to identify key entities in customer emails or the sentiment of customer reviews, and use the entities as categorical variables and the sentiment as a numeric feature.

You also might be able to turn unstructured data into structured data through string functions or machine learning APIs. Splitting a text field into individual words and treating the presence/absence of individual words as features is a common technique, often called *bag of words*. In the movie title example, if you had a movie called *The Spy Who Loved Me*, you might have two features, has_spy and has_love, as True, and all other features would be false (you'd probably drop "the," "Who," and "Me" as being too common to be helpful in prediction). Or you might use the number of words in the title (maybe wordy titles are more likely to be indie films and more likely to appeal to different audiences).

If the label itself is unstructured (e.g., you want the model to craft the ideal response to customer questions based on a dataset of historical responses), this is a natural language generation problem—it's outside the scope of what BigQuery can handle.

Summary of model types

Table 9-1 summarizes the machine learning problem types. We discuss the BigQuery model types in the following sections.

Table 9-1. Machine learning model types and how to implement them in BigQuery

Problem characteristic	Machine learning problem type	BigQuery model_type
Labels unavailable and data cannot be labeled	Clustering	kmeans
Label is a number	Regression	linear_reg dnn_regressor boosted_tree_regressor
Predict future value of a time series of numbers	Time Series Prediction	ARIMA
Recommend products to users	Recommender	matrix_factorization
Recommend users for product	Customer targeting	matrix_factorization
Label is 1/0, True/False (or two categories)	Binary classification	logistic_reg dnn_classifier boosted_tree_classifier

Problem characteristic	Machine learning problem type	BigQuery model_type

Label is in a fixed set of strings	Multiclass classification	`logistic_reg`
		`dnn_classifier`
		`boosted_tree_classifier`

Input feature is unstructured	Image classification Text classification Sentiment analysis Entity extraction	Use output of Cloud Vision API or Cloud Natural Language API as input to any of the standard BigQuery models above
Label is unstructured	Question answering Text summarization Image captioning	Use Cloud AutoML products

Building a Regression Model

As an example of building a regression model, let's use the `london_bicycles` dataset. Let's assume that we have two types of bicycles: hardy commuter bikes, and fast but fragile road bikes. If a bicycle rental is likely to be for a long duration, we need to have road bikes in stock, but if the rental is likely to be for a short duration, we need to have commuter bikes in stock. Therefore, to build a system to properly stock bicycles, we need to predict the duration of bicycle rentals.

Choose the Label

The first step of solving a machine learning problem is to formulate it—to identify features of our model and the label. Because the goal of our first model is to predict the duration of a rental based on our historical dataset of cycle rentals, the label is the duration of the rental.

However, is this the correct objective for the problem? Should we be predicting the duration of each rental, or should we be predicting the total duration of all rentals at a station over, for instance, an hour? If the latter is the better formulation, the label should be the sum of all the rentals in a specific hour. Talking to our business, though, we learn that a station with 1,000 rentals of 20 minutes each should get commuter bikes, whereas a station that has 100 rentals of 200 minutes each should get road bikes. So predicting the total duration will not help the business make the right decision; predicting the duration of each rental will help them.

Another option is to predict the likelihood of rentals that last less than 30 minutes. In that case, the label is True/False depending on whether the duration was long (more than 30 minutes) or short (less than 30 minutes). This might help the business even more because the probability might indicate the relative proportion of commuter bikes to road bikes to have on hand at each station.

It is quite common to have to make a choice between multiple objectives. In some cases, we could create a weighted combination of these objectives as the label and train a single model. In other cases, you might find it helpful to train multiple models, one for each objective, and use different models in different scenarios. In yet other situations, the best approach might be to present to the end user the results of all the models and have the end user choose. It all depends on your business case.

In this use case, let's decide that we need to build two models: one in which we predict the duration of a rental, and the other in which we predict the probability that the rental will be longer than 30 minutes. Then we have the end user make their decision based on the two predictions.

Exploring the Dataset to Find Features

If we believe that the duration will vary based on the station at which the bicycle is being rented, the day of the week, and the time of day, those could be our input features. Before we go ahead and create a model with these three features, though, it's a good idea to verify that these factors do influence the label.

Coming up with features for a machine learning model is called *feature engineering*. Feature engineering is often the most important part of building accurate machine learning models, and it can be much more impactful than deciding which algorithm to use or tuning hyperparameters. Good feature engineering requires deep understanding of the data and the domain. It is often a process of hypothesis testing; you have an idea for a feature, you check to see whether it works (has mutual information with the label), and then you add it to the model. If it doesn't work, you try the next idea.

Impact of station

To check whether the duration of a rental varies by station, you can visualize the result of the following query in Data Studio using the `start_station_name` as the dimension and `duration` as the metric:[3]

```
SELECT
  start_station_name
  , AVG(duration) AS duration
FROM `bigquery-public-data`.london_bicycles.cycle_hire
GROUP BY start_station_name
```

This yields the result shown in Figure 9-2.

---

3 In the BigQuery web user interface, click Explore in Data Studio.

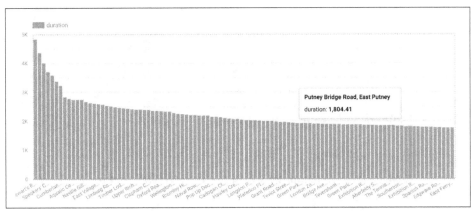

Figure 9-2. It appears that there are a few stations that are associated with long-duration rentals

From Figure 9-2, it is clear that a handful of stations are associated with long-duration rentals (over 3,000 seconds), but that the majority of stations have durations that lie in a relatively narrow range. Had all the stations in London been associated with durations within a narrow range, the station at which the rental commenced would not have been a good feature. But in this problem, as the graph in Figure 9-2 demonstrates, the start_station_name does matter.

Note that you cannot use end_station_name as a feature because at the time the bicycle is being rented, you won't know to which station the bicycle is going to be returned. Because we are creating a machine learning model to predict events in the future, you need to be mindful of not using any columns that will not be known at the time the prediction is made. This time/causality criterion imposes constraints on what features you can use.

Day of week

For the next candidate features, the process is similar. You can check whether dayofweek (or, similarly, hourofday) matters:

```
SELECT
  EXTRACT(dayofweek FROM start_date) AS dayofweek
  , AVG(duration) AS duration
FROM `bigquery-public-data`.london_bicycles.cycle_hire
GROUP BY dayofweek
```

Figure 9-3 shows the visualized result.

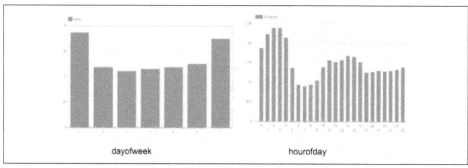

Figure 9-3. Longer duration rentals tend to happen on weekends and in the morning and early afternoon

From Figure 9-3, it is clear that the duration varies depending both on the day of the week and on the hour of the day. It appears that durations are longer on weekends (days 1 and 7) than on weekdays. Similarly, durations are longer early in the morning and in the midafternoon. Hence, both dayofweek and hourofday are good features.

Number of bicycles

Another potential feature is the number of bikes in the station. Perhaps, we hypothesize, people keep bicycles longer if there are fewer bicycles on rent at the station from which they rented. You can verify whether this is the case by using the following:

```
SELECT
  bikes_count
  , AVG(duration) AS duration
FROM `bigquery-public-data`.london_bicycles.cycle_hire
JOIN `bigquery-public-data`.london_bicycles.cycle_stations
ON cycle_hire.start_station_name = cycle_stations.name
GROUP BY bikes_count
```

Figure 9-4 presents the result via Data Studio.

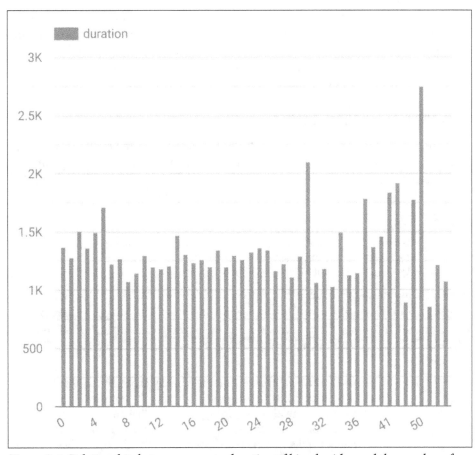

Figure 9-4. Relationship between average duration of bicycle rides and the number of bicycles at the station the bicycle was rented from

In Figure 9-4, notice that the relationship is noisy with no visible trend (compared against hour-of-day, for example). This indicates that the number of bicycles is not a good feature. You can confirm this quantitatively by computing the Pearson correlation coefficient:

```
SELECT
  CORR(bikes_count, duration) AS corr
FROM `bigquery-public-data`.london_bicycles.cycle_hire
JOIN `bigquery-public-data`.london_bicycles.cycle_stations
ON cycle_hire.start_station_name = cycle_stations.name
```

The result, −0.0039, indicates that the bikes_count and duration are essentially independent, because the Pearson coefficient will have an absolute value of 1.0 if they are linearly dependent, and 0.0 if they are linearly independent.

The Pearson correlation coefficient isn't a perfect test for whether a feature is useful because it looks only at linear dependence. Sometimes, a feature might have a nonlinear dependence with the label. Still, the Pearson coefficient is a good starting point. Machine learning scientists often use more sophisticated statistical tests like mutual information, which computes the randomness of the feature with respect to the label.

Creating a Training Dataset

Based on the exploration of the london_bicycles dataset and the relationship of various columns to the label column, we can prepare the training dataset by pulling out the selected features and the label:

```
SELECT
  duration
  , start_station_name
  , CAST(EXTRACT(dayofweek FROM start_date) AS STRING) as dayofweek
  , CAST(EXTRACT(hour FROM start_date) AS STRING) AS hourofday
FROM `bigquery-public-data`.london_bicycles.cycle_hire
```

Feature columns have to be either numeric (INT64, FLOAT64, etc.) or categorical (STRING). If the feature is numeric but needs to be treated as categorical, we need to cast it as a STRING—this explains why we cast the dayofweek and hourofday columns, which are integers (in the ranges 1 to 7 and 0 to 23, respectively), into strings.[4]

> If preparing the data involves computationally expensive transformations or joins, it might be a good idea to save the prepared training data as a table so as to not repeat that work during experimentation. If the transformations are trivial but the query itself is long-winded, it might be convenient to avoid repetitiveness by saving it as a view.

In this case, the query is simple and short, and so (for clarity) we'll simply repeat the query in later sections.

---

4 We could have treated these variables as continuous, but we would then be faced with unappealing choices about how to deal with the fact that dayofweek=7 is closer to dayofweek=1 than to dayofweek=5. For the record, some of these unappealing choices include: (a) storing the dayofweek twice, one in its current form and the other as MOD(dayofweek+3,7); and (b) replacing dayofweek by sin(2n * dayofweek / 7.0). They are unappealing because of how difficult they are to explain to stakeholders. If this is not a concern and you are solving a similar problem, it is worth experimenting with all three representations to see which one performs best.

Training and Evaluating the Model

To train the machine learning model and save it into the dataset ch09eu,[5] we need to call CREATE MODEL, which works similarly to CREATE TABLE:

```
CREATE OR REPLACE MODEL ch09eu.bicycle_model
OPTIONS(input_label_cols=['duration'], model_type='linear_reg')
AS

SELECT
  duration
  , start_station_name
  , CAST(EXTRACT(dayofweek FROM start_date) AS STRING) as dayofweek
  , CAST(EXTRACT(hour FROM start_date) AS STRING) AS hourofday
FROM `bigquery-public-data`.london_bicycles.cycle_hire
```

Note that the label column and model type are specified in OPTIONS. Because the label is numeric, this is a regression problem. This is why we picked linear_reg as the model type (we discuss other supported model types later in the chapter). As discussed in the previous section, the SELECT statement above prepares the training dataset and pulls in the label and feature columns.

Evaluating the model

This query took 2.5 minutes and was trained in just one iteration,[6] something we can learn by looking at the "Training" tab in the BigQuery section of the GCP Cloud Console. The mean absolute error (available from the evaluation tab) is 1,026 seconds, or about 17 minutes.[7] This means that you should expect to be able to predict the duration of bicycle rentals with an average error of about 17 minutes.

In addition to looking at the evaluation tab, you can obtain the evaluation results by running the following SQL query:

```
SELECT * FROM ML.EVALUATE(MODEL ch09eu.bicycle_model)
```

Note that the query OPTIONS also identifies the model type. Here, we have picked the simplest regression model that BigQuery supports. We strongly encourage you to pick the simplest model and to spend a lot of time considering and bringing in alternate data choices, because the payoff of a new/improved input feature greatly

---

5 Create it if necessary; it needs to be in the EU region because the data we are training on is in the EU.

6 This is because BigQuery is able to compute a closed-form solution to this linear regression problem. For more details, see *https://oreil.ly/0svPQ*.

7 Other error measures (mean squared error, mean squared log error, median absolute error, etc.) are also reported. For most regression problems, the mean absolute error strikes a good balance between insensitivity to outliers and sensitivity to iterative improvements. Use the mean absolute error unless you have a strong reason not to do so.

outweighs the payoff of a better model. Only when you have reached the limits of your data experimentation should you try more complex models.

Combining days of the week

There are other ways that you could have chosen to represent the features that you have. For example, recall that when we explored the relationship between dayofweek and the duration of rentals, we found that durations were longer on weekends than on weekdays. Therefore, instead of treating the raw value of dayofweek as a feature, you can employ this insight by fusing several dayofweek values into the weekday category:

```
CREATE OR REPLACE MODEL ch09eu.bicycle_model_weekday
OPTIONS(input_label_cols=['duration'], model_type='linear_reg')
AS

SELECT
  duration
  , start_station_name
  , IF(EXTRACT(dayofweek FROM start_date) BETWEEN 2 and 6,
       'weekday', 'weekend') as dayofweek
  , CAST(EXTRACT(hour FROM start_date) AS STRING) AS hourofday
FROM `bigquery-public-data`.london_bicycles.cycle_hire
```

This model results in a mean absolute error of 967 seconds, which is less than the 1,026 seconds for the original model. So let's go with the weekend-weekday model instead.

Bucketizing the hour of day

Again, based on the relationship between hourofday and the duration, you can experiment with bucketizing the variable into four bins—(–inf,5), [5,10),[8] [10,17), and [17,inf):

```
CREATE OR REPLACE MODEL ch09eu.bicycle_model_bucketized
OPTIONS(input_label_cols=['duration'], model_type='linear_reg')
AS

SELECT
  duration
  , start_station_name
  , IF(EXTRACT(dayofweek FROM start_date) BETWEEN 2 and 6, 'weekday', 'weekend')
    as dayofweek
  , ML.BUCKETIZE(EXTRACT(hour FROM start_date), [5, 10, 17]) AS hourofday
FROM `bigquery-public-data`.london_bicycles.cycle_hire
```

---

[8] The interval [a,b) means that a is included and b is not; in other words, this is the interval a ≤ x < b.

`ML.BUCKETIZE` is an example of a preprocessing function supported by BigQuery—we are passing in the number to bucketize and the bounds of the bins with –infinity and +infinity being assumed to be on either extremity. This model results in a mean absolute error of 901 seconds, which is less than the 967 seconds for the weekday-weekend model. So let's choose the bucketized model.

Predicting with the Model

We can try out the prediction by passing in a set of rows for which to predict. For example, you can obtain the predicted duration of a rental in Hyde Park at 5 p.m. on a Tuesday by using this code:

```
-- INCORRECT! (see next section)
SELECT * FROM ML.PREDICT(MODEL ch09eu.bicycle_model_bucketized,
    (SELECT 'Park Lane , Hyde Park' AS start_station_name

            , 'weekday' AS dayofweek, '17' AS hourofday)
)
```

This returns a predicted duration of 2,225 seconds, but this is wrong. Do you see the problem?

The need for TRANSFORM

In the previous prediction query, we had to pass in `'weekday'` rather than `'3'` for `dayofweek` because the model was trained with `dayofweek` being either `weekday` or `weekend`. It is incorrect to pass in the raw data value of `'17'` for `hourofday`—we should be passing in the name of the bin that represents 5 p.m. The prediction code will need to carry out the same transformations on the raw data that the training code did in order to get these values correct.

Wouldn't it be nice if BigQuery could remember the sets of transformations you did at the time of training and automatically apply them at the time of prediction? It can—that's precisely what the TRANSFORM clause does!

You can even move the extraction of hour-of-day and day-of-week into the TRANS FORM clause so that the client code needs to give us only the timestamp at which the bicycle is being rented:

```
CREATE OR REPLACE MODEL ch09eu.bicycle_model_bucketized
TRANSFORM(* EXCEPT(start_date)
        , IF(EXTRACT(dayofweek FROM start_date) BETWEEN 2 and 6,
'weekday', 'weekend') as dayofweek
        , ML.BUCKETIZE(EXTRACT(HOUR FROM start_date), [5, 10, 17]) AS hourofday
)
OPTIONS(input_label_cols=['duration'], model_type='linear_reg')
AS

SELECT
```

```
  duration
  , start_station_name
  , start_date
FROM `bigquery-public-data`.london_bicycles.cycle_hire
```

Use the TRANSFORM clause and formulate the machine learning problem in such a way that anyone requiring prediction needs to provide just the raw data.[9]

If a TRANSFORM clause is specified, the model is trained on the output of the TRANSFORM clause. So here, the TRANSFORM clause passes on all of the features and labels from the original SELECT query, except for the start_date, and then adds a couple of features (dayofweek and hourofday) extracted from the start_date.

The resulting model requires just the start_station_name and start_date to predict the duration. The transformations are saved and carried out on the provided raw data to create input features for the model.

 The advantage of placing all preprocessing functions inside the TRANSFORM clause is that clients of the model do not need to know what kind of preprocessing has been carried out—BigQuery takes care of automatically applying the necessary transformations to the raw data during prediction. Best practice, therefore, is to have the SELECT statement in a training query return just the raw data, and have all transformations done in the TRANSFORM clause.

With the TRANSFORM clause in place, the prediction query becomes:

```
SELECT * FROM ML.PREDICT(MODEL ch09eu.bicycle_model_bucketized,
  (SELECT 'Park Lane , Hyde Park' AS start_station_name
          , CURRENT_TIMESTAMP() AS start_date)
)
```

The result (yours will vary because presumably the timeofday and dayofweek are different) is something like the following:

Row	predicted_duration	start_station_name	start_date
1	3498.804224263982	Park Lane, Hyde Park	2019-05-19 04:24:03.376064 UTC

---

9 Indeed, this is the default behavior of BigQuery if the input feature is a TIMESTAMP. Just as the default behavior of BigQuery to string values is to one-hot encode it, the default behavior of BigQuery when supplied a TIME STAMP is to extract pieces such as day-of-week from it. Specifying the transformation ourselves gives us more granular control.

Generating batch predictions

You could also create a table of predictions for every hour at every station, starting at 3 a.m. the next day, using array generation:

```
DECLARE tomorrow_3am TIMESTAMP;
SET tomorrow_3am = TIMESTAMP_ADD(
  TIMESTAMP(DATE_ADD(CURRENT_DATE(), INTERVAL 1 DAY)),
  INTERVAL 3 HOUR);

WITH generated AS (
  SELECT
    name AS start_station_name
    , GENERATE_TIMESTAMP_ARRAY(
        tomorrow_3am,
        TIMESTAMP_ADD(tomorrow_3am, INTERVAL 24 HOUR),
        INTERVAL 1 HOUR) AS dates
  FROM
    `bigquery-public-data`.london_bicycles.cycle_stations
),

features AS (
  SELECT
    start_station_name
    , start_date
  FROM
    generated
    , UNNEST(dates) AS start_date
)

SELECT * FROM ML.PREDICT(MODEL ch09eu.bicycle_model_bucketized,
  (SELECT * FROM features)
)
```

This returns nearly 20,000 predictions, some of which include the following:

6	2707.621807505363	Palace Gate, Kensington Gardens	2019-05-19 15:00:00 UTC
7	2707.621807505363	Palace Gate, Kensington Gardens	2019-05-19 16:00:00 UTC
8	2571.887817969073	Palace Gate, Kensington Gardens	2019-05-19 17:00:00 UTC
9	2571.887817969073	Palace Gate, Kensington Gardens	2019-05-19 18:00:00 UTC

The entire process of machine learning, from creating the training dataset to training and prediction, has thus been carried out without the need to move the data out of BigQuery.

Examining Model Weights

A linear regression model predicts the output as a weighted sum of its inputs. You can examine (or export) these weights by using this command:

```
SELECT * FROM ML.WEIGHTS(MODEL ch09eu.bicycle_model_bucketized)
```

Numeric features receive a single weight, whereas categorical features receive a weight for each possible value. For example, the dayofweek feature has the following weights:

Row	processed_input	weight	category_weights.category	category_weights.weight
2	dayofweek	*null*	weekday	1709.4363890323655
			weekend	2084.400311228229

This means that if the day is a weekday, the contribution of this feature to the overall predicted duration is 1,709 seconds (the weights that provide the optimal performance are not unique, so you might get a different value). The weights of different input features are not very meaningful—pretty much the only reason you might need to examine the weights in this manner is if you want to carry out predictions outside of BigQuery.

 Do not use the magnitude or sign of the weights as a handy way to explain what the model is doing. Unless the input features are linearly independent (in real-world datasets, this is not very likely), the magnitudes and signs of the weights are not meaningful. For model explainability, consider using the What-If Tool (*https://ai.google blog.com/2018/09/the-what-if-tool-code-free-probing-of.html*) or a model explainability package like LIME (*https://www.oreilly.com/ learning/introduction-to-local-interpretable-model-agnostic-explanations-lime*).

Because a linear model is so simple (it's a weighted average of the inputs), it is possible to extract the model weights and write out the math to compute the prediction in, for example, a Python application (*https://towardsdatascience.com/how-to-do-online-prediction-with-bigquery-ml-db2248c0ae5*):

```
def compute_regression(rowdict,
        numeric_weights, scaling_df, categorical_weights):
  input_values = rowdict
  # numeric inputs
  pred = 0
  for column_name in numeric_weights['input'].unique():
    wt = numeric_weights[ numeric_weights['input'] == column_name
][ 'input_weight'].values[0]
    if column_name != '__INTERCEPT__':
      meanv = (scaling_df[ scaling_df['input'] ==
        column_name ]['mean'].values[0])
      stddev = (scaling_df[ scaling_df['input'] ==
        column_name ]['stddev'].values[0])
      scaled_value = (input_values[column_name] - meanv)/stddev
    else:
      scaled_value = 1.0
```

```
        contrib = wt * scaled_value
        pred = pred + contrib
    # categorical inputs
    for column_name in categorical_weights['input'].unique():
        category_weights = categorical_weights[ categorical_weights['input'] ==
column_name ]
        wt = category_weights[ category_weights['category_name'] ==
input_values[column_name] ]['category_weight'].values[0]
        pred = pred + wt
    return pred
```

In this code, the `numeric_weights` are obtained from the query:

```
SELECT
  processed_input AS input,
  model.weight AS input_weight
FROM
  ml.WEIGHTS(MODEL dataset.model) AS model
```

The scaling DataFrame, `scaling_df`, is obtained from the query:

```
SELECT
  input, min, max, mean, stddev
FROM
  ml.FEATURE_INFO(MODEL dataset.model) AS model
```

The `categorical_weights` are obtained from the query:

```
SELECT
  processed_input AS input,
  model.weight AS input_weight,
  category.category AS category_name,
  category.weight AS category_weight
FROM
  ml.WEIGHTS(MODEL dataset.model) AS model,
  UNNEST(category_weights) AS category
```

If you are doing `logistic_reg`, the output prediction is the result of a sigmoid function applied to the weighted average. Therefore, the output prediction can be obtained as follows:

```
def compute_classifier(rowdict,
    numeric_weights, scaling_df, categorical_weights):
        pred=compute_regression(rowdict, numeric_weights, scaling_df,
categorical_weights)
        return (1.0/(1 + np.exp(-pred)) if (-500 < pred) else 0)
```

More-Complex Regression Models

A linear regression model is the simplest form of regression model—each input feature is assigned a weight, and the output is the sum of the weighted inputs plus a constant called the intercept. BigQuery supports `dnn_regressor` and `xgboost` models as well.

Deep Neural Networks

A *Deep Neural Network* (DNN) can be thought of as an extension of linear models in which each node in the first layer consists of a weighted sum of the input features transformed through a (typically nonlinear) function. The second layer consists of nodes, each of which is a weighted sum of the outputs of the first layer transformed through a nonlinear function, and so on, as demonstrated in Figure 9-5.

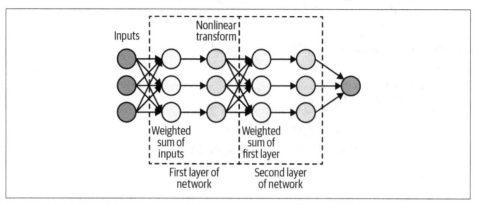

Figure 9-5. A Deep Neural Network consists of layers of "nodes." This example shows two layers between the inputs and outputs and each layer with three nodes, but we can have an arbitrary number of layers and an arbitrary number of nodes in each layer.

To train a DNN model with 64 nodes in the first layer and 32 nodes in the second layer, you would do the following:

```
CREATE OR REPLACE MODEL ch09eu.bicycle_model_dnn
TRANSFORM(* EXCEPT(start_date)
         , IF(EXTRACT(dayofweek FROM start_date) BETWEEN 2 and 6, 'weekday',
'weekend') as dayofweek
         , ML.BUCKETIZE(EXTRACT(HOUR FROM start_date), [5, 10, 17]) AS hourofday
)
OPTIONS(input_label_cols=['duration'],
        model_type='dnn_regressor',
        hidden_units=[64, 32])
AS

SELECT
  duration
  , start_station_name
  , start_date
FROM `bigquery-public-data`.london_bicycles.cycle_hire
```

This model took about 20 minutes to train. It ended with a mean absolute error of 1,016 seconds. This is, of course, worse than the 901 seconds that we achieved with the linear model. Sadly, this is par for the course—DNNs are notoriously finicky to train.

We strongly recommend that you begin with linear models, and only after you have finalized the set of features and transformations should you move on to experiment with more complex models. This is because with the dnn_regressor you will probably need to experiment with different numbers of layers and nodes (i.e., with hidden_units) and regularization settings (i.e., with l2_reg) to obtain good performance. Considering how finicky deep learning networks can be to train, varying feature representations at the same time is a surefire recipe for confusion.

One way to handle this finickiness is to perform hyperparameter tuning to search for optimal network parameters—this is supported by a full-fledged machine learning framework like Cloud AI Platform (CAIP).[10] You might be better off doing this training there, or using AutoML (we explore both of these options later in this chapter), but for now let's try using a smaller network:

```
CREATE OR REPLACE MODEL ch09eu.bicycle_model_dnn
 TRANSFORM(* EXCEPT(start_date)
          , IF(EXTRACT(dayofweek FROM start_date) BETWEEN 2 and 6, 'weekday',
'weekend') as dayofweek
          , ML.BUCKETIZE(EXTRACT(HOUR FROM start_date), [5, 10, 17]) AS hourofday
)
OPTIONS(input_label_cols=['duration'],
        model_type='dnn_regressor',
        hidden_units=[10, 5])
AS

SELECT
  duration
  , start_station_name
  , start_date
FROM `bigquery-public-data`.london_bicycles.cycle_hire
```

This yields better performance (981 seconds) but is still not as good as the linear model. More hyperparameter tuning is needed to get a DNN model that does better than the linear model we started out with. Also, in general a DNN provides superior performance only if there are many continuous features.

Gradient-boosted trees

Decision trees are a popular technique in machine learning because of their ready interpretability (they are essentially just combinations of if-then rules). However, decision trees tend to have poor accuracy because the range of functions they can

---

10 See *https://cloud.google.com/ml-engine/docs/tensorflow/hyperparameter-tuning-overview*. Cloud AI Platform Predictions allows you to submit a machine learning training job where you specify a range of values to search within.

approximate is limited and can be prone to overfitting. One way of improving the performance of decision trees (at the expense of explainability[11]) is to train an ensemble of decision trees, each of which is a poor predictor but when averaged together yield good performance. Boosting is a technique that is used to select trees in the ensemble, and XGBoost[12] is a scalable, distributed way to build boosted decision trees on extremely large and sparse datasets. XGBoost used to be considered the state-of-the-art machine learning technique until the advent of deep learning networks circa 2015. It continues to be popular on structured data problems.

You can train an XGBoost machine learning model in BigQuery by selecting the `boosted_tree_regressor` model type:

```
CREATE OR REPLACE MODEL ch09eu.bicycle_model_xgboost
TRANSFORM(* EXCEPT(start_date)
        , IF(EXTRACT(dayofweek FROM start_date) BETWEEN 2 and 6,
    'weekday', 'weekend') as dayofweek
        , ML.BUCKETIZE(EXTRACT(HOUR FROM start_date), [5, 10, 17]) AS hourofday
)
OPTIONS(input_label_cols=['duration'],
        model_type='boosted_tree_regressor',
        max_tree_depth=4)
AS

SELECT
  duration
  , start_station_name
  , start_date
FROM `bigquery-public-data`.london_bicycles.cycle_hire
```

The resulting model on this problem has poorer performance (1,363 seconds) than the linear model. The importance of the input features can be obtained by using this command:

```
SELECT * FROM ML.FEATURE_INFO(MODEL ch09eu.bicycle_model_xgboost)
```

Human insights and auxiliary data

Besides trying different model architectures and tuning the parameters of these models, we might consider adding new input features that incorporate human insights or provide auxiliary data to the machine learning model.

---

11 Many decision-tree packages provide a measure of "feature importance," which loosely means how often a feature is used in the ensemble of trees. However, if you have two features that are correlated, the importance will be split between them, and so explainability suffers in real-world datasets.

12 XGBoost stands for eXtreme Gradient Boost, where gradient boosting is the technique proposed in the paper "Greedy Function Approximation: A Gradient Boosting Machine" (*https://www.kdd.org/kdd2016/papers/files/rfp0697-chenAemb.pdf*), by Jerome H. Friedman.

For example, in the previous model, we used `ML.BUCKETIZE` to split a continuous variable (the hour extracted from the timestamp) into four bins. Another extremely useful function is `ML.FEATURE_CROSS`, which can combine separate categorical features into an `AND` condition (this sort of relationship between features can be difficult for a machine learning model to learn). In our problem, intuition dictates that the combination of weekday and morning is a good predictor of bicycle rental duration, much more so than either weekday by itself or morning by itself. If so, it might be worthwhile to create a feature cross of the two features instead of treating the day and time separately:

```
ML.FEATURE_CROSS(STRUCT(
    IF(EXTRACT(dayofweek FROM start_date) BETWEEN 2 and 6,
        'weekday', 'weekend') as dayofweek,
    ML.BUCKETIZE(EXTRACT(HOUR FROM start_date),
        [5, 10, 17]) AS hr
)) AS dayhr
```

In our models so far, we used `start_station_name` as an input to the model. This treats the stations as independent. In Chapter 8, we discussed the benefits of `ST_Geo Hash` as a way to capture spatial proximity. Let's, therefore, bring in the auxiliary information about the stations' locations and use that as an additional input to the model.

Combining these two ideas, we now have the model training query:

```
CREATE OR REPLACE MODEL ch09eu.bicycle_model_fc_geo
 TRANSFORM(duration
        , ML.FEATURE_CROSS(STRUCT(
            IF(EXTRACT(dayofweek FROM start_date) BETWEEN 2 and 6,
                'weekday', 'weekend') as dayofweek,
            ML.BUCKETIZE(EXTRACT(HOUR FROM start_date),
                [5, 10, 17]) AS hr
            )) AS dayhr
        , ST_GeoHash(ST_GeogPoint(latitude, longitude), 4) AS start_station_loc4
        , ST_GeoHash(ST_GeogPoint(latitude, longitude), 6) AS start_station_loc6
        , ST_GeoHash(ST_GeogPoint(latitude, longitude), 8) AS start_station_loc8
)
OPTIONS(input_label_cols=['duration'], model_type='linear_reg')
AS

SELECT
  duration
  , latitude
  , longitude
  , start_date
FROM `bigquery-public-data`.london_bicycles.cycle_hire
JOIN `bigquery-public-data`.london_bicycles.cycle_stations
ON cycle_hire.start_station_id = cycle_stations.id
```

This model results in a mean absolute error of 898 seconds, an improvement over the 901 seconds we saw earlier. However, the improvement is relatively minor. Because of these diminishing returns, it might be time to move on.

Time series prediction with ARIMA

Let's consider the problem of carrying out 2-week forecasts of the number of bicycle rentals that will commence at one of the bicycle stations in Hyde Park based on the past six weeks. This is a demand forecasting problem and we might want to make the prediction based purely on how the demand for bicycles varies over time.

The first step, as with any machine learning problem is to gather the training data and explore it. Assume that we have the data on rentals until mid-June of 2015 and we'd like to predict for the rest of the month. We can gather the past 6 weeks of data using:

```
SELECT
  CAST(EXTRACT(date from start_date) AS TIMESTAMP) AS date
  , COUNT(*) AS numrentals
FROM
  `bigquery-public-data`.london_bicycles.cycle_hire
WHERE start_station_name LIKE '%Hyde%'  -- all stations in Hyde Park
GROUP BY date
HAVING date BETWEEN '2015-05-01' AND '2015-06-15'
ORDER BY date
```

Plotting this, we see in Figure 9-6 a sort of weekly trend with higher rentals on weekends.

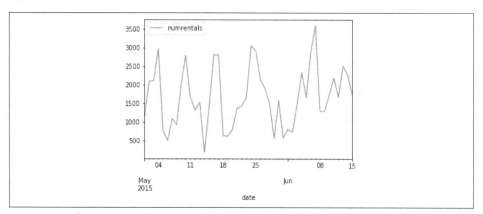

Figure 9-6. There is a weekly trend in the historical data

We can use this data to train an ARIMA (*https://en.wikipedia.org/wiki/Autoregressive_integrated_moving_average*) model *(as of May 2020, this is in alpha, so contact your GCP sales rep to get whitelisted)*, telling BigQuery which column is the data column and which one the timestamp column:

```
CREATE OR REPLACE MODEL ch09eu.numrentals_forecast
OPTIONS(model_type='ARIMA',
        time_series_data_col='numrentals',
        time_series_timestamp_col='date') AS
SELECT
   CAST(EXTRACT(date from start_date) AS TIMESTAMP) AS date
   , COUNT(*) AS numrentals
FROM
   `bigquery-public-data`.london_bicycles.cycle_hire
WHERE start_station_name LIKE '%Hyde%'  -- all stations in Hyde Park
GROUP BY date
HAVING date BETWEEN '2015-05-01' AND '2015-06-15'
```

Once the model is trained, we can evaluate it using `ML.EVALUATE()` and view the ARIMA coefficients using `ML.ARIMA_COEFFICIENTS()`. We can also forecast the number of rentals for each of the next 14 days and obtain 90th percentile confidence bounds using:

```
SELECT * FROM ML.FORECAST(MODEL ch09eu.numrentals_forecast,
               STRUCT(14 AS horizon, 0.9 AS confidence_level))
```

The history, forecast, and confidence bounds can be plotted using:

```
import matplotlib.pyplot as plt
import pandas as pd
def plot_historical_and_forecast(
         input_timeseries, forecast_output,
         timestamp_col_name, data_col_name):
  plt.figure(figsize=(20,6))
  plt.plot(input_timeseries[timestamp_col_name],
         input_timeseries[data_col_name], label = 'Historical')
  plt.xlabel(timestamp_col_name)
  plt.ylabel(data_col_name)
  forecast_output['forecast_timestamp'] = pd.to_datetime(
         forecast_output['forecast_timestamp'])
  x_data = forecast_output['forecast_timestamp']
  y_data = forecast_output['forecast_value']
  confidence_level = (forecast_output['confidence_level'].iloc[0]
         * 100)
  low_CI = forecast_output['confidence_interval_lower_bound']
  upper_CI = forecast_output['confidence_interval_upper_bound']
  # Plot the data, set the linewidth, color
  # and transparency of the
  # line, provide a label for the legend
  plt.plot(x_data, y_data, alpha = 1,
         label = 'Forecast', linestyle='--')
  # Shade the confidence interval
  plt.fill_between(x_data, low_CI, upper_CI,
         color = '#539caf', alpha = 0.4,
         label = str(confidence_level) + '% confidence interval')
  # Display legend
  plt.legend(loc = 'upper center', prop={'size': 16})
  plot_historical_and_forecast(df, fcst, 'date', 'numrentals')
```

The result is shown in Figure 9-7.

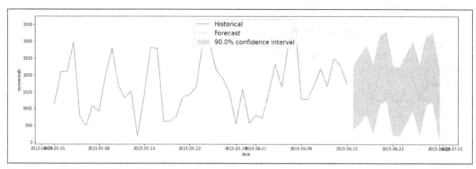

Figure 9-7. Historical and forecast data

But how well does this compare with actually happened in the latter part of June? We can pull out the data for those days and compare with the forecast time series, as shown in Figure 9-8.

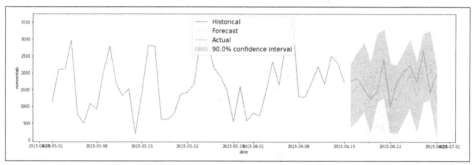

Figure 9-8. Historical and forecast data along with actual outcome

So far, we have been forecasting the overall rental volume for all the bicycle stations in Hyde Park. How do we predict the rental volume for each individual station? Use the time_series_id_col:

```
CREATE OR REPLACE MODEL ch09eu.numrentals_forecast
OPTIONS(model_type='ARIMA',
        time_series_data_col='numrentals',
        time_series_timestamp_col='date',
        time_series_id_col='start_station_name') AS
SELECT
    start_station_name
    , CAST(EXTRACT(date from start_date) AS TIMESTAMP) AS date
    , COUNT(*) AS numrentals
FROM
    `bigquery-public-data`.london_bicycles.cycle_hire
WHERE start_station_name LIKE '%Hyde%'  -- all stations in Hyde Park
GROUP BY start_station_name, date
HAVING date BETWEEN '2015-01-01' AND '2015-06-15'
```

Note that instead of training the series on 45 days (May 1 to June 15), we are now training on a longer time period. That's because aggregate time series will tend to be smoother and much easier to predict than the time series for individual stations. So, we have to show the model a longer trend-line.

Now, the model is not one ARIMA model, but a separate ARIMA model for each station name. Indeed, doing:

```
SELECT *
FROM ML.ARIMA_COEFFICIENTS(MODEL ch09eu.numrentals_forecast)
ORDER BY time_series_id
```

would give us a separate set of coefficients for each time_series_id (which is a station name). Each of the stations will have ARIMA models of different complexity because, under the hood, BigQuery ML does automatic hyper-parameter tuning. Although the model is called "ARIMA", the underlying algorithm actually includes quite a few bells-and-whistles including anomaly detection, holiday effect modeling (user needs to specify the holiday region), seasonality detection/modeling, and trend modeling. Plus, the different time series are trained in parallel.

When we do a prediction, we will get a prediction for each station and timestamp:

```
SELECT
  time_series_id AS start_station_name,
  forecast_timestamp, forecast_value
FROM ML.FORECAST(MODEL ch09eu.numrentals_forecast,
                 STRUCT(3 AS horizon, 0.9 AS confidence_level))
ORDER By time_series_id, forecast_timestamp
```

yields one time-series forecast per station. The full notebook on GitHub (*https://github.com/GoogleCloudPlatform/bigquery-oreilly-book/blob/master/blogs/bqml_arima/bqml_arima.ipynb*) has these results and plots of the forecasts by station. Some of these plots are shown in Figure 9-9.

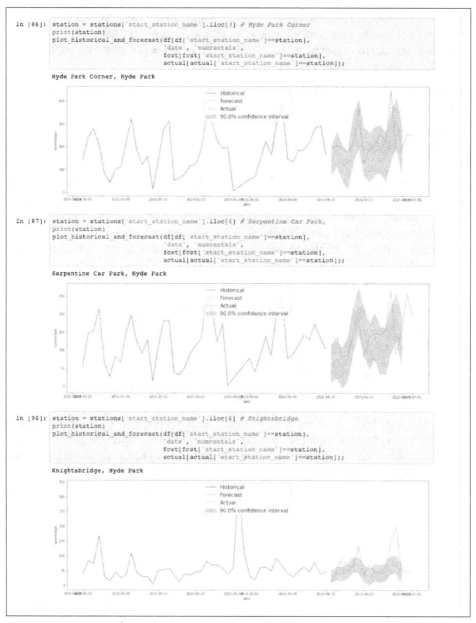

Figure 9-9. Forecasts for multiple stations

Building a Classification Model

In the previous section, we built machine learning models to predict the duration of a bicycle rental. However, over the span of one hour, many bicycles will be rented, and they will be rented for different durations. For example, take the distribution of bicycles that were rented at Royal Avenue 1, Chelsea, on weekdays in the hour starting at 14:00 (2:00 p.m.):

```
SELECT
  APPROX_QUANTILES(duration, 10) AS q
FROM `bigquery-public-data`.london_bicycles.cycle_hire
WHERE
  EXTRACT(dayofweek FROM start_date) BETWEEN 2 and 6
  AND EXTRACT(hour FROM start_date) = 14
  AND start_station_name = 'Royal Avenue 1, Chelsea'
```

Here's the result:

Row	q
1	0
	240
	420
	540
	660
	840
	1020
	1260
	1500
	2040
	386460

80% of weekday rentals at this station lasted less than 1,500 seconds. Had this been the only prediction for you to go by, you would have stocked only commuter bikes at this station on those days. However, had you known that somewhere between 10% and 20% of bicycle rentals last longer than 1,800 seconds, you might have decided to stock this station so that 15% of the bicycles are road bikes. A classification model will allow us to predict the probability that a rental will last longer than 1,800 seconds.

Training

For simplicity, let's take the set of features we used in the regression model and train a model to predict the probability that the rental will be for longer than 30 minutes:

```
CREATE OR REPLACE MODEL ch09eu.bicycle_model_longrental
TRANSFORM(* EXCEPT(start_date)
        , IF(EXTRACT(dayofweek FROM start_date) BETWEEN 2 and 6,
```

```
            'weekday', 'weekend') as dayofweek
            , ML.BUCKETIZE(EXTRACT(HOUR FROM start_date), [5, 10, 17]) AS hourofday
   )
   OPTIONS(input_label_cols=['biketype'], model_type='logistic_reg')
   AS

   SELECT
     IF(duration > 1800, 'roadbike', 'commuter') AS biketype
     , start_station_name
     , start_date
   FROM `bigquery-public-data`.london_bicycles.cycle_hire
```

Note that the model_type now is logistic regression (logistic_reg)—this is the simplest model type for classification problems. For classification with DNNs or boosted-regression trees, use dnn_classifier or boosted_tree_classifier, respectively.

We created the label by thresholding rentals at 1,800 seconds and gave the two categories the names roadbike and commuter (this is similar to how we created a categorical variable weekend/weekday from the numeric variable dayofweek). We could also have used a Boolean value (True/False), but using the actual category name is clearer.

At the end of training, you can see that the error has decreased over seven iterations through the dataset and has now converged, as depicted in Figure 9-10 (because of random seeds, your results might be somewhat different).

There are actually two loss curves in Figure 9-10: one on the training data and the other on the evaluation data (BigQuery automatically split the data for us). Here, the curves are quite similar. If the evaluation curve were much higher than the loss curve, you'd have been worried about overfitting. Switching to the table view, you can verify that the two losses were, indeed, quite similar throughout the training:

Iteration	Training Data Loss	Evaluation Data Loss	Learn Rate	Duration (seconds)
6	0.3072	0.3024	3.2000	41.59
5	0.3078	0.3029	6.4000	39.66
4	0.3119	0.3069	3.2000	40.54
3	0.3240	0.3195	1.6000	42.15
2	0.3576	0.3543	0.8000	37.96
1	0.4502	0.4483	0.4000	38.01
0	0.5812	0.5805	0.2000	22.10

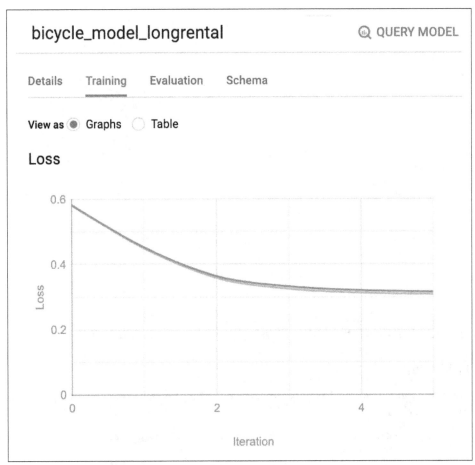

Figure 9-10. The loss curve during model training has converged

Evaluation

The loss measure used in classification is cross-entropy, so that's what the training curves depicted. You can look at more familiar evaluation metrics such as accuracy in the evaluation tab of the BigQuery web user interface (UI), as shown in Figure 9-11.

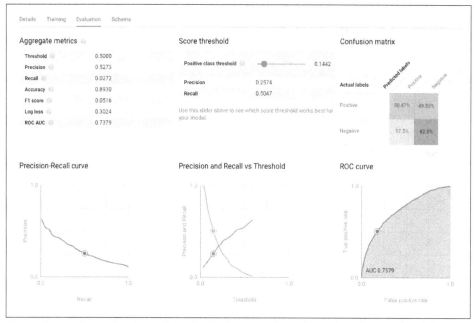

Figure 9-11. The evaluation tab in the BigQuery web UI for a classification model

Prediction

The prediction is similar to the regression case, except that you now get the probability of each class:

```
SELECT * FROM ML.PREDICT(MODEL ch09eu.bicycle_model_longrental,
    (SELECT 'Park Lane , Hyde Park' AS start_station_name
        , TIMESTAMP('2019-05-09 16:16:00 UTC') AS start_date)
)
```

This yields the following:

Row	predicted_biketype	predicted_biketype_probs.label	predicted_biketype_probs.prob	start_station_name	start_date
1	commuter	roadbike	0.4419...	Park Lane, Hyde Park	2019-05-10 16:16:00 UTC
		commuter	0.5580...		

Thus, the probability that a rental at 4 p.m. on a weekday from Hyde Park will require a road bike is 0.44, or 44%. Ideally, then, you should have 44% of your bicycles at that station at that time be road bikes.

Choosing the Threshold

In our use case, the actual probability is what is of interest. Often, though, in classification problems, the desired output is the predicted class, not just the probability. Thus, the predicted output (see previous section) includes not only the probability but also the class with the highest probability. In a binary classification problem, this is the same as thresholding the probability at 0.5 and choosing the "positive" class if the probability is more than 0.5.

Recall is the percentage of actual true values (true positives / total positives) at a particular threshold point. If the recall is high, you'll get almost all of the things you're looking for. However, setting a threshold point with a high recall can be dangerous, because you might get a lot of false positives as well. If the threshold is 0, everything is chosen, so you get a perfect recall.

The other important metric is *precision*, which is the percentage of true positives over the whole dataset. In other words, it is a way of saying, "Given I've predicted this to be true, what is the probability that I'm right?" If you set the threshold to 0, you get the proportion of true data in the dataset. (In other words, you predict everything to be true, so if 10% of the values are true, your precision will be 10%. This isn't a very good classifier.)

The aggregate metrics in the evaluation tab (e.g., `accuracy=0.89`) are calculated based on the 0.5 threshold.

If you wanted to ensure that you have a road bike in stock 50% of the times that one is required, you would want to have a recall of 0.5 because you'd need to capture half of the long rides. You can use the slider in the evaluation tab to change the threshold to 0.144, as shown in Figure 9-12, so that you obtain the desired recall metric. Note that this comes at the expense of precision; at this threshold, the model will give you a precision of 0.26—only 26% of the trips that we predict will require road bikes will actually be longer than 30 minutes.[13]

---

13 The precision (or true positive rate) is the fraction of times that the model is correct when it predicted the positive class. In other words, if the model predicted `roadbike` 100 times, it will be correct 25.7 times. The recall is the fraction of positive instances that the model predicts correctly—that is, the fraction of times a road bike is required that the model predicts `roadbike`. For multiclass problems, the reported precision (or recall) corresponds to the mean precision when treating each category as a binary classification problem.

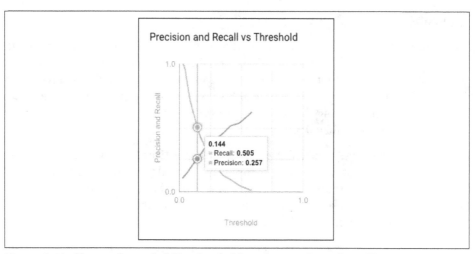

Figure 9-12. Change the probability threshold to obtain a desired recall or precision

For binary classification models, the desired threshold can be passed to ML.PREDICT:

```
SELECT * FROM ML.PREDICT(MODEL ch09eu.bicycle_model_longrental,
  (SELECT 'Park Lane , Hyde Park' AS start_station_name
         , TIMESTAMP('2019-05-09 16:16:00 UTC') AS start_date),
  STRUCT(0.144 AS threshold)
)
```

Here is the result:

Row	predicted_biketype	predicted_biketype_ probs.label	predicted_biketype_ probs.prob	start_station_name	start_date
1	roadbike	roadbike	0.4419...	Park Lane, Hyde Park	2019-05-09 16:16:00 UTC

Note that the predicted_biketype now is roadbike, even though the probability corresponding to roadbike is less than the default threshold of 0.5.

Customizing BigQuery ML

By default, BigQuery ML makes reasonable choices for learning rate,[14] scaling input features,[15] splitting the data,[16] and so on. The OPTIONS setting when creating a model provides a number of fine-grained ways to control the model creation (*https:// cloud.google.com/bigquery-ml/docs/reference/standard-sql/bigqueryml-syntax-create#model_option_list*). In this section, we discuss a few of them.

Controlling Data Split

By default on moderately sized datasets, BigQuery randomly selects 20% of the data and keeps it aside for evaluation. The training is carried out on only 80% of the data we provide. For tiny datasets (those under 500 rows), all of the data is used for training, and for large datasets (those over 50,000 rows), only 10,000 rows are used for evaluation. We can control what data is used for evaluation by means of three parameters: data_split_method, data_split_eval_fraction, and data_split_col, as listed in Table 9-2.

Table 9-2. Controlling how data is split between training and evaluation

Scenario	data_split_method	data_split_eval_fraction	data_split_col
Default	auto_split	0.2	n/a
Train on all the data	no_split	n/a	n/a
Keep aside a randomly selected 10% of data for evaluation	random	0.1	n/a
Specifically identify which rows are for evaluation	custom	n/a	colname Rows with Boolean value of True/NULL for this column are kept aside for evaluation.
Keep last 10% of rows for evaluation	seq	0.1 (default is 0.2)	colname Rows are ordered ASC on this column.

A better measure of how well the model will perform after it's deployed is to train it on the first 80% (ordered by time) of bicycle rentals in the dataset and then test it on

---

14 BigQuery estimates a good value through line search at the start of each iteration through the data.

15 Scale all numeric inputs to have zero mean and unit variance.

16 By default, randomly select 20% of the rows for evaluation.

the remaining 20%.[17] That is, rather than splitting randomly, you'd train on the older trips and test on the newer ones:

```
CREATE OR REPLACE MODEL ch09eu.bicycle_model_bucketized_seq
TRANSFORM(* EXCEPT(start_date)
          , IF(EXTRACT(dayofweek FROM start_date) BETWEEN 2 and 6, 'weekday',
'weekend') as dayofweek
          , ML.BUCKETIZE(EXTRACT(HOUR FROM start_date), [5, 10, 17]) AS hourofday
          , start_date—used to split the data
)
OPTIONS(input_label_cols=['duration'], model_type='linear_reg',
        data_split_method='seq',
        data_split_eval_fraction=0.2,
        data_split_col='start_date')
AS

SELECT
  duration
  , start_station_name
  , start_date
FROM `bigquery-public-data`.london_bicycles.cycle_hire
```

Note that the SELECT and TRANSFORM clauses both emit the column used to split the data, and that OPTIONS includes the three parameters that control how the data is split.

The mean absolute error now is 860 seconds, but we cannot compare this number with the results obtained with the random split—evaluation metrics depend quite heavily on what data is used for evaluation, and because we are using a different evaluation dataset now, we cannot compare these results to the ones obtained earlier. Also, our earlier results were contaminated by leakage—for example, of Christmas days.

Balancing Classes

In our classification problem, less than 12% of rentals last longer than 1,800 seconds. This is an example of an unbalanced dataset. It can be helpful to weight the rarer class higher, and we can do that either by passing in an explicit array of class weights or by asking BigQuery to set the weights of classes based on inverse frequency.

Here's an example of using this autobalancing method:

---

17 This is better because it is possible that days on which station A is busy are the days on which station B is also busy. A random split might end up causing leakage of this information if Christmas 2009 at station A is in training and Christmas 2009 at station B is in evaluation. By controlling the split to happen so that the last few days of the dataset are not seen in training, we are able to more closely model how we plan to train our model on historical data and then deploy it.

```
CREATE OR REPLACE MODEL ch09eu.bicycle_model_longrental_balanced
TRANSFORM(* EXCEPT(start_date)
          , IF(EXTRACT(dayofweek FROM start_date) BETWEEN 2 and 6, 'weekday',
'weekend') as dayofweek
          , ML.BUCKETIZE(EXTRACT(HOUR FROM start_date), [5, 10, 17]) AS hourofday
          , start_date
)
OPTIONS(input_label_cols=['biketype'], model_type='logistic_reg',
        data_split_method='seq',
        data_split_eval_fraction=0.2,
        data_split_col='start_date',
        auto_class_weights=True)

AS

SELECT
  IF(duration > 1800, 'roadbike', 'commuter') AS biketype
  , start_station_name
  , start_date
FROM `bigquery-public-data`.london_bicycles.cycle_hire
```

Note that after you balance the weights, the probability that comes from the model is no longer an estimate of the actual predicted occurrence frequency. This is because the probability estimate that comes out of logistic regression is based on the frequency of occurrence in the data seen by the model, and we have artificially boosted the occurrence of rare events.

Regularization

Recall that in our data exploration, we discovered that except for a handful of stations which had unusually long durations, most of the stations had nearly identical durations, and many of these stations had very few rentals. Categorical features with such long-tailed distributions can cause *overfitting*. Overfitting is when the model learns noise (arbitrary variation) in the data, not the signal. In other words, the model can become so elaborate that it represents the dataset itself, not the underlying qualities of the dataset.

Regularization avoids overfitting because it penalizes complexity, in part by assigning penalties to large weight values. Large weight values are often a sign of overfitting because they can turn on suddenly when exactly one datapoint is encountered.

BigQuery ML supports two types of regularization: L1 and L2. L1 regularization tries to push individual weights to zero and is better for interpretability, whereas L2 tries to keep all the weights relatively similar and does better at controlling overfitting.[18] You can control the amount of L1 or L2 regularization when creating the model:

---

18 For more information about L1 and L2, see www.robotics.stanford.edu/~ang/papers/icml04-l1l2.ps.

```
CREATE OR REPLACE MODEL ch09eu.bicycle_model_bucketized_seq_l2
TRANSFORM(* EXCEPT(start_date)
          , IF(EXTRACT(dayofweek FROM start_date) BETWEEN 2 and 6,
               'weekday', 'weekend') as dayofweek
          , ML.BUCKETIZE(EXTRACT(HOUR FROM start_date), [5, 10, 17]) AS hourofday
          , start_date—used to split the data
)
OPTIONS(input_label_cols=['duration'], model_type='linear_reg',
         data_split_method='seq',
         data_split_eval_fraction=0.2,
         data_split_col='start_date',
         l2_reg=0.1)
AS

SELECT
  duration
  , start_station_name
  , start_date
FROM `bigquery-public-data`.london_bicycles.cycle_hire
```

In this case, though, the resulting mean absolute error is 857 seconds, nearly identical to what was obtained without L2 regularization; this is most likely because we have a large-enough dataset and a model with few enough parameters to tune that overfitting was not happening. L2 regularization is generally considered a best practice, particularly if you don't have a large amount of data or if you are using a more sophisticated model (such as a DNN) with many more parameters.

k-Means Clustering

The machine learning algorithms that we have considered so far have been supervised learning methods—we needed to provide BigQuery a label column. BigQuery also supports unsupervised learning in that you can apply the k (*https://en.wikipedia.org/wiki/K-means_clustering*)-means algorithm (*https://en.wikipedia.org/wiki/K-means_clustering*) to group your data into clusters based on similarity. The algorithm is called k-means because it identifies k clusters, each of which is described in terms of the mean of the members of the cluster. Unlike supervised machine learning, which helps you predict the value of the label column when given values for the futures, unsupervised learning is descriptive. Use model_type=kmeans in BigQuery to understand your data in terms of centroids of the k clusters that have been determined from the data, and to make decisions about the members of each cluster based on the attributes of its centroid.

What's Being Clustered?

The first step in using k-means clustering is to determine what is being clustered and why you are doing it. Because tables in BigQuery tend to be flattened and describe multiple aspects, it helps to be clear about what each member of the cluster represents.

Suppose that you have data in which each row represents a retail customer transaction. There are several ways in which you could do the clustering on this table, and which one you choose depends on what you want to do with the clusters:

- You could find natural groups among your customers. This is called *customer segmentation*. Data we use to perform the customer segmentation would be attributes that describe the customer making the transaction—these might include things like which store they visited, what items they bought, how much they paid, and so on. The reason to cluster these customers is that you want to understand what these groups of customers are like (these are called *personas*) so that you can design items that appeal to members of one of those groups by understanding the "centroid customer" of each cluster.

- You could find natural groups among the items purchased. These are called *product groups*. Data we use to perform the product groups would be attributes that describe the item(s) being purchased in the transaction—these might include things like who purchased them, when they were purchased, which store they were purchased at, and so forth. The reason to cluster these items is that you want to understand the characteristics of a product group so that you can learn how to reduce *cannibalization* or improve *cross-selling*.

In both of these cases, we are using clustering as a heuristic to help make decisions—it's too difficult to design individualized products or understand product interactions, so you design for groups of customers or groups of items.

Note that for the specific use case of product recommendations (recommending products to customers or targeting customers for a product), it is better to train a `matrix_factorization` model as described later in this chapter. But for other decisions for which there is no readily available predictive analytics approach, *k*-means clustering might give you a way to make a data-driven decision.

Clustering Bicycle Stations

Suppose that you often make decisions about bicycle stations—which stations to stock with new types of bicycles, which ones to repair, which ones to expand, and so on, and you want to make these decisions in a data-driven manner. This means that you are going to cluster bicycle stations, and you could group stations that are similar based on attributes such as the duration of rentals from the station, the number of trips per day from the station, the number of bike racks at the station, and the distance of the station from the city center. Because the first two attributes vary based on whether the day in question is a weekday or a weekend, let's compute two values for those.

Because the query is quite long and cumbersome, let's also save it into a table:

```
CREATE OR REPLACE TABLE ch09eu.stationstats AS

WITH hires AS (
  SELECT
    h.start_station_name as station_name,
    IF(EXTRACT(DAYOFWEEK FROM h.start_date) BETWEEN 2 and 6,
             "weekday", "weekend") as isweekday,
    h.duration,
    s.bikes_count,
    ST_DISTANCE(ST_GEOGPOINT(s.longitude, s.latitude),
             ST_GEOGPOINT(-0.1, 51.5))/1000 as distance_from_city_center
  FROM `bigquery-public-data.london_bicycles.cycle_hire` as h
  JOIN `bigquery-public-data.london_bicycles.cycle_stations` as s
  ON h.start_station_id = s.id
  WHERE EXTRACT(YEAR from start_date) = 2015
),

stationstats AS (
  SELECT
    station_name,
    AVG(IF(isweekday = 'weekday', duration, NULL)) AS duration_weekdays,
    AVG(IF(isweekday = 'weekend', duration, NULL)) AS duration_weekends,
    COUNT(IF(isweekday = 'weekday', duration, NULL)) AS numtrips_weekdays,
    COUNT(IF(isweekday = 'weekend', duration, NULL)) AS numtrips_weekends,
    MAX(bikes_count) as bikes_count,
    MAX(distance_from_city_center) as distance_from_city_center
  FROM hires
  GROUP BY station_name
)

SELECT *
from stationstats
```

The resulting table has 802 rows, one for each station operating in 2015, and looks something like this:

Row	station_name	duration_weekdays	duration_weekends	numtrips_weekdays	numtrips_weekends	bikes_count	distance_from_city_center
1	Borough Road, Elephant & Castle	1109.932...	2125.095...	5749	1774	29	0.126...
2	Webber Street, Southwark	795.439...	938.357...	6517	1619	34	0.164...
3	Great Suffolk Street, The Borough	802.530...	1018.310...	8418	2024	18	0.193...

Carrying Out Clustering

As with supervised learning, carrying out clustering simply involves a CREATE MODEL statement on the table created in the previous section, but taking care to remove the station_name field because it uniquely identifies each station:

```
CREATE OR REPLACE MODEL ch09eu.london_station_clusters
OPTIONS(model_type='kmeans',
        num_clusters=4,
        standardize_features = true) AS

SELECT * EXCEPT(station_name)
from ch09eu.stationstats
```

The model_type is kmeans. If the num_clusters option is omitted, BigQuery will choose a reasonable value based on the number of rows in the table. The other option, standardize_features, is necessary for this dataset because the different columns all have very different ranges. The distance from the city center is on the order of a few kilometers, whereas the number of trips and duration are on the order of thousands. Therefore, it is a good idea to have BigQuery scale these values by making them zero-mean and unit-variance.

Understanding the Clusters

To find which cluster a particular station belongs to, use ML.PREDICT. Here's a query to find the cluster of every station that has "Kennington" in its name:

```
SELECT * except(nearest_centroids_distance)
FROM ML.PREDICT(MODEL ch09eu.london_station_clusters,
(SELECT * FROM ch09eu.stationstats
 WHERE REGEXP_CONTAINS(station_name, 'Kennington')))
```

This yields the following:

Row	CENTROID_ ID	station_ name	duration_ weekdays	duration_ weekends	numtrips_ weekdays	numtrips_ weekends	bikes_ count	distance_ from_city_ center
1	2	Kennington Road, Vauxhall	1209.433...	1720.598...	8135	2975	26	0.891...
2	2	Kennington Lane Rail Bridge, Vauxhall	979.391...	1812.217...	20263	5014	28	2.175...
3	2	Cotton Garden Estate, Kennington	1572.919...	997.949...	5313	1600	14	1.117...

Row	CENTROID_ ID	station_ name	duration_ weekdays	duration_ weekends	numtrips_ weekdays	numtrips_ weekends	bikes_ count	distance_ from_city_ center
4	3	Kennington Station, Kennington	1689.587...	3579.285...	4875	1848	15	1.298...

A few of the Kennington stations are in centroid #2, whereas others are in centroid #3.[19] To understand these groups, you can examine the centroid attributes:

```
SELECT *
FROM ML.CENTROIDS(MODEL ch09eu.london_station_clusters)
ORDER BY centroid_id
```

This returns a table that contains one row for each attribute of the cluster:

Row	centroid_id	feature	numerical_value	categorical_value .category	categorical_value .value
1	1	distance_from_city_center	2.978...		
2	1	bikes_count	10.013...		
3	1	numtrips_weekends	8273.849...		

You can pivot the table as follows:

```
CREATE TEMP FUNCTION cvalue(x ANY TYPE, col STRING) AS (
  (SELECT value from unnest(x) WHERE name = col)
);

WITH T AS (
  SELECT
  centroid_id,
  ARRAY_AGG(STRUCT(feature AS name,
                ROUND(numerical_value,1) AS value)
          ORDER BY centroid_id) AS cluster
  FROM ML.CENTROIDS(MODEL ch09eu.london_station_clusters)
  GROUP BY centroid_id
)
SELECT
  CONCAT('Cluster#', CAST(centroid_id AS STRING)) AS centroid,
  cvalue(cluster, 'duration_weekdays') AS duration_weekdays,
  cvalue(cluster, 'duration_weekends') AS duration_weekends,
  cvalue(cluster, 'numtrips_weekdays') AS numtrips_weekdays,
  cvalue(cluster, 'numtrips_weekends') AS numtrips_weekends,
  cvalue(cluster, 'bikes_count') AS bikes_count,
  cvalue(cluster, 'distance_from_city_center') AS distance_from_city_center
```

---

19 The k-means algorithm is sensitive to the initial starting point, and because starting points are chosen randomly, your results might be different.

```
FROM T
ORDER BY centroid_id ASC
```

The pivot gives you the following result:

Row	centroid	duration_ weekdays	duration_ weekends	numtrips_ weekdays	numtrips_ weekends	bikes_count	distance_from_ city_center
1	Cluster#1	1362.6	1968.4	25427.3	8273.8	10.0	3.0
2	Cluster#2	1193.5	1738.1	8457.4	2584.3	21.0	3.0
3	Cluster#3	1675.0	2460.5	4702.4	2136.8	14.9	6.7
4	Cluster#4	1124.0	1543.1	8519.0	2342.1	5.7	4.1

To visualize this table, in the BigQuery web UI, click "Explore in Data Studio" and then select "Table with bars." Make the centroid column the "dimension" and the remaining columns the metrics. Figure 9-13 shows the result.

Figure 9-13. Cluster attributes

From Figure 9-13, you can see that Cluster #1 consists of extremely busy stations (see the number of trips) that are close to the city center, Cluster #2 consists of less busy stations close to the city center, Cluster #3 consists of stations that are far away from the city center and seem to be used more on weekends on long trips (these are the only stations with more weekend trips than weekday trips), and Cluster #4 consists of tiny stations (see bikes_count) in the outer core of the city, probably in residential areas. Based on these characteristics and some knowledge of London, we can come up with descriptive names for these clusters. Cluster 1 would probably be "Tourist areas," Cluster 2 would be "Business district," Cluster 3 would be "Day trips," and Cluster 4 would be "Commuter stations."

Data-Driven Decisions

You can now use these clusters to make different decisions. For example, suppose that you just received funding and can expand the bike racks. In which stations should you install extra capacity? If you didn't have the clustering data, you might be tempted to go with stations with lots of trips and not enough bikes—stations in Cluster #1. But you have done the clustering and discovered that this group of stations mostly serves tourists. They don't vote, so let's put the extra capacity in Cluster #4 (commuter stations).

To take another example, suppose that you need to experiment with a new type of lock. In which cluster of stations should you conduct this experiment? The business district stations seem logical, and sure enough, those are the stations with lots of bikes and that are busy enough to support an A/B test. If, on the other hand, you want to stock some stations with road (racing) bikes, which ones should you select? Cluster #3, comprising stations that serve people who are going on day trips out of the city, seems like a good choice.

Obviously, you could have made these decisions individually by doing custom data analysis each time. But clustering the stations, coming up with descriptive names, and using the names to make decisions is much simpler and more explainable.

Recommender Systems

Collaborative filtering provides a way to generate product recommendations for users, or user targeting for products. The starting point is a table with three columns: a user ID, an item ID, and the rating that the user gave the product. This table can be sparse—users don't need to rate all products. Based on just the ratings, the technique finds similar users and similar products and determines the rating that a user would give an unseen product. Then we can recommend the products with the highest predicted ratings to users, or target products at users with the highest predicted ratings.

The MovieLens Dataset

To illustrate recommender systems in action, let's use the MovieLens dataset. This is a dataset of movie reviews released by GroupLens (*https://grouplens.org/about/what-is-grouplens/*), a research lab in the Department of Computer Science and Engineering at the University of Minnesota, through funding from the US National Science Foundation.

In Cloud Shell, download the data and load it as a BigQuery table using the following:

```
curl -O 'http://files.grouplens.org/datasets/movielens/ml-20m.zip'
unzip ml-20m.zip
bq --location=EU load --source_format=CSV \
    --autodetect ch09eu.movielens_ratings ml-20m/ratings.csv
bq --location=EU load --source_format=CSV \
    --autodetect ch09eu.movielens_movies_raw ml-20m/movies.csv
```

The resulting ratings table has the following columns:

Row	userId	movieId	rating	timestamp
1	70141	6219	2.0	1070338674
2	70159	2657	2.0	1427155558

Here's a quick exploratory query:

```
SELECT
 COUNT(DISTINCT userId) numUsers,
 COUNT(DISTINCT movieId) numMovies,
 COUNT(*) totalRatings
FROM ch09eu.movielens_ratings
```

This reveals that the dataset consists of more than 138,000 users, nearly 27,000 movies, and a little more than 20 million ratings, confirming that the data has been loaded successfully.

Let's examine the first few movies using the following query:

```
SELECT *
FROM ch09eu.movielens_movies_raw
WHERE movieId < 5
```

We can see that the genres column is a formatted string:

Row	movieId	title	genres
1	3	Grumpier Old Men (1995)	Comedy|Romance
2	4	Waiting to Exhale (1995)	Comedy|Drama|Romance
3	2	Jumanji (1995)	Adventure|Children|Fantasy

We can parse the genres into an array and rewrite the table as follows:

```
CREATE OR REPLACE TABLE ch09eu.movielens_movies AS
SELECT
* REPLACE(SPLIT(genres, "|") AS genres)
FROM
ch09eu.movielens_movies_raw
```

Now the table looks as follows:

Row	movieId	title	genres
1	4	Waiting to Exhale (1995)	Comedy
			Drama
			Romance
2	3	Grumpier Old Men (1995)	Comedy
			Romance
3	2	Jumanji (1995)	Adventure
			Children
			Fantasy

With the MovieLens data now loaded, we are ready to do collaborative filtering.

Matrix Factorization

Matrix factorization is a collaborative filtering technique that relies on factorizing the ratings matrix into two vectors called the *user factors* and the *item factors*. The user factors vector is a low-dimensional representation of a user_col, and the item factors vector similarly represents an item_col.

You can create the recommender model using the following:

```
-- not the final model; see movie_recommender_16
CREATE OR REPLACE MODEL ch09eu.movie_recommender
options(model_type='matrix_factorization',
        user_col='userId', item_col='movieId', rating_col='rating')
AS

SELECT
userId, movieId, rating
FROM ch09eu.movielens_ratings
```

Note that you create a model as usual, except that the model_type is matrix_factori zation and that you need to identify which columns play what roles in the collaborative filtering setup.

Use Flat-Rate Pricing or Flex Slots for Machine Learning Workloads

If you are on an on-demand pricing plan, you may get an error message that training Matrix Factorization models is not available for on-demand usage. You will be asked to set up a reservation (flex or regular).You can use flex slots for as little as 60 seconds.

With on-demand pricing, you will pay for the amount of data processed by your query. If you are just doing some basic SELECT, WHERE, JOIN, and GROUP BY, then both on-demand and flat-rate work out to the same. On-demand pricing is a bargain for computationally expensive queries such as GIS, regular expression parsing, JSON extraction, ORDER BY, etc.

Machine learning queries are the exception to this. Training a machine learning model requires iterating over the data multiple times, and so in on-demand, you will get charged based on the number of iterations the ML model might have to do. This means that, if you know (*https://medium.com/google-cloud/bigquery-ml-gets-faster-by-computing-a-closed-form-solution-sometimes-1baa5a838eb6*) your ML model won't (*https://towardsdatascience.com/k-means-clustering-in-bigquery-now-does-better-initialization-3d7e7567bad3*) take the maximum amount of time, you are better off using either a flat rate reservation or flex slots—ML in BigQuery is cheaper if you pay for the compute that you actually use.

In particular, recommendation models would be too expensive when charged by data and iterations—common matrix factorization models have millions of users and tens

---

of thousands of products. Matrix factorization is an $O(N^3)$ algorithm. In practice, though, the convergence is faster because your matrix is probably quite sparse. For this reason, BigQuery may refuse to do matrix factorization if you are on-demand and tell you to buy flex slots so that you can pay for the compute that you actually use.

The resulting model took an hour to train, and the training data loss starts out extremely bad and is driven down to near-zero over the next four iterations:[20]

Iteration	Training Data Loss	Evaluation Data Loss	Duration (seconds)
4	0.5734	172.4057	180.99
3	0.5826	187.2103	1,040.06
2	0.6531	4,758.2944	219.46
1	1.9776	6,297.2573	1,093.76
0	63,287,833,220.5795	168,995,333.0464	1,091.21

However, the evaluation data loss is quite high—much higher than the training data loss. This indicates that overfitting is happening, and so you need to add some regularization. Let's do that next:

```
-- not final model. See movie_recommender_16
CREATE OR REPLACE MODEL ch09eu.movie_recommender_l2
options(model_type='matrix_factorization',
        user_col='userId', item_col='movieId',
        rating_col='rating', l2_reg=0.2)
AS

SELECT
userId, movieId, rating
FROM ch09eu.movielens_ratings
```

Now you get faster convergence (three iterations instead of five) and a lot less overfitting:

Iteration	Training Data Loss	Evaluation Data Loss	Duration (seconds)
2	0.6509	1.4596	198.17
1	1.9829	33,814.3017	1,066.06
0	481,434,346,060.7928	2,156,993,687.7928	1,024.59

By default, BigQuery sets the number of factors to be the $\log_2$ of the number of rows. In this case, because we have 20 million rows in the table, the number of factors

---

20 The reason the duration of iterations swings back and forth is because the underlying optimization algorithm processes users in one iteration and movies in the next, and there are so many more users than movies.

would have been chosen to be 24. As with the number of clusters in k-means clustering, this is a reasonable default, but it is often worth experimenting with a number about 50% higher (36) and a number that is about a third lower (16):[21]

```
CREATE OR REPLACE MODEL ch09eu.movie_recommender_16
options(model_type='matrix_factorization',
        user_col='userId', item_col='movieId',
        rating_col='rating', l2_reg=0.2, num_factors=16)
AS

SELECT
userId, movieId, rating
FROM ch09eu.movielens_ratings
```

When we did that, we discovered that the evaluation loss was lower (0.97) with num_factors=16 than with num_factors=36 (1.67) or num_factors=24 (1.45). We could continue experimenting, but we are likely to see diminishing returns with further experimentation. So let's pick this as the final matrix factorization model and move on.

Making Recommendations

With the trained model, you can now provide recommendations. For example, let's find the best comedy movies to recommend to the user whose userId is 903:

```
SELECT * FROM
ML.PREDICT(MODEL ch09eu.movie_recommender_16, (
  SELECT
    movieId, title, 903 AS userId
  FROM ch09eu.movielens_movies, UNNEST(genres) g
  WHERE g = 'Comedy'
))
ORDER BY predicted_rating DESC
LIMIT 5
```

In this query, we are calling ML.PREDICT, passing in the trained recommendation model and providing a set of movieId and userId on which to carry out the predictions. In this case, it's just one userId (903), but all movies whose genre includes Comedy. Here is the result:

---

21 This might sound weird. Why a third lower and not half? Essentially, the idea is that, starting from 16, 24 is 50% higher. We want to try a geometric progression of candidate values for num_factors so that we cover the candidate space quickly. If you are trying more than three possible num_factors, consider trying a sequence of num_factors, each of which is about sqrt(2) times higher than the previous. For example, you could try 4, 6, 8, 12, 16, 24, 32, 48, 64, and so on.

Row	predicted_rating	movieId	title	userId
1	4.747231361947591	107434	Diplomatic Immunity (2009–)	903
2	4.372639637398302	62206	Supermarket Woman (Sûpâ no onna) (1996)	903
3	4.325021974040314	122441	Tales That Witness Madness (1973)	903
4	4.296062517241643	120313	Otakus in Love (2004)	903
5	4.277251207896746	130347	Bill Hicks: Sane Man (1989)	903

Filtering out previously rated movies

Of course, this includes movies the user has already seen and rated in the past. Let's remove them:

```
SELECT * FROM
ML.PREDICT(MODEL ch09eu.movie_recommender_16, (
  WITH seen AS (
    SELECT ARRAY_AGG(movieId) AS movies
    FROM ch09eu.movielens_ratings
    WHERE userId = 903
  )
  SELECT
    movieId, title, 903 AS userId
  FROM ch09eu.movielens_movies, UNNEST(genres) g, seen
  WHERE g = 'Comedy' AND movieId NOT IN UNNEST(seen.movies)
))
ORDER BY predicted_rating DESC
LIMIT 5
```

For this user, this happens to yield the same set of movies—the top predicted ratings didn't include any of the movies the user has already seen.

Customer targeting

In the previous section, we looked at how to identify the top-rated movies for a specific user. Sometimes we have a product and need to find the customers who are likely to appreciate it. Suppose, for example, you want to get more reviews for movieId=96481, which has only one rating, and you want to send coupons to the 100 users who are likely to rate it the highest. We can identify those users by using the following:

```
SELECT * FROM
ML.PREDICT(MODEL ch09eu.movie_recommender_16, (
  WITH allUsers AS (
    SELECT DISTINCT userId
    FROM ch09eu.movielens_ratings
  )
  SELECT
    96481 AS movieId,
    (SELECT title FROM ch09eu.movielens_movies WHERE movieId=96481) title,
```

```
        userId
  FROM
      allUsers
))
ORDER BY predicted_rating DESC
LIMIT 100
```

The result gives us 100 users to target, the top 5 of whom we list here:

Row	predicted_rating	movieId	title	userId
1	4.8586009640376915	96481	American Mullet (2001)	54192
2	4.670093338552966	96481	American Mullet (2001)	84240
3	4.544395037073204	96481	American Mullet (2001)	109638
4	4.422718574118088	96481	American Mullet (2001)	26606
5	4.410969328468145	96481	American Mullet (2001)	138139

Batch predictions for all users and movies

What if you want to carry out predictions for every user and movie combination? Instead of having to pull distinct users and movies as in the previous query, a convenient function is provided to carry out batch predictions for all movieId and userId encountered during training:

```
SELECT *
FROM ML.RECOMMEND(MODEL ch09eu.movie_recommender_16)
```

As seen in an earlier section, it is possible to filter out movies that the user has already seen and rated in the past. The reason previously viewed movies aren't filtered out by default is that there are situations (think of restaurant recommendations, for example) for which it is perfectly expected that we would need to recommend restaurants the user has liked in the past.

Incorporating User and Movie Information

The matrix factorization approach does not use any information about users or movies beyond what is available from the ratings matrix. However, we will often have user information (such as the city they live in, their annual income, their annual expenditure, etc.), and we will almost always have more information about the products in our catalog. How do we incorporate this information into our recommendation model?

The answer lies in recognizing that the user factors and product factors that result from the matrix factorization approach end up being a concise representation of the information about users and products available from the ratings matrix. We can concatenate this information with other information we have available and train a regression model to predict the rating.

Obtaining user and product factors

You can get the user factors or product factors from `ML.WEIGHTS`. For example, here's how to get the product factors for `movieId=96481` and user factors for `userId=54192`:

```
SELECT
    processed_input
    , feature
    , TO_JSON_STRING(factor_weights)
    , intercept
FROM ML.WEIGHTS(MODEL ch09eu.movie_recommender_16)
WHERE
(processed_input = 'movieId' AND feature = '96481')
OR
(processed_input = 'userId' AND feature = '54192')
```

The result is as follows:

Row	processed_input	feature	f0_	intercept
1	movieId	96481	[{"factor":16,"weight":0.01274324364248563}, {"factor":15,"weight":-0.026002830400362179}, {"factor":14,"weight":-0.0088894978851240675}, {"factor":13,"weight":0.010309411637259363}, {"factor":12,"weight":-0.025990228913849212}, {"factor":11,"weight":0.0037023423385396021}, {"factor":10,"weight":-0.0016743710047063861}, {"factor":9,"weight":0.018434530705228803}, {"factor":8,"weight":-0.0016500835388799462}, {"factor":7,"weight":-0.021652088589080184}, {"factor":6,"weight":-0.00097969747732716637}, {"factor":5,"weight":-0.056352201014532581}, {"factor":4,"weight":-0.025090456181039382}, {"factor":3,"weight":0.015317626028966519}, {"factor":2,"weight":-0.00046084151232374118}, {"factor":1,"weight":-0.0009461271544545048}]	-1.1915305828542884

Row	processed_input	feature	f0_	intercept
2	userId	54192	[{"factor":16,"weight":-0.66257902781387934}, {"factor":15,"weight":-0.089502881890795027}, {"factor":14,"weight":-0.14498342867805328}, {"factor":13,"weight":0.57708118940369757}, {"factor":12,"weight":-0.25409266698347688}, {"factor":11,"weight":0.243523510689305}, {"factor":10,"weight":0.48314159427498959}, {"factor":9,"weight":0.21335694312220596}, {"factor":8,"weight":0.34206958377350211}, {"factor":7,"weight":-0.076313491055098021}, {"factor":6,"weight":0.21214183741037482}, {"factor":5,"weight":0.19387028511697624}, {"factor":4,"weight":-0.42699681695332414}, {"factor":3,"weight":0.046570444717220438}, {"factor":2,"weight":0.25934273163373722}, {"factor":1,"weight":-0.18839802656522864}]	2.511409230366029

Multiplying these weights and adding the intercept is how you get the predicted rating for this combination of movieId and userId in the matrix factorization approach.

These weights also serve as a low-dimensional representation of the movie and user behavior. You can create a regression model to predict the rating given the user factors, product factors, and any other information that we know about our users and products.

Creating input features

The MovieLens dataset does not have any user information and has very little information about the movies themselves. To illustrate the concept, therefore, let's create some synthetic information about users:

```
CREATE OR REPLACE TABLE ch09eu.movielens_users AS
SELECT
  userId
  , RAND() * COUNT(rating) AS loyalty
  , CONCAT(SUBSTR(CAST(userId AS STRING), 0, 2)) AS postcode
FROM
  ch09eu.movielens_ratings
GROUP BY userId
```

Input features about users can be obtained by joining the user table with the machine learning weights and selecting all of the user information and the user factors from the weights array:

```
WITH userFeatures AS (
  SELECT
    u.*,
    (SELECT ARRAY_AGG(weight) FROM UNNEST(factor_weights)) AS user_factors
```

```
FROM
    ch09eu.movielens_users u
JOIN
    ML.WEIGHTS(MODEL ch09eu.movie_recommender_16) w
  ON
    processed_input = 'userId' AND feature = CAST(u.userId AS STRING)
)

SELECT * FROM userFeatures
LIMIT 5
```

This yields user features like these (you will need to remove the `userId` itself before feeding it into the regression model):

Row	userId	loyalty	postcode	user_factors
1	65536	72.51794801197904	65	0.038901538776462
				0.0019075355240976716
				0.011537776936285278
				-0.0322503841197857
				0.046464397209825425
				-0.015348467879503527
				0.05865111283285229
				0.04859058815259179
				0.017664456774125117
				0.006847553039523945
				0.012585216564478762
				-0.06506297976701378
				-0.005041156227839918
				-0.04187860699038322
				0.006216526560890197
				0.02711744261644579

Similarly, you can get product features for the movies data, except that you need to decide how to handle the genre because a movie could have more than one. If you decide to create a separate training row for each genre, you can construct the product features using the following:

```
WITH productFeatures AS (
  SELECT
      p.* EXCEPT(genres)
      , g
      , (SELECT ARRAY_AGG(weight) FROM UNNEST(factor_weights)) AS product_factors
  FROM
      ch09eu.movielens_movies p, UNNEST(genres) g
  JOIN
      ML.WEIGHTS(MODEL ch09eu.movie_recommender_16) w
```

```
ON
    processed_input = 'movieId' AND feature = CAST(p.movieId AS STRING)
)

SELECT * FROM productFeatures
LIMIT 5
```

This yields rows of the following form:

Row	movieId	title	g	product_factors
1	1450	Prisoner of the Mountains (Kavkazsky plennik) (1996)	War	0.9883690055578206
				1.3052751077485096
				-1.4000285383517228
				1.3901032474256991
				-0.32863748198986686
				-0.7688057246956399
				-1.1853591273232054
				-0.4553668299329251
				-0.14564591302024543
				-0.18609388556738163
				-0.3547198526732644
				0.06067380147330148
				-0.2733324088164271
				1.8302213060412562
				0.4753820155626278
				1.559946725190114

By combining these two WITH clauses and pulling in the rating corresponding to the movieId-userId combination (if it exists in the ratings table), you can create the training dataset:[22]

```
CREATE OR REPLACE TABLE ch09eu.movielens_hybrid_dataset AS

WITH userFeatures AS (
  SELECT
    u.*,
    (SELECT ARRAY_AGG(weight) FROM UNNEST(factor_weights)) AS user_factors
  FROM
    ch09eu.movielens_users u
  JOIN
    ML.WEIGHTS(MODEL ch09eu.movie_recommender_16) w
```

---

22 See *09_bqml/hybrid.sql* in the GitHub repository for this book (*https://github.com/GoogleCloudPlatform/bigquery-oreilly-book*).

```
ON
    processed_input = 'userId' AND feature = CAST(u.userId AS STRING)
),

productFeatures AS (
  SELECT
      p.* EXCEPT(genres)
      , g
      , (SELECT ARRAY_AGG(weight) FROM UNNEST(factor_weights)) AS product_factors
  FROM
      ch09eu.movielens_movies p, UNNEST(genres) g
  JOIN
      ML.WEIGHTS(MODEL ch09eu.movie_recommender_16) w
  ON
      processed_input = 'movieId' AND feature = CAST(p.movieId AS STRING)
)

SELECT p.* EXCEPT(movieId), u.* EXCEPT(userId), rating
FROM productFeatures p, userFeatures u
JOIN
    ch09eu.movielens_ratings r
ON
    r.movieId = p.movieId AND r.userId = u.userId
```

One of the rows of this table looks like this:

1 Hunted, The (2003)	Action	2.6029616190628015	692.7156232519949	70	0.026523240535672774	2.0
		0.33485455845698525			0.0019319939217823622	
		0.31628840722516194			-0.0020145595411925534	
		-0.3075233831543138			-0.002646563034985453	
		-0.4473419662482839			-0.01594551937825673	
		-1.0222758233057185			-0.010801066706191506	
		-0.42418301494313826			4.772572135005211E-4	
		-1.2447809221572947			0.014766024570817101	
		-0.20242685993451942			-0.007500869241538576	
		1.330350771422776			-0.020383420117709883	
		-0.3354935275410769			-0.007863867111381763	
		0.32404375319192513			0.019901597021923123	
		1.402657314320568			-0.003178194776711233	
		0.4728896971092763			0.013146874239054253	
		-0.5743444547904143			-0.0017117741950437	
		0.35632448579921905			-0.030130776462043048	

Essentially, you have a couple of attributes about the movie, the product factors array corresponding to the movie, a couple of attributes about the user, and the user factors array corresponding to the user. These form the inputs to the "hybrid" recommendations model that builds off the matrix factorization model and adds in metadata about users and movies.

Training hybrid recommendation model

As of this writing, BigQuery ML cannot handle arrays as inputs to a regression model. Let's therefore define a function to convert arrays to a struct for which the array elements are its fields:

```
CREATE OR REPLACE FUNCTION ch09eu.arr_to_input_3(a ARRAY<FLOAT64>)
RETURNS STRUCT<a1 FLOAT64, a2 FLOAT64, a3 FLOAT64> AS (
STRUCT(
    a[OFFSET(0)]
    , a[OFFSET(1)]
    , a[OFFSET(2)]
));
```

Now you can do the following:

```
SELECT
  ch09eu.arr_to_input_3(a).*
FROM
(SELECT [34.23, 43.21, 63.21] AS a)
```

And here's your result:

Row	a1	a2	a3
1	34.23	43.21	63.21

You can create a similar function named ch09eu.arr_to_input_16_users to convert the user factor array into named columns, and a similar function for the product factor arrays.[23] Then you can tie together metadata about users and products with the user factors and product factors obtained from the matrix factorization approach to create a regression model to predict the rating:

```
CREATE OR REPLACE MODEL ch09eu.movielens_recommender_hybrid
OPTIONS(model_type='linear_reg', input_label_cols=['rating'])
AS

SELECT
  * EXCEPT(user_factors, product_factors)
  , ch09eu.arr_to_input_16_users(user_factors).*
  , ch09eu.arr_to_input_16_products(product_factors).*
FROM
  ch09eu.movielens_hybrid_dataset
```

---

23 See *09_bqml/arr_to_input16.sql* in the GitHub repository for this book.

There is no point in looking at the evaluation metrics of this model, because the user information we used to create the training dataset was fake (note the RAND() in the creation of the loyalty column)—we did this exercise to demonstrate how it could be done. And of course, we could train a dnn_regressor model and optimize the hyperparameters if we want a more sophisticated model. But if we are going to go that far, it might be better to consider using AutoML tables, which we cover in the next section.

Custom Machine Learning Models on GCP

Whereas BigQuery ML provides you a choice of models[24] that can be built and iterated over very quickly, AutoML provides you with a state-of-the-art, high-quality model for the task, with the trade-off being that the model takes hours or even days to train. Keras and TensorFlow provide lower-level control of machine learning model architectures and allow you to design, develop, and deploy custom machine learning models. We recommend that you begin with BigQuery ML for machine learning on structured or semi-structured data and, depending on your skill set and the value of the problem being solved, use AutoML or Keras to fine-tune the machine learning problem.

Hyperparameter Tuning

When you're carrying out machine learning, there are many parameters that you choose rather arbitrarily. These include factors such as the learning rate, the level of L2 regularization, the number of layers and nodes in a neural network, the maximum depth of a boosted tree, and the number of factors of a matrix factorization model. It is often the case that choosing a different value for these could result in a better model (as measured by the error on a withheld evaluation dataset). Choosing a good value for these parameters is called *hyperparameter tuning*.

Hyperparameter tuning using scripting

Take the *k*-means clustering model. The evaluation tab in the BigQuery web UI (as well as SELECT * from ML.EVALUATE) shows the Davies-Bouldin index, which is useful for determining the optimal number of clusters supported by the data (the lower the number, the better the clustering).

For example, here's a script to try varying the number of clusters:

```
DECLARE NUM_CLUSTERS INT64 DEFAULT 3;
DECLARE MIN_ERROR FLOAT64 DEFAULT 1000.0;
DECLARE BEST_NUM_CLUSTERS INT64 DEFAULT -1;
```

---

24 By the time you are reading this, automl might well be one of the supported model types in BigQuery.

```
DECLARE MODEL_NAME STRING;
DECLARE error FLOAT64 DEFAULT 0;

WHILE NUM_CLUSTERS < 8 DO

    SET MODEL_NAME = CONCAT('ch09eu.london_station_clusters_',
                            CAST(NUM_CLUSTERS AS STRING));

    EXECUTE IMMEDIATE format("""
    CREATE OR REPLACE MODEL %s
      OPTIONS(model_type='kmeans',
              num_clusters=%d,
              standardize_features = true) AS
      SELECT * except(station_name)
      from ch09eu.stationstats;
    """, MODEL_NAME, NUM_CLUSTERS);

    EXECUTE IMMEDIATE format("""
      SELECT davies_bouldin_index FROM ML.EVALUATE(MODEL %s);
    """, MODEL_NAME) INTO error;

    IF error < MIN_ERROR THEN
        SET MIN_ERROR = error;
        SET BEST_NUM_CLUSTERS = NUM_CLUSTERS;
    END IF;
    SET NUM_CLUSTERS = NUM_CLUSTERS + 1;

END WHILE
```

Hyperparameter tuning in Python

Alternatively, you could do this using Python and its multithreading capability to limit the number of concurrent queries:[25]

```
def train_and_evaluate(num_clusters: Range, max_concurrent=3):
    # grid search means to try all possible values in range
    params = []
    for k in num_clusters.values():
        params.append(Params(k))

    # run all the jobs
    print('Grid search of {} possible parameters'.format(len(params)))
    pool = ThreadPool(max_concurrent)
    results = pool.map(lambda p: p.run(), params)

    # sort in ascending order
    return sorted(results, key=lambda p: p._error)
```

---

25 For the full code, see *09_bqml/hyperparam.ipynb* in the GitHub repository for this book.

In this code, the run() method of the Params class invokes the appropriate training and evaluation queries:

```
class Params:
    def __init__(self, num_clusters):
        self._num_clusters = num_clusters
        self._model_name = (
            'ch09eu.london_station_clusters_{}'.format(num_clusters))
        self._train_query = """
          CREATE OR REPLACE MODEL {}
          OPTIONS(model_type='kmeans',
                  num_clusters={},
                  standardize_features = true) AS
        SELECT * except(station_name)
        from ch09eu.stationstats
        """.format(self._model_name, self._num_clusters)
        self._eval_query = """
          SELECT davies_bouldin_index AS error
          FROM ML.EVALUATE(MODEL {});
        """.format(self._model_name)
        self._error = None

    def run(self):
        bq = bigquery.Client(project=PROJECT)
        job = bq.query(self._train_query, location='EU')
        job.result() # wait for job to finish
        evaldf = bq.query(self._eval_query, location='EU').to_dataframe()
        self._error = evaldf['error'][0]
        return self
```

When searching in the range [3,9], you find that the number of clusters at which the error is minimized is 7:

```
ch09eu.london_station_clusters_7    1.551265    7
ch09eu.london_station_clusters_9    1.571020    9
ch09eu.london_station_clusters_6    1.571398    6
ch09eu.london_station_clusters_4    1.596398    4
ch09eu.london_station_clusters_8    1.621974    8
ch09eu.london_station_clusters_5    1.660766    5
ch09eu.london_station_clusters_3    1.681441    3
```

Hyperparameter tuning using AI Platform

In both of the hyperparameter tuning methods that we've considered so far, we tried out every possible value of a parameter that fell within a range. As the number of possible parameters grows, a grid search becomes increasingly wasteful. It is better to use a more efficient search algorithm, and that's where Cloud AI Platform's hyperparameter tuning can be helpful. You can use the hyperparameter tuning service for any model (not just TensorFlow). Let's apply it to tuning the feature engineering and number of nodes of a DNN model.[26]

First, create a configuration file that specifies the ranges for each of the parameters, the number of concurrent queries, and the total number of trials:

```
trainingInput:
  scaleTier: CUSTOM
  masterType: standard    # See: https://cloud.google.com/ml-
engine/docs/tensorflow/machine-types
  hyperparameters:
    goal: MINIMIZE
    maxTrials: 50
    maxParallelTrials: 2
    hyperparameterMetricTag: mean_absolute_error
    params:
    - parameterName: afternoon_start
      type: INTEGER
      minValue: 9
      maxValue: 12
      scaleType: UNIT_LINEAR_SCALE
    - parameterName: afternoon_end
      type: INTEGER
      minValue: 15
      maxValue: 19
      scaleType: UNIT_LINEAR_SCALE
    - parameterName: num_nodes_0
      type: INTEGER
      minValue: 10
      maxValue: 100
      scaleType: UNIT_LOG_SCALE
    - parameterName: num_nodes_1
      type: INTEGER
      minValue: 3
      maxValue: 10
      scaleType: UNIT_LINEAR_SCALE
```

Note that we have specified minimum and maximum values for each of the parameters and the metric (mean absolute error) to be minimized. We are asking for optimization to happen using just 50 trials, whereas a grid search would have required trying out 4×4×90×7, or more than 10,000 options. So using the AI Platform hyperparameter tuning service results in a 200-fold savings!

Next, you create a Python program that invokes BigQuery to train and evaluate the model given a single set of these parameters:

---

26 The full code is available at *https://github.com/GoogleCloudPlatform/bigquery-oreilly-book/blob/master/09_bqml/hyperparam.ipynb*.

```
def train_and_evaluate(args):
    model_name = "ch09eu.bicycle_model_dnn_{}_{}_{}_{}".format(
        args.afternoon_start, args.afternoon_end, args.num_nodes_0,
args.num_nodes_1
    )
    train_query = """
        CREATE OR REPLACE MODEL {}
        TRANSFORM(* EXCEPT(start_date)
                , IF(EXTRACT(dayofweek FROM start_date) BETWEEN 2 and 6,
'weekday', 'weekend') as dayofweek
                , ML.BUCKETIZE(EXTRACT(HOUR FROM start_date), [5, {}, {}]) AS
hourofday
        )
        OPTIONS(input_label_cols=['duration'],
            model_type='dnn_regressor',
            hidden_units=[{}, {}])
        AS

        SELECT
          duration
          , start_station_name
          , start_date
        FROM `bigquery-public-data`.london_bicycles.cycle_hire
    """.format(model_name,
            args.afternoon_start,
            args.afternoon_end,
            args.num_nodes_0,
            args.num_nodes_1)
    logging.info(train_query)
    bq = bigquery.Client(project=args.project,
                        location=args.location,
                        credentials=get_credentials())
    job = bq.query(train_query)
    job.result() # wait for job to finish

    eval_query = """
        SELECT mean_absolute_error
        FROM ML.EVALUATE(MODEL {})
    """.format(model_name)
    logging.info(eval_info)
    evaldf = bq.query(eval_query).to_dataframe()
    return evaldf['mean_absolute_error'][0]
```

Note that this code uses a specific value for each of the tunable parameters and returns the mean absolute error, which is the metric being minimized.

This error value is then written out:

```
hpt.report_hyperparameter_tuning_metric(
    hyperparameter_metric_tag='mean_absolute_error',
    metric_value=error,
    global_step=1)
```

The training program is submitted to the AI Platform Training service:

```
gcloud ai-platform jobs submit training $JOBNAME \
  --runtime-version=1.13 \
  --python-version=3.5 \
  --region=$REGION \
  --module-name=trainer.train_and_eval \
  --package-path=$(pwd)/trainer \
  --job-dir=gs://$BUCKET/hparam/ \
  --config=hyperparam.yaml \
  -\
  --project=$PROJECT --location=EU
```

The resulting output, shown in the AI Platform console, contains the best parameters.

AutoML

AutoML consists of a family of products that provide a code-free way to automatically create and deploy state-of-the-art machine learning models. They tend to rely on applying a variety of feature engineering, hyperparameter tuning, neural architecture search, transfer learning, and ensembling methods to build models that have comparable quality to models manually crafted by top machine learning experts.

> Use BigQuery ML to formulate your machine learning problems—to identify the features and labels, to quickly diagnose whether some new dataset improves accuracy, to detect mistakes in assumptions about time-dependence, and to determine the best way of representing some piece of domain knowledge. The fast iteration capability that BigQuery ML provides is invaluable, as is the ability to train models without moving data outside the data warehouse. After you have identified a feasible machine learning problem, you can use AutoML to get a very accurate model on the specific training dataset (features and labels). In our experience, AutoML infused with features that represent the insights of domain experts is hard to beat either in terms of accuracy or in terms of time to deployment.

AutoML Vision, for example, provides a web-based interface to upload images (or point to images on Google Cloud Storage), identify their labels, and launch the training of image classification or object detection models.

Because the data in BigQuery tends to be structured or semi-structured, the AutoML models that are relevant tend to be AutoML Natural Language (to do tasks such as text classification and entity detection), AutoML Tables (to do tasks such as regression, classification, and time-series forecasting on structured data), and AutoML Recommendations (to build state-of-the-art recommendation models).

To use AutoML Tables (Figure 9-14), simply visit the starting point on the GCP console, point it at a BigQuery table, select the feature columns and label column, and then click Train. Although training will take much longer (on the order of 12 to 24 hours), the resulting accuracy tends to be higher than what you might have achieved on the same dataset with BigQuery ML.

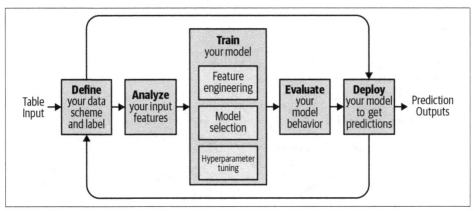

Figure 9-14. AutoML Tables can start from a BigQuery table, the same training dataset that was built through iterative exploration and experimentation in BigQuery ML. In our experience, AutoML Tables applied to thoughtfully created training datasets provides state-of-the-art performance.

Support for TensorFlow

Even though BigQuery ML is scalable and convenient, and AutoML powerful and accurate, there are times when you might want to build your own custom models using Keras or TensorFlow. You might also find it advantageous to train models using TensorFlow and predict using BigQuery, or to train models in BigQuery but deploy into TensorFlow Serving.

It is possible to access BigQuery directly from TensorFlow code and to export BigQuery tables to TensorFlow records, transforming the data along the way. There is also interoperability between BigQuery and TensorFlow models—it is possible to load a TensorFlow model into BigQuery and to export a BigQuery model in TensorFlow's SavedModel format. We cover these capabilities in this section.

TensorFlow's BigQueryClient

TensorFlow's BigQueryClient (*https://github.com/tensorflow/io/tree/master/tensorflow_io/bigquery*) uses the Storage API to efficiently read data directly out of BigQuery storage (i.e., without having to issue a BigQuery query). We can use this class in a Keras/TensorFlow 2.0 model to create a `tf.data Dataset`.

First import the necessary packages:

```
import tensorflow as tf
from tensorflow.python.framework import dtypes
from tensorflow_io.bigquery import BigQueryClient
from tensorflow_io.bigquery import BigQueryReadSession
```

Then create a BigQueryClient and call read_session on it, providing the project id to be billed, and details about the dataset to be read:

```
client = BigQueryClient()

GCP_PROJECT_ID='your_project_name'  # The project to bill
COL_NAMES = ['Time', 'Amount', 'Class'] # list of columns desired
COL_TYPES = [dtypes.float64, dtypes.float64, dtypes.int64]
ROW_RESTR = 'Time <= 144803'
DATASET_GCP_PROJECT_ID, DATASET_ID, TABLE_ID = (
    'bigquery-public-data.ml_datasets.ulb_fraud_detection').split('.')

bqsession = client.read_session(
        "projects/" + GCP_PROJECT_ID,
        DATASET_GCP_PROJECT_ID, TABLE_ID, DATASET_ID,
        COL_NAMES, COL_TYPES,
        requested_streams=2,
        row_restriction=row_restriction)
```

Note that in the code above, we are specifying the columns to read (because Big-Query's storage is columnar, we don't have to read the entire table), specifying the data types of those columns, and also specifying a row restriction. In the case of clustered tables, this allows the Storage API to be efficient and read only a subset of even the columnar files.

We can then read a `tf.data.Dataset` using the session. The common optimizations and practices such as label popping, prefetching, batching, and shuffling can be applied as well:

```
def features_and_labels(features):
  label = features.pop('Class') # this is what we will train for
  return features, label

batch_size=1024
dataset = (bqsession.parallel_read_rows()
            .prefetch(1)
            .map(features_and_labels)
            .shuffle(batch_size*10)
            .batch(batch_size))
```

This approach allows us to read `batch_size` records at once, shuffle the read order across workers, prefetch records, and so on. Hence, we recommend that you follow this approach when training TensorFlow models on BigQuery data. Do not duplicate the data by exporting it into CSV files and the like.

Using pandas

If the BigQuery table is small enough, read it directly into an in-memory pandas DataFrame:

```
query = """
SELECT
  start_station_name
  , duration
FROM `bigquery-public-data`.london_bicycles.cycle_hire
GROUP BY start_station_name
"""
df = bq.query(query, location='EU').to_dataframe()
```

Use the tf.data API to read from pandas:

```
tf.estimator.inputs.pandas_input_fn(
    df,
    batch_size=128,
    num_epochs=10,
    shuffle=True,
    num_threads=8,
    target_column='duration'
)
```

Apache Beam/Cloud Dataflow

If the table is too large to fit into memory, use the BigQueryClient as suggested in a previous section. An alternative is to export the BigQuery data into TensorFlow records on Google Cloud Storage using Cloud Dataflow (see Chapter 5 for more details):

```
_ = (
        examples
        | 'get_tfrecords' >> beam.Map(lambda x: x['tfrecord'])
        | 'writetfr' >> beam.io.tfrecordio.WriteToTFRecord(
            os.path.join(options['outdir'], 'tfrecord', step)))
```

Each of the previous examples is created by pulling the necessary records from BigQuery:

```
tfexample = tf.train.Example(
        features=tf.train.Features(
            feature={
                'start_station_name': _bytes_feature(row['start_station_name']),
                'duration': _int64_feature(row['duration']),
            }))
```

Along the way, if necessary, you can transform the records using tf.transform (*https://www.tensorflow.org/tfx/transform/get_started*). Then, in TensorFlow, you can use the high-throughput methods provided by tf.data.tfrecorddataset to read in the data.

Exporting to TensorFlow

The TensorFlow ecosystem for serving is very powerful—it is possible to carry out predictions of TensorFlow models in a web browser using JavaScript and *tensor-flow.js*, on an embedded device or mobile application using TensorFlow Lite, in Kubernetes clusters using Kubeflow, as a REST API using AI Platform Predictions, and more. Therefore, you might find it advantageous to export your BigQuery ML model as a TensorFlow SavedModel. After the BigQuery ML model has been exported, you can use it in any of the environments that can serve TensorFlow models.

To export the BigQuery model ch09eu.bicycle_model_linear as a TensorFlow SavedModel to Google Cloud Storage, use bq extract:

```
bq extract -m ch09eu.bicycle_model_linear \
           gs://${BUCKET}/bqml_model_export/bicycle_model_linear
```

The result will be a set of files including a protobuf file that has the extension .pb. On Google Cloud, the fully managed serving environment for TensorFlow/xgboost/PyTorch/etc. models is Cloud AI Platform (CAIP) Predictions.

To deploy the model, download deploy.sh from the GitHub (*https://github.com/GoogleCloudPlatform/bigquery-oreilly-book/blob/master/blogs/bqml_model_export/deploy.sh*) repository for the book and run it:

```
./deploy.sh gs://${BUCKET}/bqml_model_export/bicycle_model_linear \
           europe-west1 london_bicycles bqml
```

What deploy.sh does is to create a model and model version in CAIP Predictions and then deploy to it.

To try out the deployed model, create a file named input.json with the following contents (all on one line):

```
{"start_station_name": "Vauxhall Cross, Vauxhall",
 "dayofweek": "weekend", "hourofday": "17"}
```

Then, send it to Cloud AI Platform Predictions using:

```
gcloud ai-platform predict --model london_bicycles \
       --version bqml --json-instances input.json
```

You should get back something like:

```
PREDICTED_LABEL
[1329.178180269723]
```

Cloud AI Platform Predictions exposes a REST API that takes JSON and so it can be invoked from any language that can make a web service call. The complete code (*https://github.com/GoogleCloudPlatform/bigquery-oreilly-book/tree/master/blogs/bqml_model_export*) in Keras for this example is available on GitHub.

Predicting with TensorFlow models

If you have trained a model in TensorFlow and exported it as a SavedModel, you can import the TensorFlow model into BigQuery and use the ML.PREDICT SQL function in BigQuery to make predictions. This is very useful if you want to make batch predictions (e.g., to make predictions for all the data collected in the past hour), given that any SQL query can be scheduled in BigQuery.

Importing the model into BigQuery is simply a matter of specifying a different model_type and pointing it at the model_path from which the SavedModel was exported (note the wildcard at the end to pick up the assets, vocabulary, etc.):

```
CREATE OR REPLACE MODEL ch09eu.txtclass_tf
OPTIONS (model_type='tensorflow',
        model_path='gs://bucket/some/dir/1549825580/*')
```

This creates a model in BigQuery that works like any built-in model, as illustrated in Figure 9-15. Here, the schema indicates that the required input to the model is called "input" and is a string.

txtclass_tf

Details   Training   Evaluation   Schema

Labels

Field name	Type	Mode	Description
dense_1	FLOAT	NULLABLE	

Features

Field name	Type	Mode	Description
input	STRING	NULLABLE	

Figure 9-15. The schema of the imported TensorFlow model

Given this schema, we can now do a prediction:

```
SELECT
  input,
  (SELECT AS STRUCT(p, ['github', 'nytimes', 'techcrunch'][ORDINAL(s)])
          prediction
```

```
FROM
    (SELECT p, ROW_NUMBER() OVER() AS s FROM
        (SELECT * FROM UNNEST(dense_1) AS p))
    ORDER BY p DESC LIMIT 1).*
FROM ML.PREDICT(MODEL advdata.txtclass_tf,
(
SELECT 'Unlikely Partnership in House Gives Lawmakers Hope for Border Deal' AS
input
UNION ALL SELECT "Fitbit\'s newest fitness tracker is just for employees and
health insurance members"
UNION ALL SELECT "Show HN: Hello, a CLI tool for managing social media"
))
```

This is very powerful because we can now train a machine learning model, save it to Google Cloud Storage, import it into BigQuery, and carry out periodic predictions without the need to move the data for predictions out of the data warehouse.

Summary

In this chapter, we did a whirlwind tour of machine learning in BigQuery. We began by discussing different types of machine learning problems that work on structured and semi-structured data and how to train and predict machine learning models for all of those problems in BigQuery.

To train a regression model in BigQuery, we created a training dataset consisting of features and a label. Next, we were able to create a trained model, evaluate it, and then use it for predictions. We also iterated through a variety of improvements to the basic model and discussed how to extract the model weights. Finally, we examined how to train not just linear models but also DNNs, time series models, and boosted regression trees.

Training a classification model in BigQuery was similar, except that the evaluation metrics were more sophisticated—we discussed how to choose the threshold in a binary classification problem to obtain a desired value of precision or recall.

We also looked at various customizations that might prove important on specific problems—things like changing the way the data is split between training and evaluation, balancing classes when one class is rarer than the other, and regularization to limit overfitting.

We also showed how to find clusters from structured data using the k-means algorithm and how to visualize the cluster attributes using Data Studio and make data-driven decisions.

The final type of machine learning model we examined in this chapter was on recommendation systems. We built a matrix factorization model to solve both product recommendation and customer targeting problems. We also discussed how to use the user factors and item factors that result from matrix factorization to train a more sophisticated model that includes data about users and products beyond their rating behavior.

Finally, we looked at the rest of the GCP ecosystem for custom models—hyperparameter tuning, AutoML, and TensorFlow. We discussed the interoperability between these different ways of building machine learning models, and when you would use which.

Administering and Securing BigQuery

One of the reasons to use a fully managed serverless product like BigQuery is to take advantage of the security infrastructure of public cloud services. In Google Cloud Platform (GCP), data is encrypted at rest and in transit, and the API-serving infrastructure is accessible only over encrypted channels. To access BigQuery resources, users and applications must be authenticated and authorized using Identity and Access Management. You can perform this administration (of users, tables, jobs, views, etc.) by using the BigQuery web user interface (UI), using the bq command-line tool, or using the REST API.

In this chapter, we discuss how BigQuery's infrastructure is secured, how to configure Cloud IAM, and a range of administration tools that you use to monitor jobs and authorize users. We end this chapter with a discussion of BigQuery support for a variety of tools that you might be able to use to help fulfill your regulatory and compliance needs based on the strong foundations established by the infrastructure security measures, Identity and Access Management, and administrative tools. It is always your responsibility to work with your legal counsel to determine whether implementing any of these tools and capabilities will satisfy your regulatory or compliance requirements.

Infrastructure Security

The security infrastructure that BigQuery relies on is end to end—starting with the people and continuing through the datacenter, server hardware, software stack, logging, encryption, and intrusion detection, and finally to the cloud platform itself.

Google's Information Security Team develops security review processes, builds security infrastructure, and implements Google's security processes. This team consists of top security experts and was responsible for discovering and coming up with fixes for problems including the *Heartbleed vulnerability* (*https://www.owasp.org/index.php/ Heartbleed_Bug*) and the *SSL 3.0 exploit* (*https://www.us-cert.gov/ncas/alerts/ TA14-290A*). Google's datacenters employ a layered physical security model with custom-designed safeguards, high-resolution cameras capable of tracking intruders, access logs, and routine patrols.

Server security is enhanced by using tens of thousands of identical, custom-built servers. This homogeneity, along with having built the entire stack including hardware, networking, and custom Linux software, reduces the security footprint and promotes agile responses to security threats. The servers themselves include a custom chip called *Titan* to provide verification of system firmware and software components, thus providing a strong, hardware-rooted system identity.

The security of customer information is protected through a variety of controls and practices. Every layer of the Google application and storage stack authenticates and verifies the authorization of requests coming from other components. Engineers' access to production services and production environments is defined and controlled by a centralized group and role management system. The practices include using a security protocol that authenticates engineers through the use of short-lived personal public key certificates, the issuance of which is in turn guarded by two-factor authentication. Hard disks that are retired from Google's systems are subjected to a data destruction process to safeguard customer information before leaving Google's premises. The disks are wiped, checked, and tracked by multiple individuals before being released.

BigQuery, like other Google services, is managed through a secured global API gateway infrastructure that is accessible only over encrypted Secure Sockets Layer (SSL)/ Transport Layer Security (TLS) channels. Every request must include a time-limited authentication token generated via human login or private key-based secrets in order to be serviced. All API requests are logged, and using GCP tools, a project administrator can read operations and access logs for BigQuery.

Any new data stored in persistent disks is encrypted under the 256-bit Advanced Encryption Standard (AES-256), and each encryption key is itself encrypted with a regularly rotated set of master keys. These are the same encryption and key management policies, cryptographic libraries, and root of trust used by many of Google's production services, including Gmail. This sharing of infrastructure extends to network infrastructure. Google's global network helps to improve the security of data in transit by limiting hops across the public internet. By using Cloud Interconnect and a managed Virtual Private Network (VPN), it is possible to create encrypted channels between an on-premises private IP environment and Google's network.

BigQuery builds on these capabilities. However, it is still your responsibility to enforce appropriate access to data and analyze request logs. This includes preventing your end users from sharing critical information outside of your corporate network/

public cloud infrastructure (i.e., data loss prevention) and ensuring that you keep safe any data that could identify a specific individual—that is, Personally Identifiable Information (PII). In the rest of this chapter, we discuss the tools that GCP and Big-Query provide to accomplish these goals.

Identity and Access Management

Cloud Identity and Access Management (IAM) allows users of BigQuery to manage access control by defining three things: identity, role, and resource. Essentially, we need to specify who (identity) has what access (role) to what resource.

Identity

The identity specifies who has access. This could be an end user who is identified by a Google account (such as a @gmail.com account or an @example.com account, where example.com is a G Suite domain) or an application identified by a service account. Service accounts are essentially GCP-assigned email addresses and can be created (for example, using the Cloud Console)[1] to have a subset of the permissions held by the creator of the service account in that project. Typically, we create them to embody the (limited) set of permissions required by applications that are run on our behalf.

Members to whom access is granted can also include virtual groups of Google accounts such as Google groups, G Suite domains, or Cloud Identity[2] domains. You should prefer providing access to Google groups over providing access to individuals because it is easier to add members to and remove members from a Google group instead of updating multiple Cloud IAM policies to onboard or remove users. Even if access control is provided to a virtual group, you don't lose auditability: logging and auditing will resolve to the actual Google account or service account that is accessing BigQuery.

It is also possible to provide access to allAuthenticatedUsers (a special identifier for anyone who is authenticated with a Google account or service account).[3] A common use is to publish a public dataset—the london_bicycles dataset that we used throughout this book was published in this manner. You should note that allAuthen

---

1 For information, see *https://console.cloud.google.com/apis/credentials/serviceaccountkey* and *https://cloud.google.com/iam/docs/creating-managing-service-accounts#creating_a_service_account*.

2 These are essentially like G Suite domains, but they don't have access to G Suite applications. To manage users who don't need G Suite or premium features like mobile device management, you can create free Cloud Identity accounts for them—see *https://support.google.com/cloudidentity/answer/7319251*.

3 Note that allUsers, although allowed by GCP, doesn't have any effect in BigQuery because all BigQuery users must be authenticated.

ticatedUsers allows any authenticated user, not just users in your domain, to have access.

Role

The role determines what access is allowed to the identity in question. A role consists of a set of permissions. It is possible to create a custom role to provide granular access to a custom list of permissions. However, most commonly, you will use predefined roles.

Predefined roles

Roles, such as the BigQuery dataViewer role, are predefined and consist of a combination of permissions that are frequently required. For example, the dataViewer role provides, among others, the bigquery.datasets.get permission to get metadata about a dataset, and bigquery.tables.getData to get table data, but not the big query.datasets.delete, which would allow any identity with that permission to delete the dataset.

As of this writing, there are eight predefined roles, including four roles associated with access to datasets and associated tables and views. Loosely, in order of increasing capability, these are:

1. metadataViewer (the fully qualified name is roles/bigquery.metadataViewer) provides metadata-only access to datasets, tables, and/or views.
2. dataViewer provides permissions to read data as well as metadata.
3. dataEditor provides the ability to read a dataset and list, create, update, read, and delete tables in that dataset.
4. dataOwner adds the ability to also delete the dataset.
5. readSessionUser provides access to the BigQuery Storage API sessions that are billed to a project.
6. jobUser can run jobs (including queries) that are billed to the project.
7. user can run jobs and create datasets whose storage is billed to the project.
8. admin can manage all data within the project and cancel jobs by other users.

Treat these two sets of roles as being independent and orthogonal. Users granted the bigquery.readSessionUser do not have access to table data—it might be that they need to read data from datasets belonging to a different project! To read data, you must also grant them bigquery.tables.getData permissions. Similarly, having the jobUser role does not grant the ability to create, modify, or delete tables (only to do a SELECT from them); you need to specifically assign the dataEditor role in addition to the `jobUser` role if you want the user to be able to run Data Definition Language (DDL)/Data Manipulation Language (DML) queries.

It is also quite conceivable that you might want to provide only the `dataViewer` role without providing the `user` role. This will be the situation when you want users to pay for their own queries (i.e., to create query jobs in their own projects, but be able to query datasets that belong to you). For the specific capabilities of each role, the full set of permissions, and which REST API methods require what permissions, refer to the BigQuery documentation (*https://cloud.google.com/bigquery/docs/access-control*).

Primitive roles

In addition to predefined roles and custom roles, BigQuery supports *primitive roles*, which date back to before GCP had support for Cloud IAM. Mostly, you will use the aforementioned predefined roles, but in some cases, it can be more convenient to assign users a role in the project (viewer, editor, or owner) and have the permissions for all BigQuery datasets and jobs in the project be inherited from this project role.

Identities that have viewing rights on the project get `dataViewer` on all datasets in the project as well as the ability to create jobs (i.e., run queries) that are billed to the project. Project editors get the `dataEditor` role in addition to project viewer privileges, and project owners get the `dataOwner` role in addition to project editor privileges. One exception is that only the user who runs a query has access to the cached results table (because of the implications of sharing access to the results of queries that join against datasets to which other project owners might not have access). To grant or revoke primitive roles for projects, use the GCP console.

The primitive roles that provide reading, writing, or ownership access to datasets translate neatly to `dataViewer`, `dataEditor`, or `dataOwner` roles, respectively. As such, they can be granted in all the ways that predefined roles can be granted, but the simplest way is to click the link to share a dataset from the BigQuery web UI.

Custom roles

If the predefined roles don't meet your specific needs, consider creating a custom role, but note that needing to grant multiple roles (such as `jobUser` as well as `data Viewer`) to groups of people is not a good reason to create a custom role.

If you need to grant multiple roles to allow a particular task, create a Google group, grant the roles to that group, and then add users or other groups to that group. You might find it helpful to create Google groups for different job functions within your organization and give everyone in those groups a set of predefined roles. For example, all members of your data science team might be given Big-Query `dataViewer` and `jobUser` permissions on data warehousing datasets. This way, if people change jobs, we need to just update their membership in the appropriate groups instead of updating their access to datasets and projects one dataset or project at a time.

One reason to create a custom role is to subtract permissions from the predefined roles. For example, the predefined role `dataEditor` allows the possessor to create, modify, and delete tables. Suppose that you want to allow your data suppliers to create tables but not to modify or delete any existing tables. In that case, you could create a new role named `dataSupplier` and provide it with the specific list of permissions. You would start by creating a YAML file (called, for instance, `dataSupplier.yaml`) with the following contents:

```
title: "Data Supplier"
description: "Can create, but not delete tables"
stage: "ALPHA"
includedPermissions:
- bigquery.datasets.get
- bigquery.tables.list
- bigquery.tables.get
- bigquery.tables.getData
- bigquery.tables.export
- bigquery.datasets.create
- bigquery.tables.create
- bigquery.tables.updateData
```

Then you would run the following `gcloud` command to create the custom role:

```
PROJECT=$(gcloud config get-value project)
gcloud iam roles create dataSupplier --project $PROJECT \
       --file dataSupplier.yaml
```

You can verify the permissions associated with this role by obtaining its current definition using:

```
gcloud iam roles describe dataSupplier --project $PROJECT
```

This works for predefined roles also.

It's a good idea when creating a new role to set its stage to be ALPHA and try it out on a smaller set of users before upgrading the stage to BETA or GA. This way, you can fine-tune the set of permissions (start with the most restrictive set) before rolling it out widely.

Resource

Access to resources is managed individually, resource by resource. An identity does not get the dataViewer role or the bigquery.tables.getData permission on all resources in BigQuery; rather, the permission is granted on specific datasets or tables.

Because the dataViewer role is provided on tables or datasets, it is not possible for someone with just the dataViewer role to obtain information about jobs, for example; jobs are a separate resource and require a different set of permissions. An identity can, of course, have both the role dataViewer and the role jobUser, which would give them the ability to create jobs (including running queries) and cancel self-created jobs in addition to being able to view table data.

As much as possible, avoid permission/role creep; err on the side of providing the least amount of privileges to identities. This includes restricting both the roles and the resources on which they are provided. Balance this against the burden of updating permissions on new resources as they are created. One reasonable compromise is to set trust boundaries that map projects to your organizational structure and set roles at the project level—IAM policies can then propagate down from projects to resources within the project, thus automatically applying to new datasets in the project.

Administering BigQuery

It is possible to administer BigQuery from the BigQuery web UI, using the REST API, or using the bq command-line tool. In this section, we assume that you have the admin role in BigQuery, either by virtue of being the BigQuery point person in your company or by being an admin on the project with the resources (either jobs or datasets) in question. Let's look at common tasks that administrators might need to do, focusing on the bq command line.

Job Management

When a job has been submitted to BigQuery, it goes into three states in succession: PENDING, meaning that it is scheduled but not yet started; RUNNING, meaning that it has started; and either SUCCESS or FAILURE depending on the final status.

You can list all jobs created within the project in the past 24 hours by using the following:

```
NOW=$(date +%s)
START_TIME=$(echo "($NOW - 24*60*60)*1000" | bc)
bq --location=US ls -j -all --min_creation_time $START_TIME
```

bq requires a Unix timestamp in milliseconds, so we obtain the `min_creation_time` by subtracting one day (24*60*60 seconds) from the current timestamp and converting it into milliseconds using the command-line calculator tool, bc.[4]

As soon as you know the job ID, it is possible to cancel[5] a running job:

```
bq --location=US cancel bquxjob_180ae24c_16b04a8d28d
```

Note that you will sometimes have a fully qualified job ID that will include both the project name and the location,[6] for example, from logs (or from the BigQuery web UI). In that case, you can omit the location to the cancel call:

```
bq cancel someproject:US.bquxjob_180ae24c_16b04a8d28d
```

Anyone with the `jobUser` or `user` role has the ability to run and cancel their own jobs; they don't need `admin` access unless it is to list or cancel jobs started by other users.

Authorizing Users

We recommend creating Google groups and adding members to Google groups instead of providing individual users access to BigQuery resources. If you follow this recommendation, you will be authorizing access to resources only to Google groups, and you can do this from the Cloud Console. There are several convenient ways to add and remove multiple users to a Google group. For details, see the G Suite help page (*https://support.google.com/a/answer/6191469?hl=en*).

On a one-off basis, use the Cloud Console IAM page (*https:// console.cloud.google.com/iam-admin/iam*) to provide individual users, service accounts, or Google groups permissions to BigQuery. To share specific resources, in the BigQuery web UI, select the dataset and then click "Share dataset."

Restoring Deleted Records and Tables

If a user has messed up the contents of a table by loading in duplicate data or by deleting necessary records, it is possible to recover as long as it is within seven days. Deleted tables (as opposed to deleted records within existing tables) can be recovered for up to two days only.

---

4 If bc is not already installed in your shell, you can install it using `sudo apt install bc` or a similar installation command.

5 Cancelled jobs are still charged.

6 Recall that BigQuery data is stored in a specific region or multiregion. Queries will need to run where the data is located, and the job metadata is also stored regionally.

To recover the state of a table as it existed 24 hours earlier, for example, you can use SYSTEM_TIME AS OF and the DDL:[7]

```
CREATE OR REPLACE TABLE ch10eu.restored_cycle_stations AS
SELECT
    *
FROM `bigquery-public-data`.london_bicycles.cycle_stations
FOR SYSTEM_TIME AS OF
    TIMESTAMP_SUB(CURRENT_TIMESTAMP(), INTERVAL 24 HOUR)
```

For up to two days, you can also recover a deleted table. For example, let's delete the table you created a moment ago:

```
bq rm ch10eu.restored_cycle_stations
```

Now recover it from a snapshot as of 120 seconds ago:

```
NOW=$(date +%s)
SNAPSHOT=$(echo "($NOW - 120)*1000" | bc)
bq --location=EU cp \
    ch10eu.restored_cycle_stations@$SNAPSHOT \
    ch10eu.restored_table
```

 You can recover a deleted table only if another table with the same ID in the dataset has not been created in the meantime.[8] In particular, this means that you cannot recover a deleted table if it is receiving streamed data and the create-disposition is to create the table if it doesn't exist. Chances are that the streaming pipeline would have created an empty table and started to push rows into it. This is also why you should be careful about using CREATE OR REPLACE TABLE: it makes the table irrecoverable.

Continuous Integration/Continuous Deployment

It might be important to have SQL queries under version control so as to be able to obtain the version of a script as of a certain time and track changes in the script over time. If this is the case, consider using Cloud Source Repositories and Cloud Functions (or Cloud Run if you have more complex dependencies) to execute the queries.

Invoking BigQuery from a Cloud Function

In your Cloud Source Repository, create an *.sql* file containing the BigQuery SQL query and a Python file implementing the Cloud Function and place both under version control. The Cloud Function could then use the BigQuery client library to

---

7 Create the output dataset ch10eu in the EU location first.

8 Also, the encompassing dataset should not have been deleted or re-created. See *https://cloud.google.com/ bigquery/docs/managing-tables#undeletetable*.

submit the query to BigQuery and export results to Google Cloud Storage as long as the query time is less than the timeout of the Cloud Function.[9]

You can create a Cloud Function from the GCP Cloud Console. In the text window, type this code:

```
from google.cloud import bigquery
def query_to_gcs():
client = bigquery.Client()

# Run query and wait for it to complete
query_job = client.query("""
    ...
    """)
query_job.result()

# Extract to GCS, and wait for it to complete
extract_job = client.extract_table(
    query_job.destination, "gs://bucket/file.csv")
extract_job.result()
```

Now, instead of scheduling the query, you will schedule the Cloud Function using Cloud Scheduler (*https://cloud.google.com/scheduler/*).

 Note that the preceding code is invoking `extract_table` on the temporary table created as a result of executing the query. This is a fast way to quickly export the result of a query into a comma-separated values (CSV) file.

Putting table, view, and function creation under version control

Having version control and repeatability is important not just for queries but also for tables, views, models, stored procedures, and functions. It is preferable, therefore, to put all creation code into a script that you can invoke every time you want to re-create the table, view, model, or function in question.

To create a table from a query result, you can use the BigQuery client library and set the job destination to be the desired table:

```
from google.cloud import bigquery
client = bigquery.Client()
sql = """
WITH stations AS (
    SELECT [300, 314, 287] AS closed
)
SELECT
```

---

9 Cloud Functions have a configurable timeout, but the maximum value as of this writing is nine minutes.

```
    station_id
    , (SELECT name FROM `bigquery-public-data`.london_bicycles.cycle_stations WHERE
id=station_id) AS name
FROM
    stations, UNNEST(closed) AS station_id
"""

job_config = bigquery.QueryJobConfig()
job_config.destination = (
client.dataset('ch10eu').table('stations_under_construction'))
query_job = client.query(sql, location='EU', job_config=job_config)
query_job.result() # Waits for the query to finish
```

Here's the equivalent using the DDL approach:

```
CREATE OR REPLACE TABLE -- or TABLE/MODEL/FUNCTION
ch10eu.stations_under_construction
(
    station_id INT64 OPTIONS(description = 'Station ID'),
    name string OPTIONS(description = 'Official station name')
)
OPTIONS(
    description = 'Stations in London.',
    labels=[("pii", "none")] -- Must be lowercase.
)
AS

WITH stations AS (
    SELECT [300, 314, 287] AS closed
)

SELECT
    station_id
    , (SELECT name FROM `bigquery-public-data`.london_bicycles.cycle_stations WHERE
id=station_id) AS name
FROM
    stations, UNNEST(closed) AS station_id
```

Note in this example how the table and column descriptions are stored directly within the CREATE statements in version control. If you already have existing Big-Query tables, you can query the list of tables and columns in your metadata and programmatically create those SQL DDL statements through functions (*https:// cloud.google.com/bigquery/docs/information-schema-tables#advanced_example*).

 Be careful about using scheduled Cloud Functions that create or replace tables: if you have a Cloud Function that schedules and reruns the previous statement to REPLACE the table, any changes to the table (including updated rows and schema descriptions) will be overwritten.

Slot Reservations

There are, broadly, two different pricing plans for BigQuery based on what you value more: predictable cost or efficiency.

Flat-rate pricing is predictable. You buy a certain number of slots and pay the same amount regardless of how many queries you submit. This is great for enterprises that want predictable costs. The drawback is that if you buy 1000 slots, and have a spiky workload that usually uses 500 slots and sometimes needs 1500 slots, slots go unused when you are using only 500 and queries run slower when it would have been nicer to have 1500 slots.

On-demand pricing is efficient both in terms of price and in terms of performance. You pay for the amount of data processed by your queries. This is the original cloud promise—pay for exactly what you use. It is perfect for spiky workloads since you never pay for unused slots, and your queries use all the compute power available at the time they run. However, even though you can set up cost controls, per-day limits on price, etc. to limit your exposure, many enterprises don't like this because (a) it is hard to budget for something that varies month-to-month, and (b) Cost controls and daily limits add friction.

In general, we find that larger enterprises prefer flat-rate and smaller digital natives prefer on-demand pricing.

Flex slots

Assume that you are on flat-rate pricing because you want predictable costs, but you have a spiky workload. Moreover, you know exactly when you need that extra capacity.

Let's say that you train a recommendations model once a day and that is when you need 1500 slots. The rest of the time, you need only 500 slots. Wouldn't it be nice to buy a 500-slot flat-rate plan, but buy an extra 1000 slots for just an hour every day that the recommendations model training happens? That way, your regular workload is unaffected and the recommendations model has 1000 slots so it is not running slower.

This is called flex slots. You can buy flex slots for as little as 60 seconds. Most commonly, flex slots are used to add flexibility on top of flat-rate pricing. However, flex slots also allow an organization that uses on-demand pricing to create a hybrid pricing model, where a few tasks are paid in terms of their computational overhead.

Commitments

You can purchase dedicated BigQuery slots by procuring commitments. These commitments can be annual, monthly, or flex. An annual or monthly commitment can not be canceled until the time period is complete. A flex slot can be canceled after 60 seconds.

You can purchase slots from the web console, using the REST API or from the command line. For example, to purchase 5000 flex slots in the US, the IT department might do:

```
IT_PROJECT=... # The billing account of this project is charged
bq mk --project_id=${IT_PROJECT} --location=US \
    --capacity_commitment --slots=5000 --plan=FLEX
```

Reservations

Optionally, the committed BigQuery slots can be placed into reservations for workload management purposes. To put 4000 of the purchased slots into a reservation named bi_team, we can do:

```
bq mk --reservation --project_id=${IT_PROJECT} --slots=4000 \
    --location=US bi_team
```

Organizations that choose flat-rate billing for BigQuery can divide their reservation into sub-reservations , and assign one or more projects to each of those sub-reservations. For instance, after purchasing 5,000 slots, you might decide to allocate several of the BI team's projects to the sub-reservation of 4,000 slots for "bi_team," and assign other projects to a different sub-reservation of 1,000 slots for "ETL", as shown in Figure 10-1. When all of the slots are in use, the BI projects are limited to those 4,000 slots, whereas the ETL projects are limited to 1,000 slots. If the current BI workloads are using up only 2,000 slots, the ETL workloads can use up the remaining 3,000 slots (and vice versa).

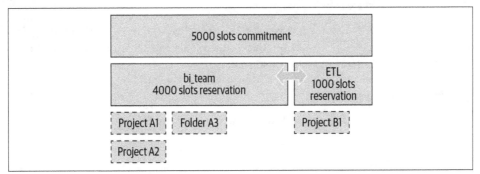

Figure 10-1. A slots commitment can be divided among several reservations. Projects and folders can be assigned to these reservations.

A common strategy is to set up a reservation for high-priority projects only—this reservation is the minimum slot count you want a project to get. If there are idle slots available in your reservation, they are available to all the projects in your organization. If the reservation is getting fully used, each high-priority project will get the minimum specified by its reservation and lower-priority projects will be restricted to left-over capacity in the root reservation. If the reservations fully use up the total slot count paid for through the reservation, the fairness scheduler kicks in and each running query will get a proportionate amount. This proportion is divided fairly among the reservations, then among the projects in each reservation, and finally among the running queries within each project.

Here's how the IT department can allow one of the BI team's projects to use a reservation:

```
BI_PROJECT=... # Queries from this project can use reservation
bq mk --reservation_assignment \
    --reservation_id=${IT_PROJECT}:US.bi_team \
    --job_type=QUERY --assignee_type=PROJECT \
    --assignee_id=${BI_PROJECT}
```

Cost/Billing Exports

It is possible to export your daily usage of GCP services as well as cost estimates automatically throughout the day to a BigQuery dataset. Watch out, though: this billing export will include your usage of BigQuery as well!

To enable billing exports, in the GCP Cloud Console, start at the Billing section, select your billing account and project, select the BigQuery dataset[10] to which to export the billing data, and then enable BigQuery export.

The billing data is loaded into BigQuery at regular intervals, so it could be a few hours before you see anything. The frequency of updates in BigQuery varies depending on the GCP services you're using.

As with any BigQuery table, you can examine the schema of the exported billing data in BigQuery and figure out what queries you can run and what dashboards you can populate. Here are a few places to get started.

Costs by month by product

To get the monthly invoice amount by product, use this query:

```
SELECT
  invoice.month
, product
, ROUND(SUM(cost)
        + SUM(IFNULL((SELECT SUM(c.amount) FROM UNNEST(credits) c),
            0))
        , 2) AS monthly_cost
```

---

10 Create a dataset if necessary.

```
FROM ch10eu.gcp_billing_export_v1_XXXXXX_XXXXXX_XXXXXX
GROUP BY 1, 2
ORDER BY 1 ASC, 2 ASC
```

The monthly cost is the sum of the costs for that product corrected by the sum of the credits.

Visualizing the billing report

As illustrated in Figure 10-2, a starter Data Studio dashboard for visualizing the billing data is available.

For details on how to make a copy and start working in Data Studio, see *https:// cloud.google.com/billing/docs/how-to/visualize-data*.

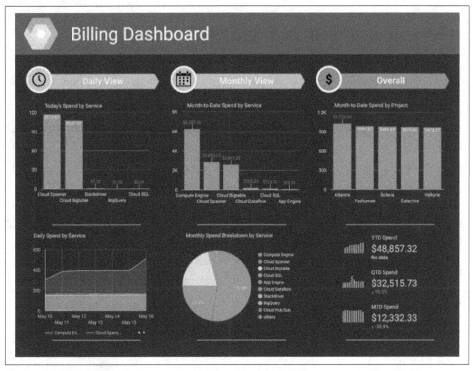

Figure 10-2. Example Data Studio dashboard of the billing export data in BigQuery

Labels

Although obtaining a cost breakdown by product is useful, what you often want is a cost breakdown by cost center within your organization. To enable this level of detail in your billing reports, you need to apply labels (which are key/value pairs) to your GCP resources. Then each row in the billing export will contain values for two columns, `labels.key` and `labels.value`, that correspond to the label applied to the GCP resource usage for which you're being billed.

If the labels are based on team or cost center, the key could be `team` and the value could be `marketing` or `research`. Labels could also be based on environment (e.g., key=environment, value=production, or value=test), application, or component.

You can assign labels to GCP resources like Compute Engine virtual machines (VMs), Dataproc clusters, or Dataflow jobs. Of course, you can also assign labels to BigQuery datasets, tables, models, and even query jobs.

Here's how to apply the label "environment:learning" to the dataset ch10eu:

```
bq update --set_label environment:learning ch10eu
```

You can also apply labels to table and views in a similar way, but (as of this writing) table/view labels do not show up in the billing data:

```
bq update --set_label environment:learning ch10eu.restored_table
```

It also possible to assign a label when you submit a job through the command line:

```
bq query --label environment:learning --nouse_legacy_sql 'SELECT 17'
```

When submitting through the REST API, populate the `labels` property for the job resource.

Then the billing export will reflect query costs, and you can aggregate costs by label for the purpose of apportioning costs between environments, or cost centers, or any other label key:

```
SELECT
  invoice.month
  , label.value
  , ROUND(SUM(cost)
          + SUM(IFNULL((SELECT SUM(c.amount) FROM UNNEST(credits) c),
                0))
          , 2) AS monthly_cost
FROM
  ch10eu.gcp_billing_export_v1_XXXXXX_XXXXXX_XXXXXX
  , UNNEST(labels) AS label
WHERE
  label.key = 'environment'
GROUP BY 1, 2
ORDER BY 1 ASC, 2 ASC
```

Dashboards, Monitoring, and Audit Logging

A key aspect of security is to be able to verify that the security measures are being effective. Observability of all the resources deployed is very important.

Cloud Security Command Center

The Cloud Security Command Center (SCC) provides a comprehensive security management and data-risk platform for GCP. By providing visibility into what assets you have and what security state they are in, Cloud SCC makes it easier to prevent, detect, and respond to threats. There are built-in threat detectors that can alert you to suspicious activity.

You can access Cloud SCC from the GCP Cloud Console Security Command Center Marketplace page and launch asset discovery. After your projects have been scanned, you can use the Cloud SCC dashboard to look for common problems like an open port 22 (for Secure Shell [SSH]). After this, asset discovery runs at least once per day.

Stackdriver monitoring and audit logging

You can use Stackdriver to monitor BigQuery resources. These include visualizations of metrics such as overall query times, the number of slots available, and more. Big-Query also automatically sends audit logs to Stackdriver Logging. Stackdriver Logging allows users to filter and export messages to other services, including Cloud Pub/Sub, Cloud Storage, and BigQuery.

In addition to providing long-term log retention functionality, log exports to Big-Query are recommended as a way to provide the ability to do aggregated analysis on logs data. Here is a query that estimates costs (before any discounts are applied) by user identity (*https://cloud.google.com/bigquery/docs/reference/auditlogs/*):

```
WITH data as
  (
   SELECT
        protopayload_auditlog.authenticationInfo.principalEmail as principalEmail,
        protopayload_auditlog.servicedata_v1_bigquery.jobCompletedEvent AS
jobCompletedEvent
     FROM
        ch10.cloudaudit_googleapis_com_data_access_2019*
  )
  SELECT
    principalEmail,
    SUM(jobCompletedEvent.job.jobStatistics.totalBilledBytes)/POWER(2, 40)) AS
Estimated_USD_Cost
   FROM
     data
   WHERE
     jobCompletedEvent.eventName = 'query_job_completed'
   GROUP BY principalEmail
   ORDER BY Estimated_USD_Cost DESC
```

BigQuery audit logs are reported as the `protoPayload.metadata` within a LogEntry message. They are organized into three streams: admin activity, system events, and data access. The admin activity includes events such as job insertions and completions. System events are events such as the TableDeletion event logged when a table or partition expires and is removed. The data access stream contains information about new jobs, jobs that changed state, table data changes, and table data reading.

Availability, Disaster Recovery, and Encryption

BigQuery architecture contributes significantly to its reliability. For instance, the serverless aspect of the service means that virtually any hardware component can fail and it will have little to no impact on BigQuery's ability to run queries. Unlike many systems that are tied to particular virtual machines (VMs) or nodes, BigQuery runs in a giant shared pool of servers and can redirect traffic nearly instantaneously from one location to another.

Zones, Regions, and Multiregions

In GCP, there are three different types of service locations. *Zones* are compute clusters, generally located within a single building. Zones have fairly high availability, but if there is a major hardware failure (there's a fire, or a transformer gets fried, for example), the zone can go offline. Sometimes services have problems within a single zone that aren't related to hardware. A high rate of requests could cause some service to crash, and that will cause problems with dependent services. Resilient services, such as BigQuery, are designed to withstand any zonal problem seamlessly.

Regions, on the other hand, are metro-wide locations that consist of multiple zones with uncorrelated failures. A region tends to be spread across multiple buildings within a large campus. In general, it is very rare for an entire region to be taken offline. Natural disasters can, however, cause regions to go offline. Predictable natural disasters, like hurricanes, can generally be preceded by an ordered shutdown of the region so that no data is lost. Unpredictable disasters, like earthquakes, could cause services to lose data in a region as well as prevent the region from starting up again when the disaster has passed.

Multiregions are the most resilient; they generally imply some flexibility in their location, being spread over multiple datacenters separated by hundreds of miles. For example, the EU multiregion consists only of physical datacenters that are part of the European Union. Which specific datacenters? Is the Frankfurt datacenter in the EU? How about the Finland one? Some services, like Google Cloud Storage, are explicit about which regions comprise the multiregions. Others, like BigQuery, give only vague guidelines to where multiregional data is located in order to preserve flexibility in both compute and data placement.

BigQuery and Failure Handling

One way of predicting how well a service will handle a particular type of failure is to note how often the failure happens; if failures happen very infrequently, the service is usually untested and liable to have bugs or other problems. Services at Google are designed to be able to handle virtually any type of hardware and even software failure and keep running. Not only are they designed this way, but they are tested rigorously to make sure the failure paths are exercised routinely. Let's discuss some different types of failures and how BigQuery responds.

Disk failures

Spinning disks have moving parts, and like many things with moving parts, they fail pretty frequently. Because of the way data is encoded in Colossus (the storage infrastructure that underlies BigQuery; see Chapter 6) using erasure encoding, lots of disks can fail without any loss of data. If you have 100,000 disks, you can expect that dozens will fail every day. If you consider that routine maintenance can cause some disks to be unavailable, the number is probably in the hundreds. If there is a power outage, when disks start up again you can lose a lot more. Even with all of these factors, losing data due to hardware failure in BigQuery would be extremely rare.[11]

When a disk fails, Colossus detects it and replicates the data to another disk. Google Datacenter Hardware Operations staff will remove the disk and securely destroy it. Software and services using that disk will not notice any disruption, other than certain requests perhaps taking a few milliseconds longer to complete.

Machine failures

Despite all attempts to keep servers up and running for long periods of time, they crash. Operating systems have bugs, cosmic rays corrupt memory, CPUs die, power supplies fail, software has memory leaks, and lots of other things can go wrong. The common approach in server software is to add redundancy and hardening to prevent these types of failures. Expensive servers have backup power supplies and hot-swappable memory and CPUs, so the server never needs to go down.

Google, as a philosophy, takes a different approach. Google datacenters are set up so that they expect any machine to die at any time. Software must be written in a way that handles this. In order to allow any machine to die at any time, Google invented a number of scale-out distributed systems, like MapReduce, Google File System (GFS, the precursor to Colossus), and Dremel.

---

11 Of course, extenuating circumstances, code bugs, natural disasters, and so on could cause data loss. But as designed, the probability of data loss is very low. If you had 1 PB of data stored and every day 1,000 disks in a single zone crashed, after a million years, there would be less than 0.01% chance that you'd lose data.

BigQuery servers crash all the time. When you have hundreds of thousands or millions of independent workers running, some of those are going to hit problems. Virtually any BigQuery server can crash at any time and users will not see more than a small hiccup in their queries. The cluster management software that runs Google datacenters, Borg, will restart any tasks that don't respond to a health check within a few seconds, sometimes on a different machine. For the most part, even the software running in the query engine doesn't notice these problems; it just retries on a different task and keeps going.

Even larger problems, like rack failures or network switch failures, are handled transparently. Because of the scale of the datacenter clusters, if a rack or switch fails, it will affect only a few of the tasks running the service, so the service can route around the problem. Nobody gets paged, except perhaps the hardware operations personnel in the datacenter who will need to address the issue directly. But the service operations (SRE) staff sleep soundly.

Zonal failures

So what happens when there are larger failures in which the built-in self-healing can no longer automatically handle the problem? To be clear, these failures are pretty rare. Zones are designed for high resilience to hardware and network failures. Anything that can cause the zone to go offline, like network switches or transformers, usually has a redundant backup. But there have been cases in which someone cuts the wrong fiber cable with a backhoe, or transformers catch fire, and it causes a zone-wide outage.

Some services, like Google Compute Engine, are, as of this writing, tied to a single availability zone. If that zone goes down, the VM instances in that zone go down. BigQuery, on the other hand, is designed to be able to handle almost all zonal failures. In BigQuery, all Cloud Projects have a primary and a secondary location. If there is an outage in the primary location, BigQuery will seamlessly fail over to the secondary location.

There are two types of zonal failures: *soft* and *hard*. Soft failures mean that there are problems in the zone but things are still progressing, perhaps with degraded capacity. Soft failures are often the result of a software failure, rather than a hardware issue. Perhaps quota servers are failing, or Bigtable is stuck, or the BigQuery scheduler is taking too long to schedule. Hard failures mean that the zone is down. Maybe it had a power failure or some sort of unrecoverable hardware issue.

BigQuery reacts to soft failures by proactively *draining* the zone. A drain means that new queries are sent somewhere else, but existing queries are allowed to continue. New requests are routed to the secondary zone. Queries that are in progress might be allowed to continue; if, however, the outage is severe enough, they will be restarted in the new secondary zone.

Soft failures happen fairly frequently. BigQuery operates in dozens of availability zones around the world, and the odds of some service behaving badly on some zone somewhere is pretty high. The good news is that this allows BigQuery to exercise failover code, and users almost never actually notice any hiccup.

Hard failures are much rarer; they generally mean that the entire zone is undergoing severe problems. In the event of a hardware zonal failure, users might notice disruption; existing queries will be cancelled and restarted in the new zone, for example, so they might take up to twice as long to complete. And particularly bad zonal failures could mean that recent data has not been replicated to the secondary zone, and will be unavailable until the zone is brought back online. In the event this happens, queries to the affected tables will fail. BigQuery would rather fail queries than return inconsistent data.

Regional failures

The next level of failure type is a failure in which an entire region goes offline. This is much rarer than a zonal outage. Like zones, regions can have soft failures in which the entire region needs to be neatly shut down. Regions that are in the path of a hurricane might be shut down cleanly before the hurricane hits. By going into shutdown before the arrival of the storm, Google can minimize the chance of data loss when the region is restarted, or in the rare event that the region is damaged. A power outage shouldn't cause a region to go down because there are backup systems in place, but if the power outage lasts too long, the backup systems can run out of capacity, and so an orderly shutdown of the region would be initiated.

Regions can have hard failures, too, but these are even more rare. Like many "black swan"–type events,[12] it is difficult to estimate how rare they are in practice. A catastrophic earthquake could take down a region with little or no warning. Other extreme weather events or natural disasters could also occur unexpectedly. A hard region failure could cause damage to hardware and could mean that data not replicated offsite could be lost.

As of this writing, single-region BigQuery locations (`asia-east1`, or `europe-north1`, for example) do not store a physical copy in another site. In general, the reason is that there might not be a place to store a backup copy in another location without violating customers' requirements for their data. For example, Singapore is an island only about 30 miles across; if a customer requires that their data is not stored outside of Singapore for regulatory purposes, there isn't much opportunity to store the data

---

12 These are unexpected and very rare events of large magnitude and consequence; the name refers to a theory put forward by Nassim Nicholas Taleb in his book, *The Black Swan: The Impact of the Highly Improbable* (Random House).

elsewhere. However, before making any durability assumptions about your data, you should check the up-to-date documentation provided by Google.

Multiregional BigQuery locations, like the US and the EU, store a backup copy offsite in another region. In the event of a catastrophic failure of a region, the data would be safe. However, it might take some time before that backup becomes available.

Durability, Backups, and Disaster Recovery

To summarize the replication story for BigQuery:

- Multiregional data is replicated to at least two regions (single-region data is only in one).
- All data is replicated to two availability zones.
- Within an availability zone, data is encoded using erasure encoding.

The offsite backups are also protected by a secondary mechanism to prevent accidental deletion; they use a feature of disk firmware that prevents deletion until a certain period of time has passed. This means that if there were a code bug in BigQuery that overzealously deleted data, low-level firmware systems on the disk would prevent the data from being physically deleted immediately.

If data is accidentally deleted by a customer, BigQuery's time-travel feature can come in handy. Users can query the table as of a time before the data was deleted, using the SYSTEM_TIME AS OF syntax (see Chapter 8). Moreover, you can copy the table as of a particular time by using `tablename@timestamp` in the copy job.

This technique of copying the old snapshot of the data is useful if you need to undelete a table. To undelete, you should copy the old table name as of a timestamp that the table existed to a new destination table. Note that if you delete a table and then re-create one with the same name, it will become unrecoverable, so you should be careful. As of this writing, time travel for deleted tables is available for only 48 hours after the table was deleted, which is shorter than the normal seven-day time travel period.

Privacy and Encryption

Google takes security and privacy very seriously. All data in BigQuery is encrypted at rest and encrypted when it is transferred over the network. Encryption on disk is done transparently through Colossus file encryption. Streaming data is encrypted in Bigtable or in log files. Metadata is encrypted in Spanner. Network traffic is encrypted transparently through the use of Google's internal Remote Procedure Call (RPC) protocols. Someone with physical disk access or with a network tap wouldn't be able to access data in the clear.

Access transparency

Google takes a number of steps to safeguard access to the data. To ensure the safety and reliable running of the system, only a small number of on-call engineers can get access to user data. The Access Transparency program in GCP means that whenever someone at Google accesses your data, you are notified through audit log records. It is generally as simple as that; if someone reads your data, you can find out about it.

Virtual Private Cloud Service Controls

Virtual Private Cloud Service Controls (VPC-SC) is a mouthful to pronounce, but it is a mechanism that gives you fine-grained control over how services can be accessed and where data can flow within GCP. For example, you can limit BigQuery access to a narrow range of IP addresses from your company's network. Or you can ensure control over how data flows between services by preventing data export from BigQuery to Google Cloud Storage. Alternatively, you might allow export to Google Cloud Storage, but only to Cloud Storage buckets that are owned by your organization.

VPC-SC is not merely a BigQuery feature; it is a feature that works across a number of GCP products. This lets you create one overall policy describing data exfiltration and movement policies. You might decide that you don't want people to access Big-Query at all (that seems like a shame, though). For more information on VPC, check out the Google Cloud Documentation (*https://cloud.google.com/vpc/docs/*).

Customer-Managed Encryption Keys

All data is encrypted at rest in BigQuery, but what if you want to make sure that your data is encrypted with your own keys? In these cases, you can use Customer-Managed Encryption Keys (CMEK) in BigQuery. You can manage your keys in Cloud KMS, GCP's central key management service. You can then designate datasets or tables that you want to be encrypted using those keys.

BigQuery uses multiple layers of key wrapping; that is, the master keys aren't exposed outside of KMS. Every CMEK-protected table has a wrapped key as part of the table metadata. When BigQuery accesses the table, it sends a request to Cloud KMS to unwrap the key. The unwrapped table key is then used to unwrap separate keys for each file. There are a number of advantages to this key-wrapping protocol that reduce the risk should an unwrapped key be leaked. If you have an unwrapped file key, you can't read any other files. If you have an unwrapped table key, you can only unwrap file keys after you pass access control checks. And Cloud KMS never discloses the master key. If you delete the key from KMS, the other keys can never be unwrapped (so be careful with your keys!).

Regulatory Compliance

Most organizations are subject to government regulations of one form or another, and your organization probably defines compliance requirements for software and analysis teams so as to follow those regulations and stay on the right side of the law. In this section, we look at BigQuery features that can help you provide support for such regulatory compliance. But remember: it is always your responsibility to work with your legal counsel to determine whether implementing any of these tools and capabilities will satisfy your regulatory or compliance requirements.

Data Locality

Many governments around the world regulate where data can be stored, and Big-Query enforces that queries on any dataset are run only in a datacenter where that dataset is available. Hence, controlling data locality is done at the time a dataset is created. For example, here's how to create a dataset in the `asia-east2` region (located in Hong Kong):

```
bq --location=asia-east2 mk --dataset ch10hk
```

Two types of locations are supported by BigQuery: regional and multiregional. The Hong Kong region is an example of a regional location and represents a specific geographic place. The other type of location is a multiregional location (like the US or the EU[13]) that contains two or more regional locations. For an up-to-date list of supported locations, refer to the BigQuery documentation (*https://cloud.google.com/bigquery/docs/locations*).

As explained in Chapter 6, BigQuery determines the location to run a job based on the project defaults, reservations, and datasets referenced in the request. It is also possible to explicitly specify the location in which to run a job, whether the job is submitted through the BigQuery web UI (set Processing Location in Query Settings), the REST API (specify the `location` property in the `jobReference` section), or the bq command-line tool (specify `--location`). If a query cannot be run in the location specified (such as if the location is specified as US but the data is in the EU), Big-Query returns an error.

Moving data directly between regions is not currently possible other than with the BigQuery Data Transfer Service, but there is one exception: you can move data from a US multiregional Cloud Storage bucket to a BigQuery dataset in any region or multiregional location. If you are loading data into BigQuery from a regional Cloud Storage bucket, the bucket must be colocated with the BigQuery dataset (for example,

---

13 As of this writing, data stored in the EU multiregion is not stored in Zurich or London.

both need to be in `asia-east2`) unless the bucket in question is in the US multire-gion.

If you cannot use the BigQuery Data Transfer Service, moving BigQuery data between locations will involve a few hops: export the data from BigQuery to Google Cloud Storage in the same region, transfer the data to Cloud Storage in the target region, and load it into a BigQuery dataset. Note that you will incur extra storage costs for the time period that you have data in Cloud Storage, and network egress charges for transferring data between regions in Cloud Storage.

Restricting Access to Subsets of Data

To restrict access to an entire dataset, you can use IAM. But in many cases, tables might contain sensitive data and what you want is to restrict access to parts of a table. You can do that with authorized views or dynamic filters, or through fine-grained access control.

Authorized views

An authorized view allows you to use an SQL query to restrict the columns or rows that the users are able to query. For example, suppose that you have a set of users who are allowed to view only a specific subset of columns and rows from our `london_bicy cles` dataset. You could do this by sharing with them, not the original dataset, but the dataset `ch10eu`, which contains this view:

```
CREATE OR REPLACE VIEW ch10eu.authorized_view_300 AS
SELECT
  * EXCEPT (bike_id, end_station_priority_id)
FROM
  [PROJECTID].ch07eu.cycle_hire_clustered
WHERE
  start_station_id = 300 OR end_station_id = 300
```

Now users granted access to this view will not be able to access the `bike_id` column or information from any stations other than the one whose ID is 300. Grant users access to this view by sharing the dataset that it is part of. From the BigQuery web UI, select the target dataset (`ch10eu`) and click Share Dataset, and then share it with the desired user or Google group. To try it out, share this dataset with a second Google Account you have access to with the `BigQuery User` role, as demonstrated in Figure 10-3.

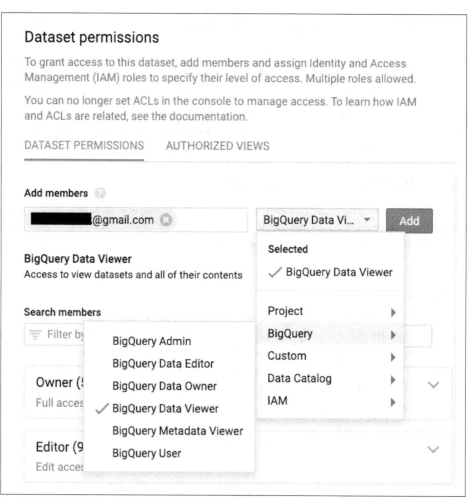

Figure 10-3. Providing access to the dataset (ch10eu) containing the authorized view

However, the authorized view itself needs to be able to access the original dataset. You can do that by selecting the source dataset (ch07eu) in the BigQuery web UI, clicking Share Dataset, and then, in the Dataset permissions panel, choosing the authorized view to allow, as shown in Figure 10-4.

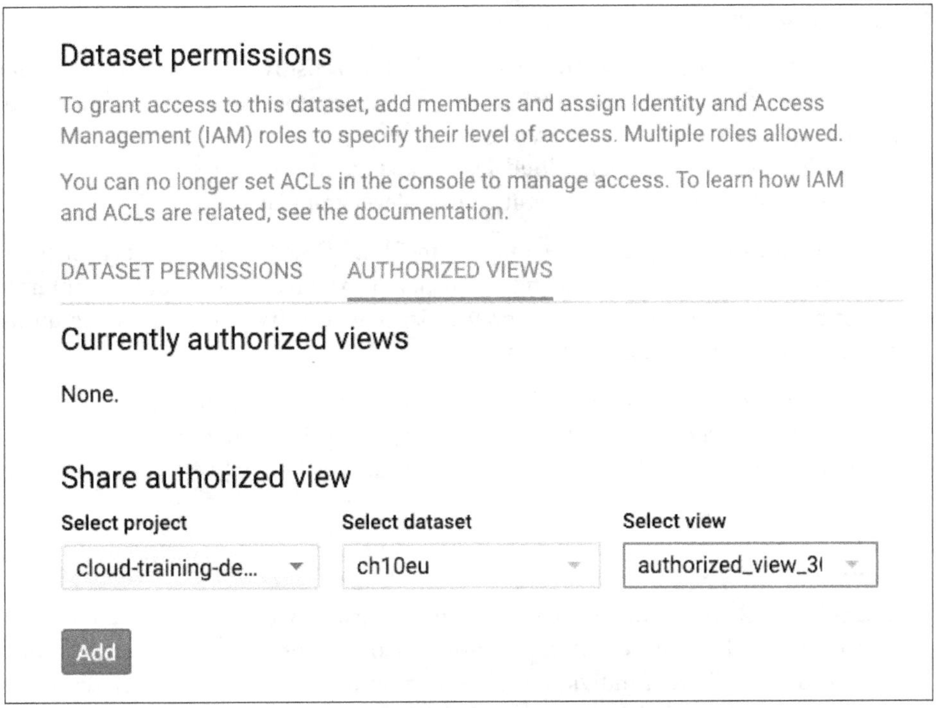

Dataset permissions

To grant access to this dataset, add members and assign Identity and Access Management (IAM) roles to specify their level of access. Multiple roles allowed.

You can no longer set ACLs in the console to manage access. To learn how IAM and ACLs are related, see the documentation.

DATASET PERMISSIONS   AUTHORIZED VIEWS

Currently authorized views

None.

Share authorized view

Select project

cloud-training-de...   ▾

Select dataset

ch10eu   ▾

Select view

authorized_view_3(▾

Add

Figure 10-4. Providing the authorized view in `ch10eu` *access to the source dataset in* `ch07eu`

Now when you visit the following URL (replace [PROJECT] by your project name):

```
https://console.cloud.google.com/bigquery?p=[PROJECT]&d=ch10eu&page=dataset
```

in a window where you are logged in as the other Google account, you will be able to view the dataset ch10eu, but not the dataset ch07eu. You will also be able to query the view:

```
SELECT AVG(duration)
FROM [PROJECT].ch10eu.authorized_view_300
```

Note that this average duration will be over trips that started or ended at station ID 300 because of the way that the view is constructed.

> Authorized views are simple only as long as you don't have layered views (views calling views calling views...). When you have layered views, the SQL effectively contains references to many tables, and those tables will often reside in different datasets. This can become challenging to administer because the Access Control Lists (ACLs) now need to be chained across all the views/datasets.

Column-level security

Sensitive data can often be scattered alongside less sensitive data within the same dataset, and managing the appropriate access to that sensitive data becomes challenging if you only look at table, dataset, or project-level permissions. BigQuery column-level security, available through Cloud Data Catalog, lets you set access controls on data classes, abstracted by policy tags at column-level granularity.

The way it works is that you create a tag set in Cloud Data Catalog and tag sensitive columns across all your datasets with that label. For example, you could tag a column as PII or related to health, and then apply consistent security policies to all columns that contain health-related information.

Policy tag hierarchies are supported. Tags in the root nodes include all the permissions for tags at the leaf nodes. If a "salary" tag is nested below a general "human_resources" tag, then anyone who can access human_resources data can access salary data.

Table Access Control

It is possible to share a table or view with specific users without sharing the dataset that contains it. This can be less cumbersome than authorized views when all what you want to do is share a individual table with an outside contributor or segregate access control at the individual table level. Authorized views, on the other hand, are more flexible in that they allow you to join multiple tables and reshape the data before sharing it.

Sharing a table, like sharing a dataset, can be accomplished through the web UI, through the REST API, or through the various client libraries.

Note that table-level access controls are not checked when querying wildcard tables. Therefore, don't set table-level access control on an individual wildcard table. Share the containing dataset instead.

Dynamic filtering based on user

Earlier in this section, we built a view that filters the full dataset to show a subset of columns and rows to anyone who has access to that view. But what if you want to filter the rows in the table based on who the logged-in user is? To accomplish that, use the built-in function SESSION_USER, as shown in the example that follows.

To illustrate, suppose that you want to create a view to flag the top 10 transactions over $1,000,000 for manual review, but you want to restrict it to the transactions from the same company as the viewer:[14]

```
CREATE OR REPLACE VIEW ecommerce.vw_large_transactions
OPTIONS(
  description="large transactions for review",
  labels=[('org_unit','loss_prevention')],
  expiration_timestamp=TIMESTAMP_ADD(CURRENT_TIMESTAMP(), INTERVAL 90 DAY)
)
AS

SELECT
  visitorId,
  REGEXP_EXTRACT(SESSION_USER(), r'@(.+)') AS user_domain,
  REGEXP_EXTRACT(visitorEmailAddress, r'@(.+)') AS customer_domain,
  date,
  totals.transactions,
  totals.transactionRevenue,
  totals.totalTransactionRevenue,
  totals.timeOnScreen

FROM `bigquery-public-data`.google_analytics_sample.ga_sessions_20170801

WHERE
  (totals.totalTransactionRevenue / 1000000) > 1000
  AND REGEXP_EXTRACT(visitorEmailAddress, r'@(.+)') =
      REGEXP_EXTRACT(SESSION_USER(), r'@(.+)')
ORDER BY totals.totalTransactionRevenue DESC
LIMIT 10
```

Notice that the view filters the transactions to reflect only transactions from the same domain as the viewer, so that someone from @example.com can review large transactions from @example.com but not those from @acme.com.

Similarly, we can also use the @@project_id system variable in scripts. This can be useful to distinguish based on which project is running the query.

Removing All Transactions Related to a Single Individual

Suppose that you are storing user transaction data in BigQuery and receive a request to remove all records of transactions by userId=xyz from the data warehouse. There are two ways you might be able to accomplish this (always check with your legal counsel whether this method is sufficient in your jurisdiction if the removal is pursuant to a legal requirement): using DML, and using crypto-shredding.

---

14 The referenced dataset is public but, for PII reasons, doesn't include visitor email addresses. So the query won't work as-is. However, it is illustrative.

DML

You can use DML to `DELETE` the rows in each table that contain user data:

```
DELETE someds.user_transactions
WHERE
  userId = 'xyz'
```

Make sure to also delete the rows in any and all of your backups and temporary tables. The deleted rows are recoverable for up to seven days, so if there is a time limit within which the erasure must be carried out, make sure to start at least seven days earlier. As discussed in Chapter 8, it is more efficient to batch up these sorts of deletes and remove records for a group of users using a `MERGE`.

Crypto-shredding

The second way to carry out erasure of records is to plan for it by assigning a unique encryption key to each `userId` and encrypting all sensitive data corresponding to a user with that encryption key. This has the advantage of maintaining user privacy as well. To remove the records for a user, you can simply delete the encryption key. This approach has the advantage that it immediately makes the user records unusable (as long as the deleted key is not recoverable) in all the tables in your data warehouse, including backups and temporary tables.

As an illustration, assume that each bike in the `london_bicycles` dataset is a "person" for whom we want to remove all data. In particular, we do not want to expose the stations that the bike is traveling between at any point in time.

The first step is to create a table of a keyset for each distinct `bike_id` in the dataset:

```
CREATE OR REPLACE TABLE ch10eu.encrypted_bike_keys AS
WITH bikes AS (
  SELECT
    DISTINCT bike_id
  FROM
    `bigquery-public-data`.london_bicycles.cycle_hire
)
SELECT
  bike_id, KEYS.NEW_KEYSET('AEAD_AES_GCM_256') AS keyset
FROM
  bikes
```

Now the `encrypted_bike_keys` table looks as follows, with a keyset for each distinct `bike_id` in the original dataset:

Row	bike_id	keyset
1	3792	CJ/erfEIEmQKWAowdHlwZS5nb29nbGVhcGlzLmNvbS9nb29nbGUuY3J5cHRvLnRpbmsuQWVzR2N0S2V5IlalBObdZJ8sfaEzaN8RyShvuCZL5rOOXf7EztsBLB9V1tMGAEQARif3q3xCCAB
2	5331	CKSmz/ILEmQKWAowdHlwZS5nb29nbGVhcGlzLmNvbS9nb29nbGUuY3J5cHRvLnRpbmsuQWVzR2N0S2V5IlalKtZqxsil9t41Sv6lTKAWEi/wxLSOcizdbCDWVPpcl8JGAEQARikps/yCyAB

We can use this keyset to encrypt any individual's data in the cycle_hire data (in our case, let's assume that data includes the stations the bike is traveling between as well as the specific timestamps). First, we create a pair of helper functions to encrypt the individual's data because some of the sensitive columns are integers and other columns are strings:

```
CREATE TEMPORARY FUNCTION encrypt_int(keyset BYTES, data INT64, trip_start
TIMESTAMP) AS (
    AEAD.ENCRYPT(keyset, CAST(data AS STRING), CAST(trip_start AS STRING))
);
CREATE TEMPORARY FUNCTION encrypt_str(keyset BYTES, data STRING, trip_start
TIMESTAMP) AS (
    AEAD.ENCRYPT(keyset, data, CAST(trip_start AS STRING))
);
```

Then we can join against the encrypted keys using the bike_id to get the encryption keyset to use for each row and invoke the encryption helper functions:

```
CREATE OR REPLACE TABLE ch10eu.encrypted_cycle_hire AS

SELECT
    cycle_hire.* EXCEPT(start_station_id, end_station_id,
      start_station_name, end_station_name)
    , encrypt_int(keyset, start_station_id, start_date) AS start_station_id
    , encrypt_int(keyset, end_station_id, start_date) AS end_station_id
    , encrypt_str(keyset, start_station_name, start_date) AS start_station_name
    , encrypt_str(keyset, end_station_name, start_date) AS end_station_name
FROM
    `bigquery-public-data`.london_bicycles.cycle_hire
JOIN
    ch10eu.encrypted_bike_keys
USING (bike_id)
```

This table was built by encrypting each column of sensitive data (here, start_sta tion_id, end_station_id, start_station_name, and end_station_name) by a key set unique to the bike_id (recall that the bike_id is the "person" whose privacy we are preserving). The third argument to the ENCRYPT function is "extra" data that can be used to ensure that decryption is allowed only in context. Here, we are using the start_date as the context. Had we not done this, it would have been possible for someone who is provided access to the table to swap in a different row corresponding to this bike and get the plain text of the bike's location. Now, because the context (`start_date`) is different, this sort of attack by an insider will not be possible.[15]

To query the encrypted table, you need to decrypt the data before querying. For example, to find stations with the longest duration rentals, you would need to do the following:

```
CREATE TEMPORARY FUNCTION
  decrypt(keyset BYTES, encrypted BYTES, trip_start TIMESTAMP) AS (
    AEAD.DECRYPT_STRING(keyset, encrypted, CAST(trip_start AS STRING))
);

WITH duration_by_station AS (
  SELECT
      duration
      , decrypt(keyset, start_station_name, start_date) AS start_station_name
  FROM
      ch10eu.encrypted_cycle_hire
  JOIN
      ch10eu.encrypted_bike_keys
  USING (bike_id)
)

SELECT
  start_station_name
  , AVG(duration) AS duration
FROM
  duration_by_station
GROUP BY
  start_station_name
ORDER BY duration DESC
LIMIT 5
```

Here is the result, as expected:

---

15 For example, suppose that a programmer uses an authorized application that displays a bike's location at the current time. If they also had the ability to modify the application, they would be able to swap the bike's encrypted current location by the encrypted location at an earlier time and get the application to map it. This way, they would get the bike's location history without ever knowing the encryption keys. If we use `start_date` as an additional field, however, this sort of attack is not possible, because the earlier location was encrypted with additional data consisting of the `start_date` of the trip being encrypted and it is not possible to decrypt it with the latest date. Any metadata that provides this sort of context can be used as extra data to the AEAD encryption function.

Row	start_station_name	duration
1	Stewart's Road, Nine Elms	4836.380090497737
2	Contact Centre, Southbury House	4364.000000000001
3	Speakers' Corner 2, Hyde Park	4006.0086554245627
4	Speakers' Corner 1, Hyde Park	3710.4661268713203
5	Black Lion Gate, Kensington Gardens	3588.0120035566083

Note that we cannot simply group by the encrypted value: because the encryption is nondeterministic (i.e., involves salting), there are many more encrypted station names than there were in the original table:

```
SELECT COUNT (DISTINCT start_station_name)
FROM ch10eu.encrypted_cycle_hire
```

This returns 24369201, whereas

```
SELECT COUNT (DISTINCT start_station_name)
FROM `bigquery-public-data`.london_bicycles.cycle_hire
```

returns just 880.

The query to compute the stations with the longest rentals is much slower (more than two times slower) than if we did not need to do decryption. The trade-off is that, if necessary, we can simply drop the keyset corresponding to a bike_id in order to forget it:

```
DELETE ch10eu.encrypted_bike_keys
WHERE bike_id = 300
```

When you need to delete all data relating to an individual, the method you use—DML or crypto-shredding—should be based on whether you want your technical overhead to be in the form of maintenance or in the form of computational complexity, respectively.

Data Loss Prevention

In many cases, you might not even know where sensitive data exists. It can therefore be helpful to scan BigQuery tables looking for known patterns such as credit card numbers, company confidential project codes, and medical information. The result of a scan can be used as a first step to ensure that such sensitive data is properly secured and managed, thus reducing the risk of exposing sensitive details. It can also be important to carry out such scans periodically to keep up with growth in data and changes in use.

You can use the Cloud Data Loss Prevention (Cloud DLP)[16] to scan your BigQuery tables and to protect your sensitive data. Cloud DLP is a fully managed service that uses more than 90 built-in information type detectors to identify patterns, formats, and checksums. It also provides the ability to define custom information type detectors using dictionaries, regular expressions, and contextual elements. Cloud DLP includes a set of tools to de-identify your data, including masking, tokenization, pseudonymization, date shifting, and more, all without replicating customer data. Besides its use in BigQuery, Cloud DLP can also be used within streams of data and files in Google Cloud Storage, and within images. Finally, it can be used to analyze structured data to help understand the risk of reidentification,[17] including computation of metrics like *k*-anonymity (*https://en.wikipedia.org/wiki/K-anonymity*).

To scan a BigQuery table, select it in the Cloud Console and then choose Export > Scan with DLP, configuring it to look for specific forms of data, as depicted in Figure 10-5.

| customers_loyalty | | | | 🔍 🗇   🗑 DELETE TABLE   ⬆ EXPORT ▼ |

				Explore with Sheets
Schema Details Preview				Explore with Data Studio
				Export to GCS
Field name	Type	Mode	Description	Scan with DLP
id	INTEGER	NULLABLE		
first_name	STRING	NULLABLE		
last_name	STRING	NULLABLE		
city	STRING	NULLABLE		
state	STRING	NULLABLE		
zip_code	INTEGER	NULLABLE		
member_since	DATE	NULLABLE		

Edit schema

Figure 10-5. Scanning a BigQuery table using Cloud DLP

---

16 See *https://cloud.google.com/dlp/docs/*. As of this writing, Cloud DLP was a global service. If you have data location requirements, check whether this is still the case.

17 See *https://en.wikipedia.org/wiki/Data_re-identification*. This is the risk that anonymized data can be matched with auxiliary data to reidentify the individual with whom the data is associated.

To redact or otherwise de-identify sensitive data that the Cloud DLP scan found, protect the data with Cloud KMS keys, which we discuss in the next section.

CMEK

BigQuery employs *envelope encryption* to encrypt table data without any additional actions on your part. In envelope encryption, the data in a BigQuery table is first encrypted using a data encryption key (DEK), and then the DEKs are encrypted by a key encryption key. For each GCP customer, any nonshared resources are split into data chunks and encrypted with keys separate from keys used for other customers. These DEKs are even separate from those that protect other pieces of the same data owned by that same customer. Key encryption keys are then used to encrypt the data encryption keys that Google uses to encrypt your data. These key encryption keys (KEKs) are managed centrally in the Google Key Management Service (KMS), as shown in Figure 10-6.

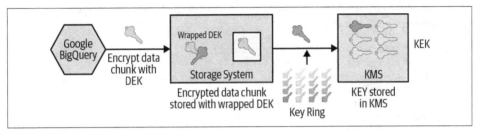

Figure 10-6. Envelope encryption with DEKs and KEKs; the KEKs are managed centrally in a KMS, which rotates keys through the use of a key ring

Encryption helps to ensure that if the data accidentally falls into an attacker's hands, they cannot access the data without also having access to the encryption keys. Even if an attacker obtains the storage devices containing your data, they won't be able to understand or decrypt it. Encryption also acts as a "chokepoint"—centrally managed encryption keys create a single place where access to data is enforced and can be audited. Finally, encryption contributes to the privacy of customer data; it allows systems to manipulate data—for backup, for example—and engineers to support the infrastructure without providing access to content.

If regulations require that you control the keys used to encrypt your data, you may find CMEK a useful tool. Recall that key encryption is used to encrypt the DEKs, which are used to encrypt the data chunks, and that the key encryption keys are stored and managed centrally. You'll typically want to do the same if you are managing key encryption yourself; you'll run the KMS in a central project and use those keys to encrypt table data in all your organization's projects.

In Cloud KMS, a key belongs to a key ring, which resides in a particular location. In the central project where you are running Cloud KMS, create a key ring and a key, specifying a rotation period of the keys:

```
gcloud kms keyrings create acmecorp --location US
gcloud kms keys create xyz --location US \
   --keyring acmecorp --purpose encryption \
   --rotation-period 30d \
   --next-rotation-time 2019-07-01T12:00:00Z
```

The key ring should be created in a location that matches the location of your Big-Query datasets. For example, a dataset in region US should be protected with a key ring from region US, and a dataset in asia-northeast1 should be protected with a key ring from asia-northeast1.

The Cloud KMS keys are used as key encryption keys in BigQuery, in that they encrypt the DEKs that encrypt your data. So, having created the key, you need to allow the BigQuery service account in every project (not the KMS project) to use the key to encrypt and decrypt data:

```
SVC=$(bq show --encryption_service_account)
gcloud kms keys add-iam-policy-binding \
   --project=[KMS_PROJECT_ID] \
   --member serviceAccount:$SVC
   --role roles/cloudkms.cryptoKeyEncrypterDecrypter \
   --location=US \
   --keyring=acmecorp \
   xyz
```

When creating tables, specify the key to be used:

```
bq mk … --destination_kms_key \
projects/[PROJECT_ID]/locations/US/keyRings/acmecorp/cryptoKeys/xyz \
mydataset.transactions
```

Beyond this configuration of tables at creation time, no special arrangements are required to query a table protected by Cloud KMS. BigQuery stores the name of the key used to encrypt the table content and will use that key when a table protected by Cloud KMS is queried. All existing tools, the BigQuery web UI, and the bq command-line interface run the same way as with default-encrypted tables, as long as BigQuery has access to the Cloud KMS key used to encrypt the table content.

Data Exfiltration Protection

Virtual Private Cloud (VPC) Service Controls allow users to define a security perimeter around Google Cloud Platform resources such as Cloud Storage buckets and Big-Query datasets, to help mitigate data exfiltration risks by constraining data to stay within the VPC perimeter. Combined with Private Google Access, it is possible to set up a hybrid cloud environment of cloud and on-premises deployments to help keep sensitive data private.

VPC Service controls provide an additional, context-based perimeter security beyond the identity-based access control offered by Cloud IAM. Using VPC Service Controls, you can mitigate security risks associated with access from unauthorized networks using stolen credentials, data exfiltration by disgruntled insiders, and inadvertent exposure of private data due to misconfigured IAM policies. It is possible to use VPC Service Controls to prevent reading data from or copying data to a resource outside the perimeter using tools such as gsutil and bq.

To set up VPC Service Controls, go to the VPC Service Controls section of the GCP console and add a new perimeter. You can then specify the projects and services within those projects that are allowed to communicate with each other within the perimeter. For example, suppose you choose only Project A and two services: Big-Query and Cloud Storage. Then it will be possible to load data from GCS into Big-Query and export data from BigQuery to GCS but only to buckets owned by the same project. It will not be possible to load data into BigQuery from buckets owned by other projects or export data from BigQuery into buckets owned by other projects. The same goes for copying data between buckets or querying datasets that are part of other projects. You can, of course, have two projects within the perimeter to allow interproject communication (but only between those two projects).

Summary

In this chapter, we described the infrastructure security that underlies BigQuery and discussed how users and applications can be authenticated and authorized using IAM. We then discussed a variety of tools that can help you fulfil your regulatory and compliance needs. We'd like to reiterate, however, that it is always your responsibility to work with your legal counsel to determine whether implementing any of these tools and capabilities will satisfy your regulatory or compliance requirements.

Thank you for sticking with us through a wide-ranging tour of BigQuery. We began with an introduction to the service in Chapter 1, delved into the SQL syntax in Chapter 2, described data types in Chapter 3, covered ingest in Chapter 4, and examined the development environment in Chapter 5. We started to go beyond the basics in Chapter 6 with a description of BigQuery's architecture. In Chapter 7, we covered a variety of performance tips, and in Chapter 8, we poked around in some of the nooks and crannies of BigQuery capabilities. Chapter 9 was devoted to machine learning in BigQuery, and in this chapter we focused on security. Because BigQuery is a server-less SQL enterprise data warehouse that was designed to be knob free, we were able to use this book to focus on analyzing data to find meaningful insights. We hope that you will enjoy working with BigQuery and be exceedingly successful with it!

Index

Symbols

! (exclamation mark), lines in Jupyter Notebook preceded by, 162
! (logical negation) operator, 57
!= (not-equals) comparison operator, 57
(pound sign), comments beginning with, 25
$ (dollar sign), end of string matching in regular expressions, 70
% (percent sign)
    enclosing named parameters, 300
    lines in Jupyter Notebook preceded by, 162
%%bigquery Magics (see Jupyter)
& (bitwise AND) operator, 54, 57
() (parentheses)
    controlling order of evaluation, 29
    enclosing subqueries, 30
    grouping in regular expressions, 69
, (comma)
    comma cross join, 47
    in correlated CROSS JOIN, 319
    leading commas in SELECT clause, 37
- (hyphen), escaping in dataset name, 26
-- (double dash), comments beginning with, 25
; (semicolon) separating statements in a script, 339
<, <=, >, >=, and != (or <>) comparison operators, 56
    using with Boolean variables, 59
<< (bitwise) operator, 54
<> (not-equals) comparison operator, 57
>> (bitwise) operator, 54
? (question mark), in positional parameters, 304
?: (capture group) in regular expressions, 69

@ (at symbol), marking named parameters, 300
@run_date parameter, 303
@run_time parameter, 303
[] (square brackets), array operator, 35
\d matching digits in regular expressions, 69
\s matching spaces in regular expressions, 69
`` (backticks), escape character in dataset name, 26
| (bitwise OR) operator, 54, 57
∧ (caret), beginning of string matching in regular expressions, 70

A

access control
    BigQuery's use of Google's IAM system, 21
    Identity and Access Management (IAM), 437-441
    on dataset, examining using dsinfo object, 146
access tokens, 140
Access Transparency program, 457
ACID operations with BigQuery, 18
admin role, 438
administering BigQuery, 435, 441-452
    authorizing users, 442
    availability, disaster recovery, and encryption, 452-457
    continuous integration/continuous deployment, 443-448
    cost/billing exports, 448-450
    dashboards, monitoring, and audit logging, 450-452
    job management, 441
    regulatory compliance, 458-471

carried out using <, <=, >, >=, and != (or
    <>) comparison operators, 56
comparison operators applied to NULL, 34
using comparison operators with Boolean
    variables, 59
compliance, 21
    (see also regulatory compliance)
compression of files, 81
    impact of, in loading data into BigQuery, 93
computation, moving to the data, 13
compute
    scaling compute in BigQuery, 16
    separation from storage in BigQuery, 9, 15
compute_fit method, 173
CONCAT function, 65, 68, 329
concatenation of arrays, 320
conda environment for Jupyter, 171
conditional expressions, 60
constants, defining, 312
container management system (Borg), 197
CONTINUE statement, 342
continuous integration/continuous deployment
    (CI/CD), 443-448
correlated CROSS JOINs, 319
correlated subqueries, 309
    for cases seeming to require a script, 339
correlation coefficients, 359
correlation, functions for, 358
costs
    controlling, 232-234
        estimating per-query cost, 233
        finding most expensive queries, 234
    cost/billing exports, 448-450
        cost by month by product, 448
        labels, using, 449
    data loaded into BigQuery, 84
    staging files on Google Cloud Storage, 94
COUNT function, counting records with, 32
COUNTIF function, using to avoid casting
    Booleans, 65
COUNT_STAR operator, 202
CRAN, bigquery library from, 171
CREATE FUNCTION IF NOT EXISTS, 307
CREATE FUNCTION statements, 307
CREATE IF NOT EXISTS statement, 121
CREATE MODEL statement, 377
CREATE OR REPLACE FUNCTION, 307
CREATE OR REPLACE PROCEDURE state-
    ment, 347

CREATE OR REPLACE TABLE statement, 121
    creating an empty table, 331
    making tables irrecoverable, 443
    OPTIONS list, using, 331
CREATE TABLE AS SELECT statement, 92,
    192
CREATE TABLE statement, 90, 121
CreateDisposition and WriteDisposition, con-
    trolling load of pandas DataFrame, 153
CROSS JOIN statement, 46, 319
cross-entropy loss measure in classification, 395
cross-region dataset copies, 124
cross-selling of product groups, improving, 403
CRUD operations
    on REST API, mapped to HTTP verbs, 138
    supported on persistent storage, 23
crypto-shredding, 464
cryptography
    BigQuery support for MD5 and SHA hash-
        ing algorithms, 361
    services provided for BigQuery by Google,
        436
CSV files, 9, 81
    compressed, loading into BigQuery, 94
    drawbacks of, for loading data into Big-
        Query, 92
    extraction format for table data using Goo-
        gle Cloud Client Library, 155
    loading into BigQuery, 82
    querying external tables created from, 96
    using Cloud Dataflow to read and write to
        BigQuery, 129
curl utility
    issuing GET request to BigQuery REST API
        URL, 140
    sending raw HTTP requests via, 188
    using in measuring query time, 235
CURRENT_TIMESTAMP function, 50, 72
custom roles, 439
customer information, security of, 436
customer segmentation, 403
customer targeting, 370, 403, 413
Customer-Managed Encryption Keys (CMEK),
    457, 469

D

dashboards, tables accessed from, using BI
    Engine with, 257
data

indexing, not needed in BigQuery, 12
infinite loops, avoiding with SQL, 13
INFORMATION_SCHEMA view, 140, 148, 328
   associated with a project, finding most expensive queries, 234
infrastructure provisioning, not needed with BigQuery, 12
INNER JOIN statement, 45, 46
   INNER JOIN EACH WITH ALL, 212
   INNER JOIN EACH WITH EACH, 213
   summary of, 48
INSERT SELECT statement, 332
INSERT statement, 91, 192, 227
INSERT VALUES statement, 92, 333
   with SELECT subquery, 334
Institute of Electrical and Electronics Engineers (IEEE), 56
INT64 type, 53, 76
   converting (coercing) to FLOAT64 or NUMERIC, 63
   decimal calculations and, 57
   returned by fingerprint function, 359
INTEGER type, detection by AUTO partitioning mode, 98
internationalization of strings, 66
intersection of geography types, 355
IS NOT NULL operator, 34
IS NULL operator, 34
IS operator
   using in comparing against built-in constants, 59
   using to check where value is NULL, 60
isolation between jobs, 12

J

Java Database Connectivity (JDBC), 174
JavaScript
   tensorflow.js, 430
   user-defined functions, 268, 336-338
JDBC/ODBC drivers, 174, 192
job management, 441
job priority, BATCH, 294
job servers, 190
   upgrades to, 192
JobConfig flags, 154
jobIds, 143, 191
jobUser role, 438, 441
job_config, 160

join+ stage
   of broadcast JOIN treaty, 211
   of hash join query, 213
joins, 42-48
   broadcast and hash, 209
   broadcast JOIN query, 209-212
   complex, support by BigQuery, 10
   CROSS JOIN, 46
   for cases seeming to require a script, 339
   hash join query, 212-213
   INNER JOIN, 45
   JOIN statement, 42
      GIS predicate functions in, 354
      how it works, 44
   joining user table and machine learning weights, 416
   OUTER JOIN, 47
   performing efficient joins, 257-266
      avoiding self-joins of large tables, 258
      denormalization, 257
      JOIN versus denormalization, 265
      reducing data being joined, 261
      using precomputed values, 263
      using window function instead of self-join, 262
   queries doing JOIN operations, 193
   summary of types of joins and their output, 48
JSON, 9
   arrays, 38
   compressed files, loading into BigQuery, 94
   converting arrays to JSON strings, 321
   creating JSON strings for dataset schema, 88
   creating table definition of data stored in newline-delimited JSON for Hive partition, 98
   GeoJSON, 350
      converting geographies to/from strings in, 351
   JSON request in body of HTTP POST sent to BigQuery REST API URL, 141
   JSON/REST interface, 138
   loading files into BigQuery, 81
   newline-delimited files, extract format using Google Cloud Client Library, 155
   response from HTTP POST request to BigQuery REST API URL, 142
   transformation of JSON HTTP request to Protobufs, 189

W

web UI (BigQuery)
>   newly inserted rows in streaming table, 151
>   one-time data loads from, 84
>   saving and sharing queries from, 50
>   transfers of data into BigQuery, 120
>   viewing persistent user-defined function, 307

weights
>   examining for linear regression model, 381-383
>   joining with user table in recommender system, 416
>   user and product factors for recommender system, 415

Well Known Text (WKT), 350
>   converting geographies to/from strings in, 351

WGS84 ellipsoid, 75, 350

What-If tool, 382

WHERE clause
>   Boolean expressions in, 59
>   casting in, 86
>   comparisons and NULL values, 57
>   correlated subqueries in, 310
>   filtering for NULL values in, 34
>   filtering results returned by SELECT, 28
>   GIS predicate functions in, 354
>   LIKE operator, 30
>   partitioning and clustering tables in, 333
>   using GROUP BY instead of, 32

WHILE loop, 342

wildcards
>   using for file paths with bq mkdef and bq load, 96
>   using to search tables, 286

window functions, 322-328
>   aggregating analytic functions, 323
>   navigation functions, 324

numbering functions, 326
>   using instead of self-join, 262

WITH clause
>   for cases seeming to require a script, 339
>   frequent use of, caching query results instead of, 254
>   holding constants, 312
>   reusing parts if queries in, 310
>   SELECT statement in, 326
>   using for subqueries, 30
>   using to abstract away expensive regex function, 256
>   using user-defined functions in, 306

worker shards
>   allocation by scheduler, 195
>   avoiding overwhelming a worker, 266-268
>   data skew, 267
>   limiting large sorts, 266
>   optimizing user-defined functions, 268
>   functions of, 197
>   JavaScript UDFs limited to single worker, 338

Workload Tester, using to measure query speed, 236-238

workloads, troubleshooting using Stackdriver, 238-240

X

XGBoost machine learning model, 386

Y

YouTube Channel, transferring data from, 122

Z

zless, 81
zones, 452
>   zonal failures, 454

About the Authors

Valliappa (Lak) Lakshmanan is Global Head for Data Analytics and AI Solutions on Google Cloud. His team builds software solutions for business problems using Big-Query and other Google Cloud data analytics and machine learning products. He is also the author of *Data Science on the Google Cloud Platform*, published by O'Reilly.

Jordan Tigani is Director of Product Management for BigQuery. He was one of the founding engineers on BigQuery and helped grow it to be one of the most successful products in Google Cloud. He wrote the first book on BigQuery and has also spoken widely on the subject. Jordan has 20 years of software development experience, ranging from Microsoft Research to machine learning startups.

Colophon

The animal on the cover of *Google BigQuery: The Definitive Guide* is a Masai ostrich (*Struthio camelus massaicus*), a subspecies of the common ostrich—the largest bird in the world. They can be found grazing along the open plains and grassy savannas of Eastern Africa.

The Masai ostrich measures between 7–9 feet tall, and although it has a wingspan of 6.5 feet, it cannot fly. Ostriches are well adapted to their flightlessness: though the filaments of their feathers grow in separately, and can't be hooked together to create airfoils (as happens in flighted birds), ostrich wings remain useful in providing lift and stabilization when they make evasive maneuvers around predators. The ostrich has long, powerful legs that can propel it to maximum speeds of 45 miles per hour, making it the fastest bird on land as well as the fastest two-legged animal.

The males are characterized by black plumage—with some white around the wings and tail—that contrast with their reddish neck and legs (which get brighter during mating). Females, on the other hand, are mostly brown and grey. And while most birds have four toes, the Masai ostrich only has two, one of which almost resembles a hoof. They travel in nomadic herds of up to 50 birds that can often include other grazing animals, such as antelopes or zebras.

There is popular belief that when in danger, the ostrich will bury its head in sand as a defense mechanism. This myth is thought to have originated from the writings of Pliny the Elder, who may have actually been observing them ingesting sand and pebbles (which help them to digest their food since they have no teeth). Another theory is that he may have seen them rotating their eggs during incubation, which they keep buried in the sand. In any case, when threatened, the Masai ostrich will either run away or lower its body toward the ground. In extreme situations they will fight back, and have even been capable of killing lions.

Many of the animals on O'Reilly covers are endangered; all of them are important to the world.

The cover illustration is by Jose Marzan, based on a black and white engraving from *Meyers Kleines Lexicon*. The cover fonts are Gilroy Semibold and Guardian Sans. The text font is Adobe Minion Pro; the heading font is Adobe Myriad Condensed; and the code font is Dalton Maag's Ubuntu Mono.

O'REILLY®

There's much more where this came from.

Experience books, videos, live online training courses, and more from O'Reilly and our 200+ partners—all in one place.

Learn more at oreilly.com/online-learning

CPSIA information can be obtained
at www.ICGtesting.com
Printed in the USA
JSHW030906111120
9479JS00003BA/121